Gendering the Knowledge Economy

Also by Sylvia Walby

GENDER TRANSFORMATIONS

THEORIZING PATRIARCHY

PATRIARCHY AT WORK

CONTEMPORARY BRITISH SOCIETY (*co-authored*)

EUROPEAN SOCIETIES: FUSION OR FISSION? (*edited*)

NEW AGENDAS FOR WOMEN (*edited*)

Also by Heidi Gottfried

FEMINISM AND SOCIAL CHANGE: BRIDGING THEORY AND PRACTICE (*edited*)

EQUITY IN THE WORKPLACE: GENDERING WORKPLACE POLICY
ANALYSIS (*edited*)

GENDER AND GLOBALIZATION IN CRITICAL SOCIOLOGY (*edited*)

Also by Karin Gottschall

BEYOND STANDARD WORK IN CRITICAL SOCIOLOGY (*edited*)

Gendering the Knowledge Economy

Comparative Perspectives

Edited by

Sylvia Walby
University of Lancaster, UK

Heidi Gottfried
Wayne State University, USA

Karin Gottschall
Bremen University, Germany

Mari Osawa
University of Tokyo, Japan

palgrave
macmillan

First published in hardback 2007

First published in paperback 2009 by
PALGRAVE MACMILLAN

Palgrave Macmillan in the UK is an imprint of Macmillan Publishers Limited, registered in England, company number 785998, of Houndmills, Basingstoke, Hampshire RG21 6XS.

Palgrave Macmillan in the US is a division of St Martin's Press LLC, 175 Fifth Avenue, New York, NY 10010.

Palgrave Macmillan is the global academic imprint of the above companies and has companies and representatives throughout the world.

Palgrave® and Macmillan® are registered trademarks in the United States, the United Kingdom, Europe and other countries

ISBN-13: 978-1-4039-9457-8 hardback
ISBN-10: 1-4039-9457-9   hardback
ISBN-13: 978-0-230-57570-7 paperback
ISBN-10: 0-230-57570-6   paperback

This book is printed on paper suitable for recycling and made from fully managed and sustained forest sources. Logging, pulping and manufacturing processes are expected to conform to the environmental regulations of the country of origin.

A catalogue record for this book is available from the British Library.

Library of Congress Cataloging-in-Publication Data

Gendering the knowledge economy : comparative perspectives / edited by Sylvia Walby . . . [et al.].
      p. cm.
   Includes bibliographical references and index.
   ISBN 1-4039-9457-9 (cloth) 0-230-57570-6 (pbk)
   1. Information technology – Economic aspects. I.Walby, Sylvia.
   HC79.I55G46 2007
   338.9'26082 – dc22

                                                          2006044696

10   9   8   7   6   5   4   3   2   1
18   17   16   15   14   13   12   11   10   09

Printed and bound in Great Britain by
CPI Antony Rowe, Chippenham and Eastbourne

Contents

v

List of Figures

List of Tables

Preface

GLOW: Globalization, Gender and Work Transformation

The international network on Globalization, Gender and Work Transformation (GLOW) is composed of scholars from the US, UK, Germany and Japan who collaborate on topics related to gender, the knowledge economy, and new employment forms in a global context.

The network has been meeting since 1998 and now holds events about twice a year, usually in the countries of network members. We have presented our work to public and academic audiences at the American Sociological Association conference in Anaheim 2001, the University of Tokyo in 2002 and 2004, the conference of the Society for the Advancement of Socio-Economics at the University of Provence in 2003, at the University of Bremen in 2003, and the University of Leeds in 2004. We have held workshops at the Sozialforschungsstelle Dortmund in 1998 and 2000, University of Tokyo in 2002 and 2004, and the University of Leeds in 2003 and 2005, in addition to meetings alongside the public presentations. A large number of grants have supported the meetings of the network including: the Council for European Studies at Columbia University, the American Sociological Association/National Science Foundation, the Hanse Institute for Advanced Studies Delmenhorst and Bremen University, the Japan Society for the Promotion of Science, the Center for Global Partnership of the Japan Foundation, the University of Tokyo, the Daiwa Anglo-Japanese Foundation, the UK Economic and Social Research Council and the University of Leeds.

The chapters in this volume represent key aspects of the current work of the GLOW network by Susan Durbin, Karin Gottschall, Ursula Holtgrewe, Daniela Kroos, Ilse Lenz, Makiko Nishikawa, Mari Osawa, Diane Perrons, Glenda Roberts, Karen Shire, Kazuko Tanaka and Sylvia Walby. We are grateful to colleagues for discussions which at various stages have contributed to the development of our ideas in the GLOW network, including: Joan Acker, Keiko Aiba, Monika Goldmann, Judith Lorber, Ronnie Steinberg, Jenny Tomlinson and Anne Witz. We would like to thank Silke Birkenstock-Niekamp and Tatiana Bezrodnaia for help with the production of the manuscript.

Sylvia Walby
Heidi Gottfried
Karin Gottschall
Mari Osawa

Notes on Authors and Editors

Susan Durbin is a Senior Lecturer in Human Resource Management at the Bristol Business School, University of the West of England, UK. Her research areas include: gendering knowledge/the knowledge economy; the gender-technology relationship; and women's careers in organizations, with a specialist focus upon call centres. Her current research analyses women's organizational networks and whether and in which ways these are utilized to create and disseminate knowledge and build social capital. Susan Durbin is a member of the international Globalization, Gender and Work Transformation network, a network that engages with comparative research in the UK, USA, Japan and Germany. She is also a member of the Employment Studies Research Unit (ESRU) at the University of the West of England. Her other recent publications include 'Gender, Skills and Careers in UK Call Centres' (in J. Burgess and J. Connell (eds), *Developments in the Call Centre Industry: Analysis, Policy and Challenges* (Taylor and Francis 2006)).

Heidi Gottfried is Professor of Sociology at Wayne State University. Her research focuses on employment regulation, gender and work in comparative perspective. She is editor of a symposium on *Feminism and Social Change: Bridging Theory and Practice* (University of Illinois Press 1996), co-editor of *Equity in the Workplace: Gendering Workplace Policy Analysis* (Lexington Press 2004), co-editor of *Gender and Globalization* (2004) and editor of *The Next Upsurge* (2005) in *Critical Sociology*. Building on previous research, a new project examines social contracts in transition.

Karin Gottschall is Professor of Sociology, Head of the 'Gender Policy in the Welfare State' Unit at the Centre for Social Policy Research and Director of the Graduate School of Social Sciences at the University of Bremen. Over the past several years her publications and research have focused on new employment forms, labour-market policy, politics of public education and welfare-state reform in comparative perspective. Currently, she participates in the newly set up EU Network on Reconciliation of Work and Welfare (RECWOWE) and is a member of the Scientific Advisory Board of the German Socio-Economic Panel. She is author of a monograph on the German sociological discourse on social inequality and gender (*Soziale Ungleichheit und Geschlecht*, Leske & Budrich 2000) and co-editor of *Beyond Standard Work*, Special Issue of *Critical Sociology* (Spring 2007).

Ursula Holtgrewe is a senior researcher at the FORBA (Forschungs- und Beratungsstelle Arbeitswelt) in Vienna, Austria, and a member of the co-ordinating team of the 'Global Call Center Industry Project'. Her main fields of study are service and knowledge work and organization, organizations and subjectivity, and the boundaries of markets and property rights in the knowledge society. Her studies of Deutsche Telekom and of telephone call centres have been funded by Deutsche Forschungsgemeinschaft, Hans-Böckler-Stiftung and the Russell Sage Foundation. Her most recent books are *Flexible Menschen in flexiblen Organisationen?* (Sigma, forthcoming in 2006), *Telekom: Wie machen die das?* (UVK 2002, with Doris Blutner and Hanns-Georg Brose) and *Re-Organizing Service Work. Call Centres in Germany and Britain* (Ashgate 2002, co-edited with Christian Kerst and Karen Shire).

Daniela Kroos is a junior research fellow at the Graduate School of Social Sciences (University of Bremen) and specializes in comparative welfare state analysis and labour market change. Her PhD project emphasizes labour market characteristics of Bismarckian welfare states and deals with non-standard employment and trajectories of employment recommodification in Germany and France.

Ilse Lenz is Professor of Social Structure and Gender Studies at the Ruhr-University Bochum, Germany, and Coordinator of the Marie Jahoda guest professorship for international gender studies. Her research areas include: globalization and transnationalism; feminism, social movements and institutional change; globalization, gender and work; as well as comparative research on the German and the Japanese new women's movement with Michiko Mae. Recent major publications include *Reflexive Körper?* as editor (VS Verlag 2003) ('Reflexive Bodies. The Modernization of Sexuality and Reproduction'), *Crossing Borders and Shifting Boundaries* (VS Verlag 2003), *Frauenbewegungen weltweit* as editor (Leske & Budrich 2000) ('Women's Movements Worldwide'), and *Getrennte Welten, gemeinsame Moderne?* as editor (Leske & Budrich 1997) ('Separated Worlds, Shared Modernity. Gender Relations in Japan').

Makiko Nishikawa is Associate Professor at the Faculty of Business Administration, Hosei University and Hosei Management School. Her research focuses on gender and employment, care-work in comparative perspective, atypical employment, and quality of working life. She is currently involved in the GLOW comparative research project on care-work as well as in a project focusing on the reconciliation of paid work and care-work in Japan.

Mari Osawa is Professor of Social Policy at the Institute of Social Science, University of Tokyo, and member of the Science Council of Japan. She specializes in welfare issues, especially in relation to gender. She has worked as a Marie Jahoda Professor (International Visiting Professorship) at the Ruhr-University of Bochum, as well as a Visiting Professor in Gender and Development Studies, Asian Institute of Technology. She is an editor of the journal *Gender, Technology and Development* (Sage). Her English publications include: 'Government Approaches to Gender Equality in the mid-1990s', *Social Science Japan Journal*, Vol. 3, No. 1, 2000; 'Koizumi's "Robust Policy": Governance, the Japanese Welfare Employment Regime and Comparative Gender Studies', Glenn D. Hook (ed.) *Contested Governance in Japan, Sites and Issues* (Routledge 2005).

Diane Perrons is Director of the Gender Institute at the London School of Economics. Her research focuses on the social and spatial implications of global economic restructuring, paying particular attention to the changing composition of employment, gender and regional inequalities and the social reproduction of daily life. Her research has been funded by the Economic and Social Research Council, the Equal Opportunities Commission and the European Union. She recently published *Globalization and Social Change. People and Places in a Divided World* (Routledge 2004) and has just finished editing the anthology *Gender Divisions and Working Time in the New Economy. Changing Patterns of Work, Care and Pubic Policy in Europe and North America* (Edward Elgar 2006) with colleagues from Oxford and Manchester.

Glenda Roberts is Professor at the Graduate School of Asia-Pacific Studies, at Waseda University in Tokyo. She is also an editorial board member of the *Social Science Japan Journal* (University of Tokyo and Oxford University Press), and Treasurer of the Section for East Asian Anthropology in the American Anthropological Association. Her main research interests are gender, work, migration and population issues, especially in regard to Japan. Her books include *Staying on the Line. Blue-Collar Women in Contemporary Japan* (University of Hawaii Press 1994) and the edited volume with Mike Douglas, *Japan and Global Migration. Foreign Workers and the Advent of a Multicultural Society* (University of Hawaii Press 2003).

Karen Shire is Professor of Comparative Sociology in the Institute of Sociology and Institute of East Asian Studies at the University Duisburg-Essen, Germany, Her comparative research on knowledge-intensive service work and employment change has been funded by the German Science Foundation and the Hans-Böckler Foundation, among others. Currently she is coordinating an interdisciplinary research project for the German Ministry of Education and Research on *Working and Learning in Project-Based Network Organizations* as part of the Ministry's *Future of Work* research focus and leading a research project on *Employment and Gender in the German New Economy* for the North Rhine Westphalian Ministry of Innovation. She is co-author of *On the Front Line. The Organization of Work in the Information*

Economy (Cornell University Press 1999 with S. Frenkel, M. Korcyznski and M. Tam) and co-editor of *Re-organizing Service Work. Call Centres in Germany and Britain* (Ashgate 2002, co-edited with Ursula Holtgrewe and Christian Kerst).

Kazuko Tanaka is Professor of Sociology in the International Studies Division, Director of the Center for Gender Studies, and Coordinator of the Program in Gender and Sexuality Studies at the International Christian University, Japan. She is editor of the journal, *Gender and Sexuality*. Her current research interests are in the fields of emotional labour in general and knowledge building of care-work in particular. Her study 'Comparative Gender Analysis of New Economy: Service and Information Oriented Aged Society' was funded by Grants-in-Aid for Scientific Research, the Japan Society for the Promotion of Science. She is currently actively involved in the networking of working women in Japan at the national level, based on the efforts from the two-year project 'US-Japan Working Women's Workshop' (which was organized by Professor H. Gottfried and Anne Zacharias-Walsh in 2004). 'Keawaaku no Senmonsei: Mienai Rodo "Kanjyo Rodo" wo Chushinni' (Professionalization of Care-Work: Emotional Labour as Invisible Labour) was published in *Jyosei Rodo Kenkyu* (Study of Women's Work), 2004. Her edited book *Passive No More. Confronting Gender Issues in Contemporary Japan* is forthcoming.

Sylvia Walby is Professor at the Department of Sociology at Lancaster University, UK. She has been Professor of Sociology at the Universities of Leeds and Bristol, and Reader at the LSE; and was the founding President of the European Sociological Association. Her recent work on gender equality has been funded by the UK Economic and Social Research Council, the UK Equal Opportunities Commission, the European Union Presidency, and the European Parliament; and she has ongoing research on the gendered knowledge economy. Her books include: *Gender Transformations* (Routledge 1997), *Theorizing Patriarchy* (Blackwell 1990) and *Patriarchy at Work* (Polity Press 1986), and she has edited special issues of both *Social Politics* (2005, 12, 3) and *International Feminist Journal of Politics* (2005, 7, 4) on 'Gender Mainstreaming'. Her next book is *Complex Social Systems in a Global Era* (Sage 2007).

Part I
Re-conceptualizing the Knowledge Economy, Gender and Regulation

1
Introduction: Theorizing the Gendering of the Knowledge Economy: Comparative Approaches

Sylvia Walby

Introduction

The knowledge economy is the future of the world of work. Its gendering is central to understanding the nature of its associated employment practices and its implications for the quality of working life. The development of knowledge economies is affected by cross-cutting global processes and national trajectories. A key issue is the conceptualization of the different forms that class and gender relations may take, in order to advance comparative analysis of these processes. The knowledge economy, gender and globalization are each key issues in contemporary social thought. In this book we challenge and revise key claims in the debates on the knowledge economy and the comparative analysis of varieties of capitalism, comparative analyses of gender relations in the context of globalization. The book is based on the work of the international network on Globalization, Gender and Work Transformation (GLOW).

This introductory chapter presents a newly developed theoretical framework to which the chapters in the book contribute in diverse ways. It critically reviews the theoretical debates pertinent to the comparative analysis of the gendering of the knowledge economy in a global era and sets out a new approach. It positions the contributions in the book within key social science debates, especially: the conceptualization of the knowledge economy and non-standard forms of employment; globalization and the varied restructuring of polities and states; the regulation and deregulation of employment; the de-gendering and re-gendering of employment practices; and the theorization of varieties of gender regime, as well as varieties of capitalism.

The definition of the knowledge economy is highly contested. We explore the implications of different definitions for the gendering of the knowledge economy. One definition of the knowledge economy is of industries predicated on information and communication technologies; another with the information sector; a third with knowledge-intensive service industries;

3

while yet others focus on the process of knowledge construction (Castells 1996; Nonaka and Takeuchi 1995). The concept of a 'knowledge' economy has become more prevalent than that of the 'new' economy. We explore the tension between the different connotations of these two concepts. The 'new' economy has more often involved a focus on the changing regulation of employment forms, especially restructuring associated with competitive global economic pressures. We investigate the nature and gendering of the new temporalities (e.g. temporary work, part-time employment), contractualities (e.g. self-employment) and spatialities (e.g. call centres).

The knowledge economy has been implicated in quite divergent processes. First, the development of a knowledge-based economy that provides higher skilled jobs with greater autonomy, flatter hierarchies, flexible schedules and improved quality of working life. Second, the development of a new economy based on new information and communication technologies (ICTs) is seen to fuel a globalization that tips the power relations between capital and labour further away from labour, leading to the degradation of the conditions of working life, especially in the increased precariousness of employment. The relative balance between these processes is addressed empirically in the chapters that follow.

There is a question as to whether these developments are common across different countries, or whether there are diverse, path-dependent patterns of development. We explore and develop the conceptualization of variations in the patterns of gender relations and variations in the forms of capitalism. We investigate the intersection of these sets of social relations in the chapters of the book. The 'varieties of capitalism' literature has made various distinctions between different forms of capitalism, including that between liberal and coordinated market economies (Hall and Soskice 2001). However, these debates have tended to focus on class relations to the relative neglect of other social divisions, such as gender. We investigate both theoretically and empirically the ways in which the varieties in the forms of gender relations should be conceptualized and analysed. A framework for the analysis of varieties of gender regime is developed, including not only the divergences noted in the gendered welfare state literature (Orloff 1993; O'Connor et al. 1999; Sainsbury 1994, 1996), but also variations in the regulation of employment relations.

Global processes cross-cut these paths of development. Often, globalization, seen through the lens of class inequality, has been understood to lead to de-regulation and to the degradation of work, as a result of intensified economic competitive pressures. Here we broaden the focus to include political as well as economic processes, gender as well as class inequalities. New polities emerging on the global stage, such as the EU, have new implications for the regulation of employment. When gender is brought into focus, some increased regulation of the workplace becomes visible, for example, the regulation of working time so as to better combine employment and caring, and the regulation of equal opportunities. There are complex patterns of regulation as well as deregulation, which differently affect class and gender relations. The consequences for gender relations of changes in patterns of regulation of emerging forms of employment are explored in the chapters.

Four countries are selected for comparison: the US, UK, Germany and Japan. These countries cross-cut the major identified forms of capitalist production, welfare state regime and gender regime. The US and the UK are examples of liberal, institutionally thin, market economies, while Germany is a corporatist, institutionally thick, market economy, and Japan somewhat hybridized between the two, though often considered corporatist. In relation to the gender regime, the four countries lie on a spectrum in which the most public is the US, followed by the UK, Germany and Japan. In terms of gendered labour market regulation, Germany and the UK are subject to the regulation of the EU, and thus have more developed regulations to support gender equality and the combination of employment and caring.

This introductory chapter sets out the conceptual issues at stake in the gendering of the knowledge economy, the development of the theoretical framework for gendered comparisons and a consideration of the range of possible implications for gender equality, as well as a comparative review of the development of non-standard work in the four countries.

Defining the knowledge economy?

What is 'knowledge'? There are many different, highly contested definitions of the knowledge economy, each of which has different implications for the gendering of the economy. One approach is distinguishing the industrial sectors that most contain 'knowledge'. A second is to treat the economy holistically and to ask what difference the development of the knowledge economy makes to different sections of the whole economy. A third is to focus on the processes by which knowledge is created.

The first approach is to define the knowledge economy as specific industrial sectors of the economy. This approach is used in a range of categorizations of the knowledge economy by EU, OECD and UN statisticians (European Commission 2001a; Eurostat 2005; OECD 2002a, 2002b, 2005a, 2005b, 2005c; UN Statistics Division 2005a, 2005b) and is developed further by Shire (in this volume). They vary significantly as to how knowledge is to be identified, especially the extent to which it is encoded in high-level technology and the extent to which it is embrained in highly educated workers. One definition of the knowledge sector of the economy restricts it to the industrial sector associated with the new information and communication technologies, extended to encompass a range of new high-level technologies, such as biotechnology. In the EU definition this is equated with high technology manufacturing, including the manufacture of relevant machinery as well as the use of ICT in industries such as telecommunications, software, publishing and data processing. A second definition shifts the focus of the knowledge-based industries towards the concept of information, including industries that process information in a variety of forms. The information sector, more narrowly defined than ICT, focuses on content industries such as publishing and media, and ICT services such as telecommunications, software publishing and data processing, innovatively straddling the conventional distinction between manufacturing and services. A third definition is of the knowledge-intensive service sector including not only high tech services, such as telecommunications and research, but also knowledge-intensive market services, such as real estate, knowledge-intensive financial services, such as insurance, and the extensive education, health and recreational sectors. This last definition is confined to the service sector, though this encompasses a higher proportion of employment than the first two measures. The first two measures focus on innovative technological developments; the third focuses on human development through education. Each of these measures has advantages and disadvantages resulting from the inclusion or exclusion of particular categories of economic activity. The gender implications of the different definitions and measures of the knowledge economy sectors are introduced later in this introduction and explored in detail by Shire (in this volume).

A second approach treats the economy holistically, considering the impact of changes on all the forms of employment, on the grounds that these are all inter-related in a functioning economy, as argued by Perrons (2003 and in this volume). The definition of the knowledge economy, as discussed above, focuses on specific newly developing sectors in the economy. Such a definitional strategy, by its restriction, implicitly lends support to the view that the knowledge economy produces high quality work. However, other ('non-knowledge') sectors of the economy may be affected by the development of the knowledge economy in quite different ways. They may be affected as a result of ICTs increasing the mobility of financial capital, increasing global competitive pressures, tilting the balance of power towards capital and away from labour (especially female and minoritized workers) and producing new lower quality employment forms. The new economy may thus have implications for the quality of jobs outside the high technology and knowledge-intensive sectors quite different from their implications for those within these sectors. Perrons (in this volume) explores the inter-relationship of gendered patterns of employment in the new and old sectors of the economy, and the re-creation of 'old' inequalities in new forms of employment.

A third approach to the definition of knowledge focuses on the process of creating knowledge and the importance of the movement of knowledge from a tacit form to one that is explicit and capable of more direct exchange and communication (Nonaka and Nishiguchi 2001; Nonaka and Takeuchi 1995). In this approach all work contains some tacit knowledge, even work that is often considered relatively low skilled, but whether it becomes explicit knowledge depends on specific circumstances. Chapters in this book discuss the way that gendered working practices place limits on the creation of knowledge. Nishikawa and Tanaka (in this volume) analyse care-work as a potential form of knowledge work, discussing the limitations on the processes of knowledge creation through exchanges between tacit and explicit knowledge caused by gendered flexible working practices, while Durbin (in this volume) explores the limitations to the creation of knowledge by women workers caused by gendered organizational practices in a call centre.

Non-standard employment forms: 'new' temporalities, spatialities and contractualities

The development of new non-standard forms of employment with implications for the quality of working life has occurred in parallel with the development of the knowledge economy. A diverse range of new employment forms has been emerging with new temporalities, contractualities and spatialities of work. These revise the ostensibly 'standard' form of working of 9–5, Monday to Friday, for one employer, at the employer's workplace, and with whom one has a direct employment contract.

Non-standard forms of temporality include part-time working hours, and a range of special and flexible working hours arrangements, including: flexitime, annualized hours contracts, term time working, job sharing, nine day fortnight, four and a half day week, and zero hours contracts. Non-standard forms of contractuality include self-employment. Temporary contracts involve non-standard forms of both temporality and contractuality. Non-standard forms of spatiality alter the organization and location of work as in call centre working, teleworking and home-based working. Call centres utilize ICTs to generate new spatialities, positioning workers who answer calls a long way from the customers to whom they speak, and are often associated with new temporalities and contractualities.

These new temporalities, contractualities and spatialities are implicated in the divergent theses about the knowledge economy. On the one hand, they have been interpreted as examples of improved quality of working conditions associated with the rise of a knowledge-based economy, especially in relation to worker autonomy and flexibility. On the other hand, they have been considered examples of worsened quality of working life associated with the postulated link between globalization and de-regulation, which has increased precarity and reduced job security.

The extent and nature of non-standard working varies substantially by country, skill level, and class, ethnic and gender location. These new non-standard forms of employment are implicated in the theses about the division between varieties of capitalist production. The coordinated variety of capitalism is associated with the regulation of the economy and working life, while the liberal variety has less regulation. For example, Hall and Soskice (2001) refer to the need and use of long-term labour contracts as part of the coordinated market economies such as Germany. Non-standard forms of employment have been implicated in theses about gender relations. They have been taken as examples of disadvantaged conditions associated with gender inequality. Different factors have been considered relevant to the amelioration of this inequality and to the production of different forms of gender regime. These include the provision of public services for care as well as the gendered regulation of the labour market by the state. The explanation of these differences requires the development of new forms of conceptualization of the intersection of varieties of capitalism and gender regimes.

The chapters in the book analyse the nature and implications of a wide range of forms of non-standard working. Durbin uncovers a plethora of working hours arrangements in call centres in the UK. The call centres in her study utilize over 100 different 'working parameters', that is, hours of work, so as to cover their twenty-four-hour, seven-day-a-week operations, thus erasing simple distinctions between full-time and part-time employment, and between standard working hours and shifts. The implications of the variable use of flexibility in German call centre working for changing patterns of gender relations is discussed by Holtgrewe (in this volume). She addresses the various modes of flexibility in call centres, their varied association with the de-gendering and re-gendering of forms of work, in which different types of call centres have diverse gender compositions, skill levels and temporalities of work. The varied implications of gendered self-employment for the quality of working life and for risk management are analysed by Gottschall and Kroos (in this volume). New forms of spatiality made possible by the new information and communication technologies are analysed in the chapters on call centres by Holtgrewe and Durbin. Key questions include whether they are associated with higher or lower quality of working life; and whether and if so in what way they are gendered. The latter part of this chapter provides data comparing the gendered nature of these developments in the US, UK, Germany and Japan. Several chapters investigate the comparative trajectories of development of gendered non-standard work and its implications for the quality of working life: Gottschall and Kroos on the new contractualities of self-employment in Germany and the UK; Perrons on the implications of new contractualities and temporalities in the new media industries in the UK; Durbin on the new spatialities of call centre work in the UK; Holtgrewe on the new spatialities of call centre work in Germany.

A key issue addressed throughout these chapters is whether and if so the extent to which changes in the spatiality, temporality and contractuality of work are associated with the knowledge-based economy, or with changes in social relations consequent on changes in capitalism associated with glob-alization that tilts the balance between capital and labour, or with changes in gender regimes associated with either welfare provision or labour market regulation associated with a move from a more domestic to a more public form.

Implications of the knowledge economy for the quality of working life

The development of the knowledge economy has been associated with divergent social processes. First, it is argued that the development of a knowledge-based economy provides higher skilled, more autonomous, more flexible, better quality jobs, coordinated through flatter hierarchies and net-works. Knowledge has newly become the primary source of productivity and competitiveness. The shift from an industrial to a knowledge-based economy affects both the content and organizational form of employment. This is because the nature of the work requires cooperation and communi-cation rather than coordination through simple hierarchies. It enables greater flexibility in the use of labour time, removes certain types of spatial constraints on where work is carried out, and facilitates the development of new forms of careers and attachments to the providers of work (Castells 1996; Drucker 1993b; Handy 1994; Lam 2002; Nonaka and Takeuchi 1995; Nonaka and Nishiguchi 2001; Quinn 1992; Reich 1991; Rodrigues 2003). The focus is on human-based knowledge, varying in emphasis from educa-tion and human capital (Reich 1991), to the creation of knowledge within firms during the dynamic relationship between the tacit and explicit knowl-edge of workers and managers (Nonaka and Takeuchi 1995; Nonaka and Nishiguchi 2001). The belief that a knowledge-based economy can provide high quality as well as more jobs underlies EU economy policy as expressed in the 2000 Lisbon European Council's adoption of the goal that the Euro-pean Union should become 'the most competitive and dynamic knowledge-based economy in the world capable of sustainable economic growth with more and better jobs and greater social cohesion' (European Commission 2000b; Rodrigues 2003).

A second approach understands the new ICT-based economy leading to a process of de-regulation and degradation of the conditions of working life as a result of the increased global interconnections consequent on new ICTs, which tilt the balance of power between capital and labour towards capital, partly because it is more mobile than labour (Castells 1996, 1997, 1998; Crouch and Streeck 1997; Standing 1999). This engages a process through which states reduce social protection and increase the flexibility of their workforces, in order to follow prevailing views about the best way to compete in a global marketplace (Cerny 1996). Martin and Schumann (1997) see global capital undermining conditions of working life, Crouch and Streeck (1997) see capital undermining national welfare states, while Sennett (1998) argues that these changes are leading to a corrosion of character, since people need the stability of the old ways of working. For example, Dex and McCulloch (1997: 187–8) conclude, on the basis of BHPS data, that 'Britain is sliding into being a low wage, low skill economy in which the quality of jobs is declining.' Similarly, Millward, Bryson and Forth (2000: 224) argue that Conservative governments sought to 'weaken the power of the trade unions, deregulate the labour market and dismantle many of the tripartite institutions of corporatism in which trade unions played a major part'.

These two processes of knowledge and ICT-based economic developments leading to enriched work and to degraded working conditions are not necessarily mutually exclusive. While some writers have focused on linking one rather than both of these processes to globalization, others have noted how both processes coexist in time, but not in space. These developments are leading to the global polarization of rich and poor according to one's position in relation to the new skills needed in the economy (Castells 1996, 1997, 1998; Standing 1999). That is, an individual's experience in the workplace depends on social location, either spatial in the sense of country, region or city zone, or social location, in the sense of class, education, ethnicity, nationality and gender. For instance, Huws, Jager and O'Regan (1999) argue that teleworking will relocate globally to those countries where there is broad access to affordable telecommunications, relatively deregulated labour markets, appropriate household sizes and structures, and a skilled workforce. Castells (1996, 1997, 1998) and Standing (1999) suggest that the consequences are likely to be beneficial to those who are able to access the relevant skills, but may be problematic to those who do not. They argue that those who have the skills needed in the knowledge-based economy, as a result of their social location, will be advantaged, while those who do not will suffer many disadvantages. There is thus a remaining empirical question as to the balance between these processes and the extent to which they take place in different locations. These locations and circumstances may be associated with path-dependent rather than generic forms of development, in which countries diverge. They may also be the result of differential insertion in global networks and processes. Indeed some of the high quality and low quality dimensions of work in new emerging occupations can occur simultaneously. Gottschall and Kroos (in this volume) analyse the self-employed cultural industry workers, as emblematic of these issues. These workers are high skill with considerable autonomy and flexibility, but also bear a higher share of the risks (such as those associated with unemployment and sickness), which in other groups are borne to a greater extent by employers and the state.

The different definitions of the knowledge economy produce quite different profiles and scales of the knowledge economy. The high technology manufacturing, ICT and information sectors constitute quite small proportions of employment, while the knowledge-intensive sector has quite a large share. The knowledge economy is usually defined as an industrial sector, rather than in terms of occupations. However, since occupations are important in shaping the quality of working life, it can be helpful to investigate the association between knowledge economy industries and the occupations that they contain. This enables the investigation of the question as to whether the knowledge economy leads to the growth of higher skilled jobs. Even when technology is cutting-edge there is no necessary reason why the associated occupations should be disproportionately high skill. This is an empirical question. There is a further question as to whether women are well or badly positioned in the knowledge industries. Although the identification of the occupations associated with the knowledge economy is difficult and there is no one set that is agreed throughout the OECD, nevertheless, OECD (2002b) has identified a provisional set using the US Current Population Survey (CPS) and the ISCO-88 occupation data from the Eurostat Labour Force Survey. It found that ICT related occupations were growing everywhere. High skill ICT workers were the most rapidly growing component of high skilled workers. Computer workers were the largest group of the high skilled ICT workers. There is considerable variation between countries. In the US, the ICT workforce were more high skilled (77 per cent) than those in the EU, in 1999, within which there was further widespread variation. In the EU (EU 14) low skill occupations made up 44 per cent of ICT related occupations as compared with 23 per cent in the US (OECD 2002b). Within the EU, almost 30 per cent of those employed in the high technology sector are high skilled, here defined as having completed tertiary education, while in the knowledge-intensive sector, 42 per cent were high skilled. This compares with 24 per cent of all those currently employed being high skilled. Thus the high technology and knowledge-intensive sectors had much higher rates of high skilled workers than other economic sectors. The high technology sector employs around 11 per cent of workers in the EU. Within the EU, between 1995 and 2001, employment growth in the high tech sector increased at 2.2 per cent a year and in the knowledge-intensive service sector by 2.9 per cent a year. Of the new jobs created in this period almost 20 per cent were in the high tech sector and about 70 per cent in the knowledge-intensive sector. The four fastest growing sectors in the EU, 1995–2000, were 'other business activities', health and social work, education, and computer and related activities, which together constituted 58 per cent of the net employment creation (European Commission 2002: 9, 23, 28, 29). These developments are consistent with the view that the development of human capital is key to the development of the knowledge economy and for economic growth. For example, de la Fuente and Ciccone (2002) argue that investment in human capital contributes significantly to productivity growth and to technological change and diffusion.

However, as Serrano-Pascual and Mósesdóttir (2003) argue, there are several reasons to be cautious about simply generalizing these processes to women and to more specifically investigate whether women are benefiting as much as men from the high skill components of these developments. There are two main types of reasons for this caution. The first is the role of occupational segregation by sex, which remains in all labour markets (Anker 1998). It is important to note that women are less prevalent than men in the ICT sector. For example, in the UK, women are a minority of those in information technology occupations, especially the higher-level occupations (Walby 2001). The second is whether women are as able as men to translate formal educational qualifications into employment assets. These remain important questions for analysis, and are considered throughout the book.

Varieties of capitalism and gender regime

Introduction

The comparative analysis of the development of the gendered knowledge economy in different countries requires a conceptualization of the variations in the forms of capitalist and gendered social relations. This integration of gender into comparative analyses of employment requires a re-thinking of the concepts traditionally used for comparative analysis. This section introduces a critical review of the literature on the varieties of capitalism and varieties of gender regime. There are several sources of variation in the forms of capitalism and gender regime. These include the level of economic development, path-dependent forms of development, and their location in international regimes, transnational polities and global political waves.

Economic development

The level of economic development may be understood in several different ways. The traditional approach is that of the level of income per person, or more precisely, GDP per capita. However, recent challenges have developed to this measure of development, not least from the human capabilities approach of Sen (1984, 1999) and Nussbaum (2000) and operationalized by the United Nations Development Programme into indices of human development (HDI). An alternative approach is to focus on the stages of the development of the economy. While this has been seen as a transition from agriculture to industry to services, Castells (1996, 2001) has argued that the information age should be regarded as the latest form of economic development.

The traditional analysis of economic development has rarely brought gender into focus. As Bakker (1998) argues, there has been a 'strategic silence' concerning gender especially in omitting domestic care-work from the concept and measurement of the economy. Rather, it can be argued that the economy includes not only paid work in the market, but also unpaid domestic work. There is an important gender dimension to economic development, not least in the extent to which women engage in paid work rather than unpaid domestic care-work (Orloff 1993; Walby 1997).

There is not one single trajectory of economic development, but rather several path-dependent variations. The relative importance of generic and path-dependent processes is addressed in the book. These generic and path-dependent processes are relevant to both the dynamics of capitalism and the dynamics of gender regimes. The conceptualization of path-dependent forms is addressed in the literature on the varieties of capitalism. Here it is argued that it is additionally necessary to address the conceptualization of the variations in patterns of gender relations and also the intersection between varieties of capitalism and varieties of gender regimes.

Varieties of capitalism

The analysis of the varieties of capitalism has had two main foci: the capitalist production system in the context of the state, and the welfare state in the context of the capitalist production system.

The analysis of varieties of capitalist production regimes has taken various forms, although they have a common focus on the institutions associated with market-based production, especially the nature of the relations between employers, labour and governmental institutions, which are key to the coordination of the economy (Boyer and Durand 1997; Crouch 1982, 1993; Hall and Soskice 2001; Hirst and Zeitlin 1997; Hollingsworth 1997; Hollingsworth and Boyer 1997a, 1997b; Jessop 2002; Lash and Urry 1987, 1994; Streeck 1992; Streeck and Yamamura 2002; Yamamura and Streeck 2003). These accounts locate an analysis of production systems in wider social contexts that cluster into distinctive groups of countries. These distinctions have often been typified in some kind of duality, though with varying conceptualization and with emphasis on different institutions. These include the distinction between corporatism and liberalism (Crouch 1982), liberal market or coordinated market economies (Hall and Soskice 2001), between institutionally thin and thick societies (Streeck 1992), liberal and non-liberal (Streeck and Yamamura 2002), and between Fordism and post-Fordist flexible specialization (Piore and Sabel 1984).

These accounts of the varieties of capitalist production regimes differ on a series of dimensions, the most significant of which are: the use of different terms to signify the duality of varieties of capitalism; whether there are further subdivisions, especially within the 'corporatist' or equivalent category; the focal institutions (especially: organizations of employers and labour and the relative importance of each; the firm; capital, labour and the state; all social institutions); the closeness and nature of the coupling of the institutions within the system; whether the difference is primarily developmental or path-dependent; whether complex inequalities other than class are included; whether globalization or other forms of international relations are included.

An early distinction was between liberal and corporatist, where the liberal form is primarily coordinated through the market and the corporatist is coordinated through institutions including the state (Crouch 1982; Olson 1982). The focus is on the role of capital and labour, especially in their organized forms, and the extent to which their relationship is mediated by the state. The duality of forms of capitalism suggested by Streeck (1992) distinguishes between societies that are institutionally 'thicker' or 'thinner', thus broadening the range of institutions considered relevant. 'Institutionally "thinner" societies are those that allow a comparatively large space for free contract and individual choice in relatively unregulated markets and hierarchies, while institutionally "thicker" societies subject the actions of rational individuals to a richer set of regulations and constraints' (Streeck 1992: 37). Streeck's distinctive contribution is to broaden the range of institutions that are considered relevant. In Streeck and Yamamura (2002), the conceptual distinction is revised to that between liberal and non-liberal forms of capitalism.

A parallel duality of forms of capitalism is made by Hall and Soskice (2001: 8) who distinguish between 'liberal market economies' (LMEs) in which 'firms coordinate their activities primarily via hierarchies and competitive market relations' and 'coordinated market economies' (CMEs) in which 'firms depend more heavily on non-market relationships to coordinate endeavours with other actors and to construct their core competencies'. In the LMEs demand and supply of the market are important, in the CMEs, strategic interactions between firms and other actors are important. The firm is placed as the central actor in this analysis, rather than the more traditional focus on the relations between organizations of capital and labour. This is in contrast to much earlier work on varieties of capitalism that focused primarily on the differential organizational strength of labour. Nevertheless, the range of institutions considered relevant still includes the traditional range of employer associations, trade unions, shareholding networks and legal systems. Thus in practice, the range of institutions is not so different, even though the dynamic of the analysis is distinctive in that it is firm-centred, not labour-centred.

Further dualistic distinctions in forms of capitalism include several that start from the distinction between Fordism and post-Fordism or flexible specialization, where Fordism is the social organization associated with mass production and mass consumption, and flexible specialization the social organization associated with craft specialization and niche consumerism (Piore and Sabel 1984). This analysis contains both a temporal notion of the process of development as well as that of divergent paths of development coexisting in time. The extent to which this distinction is treated as a temporal development process or one of path-dependency varies in related texts. Boyer and Durand (1997) distinguish between Fordism and after Fordism in their 'regulation' approach to 'production systems'. The lead element is 'sociotechnical', by which is meant the regulation of the consumption/production link based on technologies and forms of work organization, while the overall model has very close interconnections between associated social institutions. Hollingsworth (1997) and Hollingsworth and Boyer (1997b) distinguish between 'mass standardised' and 'flexible specialisation' 'systems of social production', together with further subtypes including those of 'diversified quality mass production' for Japan and 'diversified quality production' for Germany. A mass standardized system involves economies of scale and a standardized system of production, while flexible specialization is the production of goods by general-purpose resources and a production system that flexibly adapts to different market demands (Hollingsworth 1997: 271–2). The concept of 'system of social production' is used to capture the coupling of a series of institutions so as to make up a specific system. While all social institutions are potentially part of this system, including those of civil society, in practice the focus is on the nature of firms, technology, labour–management relations, relationships with other firms, skills, education and legislation, that is, not so far from the traditional trilogy of organization of capital, labour and the state.

A different focus for the analysis of variations in capitalism is that on the state, situated in the context of other social, political and economic institutions (Esping-Andersen 1990, 1997a, 1999; Huber and Stephens 2000, 2001a; Jessop 2002). Esping-Andersen distinguishes between types of welfare state regime on the basis of the extent to which they decommodify labour and links this to forms of organization of the economy. In this way he establishes that there is not a single logic to capitalist development, but significant path-dependent variations. In his early work (1990) there were three main clusters – liberal (including US and UK), conservative corporatist (including Germany) and social democratic – to which he added, following extensive debate, a residual cluster (1999), while Japan was considered a hybrid case (1997a).

The integration of these approaches to varieties of capitalism focusing either on production or the state has proven challenging (Ebbinghaus and Manow 2001), though there are significant attempts to do this (Huber and Stephens 2000, 2001a; Jessop 2002). Huber and Stephens (2000, 2001a) are important in including political institutions and gender politics in the analysis of variations. There are varying conceptions of the breadth of and relations between the elements of the system, with considerable variation in the extent to which institutions cohere and the nature of the process by which this might obtain. There is variation in the closeness of the coupling of the various institutions.

While these discussions of the varieties of capitalism have made important and subtle distinctions that enable an analysis of path-dependent as well as generic development, there are a number of limitations. The most important of these for present concerns is the relative neglect of social divisions other than class, especially those associated with gender, which, with significant exceptions (e.g. Huber and Stephens 2000, 2001a), tend to be treated descriptively or as derivative and marginal. Esping-Andersen (1990, 1999), while noting the empirical and political importance of gender relations, resists theorizing these autonomously from capitalist dynamics. The argument here is that gender cannot be reduced in a simple way to class relations.

Varieties of patterns of gender relations

Gender relations are not an absolute but vary over time and place. The theorization of these variations is one of the major issues addressed in this book. Early accounts, while empirically noting the malleability of gender relations, found it hard to theorize and explain the variations in them. This section starts by examining some of the reasons why it has been found hard to theorize variations in gender relations even when they are empirically recognized. This is followed by a review of three of the most important bodies of literature that have theorized variations in systems of gender relations, including models of variations in the extent to which families have a 'male breadwinner', gendered politics and gender regimes.

Early feminist theory tended to oscillate between simple reductionist theories of gender inequality and accounts that were so complex that they effectively constituted rich descriptions. Many early theories of gender relations used an implicit base–superstructure model in which one element, ranging from sexuality to domestic labour, was identified as key to understanding all aspects of gender inequality. This type of analysis was criticized as simplistic, essentialist and reductionist (Segal 1987). A polar opposite approach rejected the notion that different dimensions of gender relations could be understood to be systematically interrelated (Spellman 1988). Instead, priority was given to the analysis of differences, for instance, 'race', 'ethnicity' and nation (Yuval-Davis 1997). This resulted in a fragmentation of the analysis of gender and the ontologizing of difference (Felski 1997), making it impossible to theorize the sources of differences, although they may be richly described.

More recently a middle way has developed between these two poles that rejects both the base–superstructure model and the primary focus on difference, and instead theorizes gender relations as systems that contain a limited number of key elements. This has taken several forms, including analyses of variations in the extent to which a household is marked by a male breadwinner, variations in feminist politics, and the concept of the gender regime.

Male breadwinner models

The first major comparative analysis of systems of gender relations focused on variations in the extent to which households were marked by a male breadwinner or whether this was modified or contained dual earners (Hobson 1994; Jenson 1997; Lewis 1992, 1993; O'Connor, Orloff and Shaver 1999; Ostner and Lewis 1995; Sainsbury 1994, 1996). One starting point for this debate was that of Esping-Andersen's (1990, 1999) typology of three forms of welfare capitalism: liberal, social democratic and corporatist. Despite noting gender, Esping-Andersen underestimated the significance of gender relations. He underestimated the full implications of the commodification of women's labour (from domestic to wage labour) for their welfare because of a theoretical framework, which asserts that de-commodification (from dependence on the wage to support from the state) is the most effective basis of equity (Orloff 1993). The typology most used to insert this focus on the specificity of gender relations is that of Lewis (1992), developed with Ostner (Ostner and Lewis 1995), though this has been much refined and amplified in ensuing debate. In Lewis (1992) the basis of the divisions within the typology lies in the extent to which there is a 'male breadwinner–female housewife' model. This ranges from 'strong male breadwinner', 'modified male breadwinner' to 'weak male breadwinner' (sometimes referred to as 'dual earner'), with slight variations according to specific publication. Examples of each are given, though they vary a little between articles: Ireland is taken as most typical of the strong male breadwinner model, with Britain sometimes being included (Lewis 1992) while at others being seen, like Germany and France, as modified male breadwinner (Lewis 1992, 1993); and Sweden as a 'weak' male breadwinner model (Lewis 1992), sometimes, dual-earner.

Debate on Lewis' model has suggested that the distinctions are overly simple, though Lewis herself notes that it was only intended to be an initial mapping exercise (1992, 1997). This has led to suggestions for adding further sources of variation beyond that of strong, modified or weak breadwinner (Hobson 1994; Jenson 1997; Korpi 2000; Orloff 1993; Sainsbury 1994, 1996). One of these sources of variance is over whether women's family role is considered in terms of their being wives or mothers, in addition to the contrast with their being workers, leading to a threefold typology as to the bases of welfare state support to women: as wives, mothers or workers (Sainsbury 1996). A further source of variance is whether the mode of resourcing care is as a service, money to purchase services, or as money for time at home. Jenson (1997) suggests inserting a focus on care, rather than unpaid work into the framework on work and welfare, arguing that care is not the same as unpaid work since care-work may be paid. She makes distinctions between three sets of questions: Who cares? Who pays? How much is provided? A further broadening of the issues considered relevant is developed in O'Connor, Orloff and Shaver (1999) by the inclusion of the regulation of the labour market, the significance of feminist movements and the role of the state in providing or restricting access to bodily autonomy, such as rights to contraception, abortion and sexual expression. However, since the comparisons were restricted to those within liberal states, the implications of this broader range of variables for comparisons with other state formations are as yet unexplored. Gottschall and Bird (2003) argue for the importance of different forms of education system and their implications for gender relations, including a consideration of its relationship with employment. Gottfried (2000), Gottfried and O'Reilly (2002) and Gottfried and Reese (2003) argue for the importance of synthesizing the gendered welfare state analysis with that of both the schools of welfare analysis and industrial relations approaches, so as to combine the traditions of both class and gender analysis.

One of the simultaneous strengths and weaknesses of this body of literature is its focus. On the one hand, the narrow focus on a single dimension (male breadwinnerness of the household) has assisted the development of the field, providing conditions that facilitate cumulation rather than dissipation of knowledge. On the other hand, there are many aspects of gender relations that are not included, or included in only marginal ways because of a tendency to focus on issues of primary concern to working mothers (Brush 2002). Thus, a limitation to this evolving body of literature lies in its relative timidity as to the range of elements of the gender regime that are included in the models.

There are further areas that may be additionally incorporated into the analysis. First, there is a need for a greater appreciation of the nature and causes in the variance in the forms of gendered employment relations. This is a challenge to the assumption that the extent of women's employment is primarily a result of the extent to which the state socializes domestic labour. The provision of services by the state is insufficient by itself to account for the variations in women's employment. Second, it requires a consideration of democracy and political action. The nature and extent of political and especially democratic participation is curiously neglected in a framework ostensibly structured by an interest in the impact of the state on gender.

Comparative feminist politics

The second major body of comparative literature on gender relations is that concerned with the extent and nature of women's political power. This is especially developed in the context of the RNGS project, which has developed a methodology for comparative analysis of the impact of women's movements and the role of women's policy agencies (RNGS 2005; Mazur 2002). The key question for the analysis is to discover the circumstances under which women's movements are more or less likely to impact on the state. The comparative methodology draws on work on the gendering of democratic representation, in particular, the extent to which an increase in the number of elected women in national parliaments increases the substantive representation of women's interests, the role of new forms of institutions, especially those of women's units in government, as well as social movement theory, especially frame analysis. The unit of analysis for the comparative studies is that of 'policy debate' rather than nation-state, though this entails a comparison of policy debates in different countries. Impact is understood as 'problem definition, policy content and policy making process' and analysed along two dimensions following Gamson (1975), first, that of substantive responses in policy content, and second, that of the inclusion of women and women's organizations within the policy-making process, logically generating four possible outcomes. In the formal model the dependent variable is this 'impact', the independent variables those of women's movement characteristics and policy environment, while the intervening variables are the women's policy agency characteristics and women's policy agency activities. The project is a development from early comparative work on state feminism (Stetson and Mazur 1995a) and includes empirical studies of job training (Mazur 2001b), abortion (McBride 2001), prostitution (Outshoorn 2004), and political representation (Lovenduski 2005).

The RNGS project constitutes a major advance in the development of comparative analysis of gender and politics, engaging with a diverse range of forms of politics and integrating these into a remarkably cohesive theoretical framework. However, from the point of view of the present agenda the framework might be considered incomplete without greater attention to economic factors.

Comparative gender regimes

A third approach includes a wider range of elements in the model used to theorize comparative gender relations. In parallel, and independently, both Walby (1986, 1990, 1994, 1997) and Connell (1987, 2002) developed theoretical models of gender regimes (Walby) and gender orders (Connell), which included a broad but limited number of factors that shaped gender relations. In the case of both Connell and Walby, it is the plurality of key elements that enables their theoretical frameworks to be used to theorize variations in the forms taken by the gender system over time and space, unlike those models that focused on one base.

Walby's (1994, 2007) model has four levels of abstraction: system; forms – a continuum from domestic to public with the public further differentiated into market-led and state-led; three systems of economy (divided into the market and domestic economies), polity, and civil society (including gender-based violence and sexuality); and many detailed specific practices. The forms of the gender regime are ranged along a continuum from domestic to public. This makes it possible to theorize differences in gender relations in time and space. In particular, there is an analytic separation of the notion of the degree of gender inequality from that of the form of the gender regime. This creates the theoretical space for the possibility that an increase of women in the public sphere, in particular in employment, does not necessarily entail a reduction in the degree of gender inequality. Rather this was an empirical question. Walby (1990) developed the distinction between a market-led and state-led route from the domestic to the public form (always in the context of political struggle). This provided the basis for the construction of an explicit comparative framework (Walby 1994). Walby (1997, 2007) focuses on the variety of forms of gender regime and of gender inequality, across both time and space, analysing local and regional variations. In this way, Walby develops more systematic distinctions between forms of gender regime than does Connell.

The concept of gender regime is intended to capture the systematic interrelationship between different dimensions of gender relations. There is complex mutual constitution of the different gender domains. Variations in the forms of gender relations, between public and domestic forms, can be found in each of the main domains of gender relations, as well as at the level of the system as a whole. During this transformation the shift from domestic to public form takes place in each of the economy, polity and civil society, each having implications for the further transformation of the other domains. It is possible to distinguish different types of trajectory from the domestic to public form of gender regime, in particular to distinguish between a market-led and state-led trajectory, which has different implications for the degree of gender inequality. The complex forms of variation in form of gender regime between countries are constituted by these variations in domains and practices. These are not fixed systems, but fluid and changing, co-evolving with other complex adaptive systems in a changing fitness landscape. A country is not a closed system since many gender domains cross national frontiers. Collective political agency constitutes an important part of the processes by which changes in the forms of the regime change. There are multiple forms and sites of actants, not merely individual agents and social structures. Gender relations are always formed in relation to processes of class, ethnicity, nation, religion and many other forms of difference. Gender, as experienced, is an effect of the complex co-evolution of gender relations with other systems of social relations.

The inclusion of gendered relations within the economy, polity and civil society within the gender regime means that a broader range of social forces is considered to constitute gender relations than in the literatures on the 'male breadwinner' and in the RNGS approach to gender politics.

Integrating varieties of capitalism and varieties of gender regime

While all the writers in this book seek to examine the implications of the interactions of varieties of capitalism and varieties of gender relations, they do so in different ways. This is an ongoing source of creative and productive intellectual tension which drives current debates. Walby uses the concept of varieties of gender regime, and analyses the intersection with varieties of capitalism. Shire (in this volume) also uses the concept of gender regime and distinguishes between liberal and non-liberal forms of capitalism. Some of the other contributing authors prefer different concepts to capture variations in gender and class relations and their inter-relationship. Gottschall and Kroos (in this volume) use the concept of male breadwinner, though broadening the associated concept of welfare state regime to give greater prominence to the varied organization of education (see also Gottschall and Bird 2003). Osawa (in this volume) engages in debate with Esping-Andersen on the nature of the welfare state regime in Japan in comparison with other countries, using the concept of male breadwinner to capture the specificity of the Japanese livelihood security systems, and elsewhere (Osawa 1994) refers to systems of both capitalism and patriarchy. Lenz (in this volume) uses both the concept of gender regime (which is defined as comprising the gender institutions in government and women's movements) and that of gendered welfare regime to capture gender relations and considers their intersection with varieties of capitalism. In each case there is an attempt to develop a conceptual vocabulary that enables a systematic comparative account of changes in patterns of gender relations.

Employment regulations at the intersection of varieties of capitalism and varieties of gender regime

The differentiation of the gendered implications of varied forms of regulation of employment is important in the theorization of the varieties of gender regime. They also have important, if much underestimated, implications for the varieties of capitalism.

The early writings in the 'male breadwinner' and 'comparative feminism' made a tremendous contribution to the comparative analysis of gender relations. However, one element of comparison, that of variations in the regulation of gendered employment relations, was rarely included as a significant factor. Writers in the GLOW group have made various contributions to include this factor in comparisons of patterns of gender relations, including Gottfried (2000, 2003; Gottfried and O'Reilly 2002), Shire (2000) and Walby (1986, 1994, 2007).

The notion of regulation is interpreted in different ways. One is a broad concept of the social institutions in which capitalist production operates as in the definition regulation school of Marxists (Boyer and Durand 1997; Jessop 2002). Another is a narrower concept that is restricted to legally binding regulations endorsed by the state (Walby 1994, 1999a, 1999b, 2001) (used in this chapter).

The varieties of capitalism literature places considerable emphasis on the level and nature of employment regulations and their development as part of a system of social relations between capital (employers, employer organizations, and firms), labour (especially trade unions) and the state, which is embedded in a wider social system. The gendered varieties of 'male breadwinner' comparative literature focuses on policies considered 'welfare', including the provision of childcare (services, or funds), the educational system, and the tax/benefit system (see Gottschall and Kroos in this volume; Osawa in this volume).

The argument here is that there are important sets of employment regulations that have implications for gender relations. While their development has been subject to detailed specific analysis (Hoskyns 1996; Pillinger 1992), they are rarely included as central elements in either the varieties of capitalism or the varieties of male breadwinner literatures (though see Gottfried 2000; Gottfried and O'Reilly 2002). Employment regulations have direct or indirect implications for gender relations in at least four ways.

(1) There are regulations that are concerned directly with the equal treatment of women and men in employment, such as regulations for equal pay and to prevent discrimination.
(2) There are regulations concerned with the relationship between care and employment, in the context where women disproportionately provide care. Examples include the regulation of working time, especially work/life balance policies such as maternal, paternal and parental leaves, and those restricting the ability of employers to demand excessively long working hours.
(3) There are regulations of employment practices that are often but not inevitably gendered, for example, the overt application of equal treatment laws to part-time employment, which is disproportionately performed by women.
(4) There are employment regulations that have gender implications as a consequence of the uneven coverage of different categories of workers that are themselves gendered, for example the extension of employment protections to those who work over a certain number of hours or who have a direct relationship with an employer.

The social and political relations that are associated with different regulatory regimes may be differentiated by gender in some significant respects. Changes in regulations associated with class relations have been affected by globalization, which, under certain circumstances, has been associated with the tipping of the relations of capital and labour towards capital. However, different processes have been occurring in relation to gendered employment regulations, associated with the transformation of the gender regime and the increasing political voice of women as they increasingly enter the public domain (Walby 1997, 2002b, 2007), the development of the European Union in response to the perceived challenge of globalization (Hoskyns 1996; Pillinger 1992; Walby 1994, 1999a, 1999b), and political processes associated with globalization (Keck and Sikkink 1998; Lenz in this volume; Roberts in this volume). In this context, gender and class dynamics in the regulation of employment are diverging, thereby challenging the assumptions of the varieties of capitalism literature. While there have been uneven processes of de-regulation in relation to the class dimension of employment relations over the last twenty years, in relation to gender there has been a process of increased polity-based regulation of gender relations in employment.

Globalization

Globalization has a political dimension as well as economic and cultural ones. Globalization is here defined as an increase in social interactions and connections over space, especially internationally (Chase-Dunn et al. 2000). The definition of globalization used here is minimal in order to avoid conflating it with a specific cause. This avoids conflating it with resurgent neo-liberal capitalism, or with the rise of a new hegemon, or with new information and communication technologies. While sympathetic to the claim that what is really new is the increased importance of phenomena that are extra-territorial (Scholte 2000), this view underestimates the extent to which most global processes at some point have a terrestrial connection (Sassen 1999). This definition allows for globalization to be associated not only with economic processes, but also those that concern politics and civil society.

In the current global era it is not appropriate to narrowly confine a comparative analysis to processes taking place within specific countries. It is also necessary to examine transnational and global processes and their interaction with national institutions. In the context of a comparison of the US, UK, Germany and Japan, there are three main issues: first, the varied resilience of national political institutions to the imperatives of global capital; second, the development of the transnational polity of the European Union; third, the linkages provided by global social movements in the context of global institutions such as the UN.

Globalization does not have a uniform impact on all countries. Political institutions can critically mediate the impact of globalization (Hall and Soskice 2001; Swank 2002), so that globalization may lead to new sources of difference rather than homogeneity. This is because political institutions of advanced capitalist countries have different kinds of capacities to respond to the challenges of globalization as a consequence of forms of electoral system, the nature of interest group representation, relative centralization or decentralization of policy-making authority and the structuring of welfare programme provision, and only in those countries that have a more liberal political structure do pressures of globalization lead to reductions in the welfare state, while in the large welfare states of northern Europe there has been little impact (Swank 2002). To the extent that such institutions mediate the response to the pressures of globalization, so there can be no simple assertion that globalization leads to a general undermining of the conditions of employment. This mediation and resilience may also be gendered (Huber and Stephens 2000, 2001a).

First, there is the importance of the development of transnational polities, especially the European Union. The majority of the legal regulation of the economic sphere in the EU now emanates from the EU rather than member state level. While in matters of welfare provision and family policy, the principle of subsidiarity means that policies are determined at the national level, this is not the case for matters concerning the economy. This regulation includes the regulation of the labour market, including a wide range of equal treatment policies. Within the EU there has been a major increase in gender equality policies (Hoskyns 1996; Pillinger 1992; Walby 1994, 1999a, 1999b) and their mainstreaming (Pollack and Hafner-Burton 2000; Walby 2005). This produces greater similarities between the economic aspects of the gender regime in Germany and the UK than might be the case if it were not for the EU. The powers of the EU entail the moderation of the judgement that the UK has a liberal form of economic governance. However, there are still significant differences in the industrial relations systems of Germany and the UK as a consequence of historical legacy and ensuing path-dependent development.

Second, globalization has implications for the development of links between feminists in different locations. The development of feminist transnational advocacy networks (Keck and Sikkink 1998), near global feminist strategies and practices (Nelson and Chowdhury 1994), and the strengthening and gender inflecting of a discourse of universal human rights (Peters and Wolper 1995) have further developed opportunities for the institutionalization of gender equality goals in national and transnational polities (Walby 2002b).

The development of new forms of communication technologies, the development of fast cheap long-distance travel, and the development of global political institutions and networks have implications for the transfer of political ideas and practices as to the appropriate regulation of employment from one part of the globe to another (Berkovitch 1999; Moghadam 2000; Walby 2002b). This has involved the development of new forms of political and policy intervention including transnational advocacy networks (Keck and Sikkink 1998), epistemic communities and argumentation at an international level. Transnational feminist and human rights movements have played an important role in providing access to new forms of legitimation for local and national organizations seeking to change the regulation of employment so as to improve the position of women (Nelson and Chowdhury 1994). The transfer of political ideas and practices via social movements that increasingly communicate across national boundaries is complex; they are rarely simple processes of impact or transfer but can involve complex processes of hybridization and co-evolution.

Lenz (in this volume) addresses the complex interplay between local, national and international political actors in the development of regulations for gender equality at work. The development of global women's movements provides information, ideas and resources to women around the world. Different national settings produce different contexts for the development of feminist interventions, in particular, varying as to whether there is a corporatist arrangement. In Germany, where women are caught by their integration into the remnants of an eroding corporatism, the EU proved an important source of power. In Japan, the international connections, this time more global via CEDAW, also provided a valuable additional source of momentum.

A further example of the implications of globalization for policy development is that of the transfer of management policies from one country to another in the context of multinational companies with firms in more than one country (Roberts in this volume). The development of transnational corporations may mean that employment practices developed in one country may be imposed on another, though mediated by state policies and international regimes.

Gendering, de-gendering and re-gendering of employment practices

The gender composition of occupations, industries and employment forms changes in complex ways associated with the development of the knowledge economy, the regulation and de-regulation of employment associated with the intersection of the varieties of capitalism and the varieties of gender regime. The presence of women may rise or fall as a result of these complex intersections, leading to the gendering, de-gendering or re-gendering of the employment under scrutiny.

Comparisons

Introduction

The next section of the chapter compares the processes associated with gendering, de-gendering and re-gendering associated with the development of the knowledge economy in four countries, the US, UK, Germany and Japan. It sets out basic empirical data in order partly to address the theoretical issues raised in the early part of the chapter and partly to provide context for the other chapters in the book.

Methodological choices

The four countries, the US, UK, Germany and Japan, were chosen for this comparative analysis of the gendered knowledge economy for several reasons. They are the four largest economies in the developed world, so what happens in these countries matters (see Table 1.1). They are also contrasting countries, necessary in order to enable the comparative methodology in the book. The four countries differ on each of the two axes that are important to the explanations being developed. In relation to the varieties of capitalist production regime, two of the countries are 'liberal', the US and UK, while two are non-liberal or coordinated, Germany and Japan (Hall and Soskice 2001; Streeck and Yamamura 2002). In relation to varieties of the capitalist welfare state, the contrast between the liberal regimes of the US and UK with the conservative corporatist regime in Germany remains, while Japan is considered a hybrid, following Esping-Andersen (1990, 1997a, 1999) (see Table 1.2). In relation to the varieties of gender regime, the countries are spread along a continuum from most public to least public, the US being the most public, followed by the UK, Germany and least of all Japan (see below for a fuller account and Tables 1.3 and 1.4). The location of both the UK and Germany within the EU introduces an interesting cross-cutting force, since this is an increasingly regulatory polity in the arena of employment, especially gendered employment.

The level as well as the form of economic and human development is different in the four countries. As Table 1.1 shows, the US has the largest Gross

Table 1.1:   Case study countries: size and level of economic and human development

	US	UK	Germany	Japan
Population, million	294	60	84	128
Gross domestic product PPP $USD billion	11679	1875	2351	3788
GDP per capita $USD PPP	39700	31400	28500	29600
Life expectancy at birth	77.2	78.5	78.4	81.8

PPP: Purchasing Power Parity.
Data for 2004, except for life expectancy which is 2003.
Source: OECD (2005f).

Table 1.2:   Forms of capitalism

	US	UK	Germany	Japan
Liberal or coordinated capitalist production regime	Liberal	Liberal	Coordinated	Coordinated
Capitalist welfare state regime	Liberal	Liberal	Conservative corporatist	Hybrid

Sources: liberal or coordinated: Hall and Soskice (2001); welfare state regime: Esping-Andersen (1990, 1997a, 1999).

Table 1.3: Comparing gender relations

	US	UK	Germany	Japan
Female employment participation rate	69.8	68.5	66.6	64.6
Childcare coverage under 3s (public and private)	54	34	10	13
Childcare coverage 3–school age (public and private)	70	60	78	34
Ratio of female to male tertiary education	1.35	1.20	1.00	0.86
% parliamentary seats held by women, 2004	14.0	17.3	31.4	9.9
Divorce rate	6.2	4.0	3.5	3.1
% births outside of marriage	33.2	39.5	23.4	1.6

Sources: Female employment rate, 2004: OECD (2005f).
Childcare: OECD (2001a), Table 4.7. US: 1995, Japan: 1998, UK (England) and Germany: 2000.
Parliamentary seats: Inter-Parliamentary Union.
Government ministers: UNDP (2004), Table 29. Data for 2001.
Ratio of female to male tertiary education enrolment, 2000/1: UNDP *Human Development Report 2004*, Table 26.

Table 1.4: Patterns of gender relations: male breadwinner; gender regime

	US	UK	Germany	Japan
Male breadwinner model	Weak	Strong/modified	Modified	Strong
Gender regime: what degree of public?	Very public	Public	Quite public	Less public

Sources: male breadwinner model: UK: Lewis (strong 1992, modified 1993); Germany (Lewis 1993), US and Japan are extrapolated from Lewis' model (see text); gender regime Walby (1994, 2007) and text above.

Domestic Product (GDP) per person, and is conventionally considered to be the most economically developed of the four countries. The other three are closely grouped, with the UK having the next largest GDP per capita followed by Japan and then Germany. Of course, GDP per capita is not the only measure of development, being subject to challenge from the capabilities approach (Sen 1999). If the measure of human development is longevity, then the hierarchy among the four countries is reversed. Life expectancy is longest in Japan, followed by the UK and Germany, and shortest in the US. While the focus in this book is on economic development, it is important to remember that this is not the only measure of human progress.

Patterns of gender relations

There are two main ways in which the patterns of gender relations in the four countries are categorized in this book. One model is centred on whether there is a strong male breadwinner in households, or if this is modified, or weak or there is a dual earner household. In addition this addresses the extent to which women are in employment contributing to the household income and the extent to which the state socializes domestic labour to enable this. The second model, that of gender regime, with a continuum between a domestic and a public form, includes a wider range of elements than does the male breadwinner typology. Not only are the participation of women in paid employment and the extent to which the state socializes domestic care work considered relevant, but so also are the extent to which women are active in the public domain, including formal politics and education, the extent to which children are cared for outside of the family, the extent of the state regulation of gender equality in employment, and the permeability of the institution of marriage by practices such as divorce and birth outside of marriage. Data to support the indicators for both the male breadwinner and gender regime models are provided in Table 1.4. This information is used to categorize the four countries in each of the two typologies and the results are presented in Table 1.5.

Table 1.5:   Comparing the regulation of employment by class and gender

Industrial relations	US	UK	Germany	Japan
Trade union density (%)	13	29	20–29	19–24
TU bargaining coverage	18	47	92	21
Centralization of wage bargaining	1	1.5	2	1
Coordination	1	1	3	3
Employment protection legislation	0.7	0.9	2.6	2.3
Employment protection legislation and company level protections	14	25	86	76
Summary ranking of the four countries by degree of industrial relations coordination and regulation	4	3	1	2
Trade union membership, % female	44	50	31	17
Equal treatment legal regulation of employment	Weak	Moderate to strong	Moderate	Very weak
Summary ranking of gendered industrial relations and employment regulations	3	1	2	4

Sources: See Notes, note 1.

Comparing the regulation of the labour market by class and gender

A comparison of the regulation of employment by class and gender is made in Table 1.5. The appendix to this chapter discusses the sources and components used. The summary ranking of the four countries by degree of industrial relations coordination and regulation is based on a simple average of the ranking for each of the six components listed: trade union density, trade union bargaining coverage, centralization of wage bargaining, coordination, employment protection legislation, combined employment protection legislation and company level protections. It is identical, for these four countries, to that found by Estévez-Abe et al. (2001: 165). Germany is the most coordinated and regulated, followed by Japan, then the UK then the US. The summary ranking of the four countries by degree of gendered industrial relations and employment regulations is based on a simple average of the rankings obtained for each of the two elements listed: the percentage of the trade union membership that is female, and the extent of effective legal equal treatment regulation of employment. In summary, the UK has the most gendered industrial relations and employment regulations, followed by Germany, then the US, and lastly Japan. The rankings for the class-based and gender-based regulation of employment are highly divergent. The UK labour market is the most gender regulated (ranked 1), but little class regulated (ranked 3). Japan the least gender regulated (ranked 4), but second-most class regulated (ranked 2).

A comparison of the summary typology of varieties of capitalism and the typologies of gender relations (male breadwinner and gender regime) finds that the countries are similarly grouped (Tables 1.4 and 1.5). Germany and Japan are the most coordinated capitalist economies and also the least public of the gender regimes, and the strongest of the male breadwinner models, as compared with the US and UK which have the most liberal capitalist economies and the most public gender regimes and weakest male breadwinner models. Such similarities pose again the response of Esping-Andersen (1999) to the feminist criticisms of his work: what difference do they make to the allocation of countries to categories? It is argued elsewhere (Walby 2007) that there are differences in the typology relating to several countries not included in this study, including Ireland. The response here is to point to the significant differences in the manner of the regulation of the labour market by class and by gender; these do not map onto each other and this has significant consequences for the gendering of the knowledge economy sector and of new employment forms.

A comparison of the degree of coordination and regulation of employment concerning class relations and gender relations finds very little consistency. The countries with high degrees of coordination and regulation of class relations in employment (Germany, Japan) are not the same as those where there are the highest levels of regulation of gender relations (UK, US).

Japan is highly coordinated and regulated for class relations, but there are few effective interventions and regulations concerning gender relations. The UK is not coordinated or highly regulated for class relations, but is more regulated for gender relations in employment than the other three countries.

This differential class and gender regulation of employment has important consequences for the gendering, de-gendering and re-gendering of occupational and industrial niches.

Comparing the gendering of the knowledge economy

Shire (in this volume) provides unique comparative statistical data on the gendering of the different sectors of the knowledge economy in the US, UK, Germany and Japan. In these countries, the contribution of the ICT sector to employment is just 4–6 per cent, the information sector is 2–3 per cent, while the knowledge-intensive sector is 25–40 per cent. The choice of measure has important implications for the gender profile of knowledge economy workers. Shire finds that women constitute one-third (32–38 per cent) of the ICT sector workers, 39–47 per cent of the information sector, and the majority (54–61 per cent) of the knowledge-intensive sector, as shown in Table 1.6. A key component of the differences in gender composition between the different knowledge economy sectors is that women constitute the majority of health and education workers, which are only included in the knowledge-intensive sector. As Shire notes, the similarities between the countries in the gender composition of each sector of the knowledge economy are quite strong. These similarities exist despite quite wide differences in gendered education and employment levels in the different countries, such as the varied ratio of female to male tertiary education as shown in Table 1.3 above.

Comparing non-standard employment

This section discusses some of the non-standard employment forms associated with new temporalities, contractualities and spatialities, presenting summary comparisons of the four countries based on statistical data. In the chapters in the book there are in-depth analyses of several forms of non-standard employment, including self-employment (Gottschall and Kroos;

Table 1.6: Percentage of women employed in knowledge economy sectors (Shire)

	US	UK	Germany	Japan
ICT	38.4	35.4	32.0	31.2
Information	47.0	41.1	39.1	32.6
Knowledge intensive	58.0	60.4	61.0	54.0

Source: Shire (in this volume, Table 2.5).

Perrons); and new forms of spatiality (Durbin; Holtgrewe), where the nuanced implications of these practices for the quality of working life are explored, as well as more general issues concerning the development on non-standard working. I focus on three examples of non-standard working – temporary work, part-time work and self-employment – where there is robust cross-national data. Other forms not addressed include: various forms of flexible hours, such as term-time working, annualized hours contracts, four and a half day week, job sharing, zero hours contracts, and nine-day fortnights; and new forms of spatiality such as various forms of teleworking, including teleworkers, homeworkers, home-based teleworkers and occasional homeworkers (Walby 2001; Durbin 2004).

Temporary work

Temporary contracts can take various forms, which vary between countries. The majority take the form of a fixed-term contract from a specific and direct employer, but there are other kinds, such as seasonal work, and also agency work and where the relationship with the entity providing the work is more distant (OECD 2002a). Temporary employment is implicated in the knowledge economy thesis predominantly as an example of employment degradation as a result of deregulation associated with competitive globalization, which is itself partly the consequence of the knowledge economy. Temporary employment appears in the gender literature as an example of the disadvantaged employment more likely to be found among women than men, as an instance of gender inequality.

Overall, temporary work is not associated with the high education, high skill end of the labour market (though there are some special niches that are quite different) (see Table 1.7). On average, temporary work is disproportionately carried out by those with lower education, and the jobs are more likely to be low than high skilled. Temporary workers are most likely

Table 1.7: Incidence of temporary employment by individual and job characteristics, 2000

	Female	Male	Low educ	Medium educ	High educ	White collar	Pink collar	Blue collar	Unskilled
Germany	13.1	12.5	29.5	9.2	9.1	10.0	10.3	10.9	15.1
Japan	20.9	7.7							
UK	7.7	5.9	5.3	6.0	8.9	6.5	7.3	4.6	9.5
US	4.2	3.9	6.1	4.1	3.3	3.5	4.2	3.7	7.5
OECD	12.2	10.5	15.7	10.4	9.3	7.7	10.6	9.2	15.3

Note: Share of temporary employment in total dependent employment for the indicated group (percentage).
Source: OECD (2002b) Table 3.3.

to be unskilled, except in the UK, where temporary work is slightly more likely among those with higher education. However, there is considerable diversity within this category, for example, some temporary work may be training positions for high level jobs. Temporary workers are on average paid less than permanent workers (OECD 2002a: Table 3.6).

There has been a very small increase in the amount of temporary employment across the whole OECD in the period 1985–2000 (OECD 2002b: 133) (see Tables 1.8 and 1.9). Within the period 1990–2000, there has been substantial increase (11.6 per cent) in total employment within the OECD, the majority of which, 7.4 percentage points, is accounted for by an increase in permanent employment, though a minority but significant and disproportionate part, 4.2 percentage points, is due to an increase in temporary employment (OECD 2002b: Table 3.2). Although many countries follow this pattern, there are large differences between some countries. In the US there

Table 1.8:   Temporary workers as a percentage of total dependent employment

Country	1983 women	1994 women	2000 women	1983 men	1994 men	2000 men
Germany	11.5	11.0	13.1	9.0	9.8	12.5
Japan	19.5	18.3	20.9	5.3	5.4	7.7
UK	7.3	7.5	7.7	4.2	5.5	5.9
US		2.4	4.2		2.0	3.9
OECD			12.2			10.5

Note: Germany 1983 is 1985.
Source: OECD (1993: Table 1.10); OECD (2002b: Table 3.3).

Table 1.9:   Contributions of temporary and permanent jobs to total employment growth, 1990–2000

Country	Cumulative growth of total employment (percentage)	Percentage point contribution of temporary employment	Percentage point contribution of permanent employment
Germany	−2.1	2.4	−4.5
Japan	11.4	3.8	7.6
UK	6.5	1.9	4.6
US	9.3	−0.5	9.8
OECD	11.6	4.2	7.4

Note: Germany is 1991–2000; US is 1995–2001.
Source: OECD (2002b: Table 3.2).

is an increase from a very low base between 1990 and 2000, remaining low by international standards. The UK shows a small increase in the 1990s only, and remains low by international standards. Germany had stability during the 1980s and early 1990s and an increase between 1994 and 2000, and is close to the OCED average. Japan has a roughly stable pattern, close to the OECD average, but has an unusually extreme gender asymmetry with three times as many women in temporary work (OECD 1993: Table 1.10; OECD 2002b: 133). In the US the majority of the increase in employment was in permanent employment. In Germany, however, there was an increase in temporary employment and a decrease in permanent employment. Germany, with one of the most regulated labour markets and the most coordinated market economy, has seen the greatest shift away from permanent to temporary employment.

Temporary employment is thus higher in the countries with the most regulated labour markets (Japan, Germany) and is lower in the countries with least regulation (US, UK). This is contrary to much of the varieties of capitalism literature, which assumes that temporary employment would be highest where there were least regulations to prevent it. In fact there is the smallest amount of temporary employment in those countries (e.g. US) where permanent employment has the fewest protections. It is larger in those countries in which permanent employment has the most protection. It is in this latter case, where there is the most differentiation in the conditions of employment between these contract types, that temporary employment has most developed.

Temporary work is fairly evenly shared between men and women in the OCED, with it being slightly more common among women (12.2 per cent female and 10.5 per cent of male workers in the OECD) (OECD 2002b: Table 3.3). This is slightly consistent with the association of temporary work with gender inequality. There are variations in the gendering of temporary work. In Japan temporary work is three times as likely for women than for men.

The growth of temporary work is consistent with the thesis that the new employment forms are associated with poor quality working conditions, low skill, low pay and job insecurity. It is a non-standard employment form that is not associated with the newly emerging economic sectors. However, temporary work is not associated with lesser regulated economies, since it is much less common in liberal than in coordinated economies. It is slightly more common among women than men, consistent with the thesis of gender disadvantage. The gendering of temporary work is varied; for example, in Japan most temporary workers are female, suggesting something distinctively gendered about its institutional forms.

The self-employed

Self-employment has been implicated in the knowledge economy thesis in various ways, involving new forms of temporality, spatiality and contractuality, but interpreted in different ways. First, it is associated with the high-skilled, well-educated worker, new ICT-based industry scenario, with associated forms of new temporalities (freedom to choose the hours of work and preferred work-life balance), new spatialities (working from home using ICTs, travelling for work), and new contractualities (freedom from an employer, to be one's own boss). Secondly, it can be associated with the new contractualities in the sense of the ending or weakening of worker entitlements and the increased bearing of risks of unemployment and sickness by individuals rather than employers or the state; new temporalities in the sense of the increased precarity, peaks and troughs in the availability of work over time; and new spatialities in the sense of enforced mobility in search of work.

Gottschall and Kroos (in this volume) provide a detailed comparison of the experience of self-employment with a focus on Germany and the UK and on cultural industries. This explores the complex balance between improved work quality on some dimensions and high risks on others. It provides a nuanced interpretation of the circumstances in which different types of self-employment develop in some countries rather than others, pointing up the importance of including an analysis of path-dependent developments. In the German context self-employment has emerged in new forms of employment associated with the new media industries, outside of the traditional forms of work regulation. Thus despite the highly coordinated nature of the overall German economy, this employment niche has developed in a very distinctive manner.

The rest of the section provides data at a more general level so as to address more general questions. The first issue is the extent to which there have been increases or decreases in self-employment among specific groups or countries which might be associated with the development of the knowledge economy or selective de-regulation associated with the pressures of globalization. A second issue is whether the differences between countries

Table 1.10:   Self-employment, 1973–2004

	1973	1979	1990	1998	2004
Germany	9.1	8.2	7.7	9.4	10.8
Japan	14.0	14.0	11.5	9.7	10.4
UK	7.3	6.6	12.4	11.4	12.7
US	6.7	7.1	7.5	7.0	7.4
OECD		9.8	11.2	11.9	14.4

Note: OECD 1973–1998 excludes Belgium, Czech Republic, Greece, Hungary, Korea, Luxembourg, Mexico, Poland and Turkey; OECD 2004a is for 30 countries.
Source: OECD (2000a: Table 5.1); OECD (2005f: 18–19).

and groups can be accounted for by theories of the varieties of capitalism and varieties of gender regime.

While self-employment can be found across the economy, the industrial sectors and occupational groups where self-employment has grown most during the 1990s are those that are consistent with the knowledge economy thesis. While self-employment has traditionally been concentrated in wholesale and retail trade and repairs, and hotels and restaurants, the growth in the 1990s has been focused on financial intermediation, real estate, renting and business, followed by community, social and personal services (OECD 2000b: 159–60). During the 1990s the occupational groups where there was most growth in self-employment were professionals, technicians and associated professionals (OECD 2000b: 159–62).

However, the conditions under which these workers labour are less consistent with the knowledge economy thesis and more consistent with the deregulatory thesis. The self-employed are more likely to report poorer working conditions, longer hours of work, less training, less use of computers and feel that their jobs are insecure, although despite this, they report higher levels of job satisfaction (OECD 2000b: 156). There is considerable variation in the quality of working life associated with different instances of self-employment. The development of new media and new cultural industries is perhaps the example that fits the knowledge economy thesis most closely (Gottschall and Kroos, this volume; Leadbeater and Oakley 1999; Perrons 2005).

Has self-employment changed? The extent of self-employment has grown in the OECD since 1979. Between 1979 and 2004, self-employment grew from 10 per cent to 14 per cent of employment in the OECD (2000b: 158–9). The timing of the increase is consistent with both the knowledge economy and de-regulation theses.

However, within this overall pattern, there are major differences between countries, as shown in Table 1.10. The US has a relatively low and stable level of self-employment of around 7 per cent from 1973–2004. In Germany there was a small decline from 9 per cent in 1973 to 8 per cent in 1990 and a slight increase to 11 per cent in 2004. In the UK during the 1970s there was a low stable level of 7 per cent, a sharp rise during the 1980s to 12 per cent with near stability since then (12.8 per cent in 2004). In Japan there was a decline from 14 per cent in the 1970s to 10 per cent in 2004.

This differential pattern between countries challenges some of the assumptions in the varieties of capitalism literature, which divides countries according to the nature and degree of coordination and the extent of regulations of the market economy. This is because the least coordinated market economy, the US, has the smallest amount of self-employment. This is inconsistent with the notion that a liberal economy would have more self-employment than coordinated economies. The small growth in self-employment in Germany since 1990 appears to be associated with the development of specific employment niches in the emergent knowledge economy

Table 1.11:   Self-employment by gender share, and gender growth rate

	Women's share of self-employment			Growth of female self-employment		
	1973–1979	1979–1990	1990–1997	1973–1979	1979–1990	1990–1997
Germany	34.2	26.4	28.3	−3.2	−1.2	6.4
Japan	33.6	35.5	33.9	0.4	0.0	−2.8
UK	20.4	23.9	24.8	−1.9	8.9	−1.0
US	27.2	32.9	37.0	5.7	4.2	1.9
OECD	26.4	28.1	29.1	0.7	3.4	1.0

Note: OECD excludes Canada, Finland, France, Greece, Ireland, Korea, Mexico, the Netherlands and Turkey.
Source: OECD (2000a: Table 5.1).

that occurs outside the otherwise tight employment restrictions, perhaps in an attempt to circumvent them (see Gottschall and Kroos in this volume).

Women's share of self-employment has grown slightly (Table 1.11), partly, but not entirely, due to the overall increase in women's employment. The US has experienced the largest change in the gender composition of the self-employed rising from 27 per cent in the 1970s to 37 per cent in the 1990s. The growth in female self-employment has also occurred most in the particular decades in particular countries that saw substantial increases in self-employment, such as the UK during the 1980s and Germany during the 1990s. Since women previously made up a minority of the self-employed, these might be considered moves towards the de-gendering of this employment form, associated with the development of a public rather than domestic gender regime and the increased presence of women across a range of employment forms, with variations associated with variations in the gender regime.

Part-time employment

Part-time working is numerically the most important form of non-standard hours working. It can be implicated in both the account of the knowledge economy as providing more flexible worker-friendly employment practices and as an example of de-regulation and poor quality of working life. Part-time employment is a growing employment form across the OECD, though it has different forms (O'Reilly and Fagan 1998; Osawa 2001) and gender compositions in different countries and is not increasing in all the developed countries (see Tables 1.12 and 1.13) (see Appendix, note 2).

From one perspective, part-time employment may be regarded as a form of flexibility that increases the quality of working life. Most women who

Table 1.12: Part-time employment as a proportion of total employment, 1973–2004

Country	1973	1983	1990	1994	2000	2004
Germany	10.1	12.6	13.4	13.4	17.6	20.1
Japan	13.9	17.5	19.2	21.4	22.6	25.5
UK	16.0	18.4	20.1	22.4	23.0	24.1
US	15.6	15.4	14.1	14.2	12.6	13.2
OECD			11.1	11.6	12.2	15.2

Source: OECD (2000b: Table E); OECD (1996: Table E); OECD (2004a); OECD (2005f).

Table 1.13: Women's share of part-time employment

Country	1973	1983	1990	2000	2004
Germany	89.9	91.9	89.7	84.5	82.8
Japan	70.0	69.5	70.5	69.7	67.4
UK	90.9	89.3	85.1	79.4	77.8
US	66.0	68.0	68.2	68.1	68.3
OECD			73.9	72.0	72.2

Source: OECD (2000b: Table E); OECD (1996: Table E); OECD (2004a); OECD (2005f).

work part-time say when asked that they prefer to do so, despite the other associated conditions (Tomlinson 2004). Across the OECD countries, the proportion of women saying they would prefer to work full-time is well under half, and under 10 per cent in some cases, although around one-quarter of women working part-time would prefer full-time employment. However, among the relatively small number of men working part-time the majority, 59 per cent, would prefer to work full-time (OECD 1999: 32–3). Thus for women, part-time employment may be predominantly considered to fit their current preferences. These preferences are associated with care-work, especially of children.

However, the quality of part-time employment is lower than that of full-time employment on several dimensions, including pay, benefits, security and training. The median hourly earnings of those working part-time is only 76 per cent of those working full-time, the gap being larger among men (71 per cent) than among women (86 per cent) (OECD 1999: Table 1.5). This affects men as well as women, indeed more so. The gap is especially marked for the US and the UK. The pay gap is greater for those on short part-time hours of 20 or fewer per week (OECD 1999: 24).

Further, part-time workers are less likely to get some benefits than full-time workers. The extent to which this is the case varies by country, with those in the EU being better protected, for instance in regard to employer provided benefits such as paid holidays (OECD 1999: 25–6). Part-time workers are more likely to have temporary jobs than full-time workers, across the OECD (OECD 1999). This is the case for both men and women, and especially for men. Among women with part-time jobs an average of 18 per cent are temporary, as compared with 10 per cent of women with full-time jobs (OECD 1999).

Part-time working is heavily skewed to the lower level occupations for both women and men. Part-time workers are disproportionately found among clerical workers, service workers and sales workers, and elementary occupations (OECD 1999: 38). Part-time workers receive less training from their employer than do full-time workers, across the OECD (23 per cent of part-timers receive this training as compared with 36 per cent of full-timers). This is especially the case among women, where 24 per cent of part-timers receive employer provided training as compared with 50 per cent of full-timers (OECD 1999).

There is little link between part-time working and the development of a high skill knowledge-based economy in that the typical forms of employment are low skill, low paid, with little employer provided training. In addition they are insecure with a greater likelihood of being in temporary than permanent employment.

While the rate of part-time employment is increasing across the OECD as a whole (increasing from 11 per cent of total employment in 1990 to 15 per cent in 2004), there are divergent patterns between countries and there are declines in some (see Table 1.12). It might be considered consistent with the 'varieties of capitalism' distinction between liberal and coordinated economies to expect the highest rates of this form of non-standard employment in the liberal (US, UK) rather than coordinated (Germany, Japan) market economies. However, the US has one of the lowest rates of part-time employment, of 13 per cent in 2004, which is also a declining rate, in that it is lower than the 16 per cent in 1973. By contrast, the more coordinated economies of Germany and Japan have higher rates of part-time employment than the US and the OECD average. Since coordinated economies are expected to have a higher proportion of standard work than liberal economies, this finding on part-time employment challenges this categorization.

Part-time employment is disproportionately undertaken by women, though there are substantial variations between countries (see Table 1.13). In the OECD in 2004 women were 72 per cent of part-time workers, this ranging from 83 per cent in Germany to 68 per cent in the US. The proportion of part-time workers who are women is declining across the OECD. There is thus a widespread tendency to the de-gendering of part-time work, though the gender composition remains uneven.

The extent to which women's employment is part-time employment varies significantly between countries. It is a much lower proportion of

Table 1.14: Part-time employment as a proportion of women's employment

Country	1973	1983	1990	2000	2004
Germany	24.4	30.0	29.8	33.9	37.0
Japan	25.1	29.5	33.4	38.6	41.7
UK	39.1	40.1	39.5	40.8	40.4
US	26.8	22.9	20.2	18.0	18.8
OECD			19.5	20.7	25.4

Note: Part-time employment is usually defined as working less than 30 hours per week, in Japan this is less than 35 hours per week.
Source: OECD (2000b: Table E); OECD (1996: Table E); OECD (2004a); OECD (2005f).

women's employment in the US, than the other three countries, despite its liberal categorization. The extent to which women's employment takes this non-standard part-time form is declining in both the US (since 1973) and the UK (since 2000), while rising in Germany and Japan (see Table 1.14). This is consistent with the thesis that in countries with the highest levels of female employment (US and UK) further increases in women's participation in employment take place in the form of shifts from part-time to full-time work.

What are the implications of these patterns for the de-regulation thesis? Among this group of countries (US, UK, Japan, Germany), the US and UK have the most de-regulated economies and share historic traditions of lighter state regulation of their economies than is the case in the other countries. If there were a link between de-regulation and working part-time, we would expect to see a grouping in which the UK and US shared a common pattern and Japan and Germany shared another. This is not the case. The UK and the US have significantly different patterns of part-time working and trajectories of change in these. The UK has a high and continuing pattern of part-time working, especially concentrated among women. The US has a low and declining pattern of part-time working, which is less concentrated among women. These widely divergent patterns cannot be simply explained by reference to the same single phenomenon, whether the economies are liberal, face global de-regulatory pressures or experience gender inequality.

The key to the explanation of the difference, and of the early high rates of part-time working in the UK, is that the UK part-time sector was, historically, selectively non-regulated. When the regulation of the UK labour market developed under pressure from the labour movement in the 1960s and 1970s, the part-time sector was routinely exempted (Walby 1986). The development of regulations such as those on unfair dismissal, redundancy payments and maternity leave typically applied to those working full-time hours. The UK was exceptional in this regard. This differentiation of the terms and conditions of full-time and part-time workers is coming to an end as a result of EU regulations, which views such practices as illegal discrimination against women. The varieties of part-time employment can only be understood if the analysis includes the varieties of gender regime and the different routes of transition from domestic to public.

The book chapters

The chapters in the book address these theories of the development of the gendered knowledge economy and varieties of capitalism and gender relations with detailed comparative data.

Shire presents the results of a detailed comparative analysis of gender and employment in the new economy in the US, UK, Germany and Japan. In the first part of the chapter, three sectoral definitions of new economic activities developed by the UN, OECD and the EU are analysed in relation to their underlying conceptualization of economic change from a gender perspective. These include: the information and computer technology (ICT) industry; the information sector; and the knowledge-intensive service sector. The approach evaluates the comparative benefits and drawbacks of the different concepts of the knowledge economy. The second part presents the results of an empirical analysis of the gender composition of new economic sectors, patterns of occupational segmentation and the gendering of non-standard employment forms. Women participate strongly in knowledge employment in all four countries, regardless of which measure of new economic activity is used. Women represent a third of all ICT industry employment, 40 per cent of information sector employment and more than half of employment in the knowledge-intensive service sector. An analysis of the gender composition in ICT occupations suggests continuities in patterns of gendered occupational segregation in the new economy. Women dominate in very few ICT occupations, most of which are at the low end of the occupational system, while men dominate most of the occupations overall, but especially higher end jobs as computer scientists, developers, engineers, service and sales workers. The results of the gender analysis point to overwhelming similarities cross-nationally in the participation of women and to continuities in the occupational segmentation and allocation of women to non-regular employment forms in the transition from the old to the new economy.

Osawa explores development of state regulations in the field of equal employment opportunities, welfare and tax policies and their impact on the development of new forms of gendered employment relations, especially non-standard forms, in Japan, Germany, UK and US since the early 1980s. Japan is a difficult case to classify in conventional typologies of the welfare state such as that of Esping-Andersen, with low welfare state expenditure, a highly selective social policy offering little family support, and a low degree of 'de-commodification' that compelled the individual to participate in the labour market, while the division of its social insurance services by occupation and social stratification demonstrates its more 'conservative' nature. From a gender perspective the designs of policy measures and their outcomes of taxation, old age pension scheme, childcare support programme and equal employment opportunity regulation reveal similarity and difference across countries. In terms of the taxation system, the large deductions that can be claimed for dependants and co-residency designate it as a male breadwinner model. This chapter focuses on the extent to which a particular model of the welfare system is compatible with conditions and requirements of the knowledge-based economy. The Japanese welfare system of large corporate-centred male breadwinner type impedes not only the desired transition or reorganization of its economy from the late industrialization (Fordist and post-Fordist) phase to the service and knowledge-oriented stage, but also the realization of more equitable gender relations at home and work.

Lenz addresses the significance of global feminism for the regulation of gender relations in employment in different countries, specifying the mechanisms whereby global feminism either has or does not have an impact at the national level. The interplay of global factors with the national and local levels is analysed drawing on the varieties of capitalism approach and the varieties of gender regime frameworks to compare Germany, Japan, the UK and the US. Crucial factors include the gendering of corporatism as well as the level of state feminism and the political mobilization by women's movements. Women's movements have contributed to the regulations for gender equality by negotiating on the global, the national and the local levels in different ways. The chapter traces contrasting trajectories of the corporate 'coordinated market economies' of Germany and Japan. In Germany, equal opportunities legislation has mainly proceeded in a corporatist framework propelled by institutionalized feminism at the national level. The Japanese women's movements on work have used the changing international opportunity structure and the new international discursive legitimacy of gender equality at the international level in a proactive way and achieved 'soft' legislation for guidance for equality at work and in society. The 'liberal market economies' of the UK and US are different. The US national hegemonic position is linked to high barriers for negotiating at the global multilevel system. In the UK, the supranational level of the EU was influential in the enactment of regulation for equality. The chapter argues for the integration of the 'varieties of capitalism' and the 'varieties of gender' approaches to analyse these differences.

Roberts compares two routes of 'policy transfer' by which 'global' conceptions of appropriate regulation of the workplace for gender equity and work/life balance have effects in Japanese workplaces. These workplaces are affected by the pressures of globalization as well as the particular social configuration in which Japan faces a low birth rate and rapidly ageing society. It follows the regulatory frameworks through to implementation, examining the extent to which policy really makes a difference, and if not, why not. While government regulations are certainly important in legitimizing the establishment of childcare leave and gender equality initiatives, other factors, such as corporate culture, the image the corporation wishes to present to the public, the larger economic environment in which the corporation is placed, the family support systems available to workers in the larger society, norms of parenthood and worker, and firm size all impinge on the effectiveness of these regulatory frameworks. The chapter discusses the rise of flexible work arrangements and their outcomes in the United States, before entering into an analysis of Japan's situation. Case studies from a US multinational financial services firm in Tokyo, as well as a large Japanese manufacturer, illustrate the two firms' somewhat different timing and different reasons for policy implementation, though both comply with state regulatory frameworks. While workers in these two firms are afforded some opportunities to balance careers and family, however, this cannot be said of workers in the majority of firms in Japan, where enforcement mechanisms for work/life policies are not strict and other incentives towards work/life flexible arrangements are lacking.

Gottschall and Kroos examine self-employment in the new media industries as a non-standard form of employment. Self-employment is a distinctive feature of the gendered labour force in old industries and services as well as in the knowledge economy. In contemporary popular and policy debates about the new economy, self-employment has been subject to both pessimistic and optimistic interpretations as to the future of the quality of work, life and gender equality. This chapter grounds these debates through a comparative analysis of solo self-employment. It starts with a review of the volume, structure and working conditions of self-employment in the UK, US, Japan and Germany. This is followed by an analysis, through in-depth case studies of the publishing and new media industries in Germany, the UK and the US, as emblematic branches of the global new economy. The analysis finds that while self-employment has some country-specific characteristics as to its growth, distribution across industries and its gender composition, nevertheless, in both coordinated and uncoordinated market economies a significant part of solo self-employment is subject to insecure working conditions and social risks. At the same time, new risk-management strategies, at both individual and collective levels, are emerging. These strategies vary in extent and sustainability, indicating the different influence of nationally specific labour market regulations and gender regimes.

Durbin analyses the inclusion and exclusion of women in the construction of knowledge through an analysis of gender in a non-standard work arena where women predominate (the call centre). She discusses the gendering process associated with four different ways by which knowledge is constructed and institutionalized: embrained (formal, theoretical knowledge that is gained through education and/or training); embodied (knowledge acquired through involvement in practical problem-solving activities);

encoded (knowledge that is shared within organizations through written rules, procedures and measurement); and embedded (knowledge that is built into routines, habits and norms (culture) that cannot easily be transformed into information systems). Her analysis is based on four case studies of call centres set up as two of the UK's largest financial service providers. She draws on interviews with the adviser and team manager population (which is predominantly female) and the senior management population in the call centres and parent organizations (which is predominantly male). Durbin finds that access to and the sharing of different knowledge types varies according to organization position, which itself is gendered. She finds that where women have access to knowledge, it typically takes individual forms and remains an invisible and untapped resource. The way that knowledge is combined and applied in organizations creates new forms of gendered inequality in call centres.

Holtgrewe investigates contrasting processes of gendering and flexibility in call centres. Call centres are frequently cited as exemplary of neo-Taylorist standardization, automation and degradation of service work. This pattern draws on traditional conceptions of women's work as devalued. An alternative organizational perspective views call centres as parts of strategic planning to design relations and communications with customers. Moving away from traditional collective agreements, regulations and traditional HRM policies allows call centres to explore their options to recompose workforces and their potential for flexibility. Evidence from German call centres suggests that changes in gender and in employment relations do not or no longer follow a unidirectional pattern. Instead, Holtgrewe finds differentiations of gendering processes. Banks in Germany hire students regardless of gender rather than skilled women part-timers – an undoing of gender and a recasting of flexibility. In the male-dominated areas of call centre work such as technical hotlines and financial services, there is a recasting of traditionally masculine notions of skill that resists the feminized and emotional labour image of call centre work. In lower-skilled call centres such as mail-ordering the neo-Taylorist pattern is retained. A further pattern is found in small marketing call centres, where skilled women part-timers accept flexible working time and fairly low remuneration, but take over a range of enriched tasks reaching from operative telephone work to project management.

Perrons develops a framework to understand the widening social divisions in the knowledge economy. It builds upon the traditional conceptualization of the knowledge economy as linked to new information and communication technologies, but goes further by theorizing the differential economic properties of knowledge and caring goods in order to explain why old social divisions by class and gender are reproduced, although in new forms. The framework facilitates the reconciliation of optimistic accounts of the new economy, which stress the potential economic and social benefits arising

from productivity increases, with more pessimistic accounts, which emphasize deteriorating working conditions, increasing insecurity, and individualization. This framework provides the context for a comparative investigation
of working conditions in new media and childcare. Perrons finds that work
remains highly gender segregated in both cases. She finds that although new
media workers earned above average incomes they experienced paternalis-
tic employment practices and low job security. As a consequence, these
workers are beginning to think of themselves less like pioneers at the technological frontier and more like routine white-collar workers. Some are even
beginning to think about collective forms of organization to press for better
working conditions, countering some of the individualization associated
with the new economy. In this way, the new forms of employment share
similarities with what might be considered older forms of work in childcare.
Further, rather than being alternatives in the future world of employment,
childcare workers are necessary for the development of new media work.

Nishikawa and Tanaka examine the relationship between the knowledge
acquisition of the globally growing female-dominated occupation of homecare, and the development of new non-standard forms of employment,
including both part-time and on-call work in Japan. Despite the weak
economy and employment prospects, care service for the elderly has been
the fastest growing sector in the Japanese economy during the last decade.
With the increasing trend towards flexibilization of the Japanese labour
market and the privatization of service providers, the number of Japanese
homecare workers who are employed as part-timers or on-call (*Toroku*) has
increased rapidly. Because of gendered assumptions about the job content
and flexible work arrangements, middle-aged married women have been the
major suppliers of labour. Two opposing trends affect Japanese homecare
workers; first is the standardization and professionalization of their work
and the second is the gendered flexibilization of their employment. How do
these affect the knowledge acquisition and chance of advancement of the
Japanese homecare workers? By drawing on Nonaka's four modes of knowledge conversion, Nishikawa and Tanaka argue that socialization (sharing
time and space together with supervisors and colleagues) and internalization (learning by doing) are the major sources for the Japanese homecare
workers to acquire professional knowledge. However, the current system of
qualifications and the flexibilization of employment forms restrict the access
to and opportunities for socialization and internalization, which can have
a detrimental effect on the acquisition and accumulation of professional
knowledge, and hence on the chance for advancement.

Conclusions

When a gender lens is used, the processes associated with the knowledge
economy look different in several ways. Different definitions of the knowl-

edge economy produce different gender profiles of who is a knowledge worker, with implications for the discussion of the gendering of the winners and losers in the knowledge economy. While the industries associated with the new ICTs and with information have a traditional male majority among their workforces, the knowledge-intensive services have a slight female majority. When the knowledge economy is defined in terms of knowledge-intensive employment, then the recent increase in women's educational level relative to that of men may mean that women as well as men are gainers if they are employed in the knowledge economy.

The major changes in employment forms are associated both with the development of new economic sectors associated with new information communication technologies and knowledge-intensive work, and with the transformation of the gender regime as it co-evolves with varieties of capitalism. Some non-standard employment forms are associated with developments of the knowledge economy, such as self-employment in the new media industries in Germany. Others are associated with the complex path-dependent interplay between varieties of capitalism and varieties of gender regime. The mainstreaming of gender into the analysis challenges the conventional divisions between the main varieties of capitalism. Many of the non-standard employment forms are to be found not in the less regulated liberal economies, but rather in the countries that have conventionally been seen as more coordinated and more regulated.

The emergence and profile of new forms of employment in the knowledge economy need to be understood in the context of the contrast between standard and non-standard forms of employment, which is more sharply drawn in traditionally coordinated economies than in liberal economies. The variation between countries in the extent and gendering of 'new' and non-standard employment depends critically upon what was and is included within the protections that were provided by the state/polity for standard employment, the extent to which these exemptions were for gendered categories of non-standard employment, and the changes in the inclusion/exclusion and gendering of various categories of 'new'/ standard/non-standard employment. This is of importance in explaining the quality of jobs that are 'new' or non-standard, especially those that are part-time, and those that are temporary. In some countries, specific forms of non-standard employment (e.g. part-time employment in the UK) were excluded from the development of procedures and benefits to protect job quality. The extent to which particular categories of non-standard work are excluded from these protections has diminished over time, but unevenly across countries, while at the same time the average level of protections focused on class relations has diminished. The intricate patterns over time of the extent to which different forms of non-standard work have been either exempted from employment protections or included within them has enormous implications for the position of women in employment which depend not least on the extent to which these different non-standard work forms are disproportionately occupied by women and the extent to which women as women are subject to forms of disadvantage in the labour market. There are complex patterns of reciprocal causation involved, as employers, male and female workers, and a host of institutionalized interests manoeuvre for advantage in the field of employment. Historically, there was often systematic exclusion of women from the employment sectors in which male workers were strong enough to ensure that they were better regulated than the average field of employment. This occurrence was associated with the lesser representation of the interests of women as workers in the industrial relations systems, not least among organized labour. This has often led to an association of women workers with the less regulated sectors, which are more usually non-standard forms of work. For example, the greater vulnerability of women workers to exploitation can sometimes mean that the gender composition of an unregulated non-standard employment niche is a factor in that niche being a target for expansion by employers. Not infrequently, this has occurred in relation to women's part-time employment.

While in some instances new temporalities, contractualities and spatialities of employment may be associated with the development of a knowledge-based economy, these are limited. The new media and cultural industries, which utilize higher proportions of self-employment and temporal flexibility, are the main example. Most of the non-standard employment forms are associated with relative poor employment conditions, with the possible exception of part-time employment in relation to workers' temporal preferences. However, on other dimensions it is associated with poor quality employment conditions. The development of these forms cannot, however, be simply attributed to globalization and pressures to de-regulate economies. They are most commonly found in the more coordinated and regulated economies (e.g. Germany, Japan), rather than those that are liberal with fewer regulations (e.g. US, UK). Temporary work, self-employment and part-time working are to be found less in the more liberal economies and more in the coordinated economies. When comparing the US, UK, Germany and Japan in 2000–3, the liberal US has the lowest rates of temporary work, self-employment and part-time employment of the four countries. The highest rate of temporary work is in Japan and Germany. The highest rate of part-time employment is in Japan.

These non-standard employment forms can be best understood in terms of the intersection of several processes. Their growth is strongest in the ostensibly coordinated economies partly because the precarity and flexibility they provide to employers are already available to employers in the more liberal countries, especially the US. That is, the 'standard' employment in the US has fewer of the protections to employment provided in the more coordinated economies. There is thus less management incentive to develop new employment forms outside of standard employment. The non-standard forms of employment have grown in the more coordinated economies partly at least as an attempt to exploit new and less protected economic and labour niches. This requires a rethinking of the categories of liberal and coordinated market economies in the varieties of capitalism literature.

There are contrary dynamics of change in capitalism and gender regimes. While there has been de-regulation on many class issues, there has been increasing regulation on issues that are directly or indirectly gendered. Taking these into account helps to understand the gender and the differentiation of the knowledge economy. As the gender regime has undergone transition from a domestic to a public form, there has been an increased political voice of women workers in both industrial and democratic arenas. These are associated with both greater provision of regulation of discrimination and working-time associated with parenthood. Since the 1970s, but especially since the 1990s, gender relations in employment have been increasingly regulated, though with very important variations, while some forms of non-standard employment have also been regulated to some extent in some locations. At the same time, processes of globalization in some countries involve some forms of de-regulation of specific types of employment relations, especially those associated with class inequality. These will impact on women as well as men, since many women will occupy low positions in the jobs hierarchy.

The class and gender dimensions of the coordination and regulation of economies need to be distinguished because there are distinctions in the levels of protection and support provided for class-based and gender-based risks and vulnerabilities. These are of three kinds. First, regulations, indirectly or directly, can provide benefits predominantly for male rather than female workers, for example, the hours threshold for protection in the 1960s–1970s in the UK meant that part-time employment, which was overwhelmingly female, was outside of the majority of the employment protections won for full-time workers who were predominantly male. Second, the needs of carers, predominantly female, are met by a distinctive set of state and employer policies, such as publicly funded childcare, which are usually left out of focus in the capitalist production system literature. Third, policies that embed the interests of women in equal opportunities and gender mainstreaming policies are a distinct set of regulations, which are usually left out of focus in the capitalist production system literature and the gendered welfare state literature. The development of the EU, with a distinctive gender regime, is producing new path-dependent forms of development as a result of its gender equality regulations in employment which are considerably stronger and deeper than in the US and Japan.

The gendered political and policy aspects of globalization need to be included more fully. Globalization may produce similar effects on some issues, but also divergent perhaps even contrary effects on others. Globalization is a political process as well as an economic one, which has facilitated the mutual development of policies and practices by feminists around the world. These have an impact on the regulatory regimes in particular polities. Further, there are policy developments within transnational corporations that may be transferred between their plants in different countries. That is, policies developed in one country may be applied in another, although there are complex interactions with the local polity. Rather than a simple process of de-regulation, there is a significant rise in new forms of regulation of gender relations in employment, from equal opportunities policies to maternity leave and the regulation of working time. The mainstreaming of gender into the analysis of globalization demands a rethinking of the assumption that globalization and de-regulation go together in a simple manner, and a more complex consideration of the gendered political and policy processes associated with globalization. Globalization has effects that may be contradictory rather than uniform, in that it may facilitate the development of global political movements that assist the development of some regulations that improve worker conditions. This has occurred in relation to gender through discourse and practice in relation to equal opportunities, work-life balance, human rights and gender mainstreaming. The differential location of countries in global networks and the temporal sequencing of change have further implications for the effects of globalization on gendered employment forms in different countries.

In order to explain these different patterns of development in the gendered knowledge economy it has been necessary to develop more nuanced conceptualizations of varieties of capitalism and especially varieties of gender regime. A key part of this has been the development of the conceptualization of regulation, so as to bring into focus its gender as well as class dimensions. The chapters in this book utilize this new theoretical agenda in order to explain the diverse nature of the gendered knowledge economy.

Notes

1. Sources and construction of indicators for Table 1.5 Comparing the regulation of the labour market by class and gender.

Trade union density
Sources: US figure calculated from data in *Monthly Labor Review* (2004) is for 2003; UK figure is from Hicks and Palmer (2004) and is for 2003; Japan: two figures: 24 per cent is for 1994, from OECD (1997: Table 3.3); 19 per cent is for 2004 and is from Broadbent (2005). Germany is from: European Industrial Relations Observatory On-Line (EIRO) (2004) for 2003. Data is for 2003, except for Japan which is 1994/2004.

TU bargaining coverage
Source: OECD (1997: Table 3.3). Data usually for 1994.
Centralization of wage bargaining. *Source*: OECD (1997: Table 3.3). Data usually for 1994. The higher the number the more centralized is the wage bargaining. 1 is firm level; 2 is industry level; 3 is national.

Coordination
Source: OECD (1997: Table 3.3). Data usually for 1994. Coordination is slightly different from centralization in that it focuses on the degree of consensus between collective bargaining partners. The higher the number, the greater the level of coordination of collective bargaining.

Employment protection legislation
Source: OECD (1999: Table 2.5). This is a summary indicator of employment protection legislation in relation to regular employment (especially individual dismissals), temporary employment and collective dismissals. Data from the late 1990s. The higher the number the more the protection.

Employment protection legislation and company level protections
Source: Estevez-Abe et al. (2001: 165). This composite index of employment protection is made up of several components: 5/9 is associated with the 'restrictiveness of individual hiring and firing rules contained in legislation and collective agreements'; 2/9 is associated with the 'restrictiveness of collective dismissal rules contained in legislation and collective agreements'; 2/9 is associated with company level protection based on three criteria: (i) employee-elected bodies with a significant role in company labour decisions, (ii) strong external unions, (iii) systematic employee-sharing practices between firms in a group. The higher the score the more the protection (the original index has been converted from a score of 0 to 1 to one of 1–100 for presentational purposes). Ultimate *sources* include the OECD and Income Data Services.

Summary ranking of the four countries by degree of industrial relations coordination and regulation
The smaller the number, the more likely is the country to have high trade union density, large trade union bargaining coverage, centralized wage bargaining, a more coordinated industrial relations system, more employment protection legislation and more employment protection at company level (each of the measures in the table contributes equally). This ranking is the same as the ranking found by Estevez-Abe et al. (2001: 165).

Union membership, percent female
Sources: US figure calculated from data in *Monthly Labor Review* (2004); UK figure is from Hicks and Palmer (2004). Japan is for 1997 and is from Broadbent (2005). Germany from: European Industrial Relations Observatory On-Line (2004). Data is for 2003.

Equal treatment legal regulation of employment
As members of the EU, the UK and Germany substantially share a common legal framework based on binding EU Directives and Treaties including commitment to gender mainstreaming. However, there are differences in implementation practices within the EU, the nature of the engagement of the social partners, and the existence of an independent body in the UK,

the Equal Opportunities Commission, with the capacity to support legal cases, especially those with strategic importance (unlike Germany). The US and Japanese legislation is both narrower in remit and weaker in application than that of the EU, going little further than basic equal pay and anti-discrimination legislation. For example, the EU legislation provides for equal rights for part-time workers with full-timers, but this is not included in the US legislation. The US has a history of affirmative action which results in its legislative framework and practice being stronger than that in Japan.

2. Part-time employment is usually defined as working less than 30 hours per week; in Japan this is less than 35 hours per week (OECD 2000b). However, in Japan, there are in practice two definitions of part-time working, one based on hours and the other based on employer treatment, so that 10–20 per cent of those who work over 35 hours a week actually receive 'part-time' conditions of service (Osawa 2001).

2
Gender and the Conceptualization of the Knowledge Economy in Comparison

Karen Shire

This chapter poses the question of how best to conceptualize the new economic activities at the core of discourses on the transition to a knowledge-based economy from a gender perspective. The focus is on economic rather than political, social or cultural dimensions of change; nonetheless behind the available reclassifications of economic activities are understandings of the driving forces behind economic changes, which have implications for a gender analysis of the knowledge-based economy. The dominant view places the emergence of new economic activities in the context of political and economic liberalization and internationalization, driven by technological innovations, with consequences for firm organization, skills and the division of labour. The important questions from a gender perspective address the extent to which gender-based occupational and labour market segregation persists within the emerging domains of the knowledge-based economy, and whether cross-national differences in gender continuity versus gender transformation are evident.

This chapter continues the comparative focus of this volume on the four major advanced economies: Britain, Germany, Japan and the US. Several decades of comparative sociology of employment and work in industrial economies have documented the persistence of systematic and qualitatively meaningful *divergences* in the social organization of production and economic action across nations and regions of market-based capitalism. The divergence in national models of industrial capitalism contrasts with the relative *convergence* in the partial and subordinate integration of women in paid employment and women's responsibility for unpaid domestic and reproductive work. Does the relative convergence of the gendered division of labour persist in the transition to a knowledge-based economy, especially in light of the parallel transformation of gender regimes? The transformation from a domestic to a public gender regime (Walby 1997) is evident in the rising educational levels and employment rates of women in all four of the countries in this volume. Nonetheless, recent comparative work on employment regimes and welfare states from a gender perspective has advanced an

51

understanding of divergence in national gender regimes, which several of the contributions in this volume discuss as 'varieties of gender regimes' (Walby in this volume; Osawa in this volume; Lenz in this volume).

The first part of this chapter presents a historical and comparative approach for analysing economic changes in the context of the transformation of gender relations. This is followed by a discussion of the new economy as a knowledge-based economy, involving new economic activities, new occupations and new employment forms, as outlined in the introductory chapter (Walby in this volume), and in reference to three images of the new knowledge-based economy currently used by the OECD, UN and the EU as follows:

- the information and communications technology sector (ICT)
- the information sector, and the
- knowledge-intensive services sector (KIS).

The second part compares the gendered dimensions of employment and occupational segregation across the four countries included in this volume. The concluding discussion addresses continuity as well as emerging divergence in gendered employment relations of the knowledge-based economy.

Convergence and divergence in gender regimes

Studying the transformation of two parallel and complementary structures – industrial capitalism and the domestic gender regime – and doing so comparatively is a complex endeavour (even within the relatively unitary category of advanced economies). Two major questions underlying this analysis of gender and new economic activities are (1) the issue of path dependency and continuity in patterns of gender segmentation of industrial economies in the emergence of a knowledge-based economy and (2) whether there is evidence of the emergence of different models of public gender regimes from the perspective of gender and employment in new economic activities in Britain, Germany, Japan and the US.

The first question raises the issue of the relationship between economic structures and gender relations. How one conceptualizes this relationship makes a difference for an analysis of economic transformation processes. Do economic processes evolve separately from gender relations, or are gender relations part of the social fabric within which economic processes are embedded and evolve? Are changes in gender relations a consequence of economic processes (e.g. labour shortages in specific markets or demands for specific sort of skills and competencies), which increase demand for female employment? Or is the relationship between gender and economic relations in transformation the best approach from the point of view of emerging affinities between a knowledge-based economy and a public gender regime?

Gender regime theory separates the analysis of economic and gender relations, in order to explicitly conceptualize the systemic nature of gender structures as an autonomous dimension of social organization (Walby 1990, 1997). Gendered employment is theorized as one of six dimensions of a gender regime, which together with the other dimensions, form a system analytically separate from the capitalist system. The question of the embeddedness of the economic in gender relations is relevant for this one domain, but not at a societal level of analysis. Capitalism and patriarchy are conceptualized as dual social systems (Walby 1990, 1997). This approach suggests a focus on affinities between the two systems, capitalism and patriarchy.

From a methodological perspective gender regime theory is important because it provides a holistic understanding of complementarities between different spheres of gender relations, without giving primacy to the economic, the political or other spheres of social action and social structure. The comprehensiveness of gender relations and the systemic nature of complementarities between social domains of gender relations are emphasized as a result. Further, gender regime theory puts forth an analysis of the historical change in gender relations, and does so in a way which underlines how this transformation is multiply contingent rather than being a consequence of changes in any one domain of social action or social structure. Walby's analysis of the transformation of the British gender regime (1990) conceptualizes a historical shift from a 'domestic' to a 'public' gender regime, pointing to the key aspects of economy-based changes without giving the economic primacy in transformative processes. Contributing to the breakdown of the domestic gender regime is the expansion of female graduates of higher education and their entry in greater numbers into new and expanding core sectors of national economies, a development which is unitary across advanced economies. An additional strength of gender regime theory concerns the question of whether or not there is greater gender equality in the transition to a public gender regime. With the economic advancement of highly qualified women in Britain, Walby finds increasing polarization in the economic opportunities of women generally on the basis of differences in education and employment chances. New pockets of equality between men and women and a continuing legacy of gender segregation and inequality, especially for less educated women and women of colour, characterize the modernization of gender relations in contemporary Britain. Conceptually and methodologically, whether or not the transformation to a public gender regime brings greater gender equality or not remains a matter for empirical research.

The strengths of gender regime theory lie in its usefulness for a societal, historical and empirical analysis of gender relations. The analysis in this volume represents an attempt to compare national models of gender regimes, focusing on only one of the six dimensions of gender regimes as developed by Walby (1997): women's employment. Focusing specifically on gender and employment in the messy world of empirical analysis necessitates an integrated study of economic and gender processes. A focus on process in empirical gender research has been most fruitfully undertaken by developing the concept of 'gendering' in constituting social relations in specific domains, such as the workplace or public policy (Acker 1990). 'Gender is not an addition to ongoing processes, conceived as gender neutral. Rather it is an integral part of those processes, which cannot be properly understood without an analysis of gender' (Acker 1990: 146). Acker's original use of the gendering concept was aimed at understanding the gendering of organizations through seemingly mundane practices such as job evaluations, promotion procedures, task descriptions, etc. I propose to use the concept methodologically in a similar manner, to understand how the composition of core value-creating industries, recruitment to new occupations and the construction of employment types 'are patterned through and in terms of a distinction between male and female, masculine and feminine' (Acker 1990: 146).

Unlike the research of Acker, however, the empirical work in this chapter neither undertakes a specific case study of new economy work (see Holt-grewe in this volume, Durbin in this volume, and Nishikawa and Tanaka in this volume) nor does it focus on 'doing' gender in workplace contexts. Rather, the focus is on the gendering of new economic activities, new occupations and new employment forms, which, as a first step is examined in terms of gender composition. While this is certainly an under-utilization of the gendering concept, the aim is to lay out an empirical foundation for future case-study approaches focused on the dynamics within the gendered structure of the knowledge-based economy.

There is a tension between gender regime theory and the gendering concept which I attempt to overcome in this analysis in a pragmatic manner. While the concept of 'gendering' has been used to critique Walby's dual systems approach to the relationship between capitalism and gender regimes (O'Reilly 2000), the analysis in this chapter draws on the gendering concept to concretize rather than oppose gender regime theory. Gender regime theory is situated at the levels of social structural, historical and systemic units of analysis, while the concept of gendering brings us a step down and closer to institutional comparisons and (re-)structuring processes in context-specific processes and practices. Integrating these approaches is necessary, since studying the gender dimensions of the knowledge-based economy requires both an emphasis on the historical and systemic nature of change and engaging in an empirical study of specific economic activities at a specific moment of societal change.

I propose to integrate what I think are two levels of analysis by approaching economic activities as *embedded* in gender regimes. Thus, the analysis I engage in has a different methodological starting point from the dual systems approach, away from system and in the direction of process, in order to focus on the interaction of economic and gender transformations under way. This approach goes beyond a stress on the affinities between the economic and gender. To say that economic changes are embedded in gender relations is to place the economic in a specific dimension of social relations, and to subject economic processes to fields of social contestations, in this case, gender relations. Economic transformations are embedded in gender relations and are shaped by societal and historical transformations of gender relations, such that the idealized image of, as well as real aspects of, the transition to a knowledge-based economy are not autonomous from gender relations.

The methodological decision to stress the embeddedness of economic changes in gender relations is aimed at generating insights into the extent to which gender structures and processes shape the emergence of new economic activities. Such an approach contributes to the development of a broader historical and critical understanding of contemporary economic changes, critical because these changes are not seen as unfolding according to their own logic, but rather in a specific social organizational context. Most accounts of the knowledge-based economy are too narrow to pick up on the ways in which social forces, and particularly gender, matter in contemporary economic transformations. In large part this blind-spot is a result of a view of contemporary economic change which over-emphasizes technology (e.g. the internet or network economy) while under-emphasizing cultural and social dimensions of economic changes. A second concern of the analysis in this chapter (a concern with its own methodological implications), is to compare gender and economic transformations cross-nationally. How does the embeddedness of economic activities in gender relations vary across national contexts? Do variations in gender regimes result in variations in the knowledge-based economies of Britain, Germany, Japan and the US? Does it make sense to theorize 'varieties of gender regimes' from the point of view of gendered knowledge-based economies?

A wave of recent research comparing gender and employment has uncovered important differences in how skill regimes, employment forms and work hierarchies are gendered in the advanced economies. Yet most comparative research on gender and employment has fallen short of theorizing divergence. Alternatively, recent research has been concerned either with critiquing and 'gendering' mainstream approaches (O'Reilly 2000 on the societal approach; Estévez-Abe 2002, 2005 on the varieties of capitalism), filling in empirical gaps in gender differences across a broad range of employment institutions (e.g. Rubery et al. 1999 on gender and employment), providing detailed accounts of one national case (Barker and Christensen 1998; McCall 2001; Smith 2001), or more cases, but without a direct comparison between national cases (Houseman and Osawa 2003; O'Reilly and Fagan 1998). Directly comparative and historical analyses are an exception (Gottfried and O'Reilly 2002 is an important exception). A stronger contribution can be made by feminist research which attempts to integrate the historical and the comparative study of change, in order to identify ideal types of gender orders (e.g. Pfau-Effinger 2000) and to bring new sets of institutional arrangements and policies into comparative analysis (e.g. Pascall and Lewis 2004; Gottfried and O'Reilly 2002; O'Reilly 2000; Gottfried in this volume).

A central aim of comparative analysis since the societal effects approach (Maurice et al. 1986; Maurice and Sorge 2000) has been to understand how unitary historical processes are played out in specific national contexts, explaining differences (as well as similarities) through a holistic understanding of societal systems. The underlying research question for understanding the gender dimension of the knowledge-based economy is whether old inequalities based on gender are being reintroduced in new economic activities, and if so, how national gender regimes shape the nature and degree of gender-based inequalities in the 'new' economy. Such an understanding could contribute to the broader task of comparing the outcomes of national public gender regimes for the persistence of gender-based inequalities.

The new economy and gendered employment

In the dual-transition to a public gender regime and a knowledge-based economy the breakdown of old arrangements is often more evident than the emergence of new meanings and practices. In some accounts of economic and employment change, the risks have been emphasized over new chances for social actors (Sennett 1998) and the breakdown of standard work for men is seen as levelling the work biographical differences between men and women (Beck 2000).[1] Recent political changes from a gender perspective involve more than a de-regulation of established employment protections. Political advances in outlawing discriminatory practices have provided women with a powerful set of resources for de-legitimizing and transforming gender-based inequality at work. Studying the dual-transformation to a knowledge-based capitalist economy and public gender regime requires sorting out these often contradictory and countervailing tendencies. The analytical eye must make a difficult move from recognizable shapes and figures to more distant and less focused objects where the patterns cannot yet be worked out. The object of the empirically oriented conceptual and analytical work in this chapter is to bring a range of underlying economic changes into better focus, with the explicit aim of understanding economic changes as embedded in the transformation of gender relations. The empirical analysis focuses on the knowledge-based or 'new' economy despite the different meanings associated with the term, and despite an inherent bias towards higher skilled domains of work and advanced economic settings. The focus on the new economy forces a look at emerging and dynamic sectors, which are gaining importance as the new core value-creating and employment growth sectors of advanced economies. The patterns of gendering emerging in these dynamic growth sectors are likely to shape gender-based inequalities in the future.

The focus on the *new* or *knowledge-based* economy does not imply that all or even most of the economic activities subsumed in this imagery are new. While emergent industries (e.g. internet publishing) and businesses (e.g. SAP applications) play a key role in creating and transforming employment, the new economy also includes activities common to industrial economies (such as high-tech manufacturing and services, finance, telecommunications) and the full range of occupations and job roles (cleaning and security as well as money market trading and web design). The imagery of the knowledge-based economy generally signals that a shift has taken place in the nature of value-creating activities, towards the creation of value through knowledge-added (Quinn 1992; Drucker 1993a). In comparative studies of economic transformation, knowledge-based competitive business strategies are increasingly associated with market-oriented reorganization and, in most cases, liberalization of capital formation and employment practices. Liberalization pressures have impacted on traditional employment relations, placing employment de-regulation on the political agendas of even the most regulated national systems (Crouch and Streeck 1997).

There is little consensus and a lot of confusion about what constitutes the new economy, with the most narrow definition based on the new high risk technology stock markets and the broadest definition based on the shift to a fourth 'information' sector (Porat 1977). The first view is too narrowly focused on capital markets while the latter view is based too specifically on the dissemination of information technology. Other approaches have focused more on specific technological infrastructures, such as the internet (see Thompson 2004 for a critique) or the network economy (Castells 1996). A critical view challenges the existence of the knowledge economy as anything more than a managerial discourse (Casey 2004). The strategy pursued in this chapter is to focus on new definitions of economic activities which cut across the traditional division between manufacturing and services, to emphasize information dissemination and knowledge-creation activities in the economy. Following Walby (in this volume), the new economy is understood as a set of new economic activities, which can be discerned as *new sectors, new occupations* and *new employment contracts*.

The relationship between gender and the new economy is explored within this empirical field in two ways. First, the focus is on women in the new economy. The female composition of the new economy tells little of the gendering or nature of gender inequalities in the construction of new economic activities. To shift the focus from 'women in the new economy' to the 'gendering of the new economy', two traditional areas of gender inequalities in employment – gender-based occupational segregation and the structuring of women's employment as non-standard employment within new economic sectors – are investigated. This empirical strategy is taken up further and more deeply in many of the subsequent chapters, which focus systematically on the gendered regulation of work (employment regulations, social policy regulations), the gendered construction of non-standard employment (self-employed and temporary work) and gender relations within specific work settings (call centre work and elderly care-work).

Measuring the new economy: new sector categorizations of economic activity

In the late 1990s, UN statistical working groups, the OECD Directorate for Science, Technology and Industry (DSTI) and Eurostat, the statistical agency of the European Commission, began to develop specific measures designed to capture developments unfolding across the established industrial sectoral classifications and to regroup specific industries into new sectoral groupings. For the OECD-DSTI new economic sectors have become the foundation for international comparisons of trends in the knowledge-based economy published in its annual Science, Technology and Industry Scoreboard (www.oecd.org). New economic sectors are the basis for a range of UN activities on the information society and ongoing discussions on furthering the comparability of national industrial classifications and measures of new economic activities (unstats.un.org). The most consistent use of new economic sector classifications has been by the EU Directorate-General for Employment and Social Affairs in its annual Employment in Europe reports since 2000 and by Eurostat in detailed analyses of employment growth reported regularly in the Science and Technology theme of its Statistics in Focus series (europa.eu.int/comm/eurostat).

Three measures developed by the UN and EU and in use by the OECD capture the dynamic development of business and employment in advanced economies – the information and communications technology sector (ICT), the information sector, and the knowledge-intensive services sector (KIS). Both the ICT and information sector are relatively small fields of employment in advanced economies and come closer to being measures of new industries within broader sectors. Despite these differences in coverage, there is no clear conceptual reason for favouring one of these measures over the other. In some sense they complement each other, so that at this early stage of analysing the new economy, it seems wise to consider all three. The conceptual advantages and disadvantages of each of the three measures for understanding gender dimensions of work transformation are discussed in detail below. This is followed by a comparative analysis of the gender composition of the new economy in the four countries. The last part presents the analysis of available data on gender dimensions of new occupations and employment types within these new sectors. In this perhaps simplistic way, the attempt is made to understand the ongoing gendering of the new economy.

The ICT sector

The ICT sector includes measures of both manufacturing industries and service industries, compiled out of four traditional economic sectors: manufacturing, wholesale trade and repair, transport and communications, and the category most important for ICT services, business activities (Table 2.1).

Table 2.1: Economic activities comprising the information and communication technologies (ICT) sector

ISIC Rev. 3

	Manufacturing of ICT machinery and equipment
3000	Manufacture of office, accounting and computer machinery
3130	Manufacture of electrical machinery and apparatuses
3210	Manufacture of electronic valves and tubes and other electronic equipment
3220	Manufacture of television and radio transmitters and apparatus for line telephony and line telegraphy
3230	Manufacture of television and radio receivers, sound or video recording or reproducing apparatus, and associated goods
3312	Manufacture of instruments and appliances for measuring, checking, testing, navigating and other purposes, except industrial process control equipment
3313	Manufacture of industrial process control equipment

	ICT services
5151–5152	Wholesale of computers, computer peripheral equipment and software, and parts[2]
6420	Telecommunications
7123	Renting of office machinery and equipment (including computers)
72	Computer and related activities
7210	Hardware consultancy
7220	Software publishing, other software consultancy and supply
7230	Data processing
7240	Database activities
7250	Maintenance and repair of office, accounting and computing machinery
7290	Other computer related activities

Source: unstats.un.org and oecd.org, conversions based on UN table, checked against Nace rev. 1 categories and OECD definitions (2002a).

The imagery of the new economy suggested by the ICT sector is one of technology-driven economic transformation. A major advantage of this measure is the combination of manufacturing with service sectors of employment, breaking with the traditional separation of these sectors in the attempt to identify the emergence of a new sector of economic activity.[3] From a gender perspective, the inclusion of both manufacturing and services has the advantage of allowing a detailed analysis of a traditionally male-dominated (manufacturing) and new (services) sector, raising the question of how women fare in new and high-skill domains of business service activity. The OECD has identified ICT as the foremost indicator of new economic development (OECD 2002a) and the availability from the OECD of further data at the national level and in relation to occupational developments enables a closer look at the relationship between industries and the quality and skill level of work in these sectors. The OECD does not include gender in its nationally comparative analyses of the ICT sector.

The ICT sector contributes nearly 10 per cent of all business value added in Britain, Japan and the United States, and more than 5 per cent in Germany.[4] Only in Japan does the ICT manufacturing sector contribute half of all business value added. In the US and Britain three times more value is added by ICT services than by ICT manufacturing; in Germany double. According to the OECD, Japan is more specialized in ICT manufacturing than in services. A similar comparative picture is evident when employment in the ICT sector is considered. ICT manufacturing dominates overall ICT employment only in Japan, which has a relatively small share of employment in ICT services.

In all four countries, value-added in the ICT sector grew from 1995–2000 and despite business decline in the early 2000s, continues to grow (OECD 2003, B.6: 97). Employment in ICT manufacturing has stagnated since 1995 in all four countries, with a slight decline in Germany. In Japan and Germany, employment growth has also stopped in ICT services. Britain had strong growth in services-related ICT activities since 1995 (+2.4 per cent), followed by the US (1.5 per cent) (OECD 2003, B.6: 99). The US has the largest single worldwide share in overall ICT employment, making up 34 per cent of the OECD total employment in the sector, compared to 18 per cent for Japan, 9 per cent in the UK and 7 per cent for Germany. These are the four countries with the top four shares of ICT employment in the OECD. Both the US and UK had especially high growth rates in ICT service employment since 1995 (10.5 and 9.5 per cent respectively). Employment in software services alone grew 19 per cent in the UK (OECD 2003, B.6: 98).

The information sector

The imagery of the new economy that is suggested by the information sector shifts from the technology-driven change of the ICT sector, to the role of information production and networks of dissemination. The information

Table 2.2:   Economic activities comprising the information sector

ISIC Rev. 3

	Content industries
2211	Publishing of books, brochures and other publications
2212	Publishing of newspapers, journals and periodicals
2213	Publishing of music
2219	Other publishing
9211	Motion picture and video production and distribution*
9212	Motion picture projection
9213	Radio and television activities
9220	News agency activities
9231	Library and archives activities
	ICT services
6420	Telecommunications
7221	Software publishing
7230	Data processing

* The UN includes video game production under this category where national classifications make this distinction. It is expected that the planned ISIC rev. 4 for 2007 will make such distinctions more in line with the present NAICS classes.
Source: unstats.un.org, 'Information Sector' and 'Appendix 2 – Information Sector: another proposal' downloaded 24.2.04. Conversions from NAICS to ISIC by the author.

sector measure was developed by the United Nations, and elements of it overlap with the ICT measure (Table 2.2). The present ISIC classes do not allow for fine enough sub-divisions in some areas of information activities, and achieving an accurate comparative measure of the information sector is difficult for this reason. The UN is presently engaged in a further specification of specific industrial classifications to better capture a narrowly defined information sector.

In contrast to the ICT measure, the information sector excludes computer manufacturing while keeping selected activities within the computer industry specific to software publishing and data processing. Publishing and cultural activities comprise the main focus of this measure. Like the ICT measure, the construction of this sector involves a subdivision and recombination of existing ISIC classes. In its most recent attempts to improve these standards, the UN has divided the industries within the information sector into two main kinds of activities: *contents industries* and *ICT services*. Content is defined 'as a specific kind of information defined as an organised message intend [sic] for mass dissemination to human beings.' In contrast, the 'intrinsic nature of an ICT service is that of a *tool* used to handle information (processings, transmissions)' (unstats.un.org, downloaded 24.2.04).

The information economy measure avoids the overly broad association with the end-use of information technology in the original thesis on the information economy (Porat 1977), yet the focus on the production of information content and dissemination (networks) may narrow the focus too much, excluding a range of other information- and knowledge-intensive activities. Even within the ICT services industry, activities like database business and consultancy are excluded. Since the OECD does not work with this measure, there are no available analyses of value-added or employment growth of this sector in Germany, Japan, the US and UK specifically or in comparison.

An advantage of the information sector measure for an analysis of gender and the new economy is the inclusion of the culture-based industries, where women have made important inroads in high-skill employment, and where new forms of employment such as solo self-employment have expanded as well (Betzelt and Gottschall 2004; Gottschall and Kroos in this volume). On the other hand, the close association of culture industries with national culture may make the job of achieving comparable measures difficult. Qualitative case studies of women in culture industries in specific national contexts may be a more reliable research approach than quantitative attempts to compare gender composition on the basis of differently construed national classifications. Despite these problems and in light of the expected improvements in this measure by 2007, there is enough reason to include the UN's information sector measure in this initial analysis of the gendering of the new economy.

The knowledge-intensive services sector

The measure of the knowledge-intensive sector first appeared in 2001 as part of the European Commission yearly employment report (European Commission 2001a). In this report, three alternative new measures of economic activity were presented – the high-tech sector, the knowledge-intensive sector and the high education sector. From 2001 the OECD began to use a similar set of measures in analysing comparative developments in the high-tech and knowledge-intensive industries, focusing especially on two subsectors included in the KIS measure – high-tech (business) services and market-based knowledge services (e.g. OECD 2001b, 2003).[5] The extension of the OECD information economy research to these subsectors supplements rather than replaces their central concern with the ICT sector. The EU alternative measure of the high-tech sector is a reclassification of manufacturing industries only, and thus does not involve an attempt to redefine sectoral boundaries in light of new economic activities.[6]

Four subsets of industries comprise the knowledge-intensive services measure: knowledge-intensive high-tech services, knowledge-intensive market services,[7] knowledge-intensive financial services and other knowledge-intensive services (Table 2.3). Especially this last category, which

Table 2.3: Economic activities comprising the knowledge-intensive services (KIS) sector

ISIC Rev. 3	
KI high-tech services	
64	Post and telecommunications
72	Computer and related activities
73	Research and development
KI market services (excluding financial intermediation and high-tech services)	
61	Water transport
62	Air transport
70	Real estate activity
71	Renting of machinery and equipment without operator, and of personal and household goods
74	Other business activities
KI financial services	
65	Financial intermediation, except insurance and pension funding
66	Insurance and pension funding, except compulsory social security
67	Activities auxiliary to financial intermediation
Other KI services	
80	Education
85	Health and social work
92	Recreational, cultural and sporting activities

Source: European Commission 2002.

includes education, health and social work, represents a major difference to the ICT and information sector measures, including a broader range of social (and not only business-oriented), yet nonetheless knowledge-intensive, service activities.[8] The construction of the KIS measure proceeds on the basis of broader (2-digit) classifications and is potentially too heterogeneous to qualify as an indicator of new economic activities. The heterogeneity of the KIS is also an advantage, since a much larger sector of employment is captured, and the higher level of aggregation allows for cross-tabulations of sectoral employment with occupational groupings, skill levels and employment types. Such further analysis is useful for identifying key segments and developments within this dynamic sector, and for contrasting developments in the ICT and information sectors with specific subsets of knowledge-intensive services, such as finances and health.

A drawback of the KIS measure is the sole focus on services, excluding knowledge-intensive manufacturing activities, a drawback shared by the information sector measure. On the other hand, the KIS measure captures a very large proportion of employment growth and value creation in contemporary advanced economies (OECD 2003; European Commission 2002). Employment growth in the EU KIS sector remained an average 3 per cent between 1995 and 2000, led by the knowledge-intensive market service sector (5.6 per cent), followed by high-tech services (3.8 per cent), other knowledge-intensive services (2.4 per cent) and stagnating financial services (0.8 per cent) (Strack 2004). Between 1995 and 2000 KIS sector employment grew an average 3 per cent in Britain, 3.4 per cent in the US, and 1.7 per cent in Germany, but declined 11.2 per cent in Japan (Strack 2004). Within Europe, Germany and the UK have the highest numbers of people employed in the KIS sector (Strack 2003), and the London inner-city had the highest proportion of KIS employment (57 per cent) in Europe as a whole (Laafia 2002).

From a gender perspective, a major advantage of the KIS sector is the inclusion of financial services, education, health and social services and a segment at least of cultural activities where women's employment is large and growing. Some of these are sectors of public and/or non-profit employment, otherwise neglected by a focus on high-tech services and ICT. These are all traditional sectors of female employment, undergoing transformation partly through privatization and/or deregulation of employment in the public sector, partly in response to cultural change and scientific progress. The imagery of the KIS sector expands well beyond technology and information networks, to encompass aspects of cultural, political and social changes driving economic changes.

Comparing measures, comparing new economies

All three measures capture important, though different, dimensions of the transformation from an industrial to a knowledge-based economy. Underlying the differences between the measures are varying images of the sources of change and of core economic activities. The OECD focus on the ICT sector emphasizes a technologically driven understanding of economic change, which carries over in part to the focus on networks as central to the new information sector. Nonetheless, the information sector also points to cultural sources of change in the creative industries. Together with the knowledge-intensive services sector, all three measures re-mix the classification of industries (in the case of the ICT measure, overriding the industrial economic division between manufacturing and service activities), thus foregrounding service activities. The ICT and information sectors include only technology-related (ICT) services. The KIS is an exclusively services sector. The imagery of change drawn by the KIS sector goes well beyond technology-driven expansions of services. With the inclusion of old, yet knowledge-intensive sectors such as education, health and social services the measurement of economic changes becomes sensitive to advances in science (e.g. medical advances), cultural changes (e.g. the expansion of the education sector) as well as major social and political developments (e.g. the ageing of the population, the privatization of health and social services). One obvious issue, related to the use of broad industry categories (2- rather than 4-digit) for the construction of the KIS measure is the fact that non-knowledge-intensive lines of work are also included in the sector. Rather than a disadvantage, the broader occupational spectrum presents an opportunity for exploring the dynamics of social inequality within the knowledge-based economy.

In comparing business value-added and employment in the ICT and KIS sectors across the four countries, Japan emerges as somewhat of an exception. While the countries studied here are the four most important countries in terms of the worldwide shares of employment in the ICT sector (almost 70 per cent together), ICT employment in Japan is concentrated in manufacturing: in the other advanced economies, in ICT services. Germany has less employment in ICT services than Britain and the US. In both Germany and Japan employment has stopped growing in ICT services, while it continues to grow in the US and more so in the UK. A similar comparative picture emerges for the KIS sector. Only in Japan has employment declined. The strongest employment growth has been in the US and the UK, less so in Germany. As a first sketch, the economic changes associated with the transition to a knowledge-based economy are most advanced in the US and UK, followed by Germany, with Japan lagging behind.

Gender and knowledge economy sectors

The international organizations and supra-national governance organizations which have created measures of new economic activities have not considered the gender composition of these sectors[9] or gender dimensions of employment growth and practices within these sectors. The OECD and the EU both track qualification levels of workers within the KIS sector/subsectors, but without consideration of the gender composition of high-, medium- or low-qualified work. Both the EU and the UN discuss disadvantages for women in new economic activities, mainly in relation to women in science education or the gender dimension of the digital divide.[10] Most mainstream research about the knowledge-based economy has either focused on the ICT industry or ignored the availability of other new economic sector classifications.

Tables 2.4 and 2.5 present the constructions of each of the three new sector measures for the four countries, based on unpublished data from national enterprise surveys (see appendix http://www.uni-due.de/shire/research.shtml). The computation of shares of women's and men's total

Table 2.4:   Proportion of total, female and male employment in new economy sectors in Britain, Germany, Japan and the United States (female/male*) (%)

Country	Sectors		
	ICT	Information	Knowledge-intensive
Britain	3.6	3.4	40.0
	(2.8/4.4)	(3.1/3.7)	(52.6/29.3)
Germany	3.6	2.4	32.0
	(2.5/4.4)	(2.1/2.6)	(43.5/22.2)
Japan	5.0	3.0	31.0
	(3.8/5.7)	(2.4/3.3)	(41.4/24.0)
United States	4.7	2.9	35.7
	(3.8/5.6)	(2.8/3.0)	(43.0/29.1)

* The data appendix (see http://www.uni-due.de/shire/research.shtml) covers surveys used, measurement and comparative issues involved in undertaking the analysis reported in this table and in Tables 2.5 and 2.6.

Table 2.5:   Proportion of female employment in new sectors in Britain, Germany, Japan and the United States (%)

Country	Sectors		
	ICT	Information	Knowledge-intensive
Britain	35.4	41.1	60.4
Germany	32.0	39.1	61.0
Japan	31.2	32.6	54.0
United States	38.4	47.0	58.0

employment in the three sectors (Table 2.4) and the proportion of women's employment in relation to total sectoral employment (Table 2.5) provide a first snapshot of the gender composition of the knowledge-based economy.

Overall, the size of new economy sectors within national employment structures is quite similar across the four countries. ICT employment in Japan and the United States is higher, reflecting the size of Japanese ICT manufacturing and the dynamic development of ICT services in the US (OECD 2003). The information sector covers a smaller share of total employment. There are stronger similarities cross-nationally and by gender for this new economic sector. As might be expected from the broader definition and level of aggregation of the knowledge-intensive service measure, the KIS sector represents a far larger share of overall employment than either of the other two measures with total employment ranging from 31 per cent in

Japan to 40 per cent in Britain. Germany and Japan, which have maintained significant manufacturing sectors well into the 1990s, have comparatively lower proportions of employment in this sector, though the KIS sector comprises nearly one-third of employment in both countries. The importance of the three sectors for women's and men's employment differs a great deal, with the ICT sector having a greater overall share of total men's employment while the KIS sector covers more than 40 per cent of total female employment, though less than 30 per cent of men's employment in all four countries. These differences are confirmed by examining the proportions of men and women comprising employment in these sectors.

Similarities in gender composition across national contexts are quite strong. Women represent about a third of total ICT employment. A larger share of ICT service employment in Britain and the US accounts for the stronger female composition in this sector in both countries. Except in Japan, 40 per cent or more of information sector employment is female, with an especially strong female presence in the sector in the US. By far the most important new economy measure from the perspective of women's employment is the KIS sector. In all four countries KIS sector employment is female-dominated. KIS is the broadest new economy measure, and gender-based differences in employment composition are evident between and within industries comprising the sector (Table 2.6).

In all four countries, the highest shares of female KIS employment are in health and social services. Women's share of this sector of knowledge-intensive employment comprises 75 per cent or more of total employment in this sector. The gender composition of KIS employment is most similar in Britain and Germany. In Japan, the insurance industry is more important for women's knowledge-intensive employment, but other business services less so than in the other three countries. Only in the US is the education sector relatively less important for women's knowledge-intensive employment. Men dominate employment in post and telecommunications, computers and R&D in all four countries. Clearly there are important gender-based differences within the knowledge-intensive services sector, which deserve more attention in future research.

The three ways of conceptualizing the knowledge-based economy – ICT, information sector and KIS – capture very different scopes of employment and result in quite divergent gender compositions. Measures of the new economy based on either new ICT industries or the production and dissemination of information never cover more than 5 per cent of total employment, and usually a much lower share of total female than male employment. Nonetheless, women comprise about a third or more of all employment in the ICT and information sectors, so that a further analysis of patterns of occupational segregation and the quality of work is meaningful for understanding the gendering of these measures of the new economy. The KIS measure depicts quite a different image of the new

Table 2.6:   Percentage of female KIS employment by industry (female share of industry employment) in Britain, Germany, Japan and the US

Subsector (ISIC Rev. 3 two-digit code)	Britain	Germany	Japan	US
Water transport (61)	0.1	0.1	0.1	0.1
	(32)	(21)	(17)	(34)
Air transport (62)	0.6	0.3	0.2	1
	(47)	(54)	(46)	(44)
Post and telecommunications (64)	2.1	1.6	1.3	4.8
	(26)	(29)	(34)	(41)
Financial intermediation (65)	5.0	8.0	4.2	7.3
	(57)	(57)	(44)	(70)
Insurance and pension funding, except compulsory social security (66)	1.8	2.0	4.7	3.5
	(55)	(48)	(65)	(62)
Activities auxiliary to financial intermediation (67)	1.9	1.1	0.1	0.4
	(52)	(60)	(30.4)	(58)
Real estate activity (70)	2.8	2.3	4.5	1.3
	(52)	(50)	(40)	(43)
Renting of machinery and equipment w/out operator, personal and household goods (71)	0.9	0.4	1.0	1
	(39)	(35)	(32)	(33)
Computer and related activities (72)	3.2	2.0	3.0	2.7
	(43)	(30)	(27)	(37)
Research and development (73)	0.7	1.1	1	1
	(48)	(42)	(25)	(41)
Other business activities (74)	20.2	21.3	5.1	26
	(48)	(50)	(32)	(47)
Education (80)	22.1	12.6	24.2	5.3
	(71)	(66)	(50)	(60)
Health and social work (85)	33.1	44.2	45.2	39.5
	(83)	(80)	(75)	(80)
Recreational, cultural and sporting activities (92)	5.4	3.0	5.8	6.3
	(53)	(49)	(50)	(48)
TOTAL per cent (female share of sector)	99.9	100.0	100.0	99.9
	(60.4)	(61)	(54)	(58)

economy as dominated by female employment. KIS is the only one of the three measures that reaches the dimension of a *sector* rather than an industry. The importance of the KIS sector for total and for women's employment is much greater, though there is wide variation between the individual industries within the sector.

Gendering of new occupations

The ICT and the KIS sectors[11] are growth sectors for high-skilled jobs and thus present new opportunities for qualified workers in the labour force. Given the rising educational levels of women and better equal opportunity provisions in advanced economies, new economic activities potentially open new chances for women without the hurdle of overcoming established discriminatory practices. Knowledge economy jobs may not be as good as they seem, meaning that women in fact do not really benefit much in these new lines of work (Gill 2002). In knowledge economy sectors employment has also grown in low-skill occupational categories. While employment growth and expansion in the ICT and the KIS sectors are more likely to involve skilled work, these sectors also include low-skilled jobs, though these are growing at a slower pace than the top jobs. The occupational segregation of women into a small range of occupations at the lower end of the spectrum of the occupational system is a traditional way in which employment is gendered. Given the limits of the available data and the difficulty of comparing occupational systems (see data appendix http://www.uni-due.de/shire/research.shtml), a direct analysis of gender and the structure of occupations in the three sectors is not possible. Instead, other sources of data are drawn upon to study the gendering of the knowledge economy from an occupational perspective. Are the patterns of gendered occupational segregation characteristic of industrial economies being reproduced in the transition to knowledge-based economies in Britain, Germany, Japan and the US?

The OECD and EU have engaged in some analyses of the quality of jobs and employment growth in the ICT and KIS sectors. The OECD has tended to focus on high-tech occupations and created a classification of ICT high- and low-skilled jobs. According to the OECD, 'there is no internationally agreed list of ICT-related occupations' and even comparisons between the EU (labour force survey) and the US (current population survey) are minimally reliable due to differences in reporting methods, the detail of classifications and the lack of concordance between occupational classifications.[12] Furthermore, the OECD division of ICT occupations into high- and low-skilled workers is based on an implicit division between white-collar and blue-collar occupational categories. Computer operators, for example, are grouped as a 'high-skilled' ICT occupation, together with scientists and programmers. The OECD does not break down its analyses of high- and low-skilled ICT occupations by gender. Important sectors of female employment, data processors for example, are not included at all in the OECD measure, so that women's participation in the sector is under-estimated in OECD analyses.

In the absence of internationally comparable data and measures, we turned to generating data from national sources, without attempting to achieve direct concordance between occupational measures. Country-specific data on ICT occupations was gathered by the GLOW network (for the UK: Walby (2002c); Japan: Gottfried and Aiba (2002); Germany: Shire, Bialucha and Vitols (2002); and the US: Gottfried and Beydoun (2002)). Rather than following the OECD method of constructing a measure of 'high'- and 'low'-skilled ICT employment, which hardly seemed reliable at the level of aggregation of many of the individual occupational groupings, our analysis focused on the distribution of employment by gender in the full range of specific ICT occupations in comparative perspective (Table 2.7).

Wide differences in the female composition of all ICT occupations exist across the four countries, a result that may be related to the inclusion of different work activities within these specific occupational classifications. The manufacturing emphasis of the Japanese ICT sector may be the reason for the high proportion of male employment in ICT occupations (nearly 90 per cent, compared to 10.8 per cent female employment). The high proportion of women in ICT occupations in the US (56 per cent female) may likewise be a result of the service dominance of this activity in this country. In Germany, a large difference in female composition is evident between the new (former German Democratic Republic) and old (West German) federal states. The higher proportion of women in the East German compared to the West German ICT sector may be related to two factors: the fuller integration of women into regular employment overall in the new federal states (because of higher labour force participation of women in the former German Democratic Republic) and the more recent development of the sector in this region, which may involve a higher proportion of employment in ICT services. The proportions of women in ICT occupations in West Germany and Britain are similar, falling between the poles of low and high female activity in Japan and the US.

Despite these differences, cross-national similarities in the gender composition of specific ICT occupations are striking. Overall, the results point to continuities with the traditional patterns of occupational segmentation rather than to new opportunities for women in new activities – women dominate a small number of occupations, while men dominate a much broader range of ICT jobs. Few occupations are gender-mixed (defined as 40–60 per cent female). The gender-mixed occupations that are present are all related to computer operation and applications. In Japan and the US women dominate the cateogory which most likely involves low-skilled work, keypunchers/data entry.[13] In all four countries, men dominate the most highly skilled occupational groups: computer scientists, developers, engineers and programmers. In summary, while women make up a third or more of employment in the ICT sector in all four countries, they are concentrated in a relatively small number of occupations at the low-skill end of the ICT occupational structure.

Gendering of new employment forms

Next to occupational position, the most important indicator of the quality of a job is the type of employment contract governing the employment relation. The institutional structure of advanced industrial economies was

Table 2.7: Gender composition of ICT occupations

Country	Female comp. of all occupations	Gender mixed occupations (40–60%)	Female-dominated occupations (>60%)	Male-dominated occupations (>60%)
Britain	23.5%	Data processing and operators	0	Systems and processing managers Analysts and programmers Computer engineers, installation and maintenance Software engineers
Germany*	W = 21% E = 41%	Software application technicians	0	Computer scientists Software developers (various) Data processing Computer services and sales
Japan	10.8%	Others (52%) (computer operators 31%, admin and sales 27%)	Keypunchers (96%)	Systems engineers Programmers Researchers (see mixed for operators, admin and sales)
US	55.6%	Computer equipment operators	Chief communications operators** Data-entry keyers	Computer programmers Computer equipment operators and supervisors

* Reported separately for East (the new federal states) and West (the old federal states) Germany
** This is a tiny occupation in the US with only 3000 workers in total
Sources: Britain: data from 1998, Labour Market Trends; Germany: data from 1993, Mikrozensus reported in Dostal 1996; Japan: data for 1998, MITI, Tokutei saabisu sangyou jittai chousa (census data does not provide enough detail), US: data for 1999, Current Population Survey, Bureau of Labor Statistics. See Gottfried and Beydoun 2002; Shire, Bialucha and Vitols 2002; and Walby 2002c for further details on the national occupational cases.

characterized by a segmentation of the labour market, with core employees (especially in large firms, protected by trade-union bargaining) in full-time jobs with employment prospects regulated by well-established internal labour markets and job security. While there are important differences between the four countries examined here, in all cases a secondary labour market also existed, where employment prospects were more subject to market-driven demands and where trade-union protection was either less comprehensive or oriented only towards a segment of the full-time, full-year employed. As secondary labour market participants and as new entrants to the labour force from the 1970s onward, women in advanced industrial economies dominated forms of non-regular employment, characterized by short-term contracts and/or short (part-time) hours while men continued to dominate the ranks of core, protected, primary labour market employment.

The rising educational levels of women and improved equal employment opportunities observed by Walby (1997) as part of the transformation of gender relations did open core employment to at least a small segment of the female labour supply. Since the 1990s, however, internationalization and liberalization pressures have led to a political (de-regulatory) and economic (market-driven) breakdown of the institutional structure of core employment and internal labour markets. In the 1990s, even Germany and Japan (countries which had virtually regulated away most forms of temporary work) began to reform their employment systems in order to expand flexible employment on the basis of temporary work contracts. With forms of direct discrimination outlawed in most advanced economies, the regulation and demand for flexible work contracts has become a major factor in the gendering of employment. Are women in the new economy sectors more likely to be found in non-regular employment contracts? Do women continue to dominate non-regular employment forms in these sectors?

The surveys used in this analysis do not include data on the full range of non-regular employment forms. With the exception of the US data, however, the data does include part-time employment. Part-time work is not the best indicator of new employment contracts; from a gender perspective, part-time work is not a new employment form, and thus not an indicator of change in employment contracts for women. But this fact also makes examining part-time work interesting, for exploring whether traditional patterns of segmenting women into non-regular employment persist in the context of new economic activities. While broader measures of temporary work would provide a better measure of the gendering of *new* employment forms and practices, the following analysis, limited to analysing part-time employment, at least gives some insight into whether traditional labour market segregation practices play a role in the gendering of new economy employment.

Table 2.8: Proportion of part-time employment in sector, and proportion of women in part-time work (in parentheses)

Country %p-t in economy (% women in p-t work)	Sectors		
	ICT	Information	KIS
Britain 23 (80)	12.3 (73.8)	16.4 (72.4)	35 (82)
Germany 17 (84)	6.3 (69.4)	12 (69.6)	21.5 (85)
Japan 24 (67)	14.1 (73.4)	23 (70.5)	21 (70.3)
US 13 (68)	–	–	–

The proportion of part-time employment in the four national economies differs from relatively low in Germany (17 per cent) and the US (13 per cent) to relatively high in Britain (23 per cent) and Japan (24 per cent) (OECD 2000a). Despite the economy-wide differences, in the three countries for which data is available, the use of part-time employment is below average in the ICT and information sectors (though only slightly so in Japan) but above average in the KIS sector (Table 2.8).

Women dominate part-time employment in all four countries (80 per cent in Britain, 84 per cent in Germany, 67 per cent in Japan and 68 per cent in the US). There are important differences in the use of part-time labour across the three sector measures. Generally, women have lower levels of part-time employment in the ICT sector and greater rates of part-time employment in the information and KIS sectors, with several country-specific variations. Women in Japan and the UK, as could be expected, are mainly represented as part-time workers in a number of industries included in the three measures. Only in Japan are female ICT workers likely to be part-time employees: the numbers of female part-timers in two ICT industries – electrical manufacturing and database services/distribution of content – are nearly as high as levels of female full-time employment. In all three countries, women working in motion picture projection are more likely to work part-time, with part-time women outnumbering full-timers in Japan and the UK.

Especially in the information and KIS sectors in Japan and the UK, the numbers of female part-timers are greater than full-timers in the industries where women's employment is also highest: library/archive activities, recreational, cultural and sport activities, specific to Japan, news agency services and in the UK, the education industry, health and social work and recreational, cultural and sport activities. These are partly traditional domains of women's employment, and the gendering patterns of old are carried forth into the new constitution of these fields as information- and knowledge-intensive industries.

Non-regular work is far more heterogeneous than the indicator employed in this analysis (part-time work). Especially in the ICT and culture industries, temporary employment and new forms of self-employment (see Gottschall and Kroos in this volume) are encroaching upon regular full-time contracts. Further, male employment in new employment forms is also expanding, with the breakdown of core regular employment in the advanced economies. The finding that women are strongly represented in non-regular employment may be due to the exclusive focus here on part-time work. While further studies of other non-regular employment forms, such as those in this volume, are key to understanding the extent and nature of the gendering of employment in the new economy, the persistence of the female domination of part-time work, for example in the electrical manufacturing industry in the Japanese ICT sector, or in education, health and social services in the UK, or in the motion picture industry everywhere, signals a high degree of continuity between the gendering of employment in industrial economies in the transition to knowledge-based economies.

Gendering of the new economy in comparison

On balance, the analysis of women in new economic sectors and the gendering of new economic activities presented in this chapter points to greater risks than chances for women, with patterns of occupational segregation persisting and the positioning of women in non-regular employment evident. How the new economy is measured makes a difference for the participation of women, with the smallest proportion of female employment in the ICT and the largest in the KIS sectors. Within the information and KIS sectors, women in all four countries are mainly found in traditional domains of female labour, such as library services and health and social services. Interesting cases of relatively mixed-gender industries, where the gendering dynamics are likely to be more complex than represented here, are ICT services and financial services. Nonetheless, women in the ICT industry in all four countries experience occupational segregation into low-skill lines of work, while men dominate the best jobs.

With the exception of Japan, where the development of ICT services lags behind and where KIS employment has declined, the new measures of economic activity seem to capture the most dynamic sector of economic growth and employment in advanced economies. While there are variations in the proportion of female employment between the sector measures, the female share is never less than a third of total sector employment. Clearly these measures are meaningful for capturing the dual transformation of economies and gender relations. We may learn more about economic and gender transformations by using the KIS measure, which captures from 25 per cent (in Japan) to 40 per cent (in the UK) of total national employment and where women in all four countries comprise more than half of all employees.

On the basis of the analyses presented in this chapter, two tentative conclusions about the gendering of the new economy can be drawn. First, the occupational system remains a source of inequality for women in advanced economies, despite rising levels of female education and the chances opened by new lines of work. Second, new employment types and statuses, related to the liberalization and de-regulation of national employment systems, have central importance for issues of gender and inequality at work. Economic changes continue to be embedded in gender relations, despite cultural and political changes which have improved women's employment chances.

The research reported in this chapter needs to be advanced in several ways, in order to improve the empirical and comparative analyses and to better explain the gendering of the new economy. Rather than enterprise surveys, a combination of labour force surveys and population/micro-census data in and across the four countries would allow for cross-tabulations of sector, occupation and employment type by gender at the level of measurement (3- or 4-digit occupational and economic activity measures), but will require context-specific knowledge to harmonize the data cross-nationally. Given the measurement and comparative issues raised by using such data for an international analysis, such research depends on supporting resources, in terms of funds, research personnel and a cross-national network infrastructure.

Explaining the gendering of the new economy in comparison requires a broader methodological approach and a theoretical framework for comparison, the beginnings of which can be found in other chapters in this volume. Understanding gendering processes requires a qualitative and longitudinal approach, which combines institutional and organizational analyses with a micro-sociological perspective on gendering processes in workplace practice. Cross-national explanations depend on identifying the relevant institutional domains for understanding gender orders in a holistic manner at the national level, and for engaging in systematic comparisons of institutional domains across national settings. Prior research gives some strong indications about which institutional domains are most relevant for understanding the gendering of employment in cross-national perspective: skill regimes (Estévez-Abe 2002), employment regulation (O'Reilly 2000) and social care regimes (Gottfried and O'Reilly 2002), some of which are further developed in this volume (see chapters by Walby, Lenz and Osawa in this volume).

Overall, the similarities rather than differences in the gendering of new economy employment are more evident in this chapter. The limited focus in both the analyses of occupation and employment type may be the reason for these similarities, rather than the actual absence of differences. Given the under-representation of women generally in the ICT compared to the other sector measures, occupational segregation may be stronger in this technology-based sector than in activities captured by other sector measures (e.g. publishing, education, financial services) with higher shares of female employment. Likewise, the sole focus on part-time work rather than new forms of temporary and self-employment probably biases the analysis towards similarities in older patterns of labour force participation rather than in new and emerging practices, where differences in regulation may be producing quite different patterns of gendering (see Holtgrewe and Gottschall and Kroos in this volume). Further research should expand the levels of analyses, the use of methodological approaches and the range of occupations and employment types analysed in order to improve the understanding and comparison of the gendering of the new economy.

Notes

1. See Gottschall's (2000) discussion of Beck, Chapter 6.
2. This finer distinction of the broader category, wholesale and retail trade and commission, except of motor vehicles and motorcycles (G-51) became possible with the update to ISIC Rev. 3.1 in 2002. National surveys do not always allow for the distinction, in which case, the entire category G-51 is included in the computations.
3. For the OECD this classification has become the major measure of the information economy and with the advantage of breaking 'the traditional ISIC dichotomy between manufacturing and service activities' in the knowledge-based economy (OECD 2002a). In the bi-annual *OECD Science and Technology Scoreboards* and in its *Measuring the Information Economy 2002* handbook, the OECD has undertaken a range of further analyses and cross-national comparison of the ICT sector, including productivity, employment, wage and incomes information (OECD 2002a, 2003).
4. The OECD estimates of the ICT sector in Germany may be under-estimates, since the measure does not include rental of ICT goods or ICT wholesale activities (7123 and 5150).
5. The OECD measure of KIS services focuses on market-services, which are R&D intensive and have a large proportion of high-skill workforce. Based on these criteria, the OECD arrives at a much narrower selection of industries than those included by the EU. Excluded are real estate rental and the air and water transport sectors.
6. The high-tech sector does, however, include an interesting distinction between high-technology, medium-high technology, medium-low technology and low-technology, which could be more useful than simple industry-based classifications for the study of gender and employment in manufacturing contexts, especially in NICs with a greater share of overall employment in manufacturing (Strack 2004). The OECD focuses on 'high-technology manufacturing' as a measure of economic development in its comparisons of a broader grouping of national cases than is covered in this book (OECD 2003).
7. The EC excludes financial services from this subset (and relegates these to a separate subset), while the OECD includes them. The OECD excludes transport

services (water and air) and is sceptical about the inclusion of real-estate activities under knowledge-intensive market-services, while the EC includes these.

8. The third industry included under knowledge-intensive services – recreational, cultural and sporting activities – overlaps with the information sector slightly with respect to the inclusion of movie and video production industries.

9. With the partial exception of ICT, EC 2003.

10. The High Level Group on Employment and Social Dimensions of the Information Society (ESDIS) devotes three out of 54 pages of its 2003 working paper to the 'gender dimension' which nonetheless recognizes the problem of exclusion of women from a range of ICT professions and the contributions of male domination of technology production to gender-based employment inequalities. The key challenge in overcoming gender inequality is very well formulated in the annex to this report (p. 52).

11. Similar quantitative and comparative analyses on the information sector are not available.

12. The EU data is available only at the 3-digit ISCO-88 level, but there is no official concordance between ISCO 88 and the US-CPS. Occupational data from labour force surveys is based on self-declaration of household members.

13. Neither Germany nor Britain has occupational classifications for keypunchers/data-entry.

Part II
Comparative Regulation

3
Comparative Livelihood Security Systems from a Gender Perspective, with a Focus on Japan

Mari Osawa

Introduction

This chapter explores the development of livelihood security systems since the early 1980s in major industrialized countries with a particular focus on Japan. As Esping-Andersen mentions in his 'Preface to the Japanese edition' of *The Three Worlds of Welfare Capitalism* (1990), Japan is a difficult case to classify, to the extent that it has served as a touchstone for his typology. The Japanese welfare state, as of 1980, exhibited the lowest expenditure among OECD countries, and was of a 'liberalistic' nature in the sense that its 'highly selective' social policy offered insufficient family support, and that its low degree of 'de-commodification' compelled the individual to participate in the labour market. Meanwhile, the division of its social insurance schemes by occupation and social stratification (due to disparity created by the size of the enterprise, etc.) demonstrated its more 'conservative' nature.

While Japan's similarity to Switzerland, Spain and Greece could be mapped out when a gender measure such as 'female work desirability' was added (Siaroff 1994), a comparative analysis from a gender perspective of the particular designs of policy measures and the outcomes of taxation, the old age pension scheme, child care support programme as well as labour market regulations can reveal similarities and differences across countries much more clearly. The Japanese livelihood security system, based on the large corporate-centred male breadwinner model, impedes not only the desired transition or reorganization of its economy from the late industrialization (Fordist and post-Fordist) phase to the service and knowledge-oriented stage, but also the realization of more equitable gender relations at home and at work.

Gendering social policy typology

This chapter tries to review comparatively from a gender perspective the characteristics of livelihood security systems of major industrialized countries and the changes that have taken place during the 1980s and the 1990s with a focus on Japan. The various sides in the current debate on welfare regimes agree that the Japanese social policy system belongs to the 'strong male breadwinner' model, characterized by insufficient public support for the family either in cash or service benefits, and compelling participation of the individual male in the labour market (due to a low degree of 'de-commodification'). The performance as well as legitimacy of this social policy system, however, started to be questioned in the early 1990s, after the bursting of the 'bubble economy' and with the ensuing recession, and as population ageing, hand-in-hand with a declining birth rate, accelerated.

Esping-Andersen characterizes Japan as 'a difficult case to classify' (Esping-Andersen 1997a: 182; 2001: v, xiii). According to his 1980 clustering of regimes of welfare states as the system of social stratification, Japan scores in the medium range on the summary index of conservatism, in the high range on liberalism, and in the low range on socialism. Japan's score for conservatism is medium, because the degree of 'statism', measured as expenditure on pensions for government employees as percentage of GDP, is slightly over half of the mean of eighteen countries surveyed, while its degree of 'corporatism', measured as number of occupationally distinct public pension schemes, is rather high. Its score for liberalism is high, partly because the degree of means-tested poor relief, measured as a percentage of total public social expenditure, is higher than the mean, and more because degrees of market influence, measured as private-sector shares of total pension spending and of total health spending, are high. Its score for socialism is low, partly because the degree of universalism, measured as an averaged percentage of the population aged 16–64, eligible for sickness, unemployment and pension benefits, is lower than the mean and also because degree of equality in the benefit structure of these programmes is only half of the mean of eighteen countries. On the 'de-commodification' score, however, it can be seen that the Japanese welfare state regime has conformed to the conservative corporatist model (Esping-Andersen 1990: 50, 52, 54, 70–1, 74).

Social expenditures, as defined by the OECD as social security benefit expenditure and spending on education, comprised 17 per cent of GDP in Japan in 1981. This was the second lowest figure among the nineteen countries compared. Thus, the Japanese welfare state around 1980 approached something like a conservative corporatist model, with the least generous benefits possible.

The indices explained above show that classification of different welfare states is based mainly on relative size of income transfer schemes and partly on their design. Though income transfer schemes and health services are certainly major parts of the welfare state, they nevertheless do not encompass all elements of the social policy system, in which employment regulations play important roles in affecting primary distribution of income and other opportunities for the population. Actually, 'functional equivalents' between welfare states and labour market policies such as employment protection, minimum wages, extension of collective bargaining and so on have been stressed recently (Bonoli 2003).

In order to put the Japanese welfare state productively into comparative perspective, Campbell proposes to make a distinction between the 'welfare state in a narrow sense', which is an equivalent with the welfare state in Esping-Andersen's arguments, and the 'welfare state in a broader sense'. The latter refers to government programmes that aim at socio-economic equality through measures including labour market regulations, tax policy and even protectionist trade policy (Campbell 2002: 2–3). This 'welfare state in a broader sense', or social policy system, however, cannot ensure the people's daily livelihood and future security nor mitigate socio-economic inequality, unless it is finely articulated with family and enterprise institutions and practices. Hence I use the articulation of the social policy system with family and enterprise institutions and practices, named as the 'livelihood security system', as the analytical framework in this chapter.

Campbell applies Esping-Andersen's typology of welfare state (in a narrow sense) to Japanese social policy (welfare state in a broader sense), and characterizes early postwar Japanese social policy as 'social democratic', because labour market policy aimed at full employment was incorporated as an intrinsic element of the welfare state. While admitting that, as well as the sheer size of the welfare state, whether full employment policy included 'equal treatment of women' or not is among the major differences between the Scandinavian model and Japanese social policy, he still emphasizes the expansion of public day-care centres to enable female employment in the early postwar Japan, and thereby intentionally ignores gender equality in classifying social policy (Campbell 2002: 5).[1]

It is true that the overall unemployment rate in Japan had been kept lower than 3 per cent throughout the rapid economic growth period from 1955 to the early 1970s, and even in the slowed-down growth period after the first oil crisis until the mid-1990s. But if 'employment performance', defined by Miura as varying patterns of unemployment risks and income maintenance among different segments of population (Miura 2001), is examined by gender and age group, it proves to be particularly for adult male workers that employment performance had been high, under so-called Japanese-type employment practices and dismissal regulations. In the first oil crisis for example, employment of women was hit significantly harder than men's employment in Japan.[2] This was unique to Japan. According to the OECD, in no advanced country of the West did the rate of withdrawal of female workers from the labour market during the recession period of the mid-1970s exceed that of male workers (OECD 1976).

Japanese-type employment practices with three key elements such as 'lifetime' employment (long-term stable employment), a seniority wage-system for male regular workers and a company-based union, started to emerge when postwar trade unions organized white- as well as blue-collar workers on a company basis, and demanded elimination of status-based (not gender-based) discrimination, i.e. between white- and blue-collar workers (including one and the same door to shop-floor and lunch hall for all the employees, and the extension of long-term stable employment and the seniority wage system to blue-collar workers) (Nimura 1987: 92–3). Ideas of democracy and egalitarianism introduced by the US occupation were in the background (Pempel 1998: 88), but they did not develop to encompass gender equality. Trade union demands were realized through serious industrial disputes in the late 1940s and the 1950s (Nimura 1987: 93), and due to the specific demographic situation at the time with an increasing number of young people. The seniority wage system is convenient and beneficial for management as long as the age structure of employees is pyramidal so that the overall labour cost is kept low under the system.

A means of gaining better insight into the Japanese welfare state in a broader sense is by estimating the measure or score of 'female work desirability', as devised by Alan Siaroff,[3] who mapped out Japan's similarity to Switzerland, Spain and Greece, and its significant difference from a group of countries that included Australia, Canada, the US and New Zealand on the one hand, and Scandinavian as well as major continental European countries on the other hand (Siaroff 1994). (The figures used by Siaroff are averages from the 1980s.) It is a reasonable estimate that, for Japan, the 'index of female work desirability' in 1980 was very close to its average of the 1980s, while the indices of the other countries increased gradually over that same period. The main reason stems from the gender wage gap that did not narrow during the 1980s in Japan and, based on the ILO statistics that Siaroff himself used, it actually widened during that period, while there were slight increases in the female to male ratios for administrative and managerial staff and for students in higher education.

Another set of typologies of welfare state regimes exists, in which gender is used as an axis to focus on the basis of entitlement to social policy benefits and the unit of contribution/benefit, thereby setting off the 'male breadwinner' model against the 'individual' (Lewis 1992; Sainsbury 1994, 1996, 1999). In Sainsbury's 'individual' model, however, not only is care supposed to be paid work, but many reproductive (family-related) tasks are also regarded as being performed in the public sector (Sainsbury 1994, 1996: 42–3). Since care can be paid such as commercial baby-sitting or elderly care tasks, this type of social policy system should rather be called the 'work/life balance' (individual) model, to be distinguished from the 'market-oriented' (individual) model, in which the boundary between private and public spheres is strictly enforced, and caring and family-related tasks are located in the private sphere and paid through commodification.

This gendered typology of market-oriented, male breadwinner and work/life balance models largely overlaps with Esping-Andersen's three types, but differs from them in that it is a typology of livelihood security systems defined above, analysed from a gender perspective.

First, under the male breadwinner model, the livelihood security system is designed to provide men with stable employment, family wages (that is, wages sufficient to guarantee the livelihoods of entire families), and public social security. Accordingly, the labour markets are regulated to guarantee men in the prime of life with stable employment and family wages. Meanwhile the health insurance, unemployment insurance, pension and other social insurance schemes are designed to provide support when labour power of the male breadwinner, who is the head of household, cannot be sold on the labour market, that is for periods when the male breadwinner suffers sickness, injury or unemployment, and when he retires in old age. In short, the schemes are designed in accordance with the life course risks of the male breadwinner, and secure the livelihoods of women and children as his dependants. The male breadwinner model livelihood security system assumes that the wife bears family responsibilities on a full-time basis, while social services such as childcare and nursing care are only provided as exceptions to low-income families and families that cannot offer their own childcare.

In contrast, the work/life balance model assumes that men and women both actively work, care for their families, and participate in their local communities. It assumes that they both earn money and also provide (or should provide) family care. In this case men and women are both given compensation in accordance with their work and receive public social security benefits as individuals, while social services are designed to support family responsibilities as the rule, rather than the exception. Under this kind of work/life balance livelihood security system, regulations are enacted to ensure equal employment opportunities and family support is instituted through such measures as allowances for dependent children, childcare services from infancy, nursing services for the elderly and maternity or childcare leaves. Additionally, taxes and social security contributions are levied on individuals, rather than households, preferential tax treatment for families is reduced, and survivors' benefits are eliminated.

Finally, under the market-oriented livelihood security system, public policies to support family formation are minimal and the labour market provides no particular livelihood security treatments.

The routes in the 1980s: policies for 'building a Japanese-style welfare society'

Since the early 1980s, Western welfare state regimes have been challenged by a growing mismatch between existing institutions of social protection and new needs and risks on the one hand, and changing economic and demographic conditions such as slower growth, deindustrialization and population ageing on the other hand. Among the several hypotheses on the recent direction taken by various welfare regimes in responding to those challenges, Esping-Andersen emphasizes their 'divergence'. The social democratic regime adopted the 'welfare as investment' strategy and promoted more balance between work and family life for both women and men through public family support and vocational training (the Scandinavian route). In the Anglo-Saxon regime de-regulation in the labour market with wage erosion was promoted and the selectivity of social services was reinforced (the neo-liberal route). Finally, the conservative regime intensified the dual ('insider-outsider') structure of the labour market, and reduced the employment rate, especially through subsidized early retirement (the labour reduction route) (Esping-Andersen 1996: chap. 1; Esping-Andersen 1999).

Esping-Andersen noticed that 'continental Europe is the clearest case of impasse' (Esping-Andersen 1996: 24), because its labour supply reduction policies mean a growing pension and tax burden for a shrinking number of male insiders, and the inevitable continuation of dependency on the male breadwinner for women and young people. The intensified insider-outsider structure itself poses obstacles to post-industrial needs for greater flexibility of labour markets and the family (Esping-Andersen 1996: 79–80).

Though this view of three routes can be a convenient way to understand the different type and trajectory of welfare regimes, Japan is again a difficult case to classify. During the 1980s, the Japanese government made extensive 'reforms' of all measures of social security and welfare services under the slogan of 'Building a Japanese-style welfare society', thereby intensifying the big company-centred 'male breadwinner' model (Osawa 1994), but importantly without reducing labour supply. The 1990s saw the introduction of all three routes in a partial and indecisive way as will be discussed in the next section.

The reality of family life was that dual-earning households outnumbered male breadwinner households by the mid-1980s in Japan, and male age-wage profiles became flat under slower growth as shown in Figure 3.1. Those men who were born in the early 1940s could, in their fifties, earn as much as 4.5 times the wage they received in their early twenties. They were able to enjoy exceptionally higher wage increases based on seniority – owing to a large number of low-waged younger workers born post-World War Two working hard for them as subordinates. In contrast, men in their early fifties

(Index)

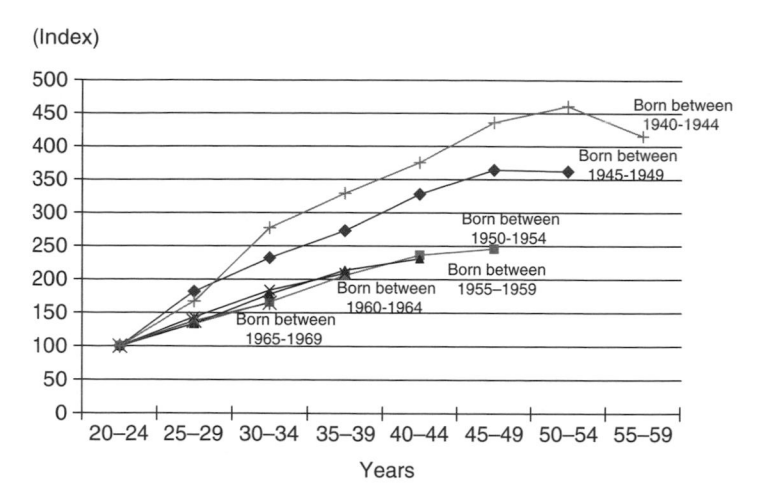

Source: Basic Statistical Survey on Wage Structure (annual edition), Ministry of Health, Labour and Welfare; Consumer Price Index, Ministry of Public Management, Home Affairs, Posts and Telecommunications.

Note: Real wages are calculated by age bracket with those regularly paid to 20–24 year olds and their annual bonuses as 100.

Figure 3.1: Growth of real wages (by cohort) (Male workers irrespective of educational background and corporate size)

today who were born in the early 1950s barely earn 2.5 times as much as compared to their younger days.

Still, according to a comparative study of the household income of employees in 1983–4 conducted by Uzuhashi, the proportion of income from wages and salary, predominantly of household head, is significantly higher in Japan than elsewhere,[4] despite women's increasing participation in the labour market. The economic basis for the household in Japan depends on a long-term 'corporate job', and the weight on the male household head is quite heavy, while the degree of dependency on the state through the social security system is very low as compared with Germany, Israel and the UK. At the same time, inter-household assistance through gifts and remittance is thin as compared with Korea and Taiwan (Uzuhashi 1997: 67).

The corporate-centred as well as gendered nature of Japanese society is thus clearly reflected in the structure of household income. Reforms in the 1980s went against both the 'de-commodification' route that reduces dependency on the labour market (the employer) by establishing the security of livelihood as an individual's social right, and the 'work/life balance' route that promotes equal employment legislation, individuals as the unit of assessments, and support for double income households. For instance, the annual income ceiling to become eligible for Spouse Deduction in the personal income tax system, which allowed tax relief to the household of a worker whose spouse's annual income remains below that ceiling, was repeatedly raised in 1984, 1987, 1988, and again in 1989. Also, the introduction of a Special Spouse Deduction added a deduction on top of the Spouse Deduction in 1987. Moreover, the 1985 Pension Reform introduced the 'Class 3 insured' category to the basic pension scheme, which exempted a worker's dependent spouse from insurance premium payments. The annual income ceiling for eligibility as a 'dependant' is equivalent to that of a 'dependent family' member in the Medical Insurance scheme, who can be provided from its fund at least 70 per cent of medical cost without paying any additional contributions.

Here let me point out the controversial issues regarding gender and pensions. Firstly, the very structure of the pension scheme can be called male breadwinner centred. The Japanese pension system consists of two tiers: a first-tier National Pension for everyone (which provides 'basic pension' benefits), and a second-tier pension for full-time employees (most commonly the Employees' Pension Insurance for corporate employees or mutual aid associations for teachers and government employees) which provides benefits proportional to the retiree's former wage level. The National Pension is divided into three categories: Class 1 for the self-employed, unemployed, etc.; Class 2 for full-time employees; and Class 3 for economically dependent spouses of Class 2 insured. The second-tier pension scheme corresponds to the Class 2 insured, of whom two-thirds are men, and is vertically divided not only into the Employee's Pension Insurance and mutual aid associations' pension, but also into various financially independent Employees' Pension Funds (company/occupational pension schemes) that act on behalf of the second-tier portion (Employees' Pension Insurance) in managing the third-tier.

This pension design represents a male breadwinner centred system. The National Pension scheme is centred around the pension for Class 2 as the standard insured. This becomes clear from the fact that Class 2 insured do not have to fill out any applications for coverage, but individuals lose their coverage when they no longer fit into this category unless they submit notifications to be re-categorized as Class 1 or 3. Moreover, among Class 2 insured, those male breadwinners who work and maintain a dependent wife (Class 3) for 40 years receive the 'model' pension benefits. The income-replacement rates reported by the Pension Bureau of the Ministry of Health, Labour and Welfare to the Pension Subcommittee of the Council of Social Security in July 2002, were 64.6 per cent for male breadwinner households, 50.5 per cent for double income households, 46.5 per cent for single male households and 56.9 per cent for single female households (for average nominal monthly earnings of full-time workers, male and female respectively), while costs to exempt dependent spouses from basic pension premiums are shared collectively by all 'Class 2 insured persons' (see Table 3.A1 in the appendix).

This pension scheme, along with the Spouse Deduction in the income tax system, encourages married women to choose limited labour force participation with an approximate annual income of about one million yen or less. It not only curbs the supply of labour by married women and their earning power, but also hinders the improvement of working conditions for women in general.

Secondly, entitlements to Survivor's Pension are explicitly gender specific (see Table 3.A1 in the appendix). When a wife dies before her husband reaches 55, the husband is not recognized as a 'survivor', but there are no similar restrictions on how old a wife must be when her spouse dies to be recognized as a 'survivor'. Widows whose earnings fell below 8 million yen per year when their husbands died are entitled to Survivors' Employees' Pensions until they reach their own pension eligibility age, regardless of their age or whether they have children (and when they have children under age 18 they also receive 'Survivors' Basic Pensions'). The benefit calculation formula assumes that their deceased husbands contributed to the system for a period of 300 months, if the husband's actual length of participation is shorter than that period.

From 1954 through 1965, women who had no children under 18 and who were under age 40 when their husbands died were not recognized as 'survivors', while those who were older than 40 when their husbands died did not receive survivors' benefits until they turned 55. In 1954 the Director of the Insurance Bureau of the Ministry of Health and Welfare explained in the Diet the government's position that widows who can work must work (Tamiya 2003: 64, 67). The viewpoint that women whose husbands have died are incapable of working (even if they have no children) actually developed through a series of revisions introduced since 1965, when the Japanese economy was growing rapidly, until 1985.

Moreover, a woman who has participated in the labour market at any time during her working life has to 'give up', on her husband's death, either her own employees' old age benefits (to receive the Survivor's Pension) or the Survivor's benefit at the level of three-quarters of the deceased husband's employees' old age benefit (to receive her own employees' old age pension). Given the gender earnings gap, it is not surprising to find that 80 per cent of working women choose to 'give up' their own benefit, even though their amounts of Survivor's Pension benefits are often less than that of a full-time housewife with no history of contribution.[5]

Thirdly, a further indication of gender bias is evident in the lack of pension provision for divorced women. Whereas a wife can receive a generous Survivor's Pension in case of her husband's death, if separated by divorce, the ex-spouse is guaranteed no portion of benefits from the husband's earnings-related pension.

Hence although financial adjustments between vertically divided pension and medical insurance schemes were introduced in the 1980s, there still is a long way to go for Japan to establish a unified system similar to the Scandinavian states.

On the other hand, reforms concerning public assistance and social welfare programmes resulted in, first, a shift away from the welfare state, that is to say, much of the responsibility for supporting a person in need shifted to his/her family and relatives and, second, lowered the upper income ceiling with regard to eligibility for receiving benefits from such programmes. In other words, public assistance and social welfare programmes became increasingly dependent on the family, and increasingly selective in their application (Osawa 1994).

Although efforts were made, in conjunction with the introduction of measures for 'solidifying the base of the home', to reform public assistance programmes, in order to give priority to the very poorest strata of the population, that is to say, lone mother households, it is clear that the living standards of those households with female heads were not thereby improved. The logic underlying these efforts may have been that the livelihood of a woman who is considered to have abandoned her role as a wife, is not worthy of public support, even where the 'base of her home' has become much less solid, because she continues to fulfil her role as a mother.[6] If this was the case, it is evident that the most important role expected of a woman, under the terms of these policy measures, is that she is to play the part of the wife, the one who is to sustain the life of a male corporate-warrior. The wholesale efforts to transform the social security system in Japan in the 1980s, thus becoming even more 'dependent on the family', can also be characterized as measures for shoring up and strengthening the male-centred orientation of the system.

It is true that the Equal Employment Opportunity Law was enacted while the 'Protection Provisions for Women' of the Labour Standard Law were relaxed in 1985. Japan ratified the UN Convention on the Elimination of All Forms of Discrimination against Women in the same year. This original EEOL stipulates only that employers 'make efforts' to treat women and men equally in recruitment, hiring, placement and promotion and prohibits (without sanction) discrimination against women only in education and training, occupational welfare, retirement and discharge. It did not introduce any new provision on wage discrimination, which has been officially prohibited by Labour Standard Law since 1947. In the Ministry of Labour's view, recruiting and hiring women only for part-time jobs or subsidiary jobs is not against the EEOL (Nakajima et al. 1994: 259–63). According to the Ministry's official interpretation, 'women only' jobs are seen to widen job opportunities of women and are consistent with the goals of the law while 'men only' jobs are unlawful. In other words, the EEOL adopted the weakest policy possible among various equal opportunity laws in different countries, one that effectively encouraged gender discrimination while, at least from an official point of view, obscuring it.

On the 'outcomes' of the original EEOL, Hanami Tadashi, then chairman of the Central Labour Standards Council, saw that private companies have been taking an increasingly greater interest in differentiating their workers into two distinctive groups to use them more effectively. One group consists of a small number of efficient, core workers (male), and the other consists of a 'large number of peripheral workers who can be readily replaced'. 'It is obvious,' Hanami concluded, 'that women and immigrant workers are expected to constitute the latter group. The gist of the problem is that laws such as the Equal Employment Opportunity Law fit in perfectly with this design' (Hanami 1991: 2000). In other words, the law effectively sanctioned the marginalization of the vast majority of female workers in non-regular, part-time or temporary jobs as well as in the general clerical dead-end track, while it nominally created a career-track for a tiny minority (Molony 1995; Shire and Imai 2000; Gelb 2003a: 52).

The lost decade

For Japan, the 1990s may have been the 'lost decade' not only in terms of structural reform and economic growth, but also as far as social security reform is concerned. Neither the 'Five-year Plan to create a Lifestyle Superpower' advocated by the Miyazawa Kiichi Cabinet (November 2001–August 2003) nor the 'Welfare Vision for the Twenty-first Century' presented under the Hosokawa Morihiro's non-LDP Cabinet (August 1993–April 1994) went beyond a mere retouching of the 'Japanese-style Welfare Society' of the 1980s. Moreover, no significant moves have been made during the 1990s to either improve the gender-based wage gap or to increase the ratio of women in managerial positions. Increase in female employment has been due to the rising number of non-regular, mostly part-time, workers (Osawa 1994, 1998).

In the meantime, Japanese-style management and employment practices have been restructured mainly by management associations amid severe global competition. Employers' associations, such as the Japan Committee for Economic Development (Keizai dôyûkai) and the Japan Federation of Employers Associations (Nikkeiren), called for 'reconstruction of the Japanese employment system and Japanese-style management' in the middle of the decade. Nikkeiren, in particular, expressed the view that 'lifetime employment and the seniority wage system' had once been effective practices, but argued that these practices were now in need of overhaul because of the rapidly changing business environment. For the future employment system, it was proposed in the interim report of 1994 that the labour force be categorized under three broad groups:

(1) the 'long-term accumulated ability utilization group' (which would be more or less equivalent to the traditional practice of long-term employment);
(2) the 'advanced specialist ability utilization group' (which would be that group of employees who would be working under limited term contracts in such areas as planning, marketing, and research and development);
(3) the 'flexible employment group' (which would also cover employees working under limited term contracts, but here would be found the generalists, technicians/engineers and salespersons).

This so-called multi-tracking (*fukusenka*) not only consisted of the above three groups, it was further argued in the interim report that 'personnel management' and 'employee compensation based on competence and performance evaluation' should also be extended to the 'long-time accumulated ability utilization' group as well. Thus, the seniority system, with regard to pay increases, would only be applicable if the employee met certain specified qualifications. Subsequent increases under the merit system, or the annual salary system, would then become applicable, and the interim report even proposed the introduction of a system of pay cuts in order to make possible the creation of wider pay differentials based on the actual job performance of employees (Nikkeiren 1994: 22–5). The implication of this would appear to be that the seniority wage system, as such, would no longer be retained.

In a nutshell, the proposed changes might be summarized in the following three phrases: *fukusenka* (multi-tracking), *tayôka* (diversification), and *ryûdôka* (flexibilization). Since long-term employment and the seniority wage system have only applied to the regular employees in large corporations and in the public services, of whom the overwhelming majority are men, representing no more than 20 per cent of the total workforce in Japan, or an estimated 12 million of the total of 50 million employees (Takanashi 1994: 21), the ranks of those males representing the most privileged class of Japanese workers would be broken up as a result of the changes proposed by the Nikkeiren.

The heyday of the 'male breadwinner' model is gone for good. Many corporations have actually revised their wage/promotion systems and shifted to meritocracy in assessing their employees' salaries. Even companies that have not opted for 'corporate restructuring' are now employing more atypical workers, e.g. mid-career recruits, part-timers and temporary staff. The employment system is gaining more flexibility and the workers are no longer as homogeneous. Nevertheless, according to indices of employment performance devised by Miura,[7] Japan in the 1990s can still be considered as a variation of continental European countries, rather than a member of Anglo-Saxon countries. She emphasizes that 'the Japanese version of the male breadwinner model is distinctive in the sense that the participation rates of women are high, but their wages are low', and that women as atypical workers constituting a low-wage sector 'sustain the co-existence of highly regulated labour market and high employment rates' (Miura 2001: 10).

Some legislation regarding the promotion of a gender-equal society, however, deserves our attention. Promoting a gender-equal society was deemed 'the key' and 'one of the pillars' of Hashimoto's Six Major Reforms[8] (Osawa 2000a). The Child/Family Care Leave Law was enforced and expanded (in 1991, 1995 and 1997), and the 'ILO 156 Convention regarding the equal opportunity/treatment of women and men with family responsibilities' was ratified in 1995. In 1997, with the call for the deregulation of employment, the 'Protection Provisions for Women' were abolished from the Labour Standards Law, which thereby led to the Equal Employment Opportunity Law being reformed and strengthened (effective as of April 1999). The Basic Law for a Gender-Equal Society, which contained the fundamental philosophy that 'no person shall be discriminated against on the basis of gender', was enacted in June 1999. These legislative measures are illustrative of Japan's possible transition towards the 'work/life balance' model. This, aside from the scale of the budget and the robustness of policy enforcement, parallels the 'Scandinavian route'.

Compared to gender equality laws and anti-discrimination laws in other countries, Japan's 'Basic Law for a Gender-Equal Society' is significant in terms of Articles 4 and 15 that highlight gender mainstreaming, and the role of the Council for Gender Equality of the Cabinet Office, which is the promoting machinery (Osawa 2000a). Article 4 stipulates that 'care should be taken so that social systems and practices have as neutral an impact as possible on the selection of social activities by women and men', which is one of the fundamental tenets of the Basic Law. Article 15 states that 'the state and local governments, when formulating and implementing policies recognized as influencing the formation of a Gender-equal Society, shall consider formation of a Gender-equal Society'. The policies to be considered here potentially extend over all sectors, for those policies with goals/measures that seem to be quite unrelated to gender equality or women's social advancement may, as an outcome, have considerable effects. As part of the administrative reforms led by Prime Minister Hashimoto, the central government offices switched over to a new system starting 6 January 2001, as seen in the reorganization of a range of key ministerial functions. Along with it, the Council for Gender Equality chaired by the Chief Cabinet Secretary became the centre in the national machinery of the Basic Law for a Gender-Equal Society, and the Bureau for Gender Equality was set up within the Cabinet Office as well.

While some trace of the Scandinavian route can be found in the above reforms, changes with regard to social security were far from the Scandinavian strategy of 'welfare as an investment'. Measures to reduce expenditure on pensions and medical care were adopted in 1994 (for further details, see Osawa 1996). During the reform of the pension system, carried out in November 1994, the minimum age of eligibility for the pension was raised from 60 years to 65 years. At the same time, the use of the current nominal wage as the base for the pension indexation was discontinued, replaced by the net wage, that is, the wage after income tax and social security contributions have been deducted. Both these measures had the aim of reducing expenditure on pensions, and the government thus continued to undermine the credibility of its pension schemes by stressing the onset of a fiscal crisis and repeatedly increasing premiums while reducing benefits.

Several proposals for medical insurance reform were made between 1995 and 1997, but substantial reform was suspended due to the tenacious objection of the Medical Association, with the exception of the 1997 revision that reduced the provision to the insured from 90 to 80 per cent (Tsuboi and Takagi 2000). Thus, the Long-term Care Insurance Law, enacted in December 1997 and enforced in April 2000, was the only major reform in the social security field during the 1990s, which is reflected in the composition of social security expenditure. Although Peng emphasizes Japan's 'social care expansion' in the 1990s, to the extent that it should be interpreted to require a revision of the productivist and developmental state perspective on East Asian welfarism (Peng 2004: 401, 416–17), the proportion of 'welfare and others' spending in the total social security expenditure stayed around 11 per cent in most of the 1990s, leaping to 14 per cent only in 2000, due to the absolute reduction in medical care spending and the introduction of the LTCI (National Institute of Population and Social Security Research 2001, 2002).[9]

Despite its many problems, the introduction of public long-term care insurance can be considered a step towards the 'Scandinavian route' or 'work/life balance' model since it is moving in the direction of 'support by the entire society' rather than relying on the unpaid care provided by female members of the family. A revision made by the coalition government parties in the latter half of fiscal year 1999, however, undermined the very core of the Long-term Care Insurance system even before it took effect.

In the autumn of 1999, the Liberal Democratic Party's policy chief, Kamei Shizuka, contended that long-term care insurance services could destroy 'Japan's admirable [*utsukushii*] tradition of children taking care of their parents'. Based on this viewpoint, the government adopted 'special measures for the smooth implementation of the long-term care insurance system' on 5 November 1999. This exempted people in the Class 1 insured category (65 years and over) from paying premiums for the first six months, and reduced their payment to 50 per cent for the following twelve months (Osawa 2000a). Kamei made a further call to impose restrictions on the provision of housework services for elderly people who are residing with their family. As of June 2000, the Ministry of Health and Welfare adopted a policy to restrict housework assistance when providing in-home visit services (*Nihon Keizai Shimbun*, 20 June 2000) (see Tanaka and Nishikawa in this volume on the implementation of the LTCI).

As explained above, the fact that Long-term Care Insurance was introduced under the terms that insurance premiums would not be collected from the insured for quite a while was a decision that could jeopardize the very foundation of the social insurance system in Japan. While the measure was adopted with the primary aim of reducing the financial burden on the elderly with a view to the general election to be held by October 2000, it no doubt slowed down the work to build the infrastructure needed to provide services. This meant that the efforts to reduce the actual burden of family caretakers, who were mostly women, were again put off. In effect, the measure stood in the way of social transition towards the 'work/life balance' model by clinging to Japanese-style welfare that relied on unpaid family (i.e. female) welfare provision on the premise of the traditional family model.

To sum up, the 'lost decade' of the 1990s saw the introduction of all three routes in a partial and indecisive way. First, it adopted elements of the 'work/life balance' model or the 'Scandinavian route' by promoting the participation of women and men in the labour force and socializing long-term care; secondly, it adopted elements of the 'neo-liberal route' by promoting certain de-regulation of the labour market; and thirdly, it adopted elements of the 'conservative route' in the sense that the restructuring of the employment practices and de-regulation of temporary employment further deepened the dual structure of the labour market.

Comparative livelihood security systems at the turn of the century

What are the comparative characteristics of the Japanese livelihood security system at the turn of the century? Figure 3.2 illustrates the trends of the overall strictness of protection against dismissal for regular workers and the overall strictness of regulation of temporary employment in the late 1980s, the late-1990s and 2003, based on the indices compiled by the OECD (OECD 2004b: 112, 115). Firstly, it is shown that in the 'liberal' countries where both kinds of strictness were low in the first place, some modest re-regulation occurred in the temporary labour market as well as in the barriers to dismissal of regular workers (with the exception of the US and Canada). Secondly, in the countries with higher barriers to the dismissal of regular workers, namely the Netherlands, Sweden, Germany, Japan and Norway, only temporary labour markets were de-regulated. Thirdly, in Italy, Belgium and Denmark, where barriers to the dismissal of regular workers were moderate, only temporary labour markets have been significantly de-regulated.

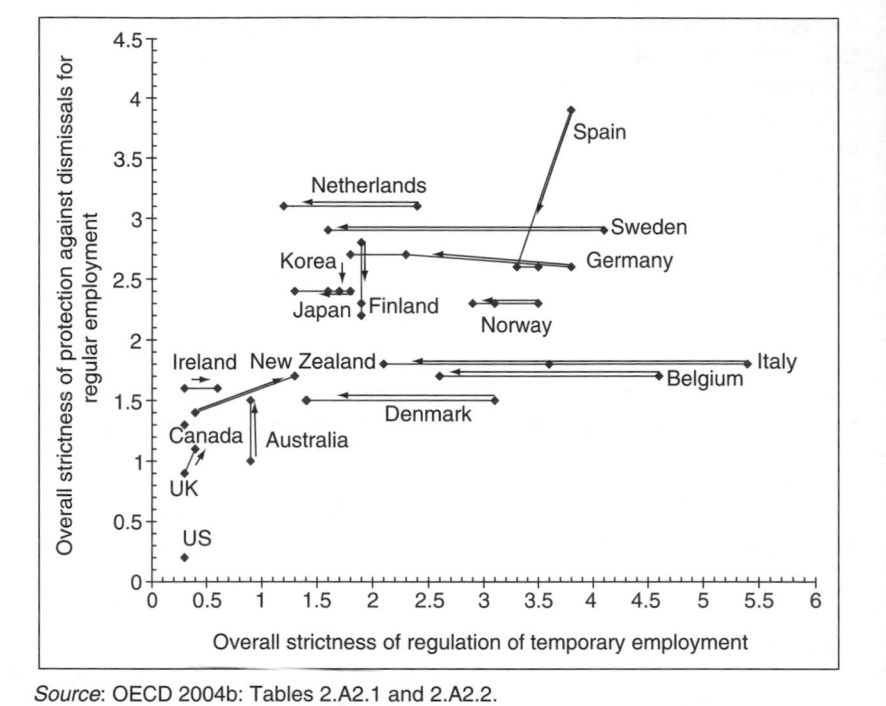

Source: OECD 2004b: Tables 2.A2.1 and 2.A2.2.

Figure 3.2:   Labour market regulations in the late 1980s, late 1990s and 2003

Notable consequences of these asymmetrical deregulations are the gender wage gap on the one hand, and an increase in non-regular employment of women and youth, particularly in Japan on the other. Although every nation exhibits a gap between men and women, Japan has a larger gender wage gap than several nations specifically compared by the Cabinet Office in 2002, namely South Korea, the Philippines, the US, Sweden, Germany and the UK.

It is well known that 'class of job position' and 'length of service years' have the most significant impacts on the gender wage gap. Japan has a lower percentage of female managerial workers than the other surveyed nations. Although women account for 40 per cent of all workers, female managerial workers account for a much lower percentage in Japan than in the Western nations and the Philippines. Japan also has a much larger gap between the female employment rate and female managerial workers rate than all the surveyed nations except South Korea. While none of the surveyed nations has shown significant changes in the percentage of female workers since 1982, the percentage of female managerial workers has been rising significantly since 1982 in the US, the Philippines and Sweden. The US has seen the most significant increase. On the other hand, Japan has shown almost no change in the female managerial-level workers rate. Male Japanese workers have, moreover, significantly longer service years (13.6 years on average) than workers in the other nations (10.7 years in Sweden, 10.6 years in Germany, 8.9 years in the UK, 7.9 years in the US and 6.8 years in Korea). Japan also has the largest gap in service years between male and female workers, that is 4.7 years as compared with gaps of smaller than two years in other countries (Cabinet Office 2003: 16–18).

Then what about unemployment risk? Japan's unemployment rate has been rising from the mid-1990s, and is higher overall for men than for women. The following points become clear from an international comparison by gender and age segment based on OECD data. First of all, the unemployment rate for young workers aged 16–24 (both men and women) has been increasing in Japan, while this rate has declined in many other OECD nations since the late 1990s. Second, in Japan the unemployment rate in 2003 is still lower for employees in the prime of life, aged 25 to 54, and in this age group the rate is lower for men than for women (the opposite holds true in the Anglo-Saxon and Northern European nations). Third, the employment/population ratio for elderly male workers aged 55 to 64 is far higher in Japan than in the other OECD nations except Switzerland (OECD 2001a: 212–20; OECD 2004b: 297–305).

The unemployment rate in Japan is higher for men than for women overall because of the high male unemployment rates for young and elderly workers. Despite this, the labour participation rate for elderly male workers is higher in Japan than in other countries. In Japan, average wages have been declining since 1998, and this drop is particularly conspicuous for men in their early 50s (according to the *Basic Survey on Wage Structure*). Regardless, the employment performance for Japanese men aged 25 and 64 may be considered as still relatively good as compared with the conditions in other nations, and for Japanese women.

Over these years there has been a substantial increase in the percentage of part-time, temporary and other 'non-regular' employees, who have not received appropriate compensation for their work. According to the *Labour Force Survey*, in Japan the percentage of female workers who are employed on a regular (permanent, full-time) basis fell from 68.1 per cent in 1985 to 48.4 per cent in 2004, while the percentage of male workers employed on a regular basis declined from 92.8 per cent to 83.7 per cent over the same period. The percentage of part-time, short-term and other non-regular employees has therefore been rising, particularly for female workers. The employment of Japanese women is rapidly becoming casualized.

How do these conditions compare with those in other nations? In 2003, 14.7 per cent of Japanese male workers were employed on a part-time basis, which is the third highest figure among all OECD nations (following Australia and the Netherlands), while 42.2 per cent of Japanese female workers were employed on a part-time basis, which is also the third highest figure in the OECD (following the Netherlands and Australia) (OECD 2004b: 310). As the percentage of part-time workers rises in Japan, the part-time labour force comes to include a greater number of individuals who are working part-time involuntarily. As companies tend to hire part-time workers as a cheap labour force, part-time workers receive significantly lower wages than full-time workers, even if they are assigned the same tasks as full-time workers. What is more, the wage differential between full-time and part-time workers has widened. Specifically, under an hourly wage index with the compensation received by full-time workers set at 100, part-time wages declined between the early 1990s and 2003 from 72.0 to 65.7 for female workers and from 57.8 to 49.9 for male workers (Danjo Kyodo Sankaku Kaigi Eikyo Chosa Senmon Chosakai 2004: charts 38-2, 68-2).

Let us now consider the wage differential between full-time and part-time female Japanese workers from an international perspective. If the median hourly wage for women who work on a full-time basis is set at 100, the hourly wages for women working part-time are 93.1 in the Netherlands, 92.3 in Sweden, 87.5 in Germany (all as of 1995), 86.8 in Australia (1997), 74.5 in the UK (2000), 66.4 in Japan (2001) and 62.5 in the US (1996) (OECD 1999: 24; Cabinet Office 2003: 28). It is important to note that while Japan has the third highest percentage of part-time employees in the OECD, following Australia and the Netherlands, the wage gap between full-time and part-time workers is relatively small in the Netherlands and Australia in particular, but quite substantial in Japan and becoming even more extreme.

Meanwhile Japan's household income distribution has been becoming unequal since as early as the mid-1970s (Tachibanaki 1998). According to a recent OECD report on income distribution and poverty in member countries in the second half of the 1990s, the Gini index of Japan in year 2000 is the tenth highest among 27 countries, while those of the US and the UK and Germany are the fourth, the ninth and the sixteenth respectively. In a composite measure of relative poverty (the poverty rate multiplied by the poverty gap) in 2000, moreover, Japan has the third highest figure among OECD nations (following Mexico and the US) (OECD 2005g). Remembering that it has been repeatedly pointed out and still is discussed that Japan is as economically egalitarian as Scandinavian countries (Campbell 2002), these facts are really alarming.

The gender gap in employment opportunities can be partly explained by opportunities for and achievements in education/learning. As for education performance of 15-year-olds, Japan is among the countries with very slight gender gaps (moderately better girls' performance in reading than boys, and

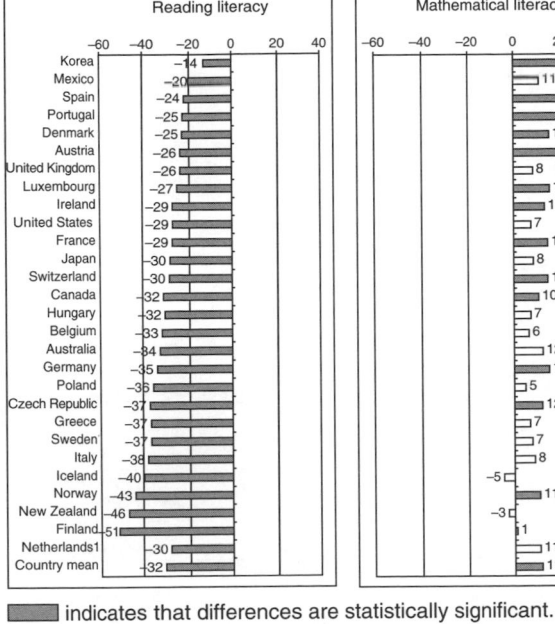
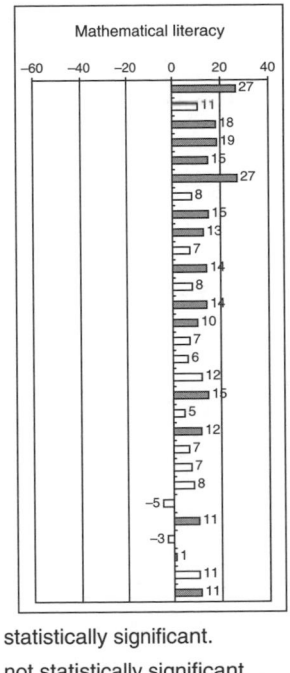
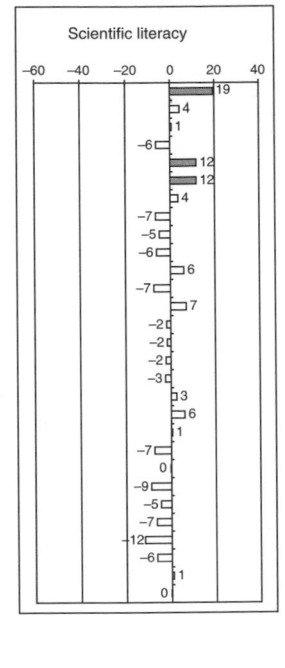

▬▬ indicates that differences are statistically significant.

☐ indicates that differences are not statistically significant.

Positive differences indicate that males perform better than females while negative differences indicate that females perform better than males.

1. Response rate is too low to ensure comparability.

Source: OECD PISA 2000 database.

Figure 3.3: Performance of 15-year-old students and gender (2000). Mean performance of 15-year-olds on the PISA reading, mathematical and scientific literacy scales

no significant gender gaps in mathematics and science, Figure 3.3). Still, there is a gap in the university (undergraduate level) enrolment rate between women (33.8 per cent) and men (47.0 per cent), and female students still tend to major in human sciences (Figures 3.4 and 3.5), even though the percentage of female students majoring in human sciences has been decreasing since 1975. The graduate school enrolment rate is rising for both men and women, with a persistent gender gap (male: 13.2 per cent; female: 6.4 per cent).

Even for those women workers who have better education and working achievements than their male counterparts, it is quite difficult to combine

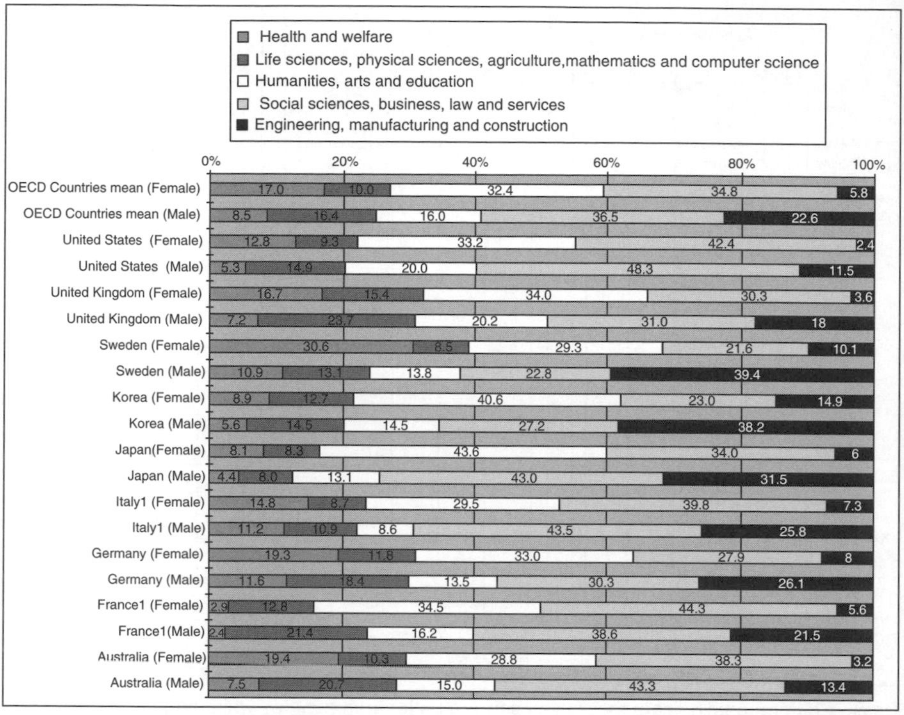

Percentage of tertiary qualifications by field of study and by gender (2002)

Legend:
- Health and welfare
- Life sciences, physical sciences, agriculture, mathematics and computer science
- Humanities, arts and education
- Social sciences, business, law and services
- Engineering, manufacturing and construction

	Health and welfare	Life sciences, physical sciences, agriculture, mathematics and computer science	Humanities, arts and education	Social sciences, business, law and services	Engineering, manufacturing and construction
OECD Countries mean (Female)	17.0	10.0	32.4	34.8	5.8
OECD Countries mean (Male)	8.5	16.4	16.0	36.5	22.6
United States (Female)	12.8	9.3	33.2	42.4	2.4
United States (Male)	5.3	14.9	20.0	48.3	11.5
United Kingdom (Female)	16.7	15.4	34.0	30.3	3.6
United Kingdom (Male)	7.2	23.7	20.2	31.0	18
Sweden (Female)	30.6	8.5	29.3	21.6	10.1
Sweden (Male)	10.9	13.1	13.8	22.8	39.4
Korea (Female)	8.9	12.7	40.6	23.0	14.9
Korea (Male)	5.6	14.5	14.5	27.2	38.2
Japan (Female)	8.1	8.3	43.6	34.0	6
Japan (Male)	4.4	8.0	13.1	43.0	31.5
Italy1 (Female)	14.8	8.7	29.5	39.8	7.3
Italy1 (Male)	11.2	10.9	8.6	43.5	25.8
Germany (Female)	19.3	11.8	33.0	27.9	8
Germany (Male)	11.6	8.4	13.5	30.3	26.1
France1 (Female)	2.9	12.8	34.5	44.3	5.6
France1 (Male)	2.4	21.4	16.2	38.6	21.5
Australia (Female)	19.4	10.3	28.8	38.3	3.2
Australia (Male)	7.5	20.7	15.0	43.3	13.4

Source: OECD 2004a 1. Year of reference 2001.

Figure 3.4:   Percentage of tertiary qualifications by field of study and by gender (2002)

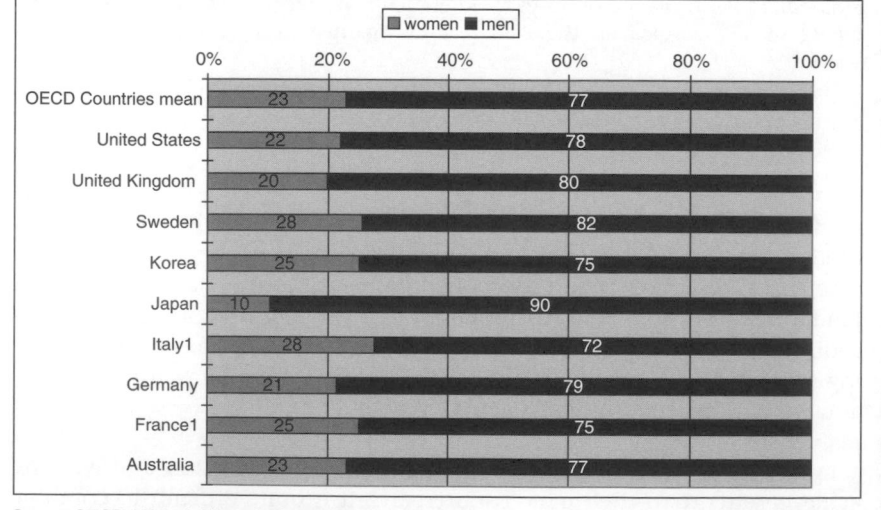

Source: OECD 2004a 1. Year of reference 2001.

Figure 3.5:   Percentage of tertiary qualifications in the field of engineering, manufacturing and construction by gender (2002)

work and family. Among women who had been employed one-year before they gave birth to their first baby, around 70 per cent lost jobs within six months of the baby's birth (Danjo Kyodo Sankaku Kaigi Eikyo Chosa Senmon Chosakai 2004: chart 27). Table 3.1, that presents respective indicators and a composite index for measures of work/family reconciliation policies and relevant flexible work arrangements, shows that Japan's rating is minus 2.9, which is the second lowest value following Greece among OECD member countries.

Finally, regarding old age pension schemes, Figure 3.6 compares the five countries and tries to identify similarities between Japan and each other country as well as the characteristics of the Japanese scheme. Particularly relevant aspects from a gender-equality perspective are income replacement rates for different types of households, pension splitting between spouses, and concrete design of Survivor's Pension (Table 3.A1 in the appendix). First, replacement rates as of July 2002 were estimated by the Pension Bureau at Japan's Ministry of Health, Labour and Welfare, as the ratio of theoretically standard monthly amount of old age benefit for households of pensioner(s) who has been insured for 40 years (the longest possible period to be insured) to average monthly regular pay for full-time male or female employees respectively. The differential in benefit levels between male breadwinner and other types of households is the greatest in the US, followed by Japan and the UK. Under the German system the pension benefits ratio is a flat 43 per cent for all households. Incidentally, in Sweden, which is said to have a high level of social welfare, the ratio is a fixed 38 per cent.

The German as well as the Swedish scheme is simply income-related without internal redistribution, and can be characterized as industrial 'achievement/performance' type in a similar sense as used by Titmuss (1974: 30–1). In contrast, there are income redistribution aspects favourable for male breadwinner households in both the US and the Japanese systems. By such redistribution, the benefit levels differ depending on the retiree's former wage-level from the viewpoint of the individual (with proportionally higher benefits given to those who earned lower wages). From the viewpoint of couples, the benefit levels vary depending on the extent of the spouse's participation in the workforce (with proportionally higher benefits given to families with spouses with lower participation). From the viewpoint of households, smaller benefits are given to single-member households. In the Japanese pension scheme the income redistribution is achieved via the basic pension benefits provided under the two-tier structure. As a result, the system provides male breadwinner households with a higher level of pension benefits than all other types of households.

Secondly, the splitting of pensions for divorced spouses was first introduced in Germany when the *Bürgerliches Gesetzbuch* (civil code) was revised in 1976 with a switch from fault to no-fault divorce (Hirowatari 1990:

Table 3.1: Summary indicators of work/family reconciliation policies and relevant flexible work arrangements

All indicators scaled so as to have mean zero and standard deviation unity, across the countries included (a)

Country	Child-care coverage for under-3s	Child-care coverage for over-3s	Maternity pay entitlement (b)	Total maternity/child-care leave	Voluntary family leave in firms (c)	Flexitime working	Voluntary part-time working	Composite index (d)	Employment rate for women aged 30-34
	(1)	(2)	(3)	(4)	(5)	(6)	(7)	(8)	(9)
Sweden	1.3	0.4	2.3	0.0	-1.9	0.6	0.2	3.3	76.7
Denmark	2.1	1.0	1.3	-0.1	-0.4	-0.3	-0.1	2.9	78.8
Netherlands	-1.0	1.3	0.0	-0.4	0.3	1.0	2.5	2.7	71.5
Australia	-0.5	-0.7	-1.4	-0.7	-0.1	2.6	1.3	1.9	64.2
United Kingdom	0.5	-0.7	-0.7	-0.9	-0.2	0.5	1.1	1.3	69.4
Germany	-0.8	0.3	-0.1	1.6	1.5	0.7	0.8	1.3	68.6
United States	1.6	-0.1	-1.4	-1.6	-0.8	2.0	1.2	1.2	72.0
Canada	1.1	-1.2	-0.7	-0.8	..	-0.5	-0.5	0.2	71.8
Belgium	0.3	1.3	-0.4	-0.4	0.4	-0.1	0.2	0.2	70.8
France	0.3	1.4	0.0	-0.4	0.2	-0.2	0.2	-0.1	65.6
Finland	-0.1	-0.3	1.9	1.6	-0.6	-0.2	-0.3	-0.3	70.7
Austria	-1.1	-0.2	0.0	0.5	1.5	-0.6	-1.2	-0.6	72.6
Ireland	0.7	-0.9	-0.5	-0.9	-0.5	-0.9	0.3	-1.1	69.1
Italy	-1.0	1.2	0.2	-0.5	1.2	-0.9	-0.7	-1.9	52.6
Portugal	-0.7	0.1	0.8	0.9	-0.1	-0.9	-1.3	-2.2	75.7
Spain	-1.0	0.6	0.0	0.9	0.6	-0.8	-1.0	-2.5	49.3
Japan	-0.6	0.0	0.0	1.6	-2.1	-0.9	0.3	-2.9	52.6
Greece	-1.1	-2.1	-0.7	-0.6	1.1	-0.5	-1.6	-3.4	57.1
Correlation with the employment rate for women aged 30-34	0.59	0.20	0.36	-0.04	-0.18	0.26	0.25	0.68	

.. Data not available.

(a) This is designed to put the indicators onto a common scale. A value of zero implies that the country concerned is at the average value for the countries in the table.

(b) Calculated as the product of the duration of maternity leave and the earnings replacement rate.

(c) Average of data for the sick child leave, maternity leave and parental leave.

(d) Calculated as the sum of the indicators in columns (1), (3), (6) and (7), plus half of that in column (5).

Source: OECD 2001a: Table 4.9.

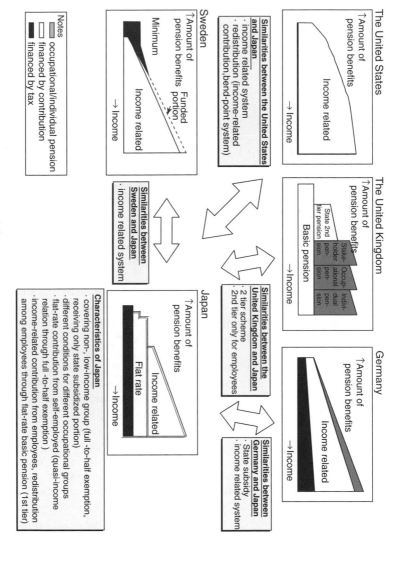

Figure 3.6: Old age pension schemes in different countries

297–9). The German system splits not only state but also occupational and individual pensions, and in 2001 it was further revised so that couples who are married for at least 25 years are free to split pensions by mutual consent (Shakai Hoken Kenkyûjo 2002: doc. V-5-7). Division of pensions at the time of divorce was introduced in the UK in 1999, and finally into Japan with the pension revisions of 2004. Under the US system, pensions are not split upon divorce, but when couples are divorced after being married for at least 10 years, the non-working ex-spouse receives 'spouse's benefits' (one half of the working ex-spouse's benefits) based on the former spouse's contributions.

Third, it is obvious that Japan has the most gender-biased Survivor's Pension scheme which is extremely generous for widows in terms of entitlement and the level and the continuity of the benefit, in which even a very young childless widow can receive life-time benefit based on her deceased husband's nominal 300 months or longer contribution, if her income was less than 8 million yen for the year that the husband died.

To summarize, the Japanese and US public pension systems exhibit the strongest male breadwinner orientation. Having wives as dependants on their husbands is rewarded by basic pension benefits for Class 3 (dependent spouses of employees) in Japan and by spouse's benefits in the US. On the other hand, the US pension system provides no rewards for childrearing, and in Japan high labour market participation by wives decreases the level of household benefits received. The German pension system is the most consistent in expressing that husbands and wives work in tandem as a couple through its provisions for splitting pensions between married couples, and provides the most benefits for childrearing. In that sense the German system best recognizes the value of women's work as mothers.

A reform friendly to working women? Concluding remarks

The coalition cabinet of Prime Minisiter Koizumi Jun'ichiro took office in April 2001, calling for an overall structural reform of Japanese society. Thus, on 26 June 2001, soon after taking office, the Koizumi Cabinet launched the so-called 'Honebuto no Hoshin' (Robust Policy) that laid down the fundamentals for a structural overhaul of Japanese society. Let us turn to examine whether the 'Robust Policy' is really moving towards the 'work/life balance' model. While the Koizumi administration has ensured that the ideal of gender equality – realizing a society where men and women can both fully participate – is reflected in the Cabinet's basic policies, there is a disparity between the administration's façade and the actual content of its reform policies. The administration has yet to seize the rudder and redirect the ship of state towards a different type of livelihood security system.

The 'Seikatsu Ishin' (lifestyle revolution) programme presented at the beginning of the Robust Policy 2001 advocates: (a) building up 'a society that is friendly to women who work outside the home', through tax and social security system reforms which shift to the individual as the unit of coverage and by 'eliminating sexual discrimination' in employment; and (b) eliminating waiting queues of children to enter day-care facilities, and preparing systems to care for children in after-school hours. Yet the specific content of the tax and social security system reforms remained unclear.

In June 2002, the basic tax reform policy of the Tax Council and the item of tax reform in the second 'Robust Policy' of the Cabinet called for a review of the treatment of spouses as dependants for income tax purposes (Cabinet decision of 25 June 2002). This review was advocated from the viewpoint of building up a gender-equal society and creating a 'neutral' tax system that does not distort tax burdens or labour market choices. And the Special Spouse Deduction was abolished as of January 2004. This second round of the 'Robust Policy' also called for pension system reforms that are consistent with the ideal of a gender-equal society. So, at any rate, the fundamental ideology of the Basic Law for a Gender-Equal Society came to be reflected in the basic Cabinet-level policies of the Koizumi administration.

Have the actual pension reform efforts upheld this ideal? The 2004 Pension Reform Law provided that: (a) The expansion of the Employees' Pension Insurance to cover part-time workers was postponed for five years as a concession to the restaurant and chain-store industries, which employ large numbers of part-time workers and voiced vehement opposition. (b) The pension splitting upon divorce was finally introduced, but without consistency as a system of pension splitting between spouses.[10] (c) The payment of Survivors' Pensions to widows was limited somewhat, but the overt gender-bias in the Survivors' Pension scheme was not rectified.[11]

So the bill made no provision for pension splitting between spouses as long as they remain married. Members of the Liberal Democratic Party's Research Commission on the Pension System, which studied this issue, reportedly emphasized 'the traditional view of the family' whereby 'married couples should be the basic unit for pensions' (*Asahi Shimbun*, 22 January 2004). While both the 'Opinion' of the Pension Subcommittee of the Council of Social Security and the proposals of the Ministry of Health, Labour and Welfare advocated a shift to the individual as the pension unit, that is to say, leaving behind the male breadwinner approach, it seems that the traditionalists' efforts to stop this advance held sway. On the whole, the government's 2004 pension reform bill maintained the male breadwinner orientation of the pension structure, and limited the individualization of the pension scheme to the absolute minimum revisions. Hence the reforms put off any break away from the male breadwinner system once again.

In July 2006, the National Police Agency reported that the suicide figures for 2004 had exceeded 30000 for eight consecutive years. Over 70 per cent of the cases were men, with an estimated 10000 cases involving men in their forties and fifties. Considering that the death toll from traffic accidents during the same year was below 9000 incidents, the suicide rate of middle-aged and older men who are 'sole breadwinners of household' is indeed alarming.

Comparatively, Japan's suicide rate in the year 2000 was the tenth highest among 99 countries for which statistics were available to the WHO in June 2004. The rate of Japanese women was the third highest among 99 countries in WHO data, following Sri Lanka and China (in selected rural and urban areas). The rate of suicide of Japanese men, on the other hand, was the eleventh highest among 99 countries, following former Soviet Union and Eastern European countries and Sri Lanka. Among these top eleven countries, the age 45–64 group has the highest rate in seven countries including Japan (Lithuania, Russia, Belarus, Ukraine, Kazakhstan, Latvia and Japan) (http://www.who.int/mental_health/prevention/suicide/suicideprevent/en/).

The curve of the suicide figures is known to run surprisingly in parallel with that of the unemployment rate in Japan. And yet, the female rate of suicide has stayed relatively unchanged for the last two decades despite increasing unemployment. Serious recession and uncertain employment prospects, which are plausible causes of the rising suicide rate, seem to hit the middle-aged and older males the hardest. In fact, the burden of the male provider has not eased much despite an increasing number of double-income households. This is because many wives have no other opportunities than part-time jobs with low wages, and even curb their annual income in order to remain eligible for tax/social insurance premium exemption. Equal treatment for atypical workers is quite difficult to attain in the Japanese version of the male breadwinner model, since the sector of low wage female atypical workers is the very cornerstone of the regime. Meanwhile the rate of real wage increase for men based on seniority has receded over time, as Figure 3.1 above indicates. Middle-aged men of today are faced with a difficult economic situation as compared with the elder generation who could enjoy steep wage increases based on seniority.

Thus, the Japanese version of the male breadwinner model is, like the continental European welfare states, 'coming into conflict with the emerging needs of a postindustrial economy' such as greater labour market flexibility and women's demand for and need of economic independence (Esping-Andersen 1996: 68). Unlike continental Europe, however, Japanese middle-aged and older men have not experienced so much labour reduction or employment deterioration as in the cases of women and younger workers. The Japanese version has a stronger male breadwinner orientation than European counterparts, and finds itself locked into a sharper negative spiral of women's ever-depressed earning power and men's growing inability to financially maintain the family, which is literally taking a death toll of 10 000 suicides from middle-aged and older men annually.

Notes

1. Pempel also characterizes Japan in the mid-1960s as 'politically conservative' but 'socially egalitarian', resembling social democratic Sweden, by virtually ignoring gender discrimination (Pempel 1998: 9, 10). Esping-Andersen himself points out that Japan's parallel to Sweden is 'superficial', because the Japanese full-employment model is very different from the Swedish model. The Japanese model is dualistic, composed of secure '"insider" male workforce' and precarious '"outsiders" (and especially among women)' (Esping-Andersen 1997a: 189).
2. The economic recession in 1974 was the sharpest one in postwar Japan except for the present one, and companies tried rigorously to reduce personnel and ratio-nalize their management. These measures were carried out in ways that were not gender-neutral. From 1974 to 1975, the female labour force decreased by 600 000, while the male labour force actually increased by 570 000. In the same two years, the average participation rate of women dropped by 2.5 per cent to 45.7 per cent, which is the lowest point in history, while that of men only slightly declined by 0.7 per cent to 81.4 per cent.
3. A measure or score of female work desirability is a composite of gender gaps of employment opportunities and wages, and female-to-male ratios of administra-tive and managerial workers as well as university and college students (Siaroff 1994: 89–90).
4. Uzuhashi (1997: 44–50) shows that the proportions of household income from wages and salary in 1983–4 were:

The proportion of household income from wages and salary

Country	wages and salary in total		of household heads	of wives of heads %
Japan	94.9		83	7.9
Korea	85.9			
Germany	Blue-collar	81.2	63	11.9
	White-collar	83.1	71	8.8
US	77.5			
UK	90.8			14.4
Israel	79.6		63	
Taiwan	85.1			
New Zealand	86.7			

5. The 1994 Pension Reform mentioned below paved a third path for working women by combining the Employees' Pension benefits for the wife and husband, and making the wives eligible to receive one half of it.
6. The labour force participation rate and poverty rate of lone mothers in Japan is quite high relative to other countries. See Kilkey 2000; Ezawa and Fujiwara 2003.
7. Miura proposes six indices that measure the degree and scope of social protec-tion for workers against volatile market forces: (1) protection of permanent

workers against dismissal, (2) regulation on atypical workers, (3) safety net towards the unemployed, (4) active labour market policies, (5) minimum wages, and (6) coverage of collective bargaining, while identifying the following six criteria to indicate employment performance: (1) unemployment rates (both standardized and long-term), (2) youth unemployment rates, (3) male employment rates (age 55–59), (4) female employment rates (age 25–54), (5) earnings dispersions among male workers, and (6) ratio of part-timers as a percentage of total employment (Miura 2001).

8. From the end of 1996 to early 1997, then Prime Minister Hashimoto Ryutaro launched the 'Six Major Reforms' (of the administrative, financial and educational systems, and of economic, fiscal and social security structures). Among them, only administrative reform (reorganizing of ministries and agencies and decentralizing power) and economic structural reform (de-regulation of employment/labour) had borne some fruit by 2000.

9. 'Welfare and others' spending in these statistics includes cash benefits to the unemployed and industrially injured. Based on the same statistics, Peng points out that, first, social security expenditure as a percentage of GDP 'nearly doubled' in the 1990s, while it actually grew from 10.8 per cent to 15.2 per cent, and second, that expansion of social care spending also 'doubled' in the decade. Comparing only figures for 1990 and 2000 as she does is misleading, since, for example, social security expenditure as a percentage of GDP grew over 5 points in the 1970s and 1.5 points in the 1980s (National Institute of Population and Social Security Research 1998).

10. The bill stipulates that the separation of pensions upon divorce under the Employees' Pension Insurance will become a mandatory equal division (giving the spouse 50 per cent) for all periods after April 2008 when the spouse was not working (i.e. when the spouse was a Class 3 insured). For periods when both spouses were working, the legislation stipulates that the divorced couple may, by mutual agreement, combine their respective pension contributions together and then divide the total between them (giving the spouse up to 50 per cent of the contribution record). When the couple cannot agree on the terms of this division, the percentage awarded to the spouse will be determined by court order.

11. The bill limits the Survivors' Pension payment period for childless wives who are under 30 when their husbands die to five years, and it raises the age that a middle-aged or elderly widow must be at the time of her husband's death to receive the additional pension benefit from 35 to 40 years old.

4
Varieties of Gender Regimes and Regulating Gender Equality at Work in the Global Context

Ilse Lenz

Globalization has been associated with economic neo-liberalism and de-regulation. In the field of gender, however, new 'soft forms of regulation' towards gender equality have emerged in the context of globalization (cf. Lenz 2003a).[1] The most important are the UN norms established during the UN decade of women and the EU Directives on gender equality at work as well as the gender equality goal in the Amsterdam Treaty of 1997 (see below). Present research has concentrated on the roles of supra-national organizations, especially the EU, and of transnational advocacy networks (Keck and Sikkink 1998; Walby 1999a, 2002b; Woodward 2004; Zippel 2004). The responses of governments and the effective results, however, have varied widely.

In this chapter a broad framework is proposed for analysing these soft forms of regulation and their national differences. It relies on the theoretical comparative framework developed in discussions with the 'Globalization, Gender and Work Transformation' (GLOW) Research Group. Three basic dimensions are compared: (1) the gendered welfare regimes, (2) the varieties of capitalism and (3) the gender regime comprising the form of state feminism (gender policy institutions in government) as well as women's movements and their mobilization (cf. Osawa and Walby in this volume). In this chapter these dimensions are discussed not as separate isolated factors, but rather with the aim of looking at their interlinkages and interdependencies. Also it should be pointed out that these dimensions are often seen as static structures without looking at their dynamics of change. The gendered welfare state, for example, is considered as a stable gendered *structure*, which evolved in national modernization. But the issue of regulation following the impulse of the international women's movement and gender politics demands a *dynamic perspective on processes*. The dynamism of regulatory development is understood in terms of social action: actors negotiate for regulations and thus the role of the main *actors* and *institutions* in negotiating these regulations has to be conceptualized. Which actors – for example, states and their women's political machineries or women's movements or

109

large interest groups – can be perceived around different phases of negotiation? How can and do they enter in the *basic aspects of policy development*, that is to say problem definition, agenda setting, policy formulation, implementation and evaluation?[2] For example, how do women's movements or the state or the UN establish that gender inequality is 'a real problem' and in which circumstances and how far are they able to set the agenda for developing more equal norms and rules? I will consider the main actor constellations at these *aspects of policy development of regulations* and the results in comparing mainly the British, the German and the Japanese welfare states (which form the basic comparative sample of this book).

This chapter will involve some travelling in time and space. First I will discuss a processual understanding of globalization beyond its widespread equation with neo-liberalism and try to shed some light on the options for regulations towards gender justice. Then I will discuss the institutional contexts of regulation in the dimensions of national welfare states and varieties of capitalism. In the next step, I will sketch the institutional contexts of the gender regimes in a comparative way. Short comparative case studies of international impulses on the regulation of work in Germany, Japan, the UK and the US will illustrate the varieties of regulations and focus on possible reasons for these differences. The main argument is the need for integrating the three dimensions of the gendered welfare regimes, the varieties of capitalism and the gender regime in a more sophisticated, but manageable framework for negotiations over regulations on equality at work.

Globalization and new global actors

Analysing the global impulses of these processes of regulation calls for a broad understanding of globalization. In a different context I introduced a concept of globalization[3] which overcomes a narrow economic focus, including the processes of political, cultural and communicative globalization (Lenz 2003a). Whereas economic and political hierarchies are powerful, globalization also leads to increasing international interdependence in view of the political supranational organizations (especially the UN and the EU) and to the reconfiguration of time and space by new technologies and forms of ICT communication. New forms of communication supported the global emergence of understandings of women's and human rights and a global civil society (Lenz 2003a).

The increasing influence of new actors beyond the nation-state, especially supra-national organizations, transnational enterprises and NGOs, is crucial for the issue of regulation. These new actors can expand and promote the range of options according to their material, organizational and power resources as well as their capacity and potential for adopting an orientation towards, reflexivity in and learning from the new complex global games.

Global orientation, communication and networking capacities become crucial capacities for organizing in global arenas. Globalization processes do not simply reinforce and carry on existing power relationships in deterministic ways. Even from asymmetric positions, actors can develop capacities for international orientation, communication and organizing. International orientation in this sense means knowledge of global economic, political and cultural structures and institutions, and of the value of engaging in transnational communication. As the global feminist networks and women's movements have shown, negotiating in asymmetric power relationships can bring incremental results (Keck and Sikkink 1998; Lenz 2001a).

Altvater and Mahnkopf (2000) have proposed the 'magic triangle' of supranational organizations/nation-states, transnational corporations and civil society as a framework for global regulation processes (cf. Figure 4.1). In their operations, they are oriented towards a specific medium of communication which Altvater and Mahnkopf call 'code'. Supra-national organizations/nation-states follow the code of power and decision-making, transnational corporations follow the code of the market and civil society follows the code of negotiation and communication. This magic triangle is useful for visualizing the changing institutional context of regulation for social movements, especially the women's movement, and for the interrelationship of the actors at the diverse corners of the triangle.

Supra-national organizations such as the UN and the EU as well as nation-states are relevant for making legitimate political decisions. Transnational corporations can deploy and use their increased options in relation to states (and supra-national organizations which are integrating them into 'private–public partnerships'). Civil society actors, NGOs as well as trade unions, are negotiating with supra-national organizations such as the UN and the EU as well as the nation-states along the global multilevel system. For example, norms like gender mainstreaming which were adopted at the global UN level become relevant for agenda setting and policy formulation at the national or local level (Lenz 2003a).

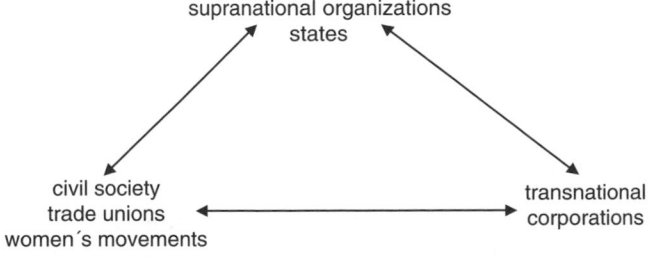

Figure 4.1:   The institutional context of regulation for the women's movement

The global women's movements and the UN decades for women: searching for egalitarian regulations and global gender democracy

The modern women's movement has continuously developed international exchange and international organizations. During the UN decades of women from 1975 to the present global feminist networks emerged in unprecedented scope (Meyer and Prügl 1999; Wichterich 1996, 2001). By discussing the issues, which they brought from local or national contexts or from global developments and by learning through 'conflicts in sisterhood', they could initiate political problem definition with a multifocal set of issues and play a proactive role in global agenda setting. For this they had to find convergent concepts in which their differences could be respected. For example, women's movements from different socio-cultural backgrounds came to share concepts like equality in work or struggling against violence against women or women's empowerment on a global level; but they associate them with different meanings and develop different strategies for realizing these concepts in their local contexts (Meyer and Prügl 1999; UN 1995). The 'women's/human rights approach' proved very productive in bridging differences and developing convergent strategies of women's movements in the South, East and West. Also, this approach could be translated into the global discourses on human rights and social issues.

Thus global feminist and transnational networks and women's movements could influence the UN processes around the decades of women and the UN social conferences – from the Rio conference on ecology in 1992 to the world social summit in 1996 – as well as put pressure on national governments. They realized significant discursive and institutional achievements: they had created global and transnational discourses which respected difference and created global concepts for converging strategies to promote equality and social peace. They had developed capacities for global orientation and could communicate around the world over the Internet.

The UN process of the women's decades for equality, development and peace can be seen as one pioneering experiment in developing flexible modes of regulation which do not follow one central set but are sensitive to different cultural contexts. The UN decades of women and its world conferences, especially the Fourth World Conference on Women (held in Beijing in 1995) provided arenas and a framework for debating and establishing universal norms on gender equality (UN 1995). The UN is the central legitimate institution for establishing universal norms as it constitutes the international community of nations. Gender perspectives were also integrated into the social UN conferences of the 1990s. The UN decades provided a rapidly expanding international opportunity structure for women's movements all over the world (Ajia josei shiryô sentâ 1997; Kramerae and Spender 2000; UN 1995; Wichterich 1996). Three results of the UN decades of women should be highlighted in this context: They provided spaces for communication and agenda setting by femocrats and by global and transnational women's networks. They established universal norms for gender equality especially at the UN World Conferences on Women. They provided for and stimulated the establishment of gender policy institutions in the national states, so-called women's political machineries (WPM) (Stetson and Mazur 1995a).

Three documents are especially relevant for the issue of gender and work:

(1) The Convention for the Elimination of all Forms of Discrimination against Women was adopted by the United Nations General Assembly 1979 (CEDAW 1979). It aimed to overcome the first fragmentary UN approaches after 1945 against 'sex discrimination' by providing an integrated framework to abolish all forms of discrimination. It has legal status in terms of international law for the states which ratified it, including a broad majority of UN member states (but not the US). In Article 2 of CEDAW, states pledged to prohibit all discrimination against women and to take all appropriate measures to eliminate discrimination against women by any person, organization or enterprise. Article 11 contains a specific commitment for eliminating all forms of discrimination in employment, including the right to work and equality in recruitment, training, promotion, wage and benefits (CEDAW 1979).

(2) The UN Women Conference in Mexico 1975 and the UN world action plan of 1980 had committed governments to establishing women's departments or focal points in the central government. Women's political machineries – women's offices or ministries, EO departments etc. – were enlarged or established in the subsequent national negotiations on UN gender norms and their tasks included implementing these norms (Unifem 2000: 37–61). From the first stage of the decade of women (1975–85) these norms and institutions contributed to an expansion of the political opportunity structure as femocrats were established in state and supranational bodies as potential allies.

(3) The UN Fourth World Conference on Women in Beijing 1995 came up with a Declaration and Platform for Action (UN 1995) which established basic norms and steps for gender equality in a process of international negotiation between governments and feminists from very different regions and approaches. The central principle of gender mainstreaming is fundamental for changing organizations and enterprises; it has been incorporated in the EU Treaty of Amsterdam (1997) and in gender policies of national states. The Platform for Action 1995 had the broader goals of empowerment and autonomy including the body and sexuality, equality in work and society, development and structural change, peace and non-violence in public as well as personal relationships and political participation. It can be seen as a charter for global gender

democracy. Feminist networking thus put on the agenda the issue of developing concepts of inclusive global gender democracy which respect gender and international justice, the differences between women and women's movements and which link up to a non-violent and sustainable development based on the empowerment of women and marginalized people. The Beijing Platform for Action also proposes goals, strategies and measures for gender equality in twelve fields of action and gives detailed time frames with specific targets for supra-national organizations, national governments and organizations from the economy and civil society.[4]

The momentum and political innovation of the UN decades have receded since the Beijing Conference 1995. The follow-up process of the 2000 conference in New York, with the next evaluation stage taking place in 2005, is characterized by inward concentration on the bureaucratic and femocrat institutions of the UN and member states, and by a decline of feminist mobilization and the intervention of strong counter-movements. The shift in international politics has changed the opportunity structure for women's movements: the transitional search for a multilateral peaceful new world order centring on the UN processes after the fall of 'real socialism' has shifted to a military safeguarded order. After the terrorist attacks of 11 September 2001 on the US by fundamentalist Islamic male networks, the US as the one remaining superpower tends to emphasize unilateral strategies and military strength in its war on terrorism and to disregard the UN as the core global legitimate institution of peace negotiation as well as to eschew international law.[5] Negotiations for gender equity regulations have relied strongly on the peaceful social UN processes of the 1990s. A reconstitution of the legitimate UN-centred resolution of conflicts and global inequality cannot be realized without a democratic reform of the UN re-establishing its global legitimation. Both democratic UN reform and more effective conflict resolution are crucial issues of global feminist politics.

Fundamentalist male-centred movements as well as armed conflicts have contributed to the renaissance of the ideals of the male warrior or 'tough single global leader' and armed violence. The militarization and trend to hegemonic aggressive masculinity in international conflicts (even if it is shared out to female soldiers) are structural barriers for global gender justice.

Civil counter-movements also mobilize aggressively against the global gender norms for equality which were decided at the UN Beijing conference. For example, fundamentalist and anti-abortionist Catholic and Islamic male-centred groups mobilize against reproductive freedom. The Vatican has even attacked the concept of *gender as a cultural category* which is basic to the Beijing Platform for Action, claiming it may promote mistrust of the family, equal positions for homosexuality and polymorph sexuality (Congregation for the Doctrine of the Faith 2004).

Whereas institutional progress appears blocked, the global women's movements are experiencing some stagnation and internal problems. One main internal problem is strategy building in view of the increasing plurality of feminisms and loss of overarching forums. Other ones are internal democracy, independence and sustainability: the democratic mechanisms of representation, feedback and accountability to the 'women back home', their local and national constituency, tend to become attenuated while lobbying in global arenas. Global women's networks are hampered by the lack of autonomous resources and the networks still largely rely on external resources like development funds or state support or women's offices. Members of feminist networks have entered political governance structures and organizations, but have not gained a firm foothold or a clear power base (Lenz 2001a; Wichterich 2001). The NGO-ization of women's groups (Alvarez 1999) reflects professionalization or routinization of organizations, and tension between logics of collective action following organizational impulses towards bureaucratization and democratic impulses. These processes are apparent in other social movements such as trade unions.[6] Global feminists are worrying about the generation gap with younger women. Coalition building with other social movements such as the critical globalization groups has been complex, siphoning off resources and energies.

Regulation for gender equality in the EU

The EU, as a regional supra-national organization with certain legislative powers, provides a different case of regulation for gender equality in an international multilevel system. One main motive of early regulations in the EU was a certain levelling of diverse national standards to avoid disadvantages for 'progressive nations'. Thus, mainly under pressure from the French government, Article 119 of the founding Treaty of Rome 1957 established equal wages for men and women. The resistance to a lowering of specifically high national standards (as in the Scandinavian countries) and fear of social 'equality dumping' later motivated some states to press strongly for gender equality regulation in the EU (Schmidt 2005; Walby 1999a, 2002b). In the 1970s further EU Directives established and strengthened the right to Equal Pay (1975) and Equal Treatment (1976); these Directives are legally binding when implemented by member states into national legislation and they are relevant for the European Court of Justice. Further Directives covered Social Security (1978 and 1986) and part-time work (Gottfried and O'Reilly 2002; Schmidt 2005; Walby 1999a).

From the middle of the 1970s, the EU broadened democratic participation by expanding the rights of the European Parliament and supported alliances with interest groups, social movements and NGOs. In this context, EU institutions (especially the Directorate General for Employment and Social

Affairs of the EU Commission) and femocrats also built up networks and alliances with academic gender experts and feminist groups. In parallel to the 'iron triangle' between bureaucracy, enterprises and trade unions, Alison Woodward analysed what she called the 'velvet triangle' looking at the opportunities as well as informal power relationships between these groups with the femocrats at the top (Woodward 2004). The EU quest for popular legitimacy and broad popular support gained momentum by the EU referenda in Nordic countries in which a gender gap emerged and women voted more critically. A number of non-binding recommendations on positive discrimination (1984), vocational training (1987) and sexual harassment (1991) reflected this strategy of creating broader popular support. Also the European Women's Lobby (EWL), the umbrella organization of the established national women's movements, is supported by the EU and accepted as the semi-official voice of women.

In a third phase after 1995, the EU deepened and strengthened gender equality regulation. For the first time gender equality and gender mainstreaming thinking was integrated in an EU Treaty, the Treaty of Amsterdam (1997). The 1976 Directive for Equal Treatment has been enlarged and concretized in 2002, now including equality in all matters of employment and prohibition of sexual harassment. The member states are requested to pass legislation for gender equality by 2005 or to 'ensure . . . that management and labour introduce the requisite provisions by way of agreement' (Directive 2002/73/EC, Article 2, 1).

During the third phase, the interplay on the global multilevel system provided an expanding opportunity structure and the interchange between EU institutions (mainly the Commission and Parliament), the EWL and women's movements and the gender experts was crucial for mobilizing inside and outside the institutions. While the gender equality circles in the EU discussed gender mainstreaming before the UN Beijing conference in 1995, they were central exponents (together with South Africa) for it at the conference. After Beijing they brought gender mainstreaming back to Europe. The principle of gender equality was integrated into the Amsterdam Treaty which is legally binding on member countries. Gender equality circles in the EU and some member states as well as outside lobbying by the EWL and experts supported this process (Schmidt 2005).

Whereas gender regulation around the UN decades of women focused on need definition and agenda setting for gender equality and on general policy formulation of 'soft rules', in the EU it gained some legal force. The EU provides strong mechanisms for implementation into national legislation and its European Court of Justice is actively proceeding with legal development by case law (Walby 1999a). But the forms of policy formation and implementation at the national level differ markedly as the short case studies below will show.

Global governance or regulation along the global multilevel system?

The approach of global governance located these processes in the negotiations of state, public and private actors (from enterprises as well as NGOs) over new global norms in a future global order. The concept was proposed by the important UN Commission on Global Governance which defined it as the ensemble of the various ways in which individuals as well as public and private institutions regulate their common affairs. It was seen as a continual process by which controversial or divergent interests can be balanced and cooperative action can be initiated (Messner and Nuscheler 1996).

This approach failed to distinguish between global governance as an analytical category which focuses on empirical processes in changing world power relationships and as a normative category which assumes an inherent positive effect for civil society or women. The question 'Is global governance really happening for women and what does this mean?' was not always separated from the statement 'Global governance is good for women'. The approach also ignored the differential power potentials of state, enterprise or civil society actors.

The approach relied on the multilateral negotiations around the UN for social rights which formed a particular trend of the 1990s in a specific historic constellation, but it projected them as the leading image of the future world order without analysing the basic power relations. Therefore it was unable to analytically come to grips with the crucial counter-developments mentioned above and has been largely consigned to oblivion in recent years.

The concept of *regulation*[7] seems more adequate to investigate the processes of norm setting for equality in a global context. Regulation is seen in the theory of action perspective. It means setting and institutionalizing norms and rules through negotiating processes in which various actors, states, organizations, networks or individuals may participate. These actors follow *perceived interests* as well as *shared interpretations of common goods and equity*. These interpretations, strategies and options of the actors are strongly influenced by the institutional contexts of the global multilevel system *and* of the national welfare states within which they negotiate global norms.

In regulation for gender equality, actors often work with global problem definitions, norms and policy approaches which are seen as legitimate for several reasons. Firstly, they provide creative or convincing knowledge and interpretations which have been proposed by global feminist expert networks (Zippel 2004). Secondly, they have been passed or propagated by prestigious global organizations like the UN or the EU. Thirdly, often national governments which are being lobbied by feminist networks have already acceded to these norms on the UN or global level and therefore can be addressed in terms of obligation and legitimacy of the demand. But the actors then *integrate* these problem definitions, norms and policy approaches with *national and local* approaches, strategies and needs. The dualistic stereo-types of 'Western feminism' versus 'other' values ignore the *cultural change and synthesis* on different levels which are after all fundamental for cultural innovation. The global norms for gender equality as in the Beijing Platform for Action have been developed by translating and bridging differences. At the national and local level, the integration and synthesis by gender equal-ity networks during the negotiation over regulation leads to new approaches and strategies which are culturally located and rooted by referring to local or national values and interpretations.[8]

Gendered welfare regimes, varieties of capitalism and new forms of gender regulation

The negotiation of global gender equality norms within national welfare states is a crucial but tricky issue as it is the touchstone for policy formation and implementation on the national level in the multilevel system. For analysing the institutional context in a comparative way, I want to use the framework of the research group on gender, globalization and work devel-oped in this volume which proposed three interrelated 'structures': (1) the gendered welfare regimes, (2) the varieties of capitalism and (3) the varieties of gender regime. The formation of these structures historically took place in the context of the respective nation-states and was basic for their national path development. In globalization, these structures and their inherent hierarchies are being eroded and reorganized. In these processes, spaces and arenas for renegotiation of the gender regimes can be opened up while the results are open and not fixed in a deterministic way.

The institutional context of regulation I: national welfare states and capitalism

These welfare states developed and were formed in the context of national varieties of capitalism as well as national modern gender regimes. Thus the formation of the basic institutions of these welfare states can be located in the context of social negotiations around the issues of capitalism and class as well as gender. Liberal reform movements and trade unions participated in these negotiations as well as various wings of the women's movements.

The liberal welfare state regimes in the comparative sample of the GLOW group (UK, US) are characterized by a liberal market economy (LME) coor-dination (Hall and Soskice 2001) and by low and thin regulation. The market is the culturally most significant form of coordination. The UK and the US have a high labour market integration of women. The state feminism varies between moderate (UK) and weak (US). In globalization, liberal welfare state initiatives are geared towards promoting global competitiveness and the shift from welfare to workfare. These policies entail the recommodification of labour power. As they include workfare measures for mothers they are influencing gender relations by subsuming unpaid care-work of mothers more directly to wage work and the labour market.

The coordinated market economies (CME) of Germany and Japan in the sample are highly regulated and institutionally thick, but in different ways. In globalization the coordination structures tend to shift towards increasing power for enterprises. Enterprises reorient their strategies on the global as well as on the national level, because their options are increasing by playing on both levels. They can use the market logic of globalization as well as the organization logic of the national coordination (Streeck 1999). Whereas they have engaged in the ICFTU and the ETUC (European Trade Union Federation), trade unions and social associations continue to concentrate on the national coordination framework as they have been constituted in this context. Their main cultural and social 'resources' such as language, communication and normative understanding are mostly nationally bound.

Looking at the dynamics of corporatist welfare states economies, it should be mentioned that basic institutions have developed in the tripartite negotiations between state, enterprises and trade unions. The Bismarck model of social security insurance is a prime example for this; but the expansion of higher education and state support for vocational training also developed by negotiation in this tripartite 'iron triangle' of state, enterprises and trade unions (Lehmbruch 2001; Streeck 1999). The negotiators in the iron triangle – including the trade unions – till recent times shared the classical breadwinner/housewife model. Therefore, it is not surprising that the corporatist institutions tended to exclude women, that regulations were centred on 'male breadwinners' and that skill formation was male-centred and gendersegregated (Gottschall 2000; Pfau-Effinger 2000).

Coming back to the institutional context of regulation for the women's movement as outlined in Figure 4.1, the hypothesis is, that *different actor constellations* can be observed in *welfare states with market coordinated or corporatist capitalism.* In liberal market coordination with low and thin regulation, the main actor constellation in the magic triangle comprises enterprises, the state, experts and civil society organizations (i.e. trade unions) (cf. Figure 4.2). In corporatist capitalism, the institutional context for regulation for gender equality is assumedly ambivalent: With the iron triangle, an institutionalized actor constellation for negotiation has evolved which has developed a framework of shared norms and beliefs (Lehmbruch 2001). As collective social rights and fairness form parts of this discursive framework, in principle the corporatist 'conflict partners' are supposedly approachable by arguments of (gender) equality (cf. Figure 4.3). But this actor constellation shares male-centred hegemonic belief systems of interests and social roles according to the breadwinner–housewife model and tends to exclude or subsume the voice and participation of women.

Nevertheless the differences between the type of corporatist welfare state regime in Germany and Japan are important; it is corporate in the German

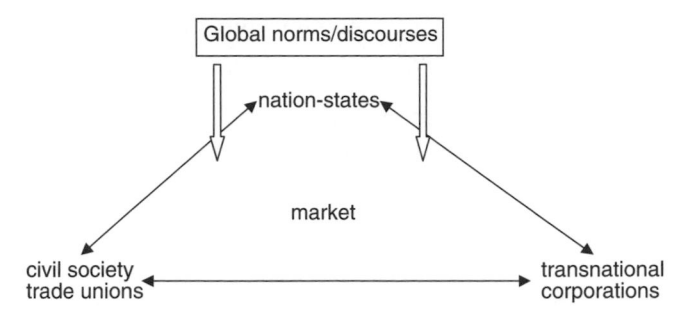

Figure 4.2:   Regulatory framework of market coordinated capitalism

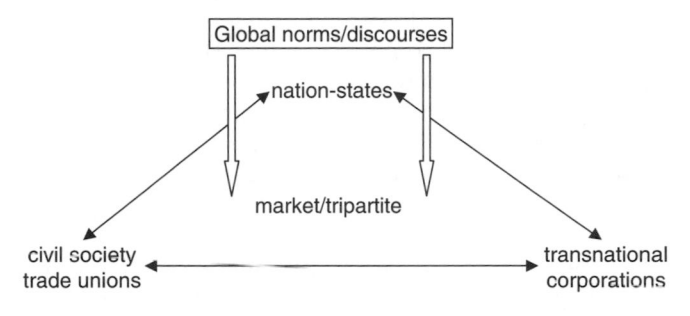

Figure 4.3:   Regulatory framework of the corporatist varieties of capitalism

case and hybrid in the Japanese case where state and enterprise are increasingly interrelated and complementary in the enterprise society after 1960 (Osawa 1994; Seifert 1997). The labour market integration of women relies heavily on part-time work. However, part-time work is a time-oriented contract form in Germany and women can go back to full-time in many cases whereas in Japan it tends to be an irreversible feminized labour status with little employment security. The state feminism also varies between moderate (Germany) and weak (Japan).

One major difference between these coordinated market economies is the structure of coordination: in Germany a *state-oriented corporatism* has integrated the negotiations between state, employers' associations and trade unions (Streeck 1999) whereas corporatism in Japan is *enterprise-oriented*.

At present German corporatism is coming under stress (Streeck 1999) from the liberal market turn of politics, from globalization and the EU internationalization and from the increasing service economy and the concurrent change in employees' consciousness, i.e. female employees in skilled and unskilled service and knowledge-intensive jobs. National corporatism is rather dwindling from a model of interest negotiation to a defensive strategy of trade unions in face of internationalization, whereas employers make use of global options.

In Japan's enterprise-centred society the enterprise and employers' associations form the focus of economic and political interest representation with the bureaucracy of the developmental state as its counterpart (Seifert 1997). The trade unions had a double orientation primarily focusing on the enterprise level but linking up in sectoral or national umbrella organizations. After 1970 they entered national politics mainly in the state-sponsored expert commissions (*shingikai*) in what can be called a latecomer weak version of corporatism, as Wolfgang Seifert has shown (cf. 1997). Thus, the *state-led corporatism*, the dominant form of coordination in the German postwar nation-state, is different from *enterprise-centred coordination* by economy and bureaucracy in the Japanese CME.

The basic argument runs that the welfare capitalism regime and institutional context related to the variety of capitalism constitutes a different institutional context and a different actor constellation in negotiating for regulation for gender equality. Other relevant factors to be considered are the institutional context of the welfare state regime and the gender regime.

The institutional context of regulation II: national welfare states and gender regimes

The development of the welfare state regimes was negotiated by women's movements among other social forces. They became influential in achieving education, the right to work and political participation for women. The modernization of gender regimes implied a shift to public participation of women especially in education and wage work. Sylvia Walby contrasts this public gender regime to the private domestic one (1990, 1997).

State feminism and women's mobilization are further important aspects of the gender regime of the welfare state (cf. Walby in this volume). Whereas comparative research on women's mobilization is only just starting, comprehensive comparative research on state feminism has been provided by the Research Network on Gender, Politics and the State (RNGS-group). Therefore I want to concentrate on state feminism in this context without wishing to disclaim the importance of women's mobilization. The RNGS-group has shown that women's institutional apparatus in the state (so-called women's political machinery, WPM) have taken up and supported feminist interests in many Western countries. The WPM form a central institutional context for regulating for gender equality in national welfare states. They mostly were set up under the double influence of global norms in the UN decade and the world action plan which made political departments for women's interests in government obligatory, and national women's movements. Thus their existence is linked to both global impact and national political change. The RNGS-group investigated the representation of women in positions of political decision-making (descriptive representation) and the incorporation of 'women friendly issues' into the policy process (substantive representation) (cf. Mazur 2002: 38). They could demonstrate that WPM contributed significantly to the success of feminist policies in both integrating women in political positions and getting feminist policies adopted (Stetson and Mazur 1995a).[9] Following their approach, the central actor constellation for gender equality regulation at the national level embraces nation-states, mainly their WPM, other interest groups and women's movements. The institutional context for regulation in the linkage of welfare state regime and gender regime can be sketched as in Figure 4.4.

The research of the RNGS-group shows that the profile and impact of the WPM do not *directly* correspond to market or corporatist coordination according to the varieties of capitalism.[10] But the historical and institutional context in which the WPM were developed reflects a certain path dependency of national development which is influenced by the varieties of capitalism. In the US the Women's Bureau was established in 1920 as a result of the first waves of the women's movement. Located in the Department of Labor, its chances depend on the 'skills and priorities of the director, the support of the secretary of labour and compatibility with the president's policy agenda' (Stetson 1995: 270). Major resources of the 'woodwork feminists' are access to and cooperation inside the bureaucracy on the one hand, and networks with feminist mobilizing circles, especially working women, as well as international expertise on the other hand (Stetson 1995). Put shortly, the Women's Bureau is negotiating within and with the bureaucracy and with women's movements/civil society.[11]

In the US, beside the Women's Bureau, two governmental agencies enforce compliance with equality laws: the Office of Federal Contract Compliance Programs (OFCCP) and the Equal Employment Opportunity Commission (EEOC). The less well-known Office of Federal Contract Compliance Programs (OFCCP) was established to monitor contractor compliance with presidential executive orders. It became more active after the 1970s when the women's movement agitated for redress of discrimination in the workplace

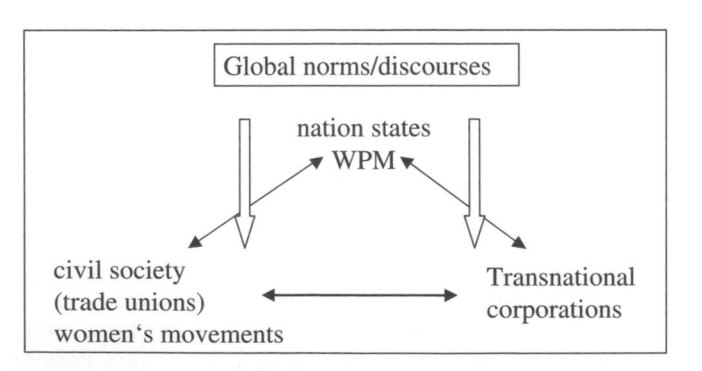

Figure 4.4:   Regulatory framework of the gender regime

and produced some positive changes such as an increase of women's representation as managers and officials (Gelb 2003a). The Equal Employment Opportunity Commission (EEOC) stands out as the agency most actively involved in enforcing equal employment opportunities and addressing sexual harassment in the workplace. The EEOC is empowered to investigate and adjudicate complaints; to grant complainants' right to seek legal remedies; to bring class action suits and to file amicus (friend of the court) briefs; and to conduct 'pattern or practice' investigations of industry or company-wide discrimination and to seek resolutions.[12]

In the UK, the Equal Opportunity Commission (EOC) was established as part of the same package of reform that included the 1970 Equal Pay Act and the 1974 Sex Discrimination Act.[13] The government reacted to pressure from women in trade unions and women parliamentarians in the 1970s, but also to influence from the EU (Lovenduski 1995: 117–18). The EOC is a semi-independent institution, but funded by the government and responsible to the Women's minister. At its start, it was limited by corporatist representation of employers and trade unions, which marginalized women's and feminist networks and by bureaucratic dominance (Lovenduski 1995). The EOC gained in strength and initiative in the context of the EU gender policy and with increasing cooperation of the women's movement with national state organizations (ibid.); now women's groups are clearly engaged with the EOC. In 1997, the ruling Labour government also established two ministers for women in the Department for Trade and Industry and the Women and Equality Unit. The WPM are anchored in the administration, but cooperate with gender experts and women's networks in issue-specific projects.

In Germany, WPM were integrated into corporatism in a specific form which may be called *differential integration*. Under the pressure of the new women's movement, state administrations from central government to regional or city administration created separate departments or desks of ombudswomen or female equal opportunity officers (Ferree 1995). Thus there was a double differentiation inside the organization on the levels of structural specialization and the highlighted *female gender* of its members: women's departments were staffed with women. The relative success in creating several thousand EO posts integrated into local administrations or in social organizations may have strengthened this orientation of the women's movements. The policies of separate women's officers and departments were also followed in major enterprises mostly as a scheme of personal development and flexibilization and by trade unions.

These groups of femocrats and organizational 'gender staff' in Germany have been called 'institutional feminism' (Lenz 2003b). While women's special departments were effective in agenda setting for equality and mobilizing, gender equality became connoted as a *special* women's issue relevant for women as *one special interest* group among many others (and was some-

times branded as irrelevant or even harmful for men). This policy of differential integration had the major advantage of making the organizational
resources (personnel and some time of the equal opportunity officers, spaces,
some money) available to activist coalitions between these departments and
the women's social movement networks. But it also implied that 'institutional feminism' has no autonomous 'voice' of its own; it has to coordinate
its voice with the interest representation of an organization's leadership or
even to remain moderate or silent.

The *differential integration* of gender issues is different from other issues
such as the environment. With respect to the latter issue, the formation of
parallel corporatism can be observed, whereby the state negotiated with management and environmental groups, which in the process tended to crys-
tallize into lobbying or interest groups. The exception to this rule is the
one existing umbrella organization of established women's organizations
(*Deutscher Frauenrat*). This umbrella organization might be seen as a case of
weak corporatism as it functions as interest representation of women in
Germany in relationship to the government and the European Women's
Lobby. It developed as a result of former waves of the women's movement
and brings together women's professional, trade union, social and volunteer
and church associations with an aggregate membership of 11 million
women. As an umbrella group with the obligation for building consensus
among diverse member organizations (e.g. church and trade union groups)
and little independent resources for organizing, it has not played a pioneering role in negotiations.

Women in Japan were excluded from the coordination mechanisms of
state and enterprises as well as from the latecomer corporatism until the mid-
1980s. They had a marginal role in government, the bureaucracy and party
politics and they had no voice in either the powerful employer's association
or the trade unions (Gottfried 2000; Lenz 1997). After 1990 women became
a more articulate political force. There were several women ministers in governments, some individual women gained leading roles in government and
opposition parties and the political culture opened somewhat to the ideas of
gender equality and feminism (Gelb 2003a; Osawa 2003). Furthermore, the
gender department in the Cabinet Office was strengthened and the accom-
panying Gender Commission (from 1994 in different forms; cf. Osawa 2003)
has been influential in problem definition and agenda setting. Again the
exception to the rule is the mini-corporatist arrangement between the state
and the umbrella organization of the established women's associations
which has lobbied the government since the 1950s and formed a League for
the International Women's Year in 1975 including some new feminist
associations to use the expanding global opportunity structures (Kokusai
fujinnen Nihon taikai no ketsugi o jitsugen suru tame no renrakukai 1989).
In the committee on the Labour Basic Law in the former Ministry of
Labour (now the Ministry of Health, Labour and Welfare) there was also

a certain representation of women after the 1980s as this law regulated the protective clauses for women (Gelb 2003a; Lam 1992).

Looking at the issue of global regulation for gender equality, the institutional contexts and the differential actor constellations have been discussed which can be derived from the varieties of capitalism and gender regimes framework.

The next section summarizes the negotiations around the fundamental UN resolutions and the EU legal norms (in the case of European countries) mentioned above in the welfare states in the sample of the GLOW group.[14] Several questions are examined, including: Which – changing – actor constellations along the triangle of state/WPM, social partners and women's movements/civil society can be observed? Which inputs of the actors can be ascertained around different aspects of policy development such as problem definition, agenda setting, policy formulation, implementation and evaluation? How far can path dependency be observed in the results according to the varieties of capitalism/gender regimes: do they remain in the framework of corporatism or market coordination or can new approaches be traced?

The benefits and limits of corporatism in Germany

The actor constellation in Germany is characterized by the classic corporatist coalition in a corporatist welfare state. State, employers and trade unions are leading actors in the iron triangle. But the actors in the velvet triangle of gender policy gained in force and participation over time. The WPM experienced differential integration into corporatism, whereas the autonomous women's movement developed outside and in opposition to this framework, forming one core of the social movements from the late 1960s (Lenz 2001b; Schulz 2002). After its consolidation from the end of the 1970s, churches, trade unions and political parties opened up to the women's movements and partially integrated it. Feminists in political parties, trade unions and other social organizations and established women's organizations formed the institutionalized wings, which gained considerable clout after 1980 (Lenz 2005). University-based women and gender studies developed from the movement in the 1970s taking up international and political impulses from global women's liberation. In contrast to Japan, the UK and the US there are no expert committees on gender equality with high public prestige or widely recognized policy planning units with academic gender expertise.

Whereas the theoretical horizon of the emerging gender experts and the movement was international (Dackweiler 2000; Schäfer 2001), political strategy was mainly oriented towards the national and local context until the mid-1990s. There was a marked differentiation between global-oriented networks in Germany which were working for global issues or the 'Third World', and the everyday work of equal opportunity on the ground which involved negotiations with national and local administrations or organizations.

As this chapter focuses on the negotiations around global norms relevant for the issue of work, it should be mentioned shortly that legislation on gender equality has been extensive and reflected many demands of the women's movements. To name but a few: childcare leave for men and women was introduced in 1986; in 1994 a constitutional amendment established the principle of gender equality as a state goal; registered partnership for homosexual couples was passed in 2001; laws were passed against sexual harassment in 1994, against rape in marriage in 1997 and against domestic violence and spouse abuse in 2001 (Lenz 2003b).

The UN decades and their basic legal norms and resolutions were mainly important for problem definition and agenda setting by the women's movements, whereas policy formulation and implementation were negotiated inside the corporatist welfare state until the increasing relevance of the EU at the end of the 1990s. The great contribution of the UN decades was in shaping global consciousness for gender inequality and for feminism in other regions. But CEDAW and even the Beijing Platform for Action 1995 hardly influenced policy formulation or implementation. Germany ratified CEDAW only in 1985 when its WPM was basically established and public discussion on its legal norms and the consequences for gender policy were negligible. Gender mainstreaming, one core norm of the Beijing Platform for Action, was introduced by way of the EU.

In contrast to the UN decades, the negotiation on the EU legal norms did lead to policy formulation and implementation at the national level in Germany. Of course, legal implementation of Directives is obligatory for EU member states, but we can see a change in the actor constellation as well as in the norms and provisions of the resulting German laws over time from the 1970s to the present. The social democratic/liberal government passed the first Law on Equal Treatment of Men and Women at Work[15] in 1980 as implementation of the EU Directives on Equal Pay (1975) and Equal Treatment (1976) after vehement discussion among employers and trade unions. The Law was incorporated into civil law (BGB § 611a, b; 612a) and contained minimal clauses which mirrored existing legal reality. In some aspects it did not even fulfil the requirements of the Directive: the EU Directive norms prohibiting indirect discrimination based on family status were not adequately incorporated (Pfarr and Bertelsmann 1989). Also effective sanctions against discrimination in recruitment were lacking as employers only had to recompense the postage and paperwork costs for discriminated candidates (the famous 'postage clause'). The European Court of Justice corrected German law clauses in a trial on treaty violation (21 May 1985), which contributed to a later revision of the law in 1994 (ibid.).

Employers and trade union participated in policy formulation in expert hearings and lobbying, whereas the women's movement and gender experts were largely excluded. Employers argued against passing the law as they considered its clauses as an excessive intervention into the freedom of contract and the constitution whereas trade unions and some feminist critics doubted its efficiency (Pfarr and Bertelsmann 1989). Basically the 1980 law with its minimal standards can be seen as a compromise in the corporatist setting favouring the employers' side. The women's movement was left out of the negotiation process, but also did not engage strongly at this time.

The second Equal Opportunity Law was passed in 1994 under the then conservative/liberal government and contained clauses on the prohibition of discrimination at work and more effective sanctions against discrimination in recruitment in reaction to the EU's critique and German public opinion. It also prohibited sexual harassment and it extended equal opportunities in vocational training and promotion to the federal administration. Now the institutionalized women's movement and gender experts participated in problem definition and agenda setting. They could gain influence in norms on sexual harassment and higher sanctions for employment discrimination. Gender experts had presented representative research on sexual harassment, which showed a startlingly high prevalence and their results served to legitimize legal prohibition (Müller et al. 1991).

While both groups lobbied for the inclusion of private enterprise into the Equal Opportunity Law, the conservative-liberal government and its Minister for Family and Women, Angela Merkel, declined this move. In view of the minimal provisions in the initial law, there is no effective equal opportunity legislation covering the private sector in Germany. The federal states passed equal opportunity laws with stronger impetus and scope than the federal legislation, but also these could not be extended to private enterprise.

Institutionalized women's movements mainly from the Social Democratic and Green Parties kept on lobbying for a more comprehensive Equal Opportunity Law covering private enterprise. Their problem definition and agenda setting was impressive and a group of legal experts proposed a bill for pubic discussion (Pfarr 2001). Further political impetus came from the new EU Directive 2002 on equal treatment revising the first version of 1976, which had been debated for some years. The Directive obliges EU member countries to pass adequate equal opportunity laws by October 2005 or 'to ensure . . . that management and labour introduce the requisite provisions by way of agreement' (Directive 2002/73/EC, Article 2, 1). By contrast to the 1970s, institutional feminists and gender experts mobilized broadly for an equal opportunity law using the EU Directive as a discursive resource.

But the Social Democratic–Green government in power since 1998 has avoided passing an Equal Opportunity Law valid for private enterprise and seems to rely on the second path of the Directive, namely the agreement of management and labour. Listening to employers' rejection of legal regulation, Chancellor Schröder proclaimed his reliance on the positive attitude of enterprise. He did not comply with his former promise of introducing more positive legal measures if enterprises would not 'deliver', although a survey in 2003 showed that only 8 per cent of enterprises introduced affirmative action policy. This can be seen as a continuation of neo-corporatism. A law is not favoured by the enterprise-side which Schröder had co-opted into his alliances for work or for the Hartz labour market reforms which were carried out after 2003. The Hartz labour market reforms were criticized as male-centred. For example they give social security only to the main breadwinner in the family (whose gender may be guessed) and disregard the need for childcare if mothers want to re-enter the labour market under the pressure of workfare.

But the decision against an Equal Opportunity Law valid for private enterprise also reflects the market and deregulation orientation of the 'third way' social democratic politics under Schröder as a reaction to globalization and thus a certain departure from corporatism. Laws and regulations in this philosophy are obstructive to the more effective market regulation and gender inequality is not given such pre-eminent importance that it merits a breach of this policy and a conflict with enterprise interests. On the institutional side, the Schröder government is subverting corporatism by installing 'councils' and 'commissions' for his market-oriented or neo-liberal reforms by co-option of persons, not mainly by representative organizations. These councils are mostly male; and they remind one of men's bonding so important to the analysis of Max Weber (*Männerbund*). They appear as networks of 'brothers' (with an occasional sister thrown in), not of fathers or patriarchs. They claim a market-oriented gender neutrality by prioritizing efficiency and innovation. The results, however, privilege the so-called male standard workers (Annacker 2005).

The institutional women's movements emphasized gender mainstreaming mainly in the context of the EU Treaty of Amsterdam 1997. At first, femocrats feared that they would lose their relative positions in the corporatist organizations and tended to resist gender mainstreaming. Women's issues, up to now in the hands of women specialists in an organizational department, could be transformed into gender equality issues of the whole organization. Then the gender mainstreaming clause on EU funds provided an incentive, as all EU funds for social programmes are supposed to be gender mainstreamed, and this gave a stronger voice to institutional feminists and equal opportunity officers at the local level where the application for and use of funds is concretized. Thus their bargaining position in the organization could be enhanced in some cases. The 'gender element' of gender mainstreaming appealed to many younger feminists who related it to concepts of gender democracy.

Gender mainstreaming after 1999 was promoted in government, management and universities. In the process, it tended to change into a concept for organizational and personnel development and thus into a technocratic concept. A small gender mainstreaming industry with specialists and trainers is developing and trying to expand their market. It remains to be seen if the *gender equality impetus* of gender mainstreaming which demands that women have one-half of decision-making power and that all affairs of organizations are reflected on their gender impact will be vitalized and developed in these contexts.

In summary, regulation for gender equality in Germany has been shaped by corporatism. The main actors, including women's movements, reacted selectively and passively towards global impulses. Corporatism with its broad integrative inter-mediation and ideology provides normative foundations of discursive negotiation (including equality and reform), which could be extended to gender equality. Institutionalized feminism and gender experts were able to gain considerable influence in problem definition and policy formulation through the use of party and parliamentary negotiations to provide expertise for government (the women's ministry) and social organizations. Thus, they could approach the state and trade unions/civil society in the corporatist triangle but had little access to employers. But feminists are caught between a rock and a hard place by their integration into the remains of corporatism as well as by the exclusionary trends in male-centred neo-liberal policy networks in the erosion of corporatism. The 'EU connection' proved the main strategy for negotiating global norms for gender equality at the national and local level.

The new women's movements in Japan: exclusion from national corporatism and global orientation

The actor constellation shifted in Japan's coordinated market economy. In the enterprise-centred corporatism of 1970, the bureaucracy, (male) academic experts and enterprise constituted the leading actors in the formulation of regulation. Policies on women's work issues in the postwar era were located in the Labour Ministry, which had a department of women and young workers' affairs, and was directed by a woman. The policy formulation process centres on deliberative committees headed by a bureaucrat in the responsible ministry: employers' representatives and experts (and in some issues trade union representatives playing a minor role) prepare legislation negotiating for compromise under the guidance of the bureaucrat (Seifert 1997). In the 1990s, gender experts and some feminist networks gained participation and an important voice in gender equality regulation inside and outside the institutional set-up (Gelb 2003a; Tsuchida 2004).

While facing exclusion on the national level during the 1970s, the actors in the velvet triangle of gender policy showed a profound global orientation and they developed a common strategy for formulation and networking in view of the new global opportunity structure. The Japanese women's movement showed a marked international, somewhat pan-Asian orientation[16] in the 1950s and 1960s, which then switched to a high global interest, especially after the start of the UN decades of women in 1975. The small feminist movements had participated in the UN decade of women from its very start in 1975 with energy, enthusiasm and rapidly increasing international expertise (cf. Lenz 2000). The established wing and the new autonomous movement met in preparation, and some activists went to the starting conference in Mexico in 1975. These groups used the new opportunities accorded by the high prestige of the UN in Japan and the new global and highly visible public spaces of the UN decades for problem definition and agenda setting in Japan. Through these efforts, the women's groups developed international networks.

In view of the UN decade, the groups also consolidated their organizational structure. Female Members of Parliament and established women's organizations formed a *Liaison Group for Realizing the Resolutions of the Japanese Conference for the International Year of Women* (abbr. *Liaison Group; Kokusai funjinnen Nihon taikai no ketsugi o kitsugen suru tame no renrakukai*; abbr. *Renrakukai*) (cf. Kokusai funjinnen Nihon taikai no ketsugi o kitsugen suru tame no renrakukai 1989). Established leaders and activists from the autonomous women's groups also formed a network for activity in the UN international year of women (abbr. *Kôdô suru kai; Kôdô* suru kai kirokshû henshû iinkai 1999). A hotbed for many of the later leading feminist lawyers, medical doctors, scientists in women studies and politicians, this group had a long and successful career with some changes, which ended in the late 1990s.

The international orientation of the Japanese women's movement was broadened from the former pan-Asian focus on Asia or the parallel focus on the West to a more detailed consciousness of global gender issues especially in the South. This growth of global consciousness was limited to a few internationally oriented activists or experts until the mid-1990s. Then, the Fourth World Conference on Women in Beijing 1995 worked like a magnet, attracting more than 5000 Japanese feminists – experts as well as grassroots activists, networks from the metropolitan areas as well as from the countryside. The Beijing conference and its preparatory and follow-up processes marked the mass sensitization of the Japanese women's movements for the Asian and the global contexts as well as its turn to politics and lobbying (Ajia josei shiryô sentâ 1997; Lenz 2000).

The impetus of the Beijing process was brought back into negotiation for regulation by a women's umbrella network, called Beijing JAC (Beijing Japan Accountability Caucus) formed by Japanese feminist networks and a part of the established women's groups who had taken the Beijing Platform for Action back home and started lobbying. Beijing JAC has twelve working groups, one for each of the issues in the Platform for Action. Beijing JAC brought together feminist experts and grassroots activists from all over Japan with long experience. They framed demands for the twelve issues in the Japanese context and have been negotiating with state and regional government on them (Gelb 2003a).

In a very interesting comparison of gender policies in Japan and the US, Joyce Gelb characterized the strategy of Japanese feminists as 'externalism' because they mobilized global norms and connections to put pressure on the Japanese government. She contrasts this with the 'insularity' of equal opportunity in the US, which is limited to the national level and disassociated from global and UN processes, e.g. manifested in the US refusal to join CEDAW (Gelb 2003a: 4, 139 passim). Whereas parts of the Japanese women's movement certainly have referred to global/external processes and built up global and regional networks, the notion of 'externalism' is somewhat problematic for several reasons. It ignores *internal* mobilization and pressure arising from the change of consciousness since the 1970s and also disregards the interplay of strategies along the global multilevel system: for example, mothers and housewives demand gender equity measures in schools at the local level and they could refer to national institutions and national legislation after 1999 (Lenz 2000), which again were lobbied for with reference to the Beijing declaration of 1995. The dualism of 'externalism' versus 'insularity' may lead to neglect of the vital local and national roots of gender equity values and norms in Japan. The issue could be reframed: How did the Japanese women's movements appropriate their international orientation and capacities? And what are the reasons for the 'opportunity value' of global norms in negotiating with the state and organizations in Japan? Then the *internal origins* for the strategies of the women's movements along the multilevel system can also be put in focus. While this is beyond the scope of this chapter, let me mention only two aspects: firstly, members have a comparatively high level of education and important social leadership positions (cf. Lenz 2000) which may account for their marked capacity for global orientation, reflexivity and learning; secondly, many local networks active in communities and negotiating 'on the spot' have linkages to global groups by Beijing JAC and other networks. Thus networks are accountable to the grassroots and the global impulses are mediated with local and national values and strategies.

In the last thirty years parallel to the UN decades of women, a shift from 'outside protest' to 'deliberative integration' of women's leaders and gender experts in gender commissions and WPM can be observed. It will be traced by looking at some issues of legal reform in the field of work and the international documents mentioned above.

Considering CEDAW, the Japanese government at first assumed a passive attitude and wanted to shirk joining. The gender policy network around the Liaison Group and internationally oriented or liberal circles made a strong appeal to public opinion and government. The government then signed the treaty in 1980. The negotiations around CEDAW and the UN decade of women also resulted in the establishment of women's political machinery, the former Women's Office in the Prime Minister's Office. The women's networks could assert themselves in problem definition and agenda setting by using the UN global legitimacy. In the dynamics of the policy processes they gained participation and weight in policy formulation as well as becoming integrated into the gender policy commissions.

CEDAW was used by the gender policy networks as well as by some local action groups of working women such as the WIN Network in Osaka (Baier 2004; Gelb 2003a). WIN formed to fight wage and promotion discrimination in the Sumitomo trading company; it appealed to CEDAW, visiting the office in Geneva and creating public response by simultaneously acting on the global and national level in the multilevel system.[17] So CEDAW was taken up by national as well by local networks aiming at strategies along the global multilevel system.

These action groups like WIN, Women's Union Tokyo and similar organizations in other cities and regions formed unions as networks outside of the traditional enterprise union structure. They raised consciousness, advocated for women's rights in the workplace, and pushed for reforms of the part-time labour law and pay equity. Working women's NGOs have consulted with their counterparts in Asia, and more recently, they have begun to network with labour feminists in the US.[18]

The shifts in the actors' constellation following the dynamics of the policy process can be seen by briefly looking at two crucial legal reforms relevant for gender and work. After a wave of trials against gender discrimination at work, the Labour Ministry installed some consecutive commissions to prepare an Equal Employment Opportunity Law (EEOL) for Men and Women (*Danjo koyô kikai kintô-hô*) which finally was passed in 1986 (Lam 1992; Gelb 2003a: 50–1). These commissions brought together bureaucrats, male liberal experts, employers and trade unions while female gender experts and the women's groups were largely excluded. Starting in the late 1970s before CEDAW, the process of regulation was motivated mainly by forces in Japan, but gained momentum through the global connection when the government signed CEDAW and the women's networks made it public in the mass media.[19]

The women's movement had a thorough debate on equality and difference as former protection clauses based on differences (e.g. the former menstruation leave) were abolished by referring to a bureaucratic equality discourse; the movement split somewhat. Its long-term orientation changed towards equality. The meaning of equality, however, was not seen in assimilation to men's hard labour, but in creating humane working conditions for women and men (Kôdô suru kai kirokushû henshû iinkai 1999: 126–38). For the first time in Japan, the EEOL contained provisions for equal opportunities for men and women in recruitment, job allocation and training even if it relied on administrative guidance and did not include sanctions. The reform of the EEOL (enacted in June 1997, enforced in April 1999) showed that it had taken root in feminist networks on gender and work. Feminists in the women's movement and trade unions lobbied widely for a more effective law. The committee in the Labour Ministry, which was in charge of the reform, had a remarkable share of women. The revised law shows clear progress in such matters as prohibition of discrimination against female workers armed with sanctions, settlement of disputes and complaints, measures for actively promoting equal treatment (so-called positive action and measures against sexual harassment) (Gelb 2003a: 51–62; Osawa 2000a: 14). Thus women's coalitions from experts, employers and trade unions gained participation and influence and could form alliances with reform forces in the policy formulation on gender equality at work.

The policy formulation of the Basic Law for a Gender-Equal Society (passed in 1999) was negotiated between the coalition government, the bureaucracy (including the WPM), gender experts and women's networks (e.g. Beijing JAC). Tsuchida Tomoko (2004) sees it as a new paradigm for citizen's participation in legislation in place of the former closed bureaucratic commissions. The LDP was in coalition with the Social Democratic Party of Japan (SDPJ) and the New Party Sakigake (NPS) for four years since July 1994; both coalition parties at that time had female leaders. The three-party accord included the expansion of the national WPM and the establishment of a basic law on gender equality (Osawa 2003: 2–3). Thus in the trend towards pluralism, political leaders and parliamentarians in the coalition government joined the actor's constellation.

When the conservative President Hashimoto (LDP) was planning administrative reform, female politicians and external and internal lobbying by feminists persuaded him to integrate the concept of the gender-equal society into the reforms. The feminist networks were able to mobilize well-known female researchers and prestigious female leaders for the government commission preparing the law and to support its debates with public lobbying and events. The small femocrat core in the Office for Gender Equality in the Prime Minister's office – women's political machinery in Japan – played an important role in coordinating efforts, especially in internal lobbying and serving as a counterpart to the feminist NGOs. The committee could come to compromises by integrating Japanese and global concepts (Osawa 2000a, 2003).

The significance of the law is its basic concept of a gender-free society and the respect for individual human rights (ibid.). As the law also regards gender equality as a means to overcome crucial economic problems such as the low birth rate or the coming labour market constraints by using women workers' potential, it appeals to broader economic and political interests in order to promote realization and concrete results (Osawa 2003). The Basic Law gives a general framework to be implemented by specific laws and rules at the national, prefectural and communal level (Osawa 2000b). It also strengthens the focal position of the Gender Equality Bureau in the Cabinet Office in administrative reforms and expands gender policy machineries at the prefectural and communal level.

In the Japanese terms of the law, gender equality is called 'joint participation of men and women' (*danjo kyôdô sankaku*) which is related to equality of opportunities whereas in English translation the phrase 'Basic Law for a Gender-Equal Society' is used. Osawa discusses the language politics of incorporating gender mainstreaming into the Japanese context of political regulations. This concept of *gender* equality had the merit of overcoming the narrow focus on women and difference in the former laws and institutions. The interpretation of 'gender-free' and 'individual human rights' is epochal indeed in Japan. Despite various problems, the Basic Law provides a framework for more equal gender regulations in work, family and politics (Osawa 2003). The actor constellation for gender regulation started with women's networks and reform-minded bureaucracy which related to the new international and national opportunity structure. From the 1980s it included the WPM, especially the Gender Office and the Gender Commission in the Prime Minister's Office (today Cabinet Office). From the 1990s it has also involved parliamentarians from all parties in establishing basic legislation for gender equity (Gelb 2003a; Osawa 2003). For some time, the dynamism has been self-reinforcing and expanding to the regional and local level.

Counter-movements close to the conservative ruling party LDP as the 'liberal historians' and arising from new religions (*Seichô no ie*) have been mobilizing against gender equity and the 'gender-free' concept and attempt to block it at the national and local level. Presently the right wing of the LDP and the extreme right are also attacking the Basic Law in a campaign to re-establish a neo-patriarchal national political culture. They even mobilized for abolishing the gender equality clauses in the 1946 constitution of Japan. Whereas global women's networks could use the global multilevel system for lobbying for regulation for equality, their achievements are vulnerable to counter-movements of conservative nationally entrenched political forces.

Equal opportunity and regulation in liberal contexts: the UK and the US

In Great Britain, the EOC and women's networks were able to use and expand the EU Directives and the gender mainstreaming clause of the Amsterdam Treaty.[20] The Equal Pay Act and the Sex Discrimination Act were passed before the EU Directives, but were reinforced and reinvigorated by them (Lovenduski 1995; Walby 1999a). For example, the burden of proof in cases of discrimination was reversed to the employer and the clause on indirect discrimination strengthened in the Sex Discrimination Act 2001 following the EU Directive (EU Directive 97/80). The government announced that the EU Directive on Equal Treatment of 2002 (2002/73/EC) will also be implemented by amending the Sex Discrimination Act and that it had already consulted on some principles (CEDAW, 5th Periodic Report of the United Kingdom 2003).

Sylvia Walby has pointed to the crucial role of the European Court of Justice: either the European Commission can take states defaulting on the implementation of its Directives to the court or citizens can take legal cases to the court after exhausting the national legal system. EU law is superior to national law and member states are obliged to comply with EU rulings on equal opportunity (Walby 2002b: 539). As it relies on strong norms of equality and on citizens' or women's support independent of large organizations, regulation by case law appears as a favourable procedure in a liberal welfare state.

The Women and Equality Unit and the EOC are cooperating with the gender policy network in the EU to push for new policies. The WEU represents the UK on the CDEG (equality between women and men) Committee of the Council of Europe and it is aiming at integrating gender equality in negotiations on the Article 13 Sex Discrimination Directive on Goods and Services which would transcend the EU focus on employment.

The influence of CEDAW on gender equality regulation in Great Britain is not clear; CEDAW was passed after the first equality laws and the establishment of the EOC and it does not seem to play a major role in agenda setting or policy formulation.

The US, the remaining global superpower, is not actively supporting global regulation for gender equality under the Bush government after 1998. The legal reforms and the equal opportunity policies which paralleled a large-scale integration of women in the labour market and management were based on internal impulses (Ferree and Hess 1994; Davis 1999; Gelb 2003a). The US has not yet ratified CEDAW (though it signed it in 1980) due to procrastination by the government (Gelb 2003a: 5).[21] The hegemonic government policy aims for an unilateral world order under US military power and tends to distance itself from the UN as well as from its efforts for global peace and equality. Thus a hegemonic government and power elite and radical conservative counter-movements have contributed to isolating the US from global gender equality regulation. US feminist networks have been crucial for the UN decades and for the human/women rights approach, but they lacked the power to basically influence US domestic and foreign policy.

Concluding remarks

Informed by global norms, welfare states established new regulations which show broad variation.[22] Therefore future research should re-embed the discussion of global norms and advocacy networks with the national welfare states, their gender regimes and the varieties of capitalism.[23] Whereas globalization was seen to propel homogenization or McDonaldization (Ritzer 2000), in the field of gender policy at least a broad variation of results has emerged. The case studies mainly focused on different actor constellations in market-oriented and corporatist welfare states with public gender regimes.

It is remarkable that the responses of liberal welfare states (Great Britain, US) are varying among themselves as well as in corporatist welfare states (Germany, Japan). The variations of capitalism/welfare states are pertinent, but not sufficient to explain the differences between regulations.

In the liberal welfare state of Great Britain women's policy networks and feminist groups and NGOs referred to citizens' equality and market efficiency in using women's capacities and linked these discourses to the EU impulses. Appeal to the European Court of Justice and case law development formed part of the strategies. The WPM developed vigorous policy networks with civil society/women's networks and gender experts. The Labour government after 1997 also took an active role in the generation and negotiation of global norms of gender equality in the EU and UN. The efficiency norms and legal strategies can be connected to the liberal welfare state, whereas the emphasis on global human and women's rights and norm generation transcends this framework. In the US, a hegemonic liberal welfare state, gender equality policy by the state is decoupled from global norms whereas feminist networks refer to them discursively.

In German corporatism, the differential integration of women's policy into corporatism led to concentration on negotiations at the national level, whereas the EU formed the main context for responding to global norms. But corporatism also provided discourses of equality and of public national integration of women. The regulation on the EU Directives on Equal Treatment (1976, 2002) was negotiated in the corporatist context. The WPM played a passive role in the generation and negotiation of global norms of gender equality compared to the active nationally centred legislation process. Still, those issues not related directly to work, as in the EU programmes against sexual violence, WPM and transnational feminist networks are taking the initiative in problem definition, agenda setting and policy formulation while transcending the corporatist framework.

In Japan, the exclusion of women from enterprise-centred corporatism paralleled the formation of concentrated and committed gender policy networks, which referred to the global level for prestige and legitimacy. Using the opportunity structure of global norms and national reform politics, they could establish their problem definition, agenda setting and strongly influence policy formulation. So while acting within corporatism (and grappling with it), gender policy networks are also transcending it. In both welfare states gender policies transcend corporatism in a phase of its decline.

Looking at the case studies, the specific formation of gender regime in a compact sense, including norms and interpretations of gender equity, women's movements, WPM and women's political participation, appears as the most relevant factor. But the gender regime is interacting with the type of welfare state and has been shaped by path dependency. It is interesting that the women's and human rights approach has contributed to transcending path dependency in the liberal as well as the corporatist welfare states (except the US).

On the whole, after the euphoria of discovering global gender equality norms and advocacy networks, a down-to-earth empirical stocktaking of the 'real regulation processes', their prospects and their risks seems timely: this is also necessary in order to see when they work (and when not). Women's networks have contributed to new forms of democratic gender equality regulation by allowing participation for civic groups and by practising supra-national consensus building. Thus they have transcended the national perspectives (as other global actors), but they still negotiate embedded in the local or national grounds.

Notes

1. This chapter grew out of the discussions of the GLOW group; especially I want to thank the group and especially Heidi Gottfried, Karin Gottschall, Mari Osawa, Karen Shire and Sylvia Walby for very constructive discussion; my thanks also go to Diane Elson, Reinhart Kössler, Verena Schmidt and Myra Marx Ferree for helpful comments and support.
2. I refer to the different aspects of the policy cycle as heuristic categories by which important aspects of policy development can be outlined, but I do not see them as phases in chronological sequence; cf. Jahn and Wegrich 2003.
3. My understanding of the concept of international, supra-national, transnational and global relations will be summarized briefly: 'international' refers to the relationships between *nations* and internationalization points to the long process of the formation of the capitalist world system and of its member nations since the sixteenth century. 'Supra-national' implies that governance institutions like the UN have been formed comprising several nations. In contrast, 'transnational' means configurations in which persons have plurilocal mobility or networks between two or more regions (Pries 2002). 'Global' presupposes the emergence of the global fields of action in the economy, politics and communication in which global actors (not only nation-states) enter and play which again influences the social relations in nation-states; therefore it points to the relative new process of globalization starting around 1965 with the New International Division of Labour and gaining broad impact and momentum since then.
4. See Unifem 2000: 47–60 for a brief overview of developments since the Beijing conference.
5. These trends are apparent in the disregard by the US government of the Geneva Convention in view of the imprisonment without legal safeguard in Guantánamo

prison as well as in its definitions of torture after 2001, especially 2003–4, which are not in accordance with international law.

6. The NGO-ization and professionalization seem somewhat dramatized in the literature; it rather seems to follow the routinization of charisma (Weber) in social movements and calls for more research from a perspective of sociology of organization.

7. This approach is different from the modes of regulation inherent to different phases of capitalist accumulation as in the school of Fordist or post-Fordist regulation.

8. The ideas of boomerang effect or ping pong effect along the multilevel governance system (Zippel 2004) neglect the cultural synthesis and 'rooting' of global norms.

9. The RNGS group classified the WPM according to the criteria whether (1) they had high or low influence in policy formulation and (2) whether they provided high or low policy access to women's movements and feminist groups. High influence in policy formulation and high policy access to women's movements are related to high profile and high impact of the WPM; cf. Mazur 2001a.

10. High influence and high access were found for Australia, the Netherlands, Norway and Denmark. In the countries in our sample the WPM in Great Britain was characterized by high influence and low access for feminist groups, whereas the WPM in Germany and the US were termed as having low influence, but giving high policy access (Stetson and Mazur 1995b).

11. Joyce Gelb states in a comparison between gender in Japan and the US, that the Women's Bureau never has been a major political actor (2003a: 152).

12. I want to thank Heidi Gottfried for information on OFCCP and EEOC.

13. I want to thank Sylvia Walby for comments and information in this section.

14. As little systematic research has been done on policy formulation and implementation following global norms at the national level, the summary is based mainly on different national case studies considering special aspects and is only a first explorative overview.

15. *Gesetz über die Gleichbehandlung von Frauen und Männern am Arbeitsplatz* (cf. Pfarr and Bertelsmann 1989).

16. Cf. note 3.

17. The women supported by WIN won their court trial in 2004 (cf. Baier 2004).

18. I want to thank Heidi Gottfried for information on this point.

19. Cf. Lam 1992 and the different interpretation of Gelb 2003a: 49–62.

20. As I am not a specialist on Great Britain and the policy institutions and there is to my knowledge no analysis of gender equality regulation of global norms, I will only sketch some results of negotiation.

21. The radical right argues that CEDAW infringes upon the sovereignty of the United States and seeks to implement a radical agenda that would undermine 'traditional' moral and social values, including marriage, motherhood, family structure (and even Mother's Day) (http://www.unausa.org/issues/cedaw/cedawfact.asp).

22. In view of the small number of cases these results can only suggest a possible research hypothesis. A comparison with social democratic welfare states based on dual earner systems would have been desirable. Certainly many other variables are relevant such as, for example, the different political cultures and normative systems.

23. Such reconsideration is also useful for understanding the different interests and logics of action among members of advocacy networks. Probably NGO leaders from liberal welfare states will have different perspectives from actors from corporatist settings. After 'discovering' gender equality advocacy networks, the differences in normative and interest inside the networks and of the other actors which are partners of alliances or of negotiations becomes an important research issue.

5

Similar Outcomes, Different Paths: the Cross-national Transfer of Gendered Regulations of Employment[1]

Glenda S. Roberts

In twenty-first-century Japan, numerous legal measures encourage both 'work/family harmonization' and gender equality at the workplace. Influenced by global (i.e. North American, UK and European) norms regarding gender equality as well as by changing demographics that have encouraged governmental reform in family/work reconciliation, corporate policies are changing, especially in large firms. This chapter will discuss the implementation of new in-house regulatory schemes for promoting work/life balance and gender equality at two large firms in Tokyo from the late 1990s to the present. Through the analysis of these two firms' strategies, one can discern different organizational cultural stances regarding the relationship between employee and firm, and between firm and government, leading to differing outcomes in the timing and structuring of work/life balance or 'family-friendly' policies.

I studied two large firms from different industries: MNF is a multinational financial services firm, based in the US, while Naruse is a multinational Japanese manufacturing firm, with sales and R&D arms.[2] Both firms operate in an environment that, until the mid-1980s, was ideologically, normatively and practically hostile to women who desired careers. The firms have responded positively to the changes in the regulatory environment, but they differ in their timing, interpretation and implementation of policy content. Differences in industry no doubt affect the work pace and climate. Differences in terms of organizational culture are perhaps even more significant and interesting, since this is a time when Japanese firms are increasingly experimenting with introducing aspects of personnel management models found in US firms. Despite differences in product and contrasting organizational cultures, however, under the larger social and infrastructural constraints of urban Japanese society, the employees of both firms share in a common difficulty of maintaining a 'fine balance' between home and work life while simultaneously striving for gender equality in the workplace.

The first section of the chaper discusses women's place in the recent employment context in Japan. The second section analyses the two case studies, both in terms of the introduction and implementation of work/life and gender equality schemes, and in terms of the workers' uptake of and response towards these schemes. In the final section, I briefly touch on issues of spousal cooperation in work and family life.

Women's employment in Japan

In what sense are my female informants part of Japan's new economy? I would argue they could be considered such in two ways. One is that they are the beneficiaries of changes wrought in Japan's employment environment for women as a result of global feminism (see Lenz in this volume). Another is that most of them are highly educated knowledge workers, with at least a university education, and some have earned either MBAs or other advanced degrees. Until the Equal Employment Opportunity Law was passed in 1985, exit from employment upon marriage was the norm for Japanese women (Ogasawara 1998, 2001; Brinton 1993). As Osawa states in this volume and elsewhere (2002), social welfare and tax codes in Japan in the postwar period have supported a class of professional homemakers, who in turn supported their salaried husbands, enabling the latter to work extremely long hours for the firm. Firms benefited by hiring young women at low wages, encouraging them to 'retire' at the time of their marriage, and then re-employing some of them as part-time or temporary staff after they had sent their youngest children off to school. Women who remained at the firm after marriage suffered discrimination, both from their younger colleagues, who felt their reasons for staying on must lie in their husbands' poor economic circumstances, and from the firm, which gave women who remained on the job neither salaried compensation nor training and promotional opportunities equal to those of men (Roberts 1994; Ogasawara 1998, 2001).

On the other hand, single and married women who managed to stay at their large firm for long years of service were not likely to be dismissed outright, as the courts had ruled this illegal in the 1960s and 1970s (Upham 1987; Cook and Hayashi 1980), and because unions in Japan's large enterprises did fight for the employment security of all employees of regular status in return for employees' total devotion to the firm. During the postwar period, large Japanese firms were characterized by the 'three pillars' of lifetime employment, the age-based seniority wage system, and the enterprise union. The union supported regular workers, both blue- and white-collar, and the system of training and promotion was internal to the firm (for example, Dore 1973; Itoh 1994; Tabata 1998). Regular staff are recruited once a year upon leaving school, each new cohort entering simultaneously. Itoh (1994) notes barriers to exit discourage mid-career separation from the firm.[3]

He also notes perverse effects of recruiting employees from other firms in mid-career. For instance, since many large firms invest in firm-specific training of young recruits and groom them for many years to become generalists in the firm, a mid-career entrant may not be as productive as an in-house person. Furthermore, those who have come up within the firm may lose motivation when newcomers are hired from outside for highly ranked positions. The job-changer might also have the reputation of being a 'bad' worker for willingly changing loyalties (Itoh 1994: 247–8). Tabata (1998: 209) also emphasizes the costs Japanese workers face when exiting from a large firm: 'the exit from a large enterprise usually results in a move to a small or medium-sized enterprise where the wage level is lower and fringe benefits such as retirement allowances are almost negligible.' Hence, it is quite deleterious for the worker to separate from the firm after the first several years of work, which is often the case with women. By and large, firms did not consider their female workers to be core employees, although as long as they continued their tenure, women's jobs were protected by the enterprise union.

Firms were able to sustain this system through the 1960s due to an expanding economy and population. In the 1970s, after the oil shocks, firms increasingly hired part-time staff (Cabinet Office 2004: 5). Large firms managed to maintain employment within their group, not the firm, by shifting employees to subsidiary small-to-medium sized firms, where lifelong wages over a career were lower and job security much less.

The situation for women employees in Japan began changing in the mid-1980s, with the passage of the Equal Employment Opportunity Law (EEOL) and increasing globalization, both economic and cultural. Although the EEOL was largely a product of pressure from the international community, it did offer women some modicum of encouragement to pursue careers. Within Japan, the first years of the EEOL brought with them some increased employment opportunities for women, though many companies responded to the EEOL by establishing a two-track system whereby the majority of women were hired on a clerical track, and only a few women were hired on a career track. There was no clerical track for men (Lam 1992; Weathers 2005; Cabinet Office 2004). The overall assessment of Japan's EEOL has not been glowing, as Osawa points out in her chapter. Still, some women did gain management experience through the opportunities opened up by the EEOL.

In recent years, foreign firms have developed a reputation of being more progressive in gender equality, and those women who were ambitious to build and maintain careers often turned to foreign-capital establishments for employment (Kelsky 2001). During the course of my research at MNF, I heard many such accounts. The following testimony is from one of my interviewees (W17), born in 1964, aged 35 at the time of the interview in 1999:

My major was economics, so . . . I had an advantage to . . . enter into a financial institution, but . . . at that time [1986], I already knew the status of Japanese financial institutions toward women because . . . I was in a seminar of economics at [x elite] university and there were many, many men and only a few females, and men were encouraged to enter into prestigious and famous Japanese international institutions, but, ah . . . we women were not welcome in such companies.

She then remarked that she knew some women who had graduated before her and who had entered prestigious Japanese financial institutions, but who had learned that they were not really welcome. Entering Japanese firms had not been to their advantage. Hence, she wanted to enter an American financial institution. Some other interviewees also observed that they had languished for several years in Japanese firms before making a career change to MNF. One example is that of Ms Hamano (W19, born 1953), a manager whom I interviewed in 1999. Ms Hamano was a four-year college graduate with an economics major. She entered a Japanese manufacturing firm in 1976, immediately upon graduating from college, and spent ten years in clerical support jobs. She noted that the Japanese firm did not know what to do with her, so they would give her something a bit challenging to do, but as soon as a new man came in, that job would be taken from her. Although the firm began hiring women for career-track jobs after the EEOL in 1986, they were not offering this to women retroactively. When she saw that MNF was hiring mid-career entrants, she applied and was hired in 1987. She remarked that upon entering MNF and seeing how women were able to build careers from when they were young, she wondered why she had put up with the Japanese firm all those years.

Even though firms such as MNF do not offer job security comparable to Japanese-based firms, and foreign firms have the reputation of offering performance-related rewards systems instead of the Japanese age-based compensation, women were attracted to the perceived greater opportunities for training and rapid advancement in foreign-owned multinational corporations.

The recession years, which began in 1991 and have lasted for over a decade, did batter Japan's lifetime employment system to some extent. Many firms have adjusted core workers' reward schemes by tying a portion of salary increases to individual productivity gains, and they increasingly have utilized temporary, dispatch, and contract staff to reduce personnel costs. The percentage of the total workforce engaged in non-standard employment has risen to 23 per cent (MHLW 2003), and part-time employment accounts for 40.7 per cent of women's non-agricultural employment in Japan. Temporary employment, although a small percentage of total employment, is one of the fastest growing 'work-styles' for women between the ages of 24 and 35 (see Shire in this volume and Gottfried 2003).The Cabinet Office (2004) notes:

> The number of female regular workers had been increasing until 1991 but has since leveled off because of the stagnant economy and ever-changing corporate employment management practices. The number of female regular workers has been decreasing since 1997. On the other hand, female workers are increasingly taking part-time positions that provide less favorable working conditions than full-time positions. In 2002, the number of non-regular female workers stood at 2.8 times those of 1985.

Even recent school-leavers increasingly cannot find full-time permanent employment and thus must settle for part-time or temporary jobs. Part-timers make up some 30 per cent of all female workers in their twenties, including many new graduates, while 'women aged 35 or older start working as a part-timer in most cases' (Cabinet Office 2004: 18). This trend is a cause of concern for several reasons. First, non-standard employment, especially part-time jobs, pays lower wages on average than regular employment, diminishing the ability of workers to be self-sufficient, and also diminishing their contributions towards national pension schemes. Second, part-time jobs do not provide the same benefits packages as regular employment. Third, and most salient to this chapter, workers in certain types of non-standard employment are not entitled to childcare leave or other 'family-friendly' provisions.

Osawa, in this volume (also see Shire in this volume), also discusses the diversification of employment types in recent years. While the recession economy has not boded well for many women's employment conditions, the status of core employee in the large firm remains, and with it, the assumption, albeit shaky, of lifetime employment (MHLW White Paper on Labour 2003). Whether the practice of 'lifetime employment' will survive in the future is a matter of current debate (Asahi Shimbun 2005; Osano and Kobayashi 2005). As we shall see, my informants at a Japanese firm were beneficiaries of the practice and expected to continue their employment.

The low birth-rate society, gender equality and 'family-friendly' workplace policy

Before presenting the data from the case studies, I explore regulatory changes related to gender equality and work/life balance policies in Japan. Much of the impetus for government initiatives on work/life balance has stemmed from a desire to shore up the falling birth-rate, which may be an artefact of the changing gender regime.[4]

Japan's continuously declining total fertility rate (TFR) fell below population replacement rate (2.07) as early as 1974. Japan's total fertility rate in

2004 stood at 1.29 (Imidas 2005: 631). Japan does not have the lowest fertility rate of the OECD; Spain, Italy and South Korea exhibit slightly lower rates. It is also well above those of Hong Kong and Singapore. As in these countries, the fertility decline set off public alarms (Roberts 2002). As the birth-rate in Japan dropped, the government began to establish legal infrastructure to uphold the principle of gender equality (Equal Employment Opportunity Law 1985, 1999; Basic Law for Gender Equality 1999), and formulated policy initiatives to relieve women of the burden of childbearing, childrearing and eldercare. Among these are the Angel Plans of 1994, 1999 and 2005, the Nursing Care Insurance Law of 2001, the Childcare Leave Law and Childcare/Family Care Leave Law of 1991 and 1999,[5] and the 'Measures Against Declining Birthrate: Plus One' policy of 2002. Like the EEOL before it, much of the 'family-friendly' legislation passed thus far has depended on the 'administrative guidance' by government ministries. According to Weathers (2005), labour bureaucrats encourage employers' compliance through 'soft' mechanisms, such as moral suasion, symbolic awards (like 'Best Family-Friendly Corporation' prizes) and subsidies. There are no penalties for non-compliance. These soft mechanisms are insufficient to induce all firms to comply. Hence, many employees cannot avail themselves of 'family-friendly' policies.

As Osawa states in Chapter 3, Japan's government has adopted elements of the work/life balance model, by promoting participation of women and men in the workforce and socializing long-term care for the infirm elderly. Yet infrastructural support is still lagging. Furthermore, pressure on corporations to implement the model has been insufficient.

Above I noted that the administrative guidance approach to enforcing 'family-friendly' legislation has had mediocre results. So far in Japan, larger firms have a higher rate of establishing such systems for their employees than do small and medium-sized firms (Sato 2001a). The tendency for large firms to incorporate the 'family-friendly' legal framework into their personnel policy systems may be a function of large firms' higher rate of unionization and generally firmer financial grounding. Since the majority of the labour force works in small and medium-sized firms, this bodes ill for the prospect that 'family-friendly' policies will catch on quickly.[6] The same tendency exists in the United States: in a study of the responsiveness of small businesses to work/family issues, researchers found that small businesses (with between 1 and 49 employees) were less likely to provide policies or programmes, whether on a formal or informal basis. They also found that large firms offered a wider variety of formal policies and programmes than smaller business. Sounder finances and economies of scale were reasons noted (Pitt-Catsouphes and Litchfield 2001).

On the other hand, firms of any size in Japan may be more likely than US firms to aim for more work/life flexibility if only because of the government's encouragement, although they are much less likely to do so, I think, during a recession. One government official told me that firms see 'family-friendly' as a luxury (*zeitaku*). Their subcontractors say, 'If you can afford to establish family-friendly policies, why can't you raise the rate you pay us for each piece we sell you?'[7] The two medium-sized manufacturing firms I visited in a north-east prefecture in February 2002, who had won Family-Friendly Awards from the Ministry of Health, Labour and Welfare, instituted their policy framework not out of a conviction that establishing such policies would be profitable for the company, nor because they should abide by the law of the land, but out of an obligation to follow the general policy trends of the parent company.

The most well-established 'family-friendly' policy in Japan's firms is Childcare Leave (CCL). By law, a full-time worker may take up to a year of leave to care for his or her newborn child. The worker receives 40 per cent of her salary: 30 per cent is paid during the leave and the remaining 10 per cent after the return to work. This leave may be taken by one parent or shared consecutively. In 2002, 81.1 per cent of firms with more than thirty employees and 61.4 per cent of all firms had employment regulations in place for CCL (Sato and Takeishi 2004: 83). I should note that Japan already had a 14-week long Maternity Leave Law for mothers, allowing 60 per cent pay, and also an additional leave (Childcare Time) allowing for two half-hour periods for nursing, until the child reached the age of one.[8] While some firms may informally allow flexible work arrangements without actual policies, Sato and Takeishi note that in firms where these practices are not institutionalized through rules and regulations, employees have difficulty in making use of them.

Both Naruse and MNF are examples of best-practices, well known in Japan for being extremely attractive places for women to work. In particular, Naruse is seen as a firm where women can work until retirement, and have a family as well. University graduate women join the firm deliberately for this reason. MNF, too, attracts university graduate women from the top Japanese universities as well as from renowned MBA programmes abroad and mid-career entrants from Japanese firms, mainly because of the perception that MNF offers women strong opportunities for advancement in their careers. Women are in the majority of employees at both firms.

Distinctions of the sample

The two firms under investigation are unusual in the sense that they allow employees to utilize the legal frameworks for gender equality and harmonization of work and life. The results are not always perfect, but the policies give female employees just enough leeway to remain working throughout their lives. The sample includes women in urban areas only. Most of the women had tertiary or postgraduate levels of education. They are the elite of the Japanese workforce. Moreover, the interviews reflected in this chapter are from current employees who are married and have children, not the majority who have chosen to 'exit' the firm or to forgo marriage and childbearing as a strategy to deal with the rigidities of the work/life balance environment.[9] According to the Ministry of Health, Labour and Welfare's 'First Profile Survey on New-Born Children in the 21st Century', as of 2001, nearly 70 per cent of women in the workforce left their jobs at the time of their first childbirth (Cabinet Office 2004). Another notable statistic from the 2002 National Institute of Population and Social Security Research's '12th Basic Survey on Birth Trends (for married couples)' is that working mothers in full-time employment make up only 10.7 per cent of those who had been married for zero to four years in 2002 (Cabinet Office 2004: 16).

Last, at Naruse I was not allowed to interview women in the frontlines of sales or manufacturing, though they make up the bulk of the workforce. I can speculate that the reason behind this refusal is that sales and manufacturing employees have far less flexibility. I did hear comments to that effect, but I am unable to confirm the accounts of the employees.

Many of the people whom I studied at these firms are managers, and access to work/life balance and gender equality policies has changed their lives, they say for the better. Their accounts show the substantial generational shifts that are taking place in Japan's corporate world, from one that took for granted that every core male employee would have a spouse supporting the household full-time, to one where the wives themselves are pursuing managerial status. Male 'corporate warriors' are beginning to get involved in childcare, but only to a limited degree, constrained by lingering public expectations of males, such as 100 per cent commitment to the firm as manifested by long work hours (over 23 per cent of salarymen in their thirties still work more than 60 hours a week[10]) and solo transfers to regional branches, that are common characteristics of the 'male breadwinner model'.

Gender equality at MNF and Naruse

What factors impelled the two firms in question to develop gender equality policies? As we shall see below, leadership in the two firms was a decisive factor contributing to the timing of the policy adoption and implementation. Furthermore, the adoption of policies took place through different pathways: MNF selectively adopted and adapted policies that had already been established in MNF's US main office, while Naruse learned through its relationship with the state.

So-called 'Japanese management' in private-sector employment has been known for treating male workers as long-term, core members in the firm, while considering female workers as peripheral and usually shorter-term support staff, with low promotion ceilings, less training, and in different job classifications than men (Roberts 1994; Ogasawara 1998, 2001; Shire 2000; Osawa 2002; Gottfried and Hayashi 1998). This has been especially true of the financial services sector. Up until the mid-1980s, MNF apparently was not an exception in this regard, despite the fact that in its home office in the US, the company had long since implemented gender-neutral employment policies. In the mid-1980s, a new top manager from the US came on board MNF Japan, saw the dearth of women in management, and said, 'Where are the women officers?'[11] Under his leadership, MNF started to promote women. This was also the decade of EEOL legislation, so the changes in the legal climate dovetailed with this CEO's inclinations to improve women's promotion opportunities in the firm. By the time of my interviews there in the late 1990s, it was not uncommon to find women among managerial staff; indeed, there were numerous female vice-presidents in various operations. In 2000, women made up 14 per cent of vice-presidents and 29 per cent of assistant vice-presidents at MNF Japan. Moreover, promotion depended on one's demonstrated abilities; employees did not have to wait years to be recognized if they were making important contributions. Factors impelling MNF to change its gender biases regarding the retention and promotion of women were: (1) the recognition by the CEO in the mid-1980s that MNF Japan, as a US multinational, was behind the times with regard to recognition of the value of female employees; (2) Japan's EEOL of 1986, which legally mandated that firms treat women and men equally; and (3) in the face of the difficulty recruiting the best male candidates who prefer to work in Japanese-owned companies, MNF sought to attract and retain the best female candidates during this period of expansion.[12]

In contrast, Naruse, while sharing with MNF the characteristic of employing more women than men, did not aggressively promote women until the mid-1990s, a full ten years after MNF's initiatives. In 2000, women made up a mere 5.3 per cent of managers at Naruse, Inc. At this time, a new president reportedly shook things up. Previously, although Naruse had been known as a firm where women could stay on after marriage (especially outside of the retail sales section), it had not been known for promoting women. As one female departmental manager, a high-school graduate who joined the firm in the 70s told me:

G.R.:   What do you think? Women were working for long years, but how did the company respond to this long span?

K: It [their response] was no good. It's recent.

G.R.:   Since when did it improve?

K: I felt it improving from about six or seven years ago [1996–7], when I was allowed to take the test for the lowest managerial rank (*sanji*) . . .

G.R.: So it was after the EEOL, wasn't it.

K: Before that, as well, we were a man's society.

G.R.: Wasn't it so everywhere?

K: What made me dissatisfied with the lack of change was that no matter how hard I tried, seven or eight years ago I felt I would never get ahead. When at last the firm started seriously considering enabling women in many areas to be promoted, I felt, 'Finally!'

G.R.: What was the impetus for the change?

K: From the top: first of all, the top of the company voiced it and I think they felt that other companies were paying attention to women. They felt they had better rid our company of its backward ways. I think they felt it did not look right for a leader in the field such as us to have such an outmoded organization . . . I have a feeling that they were driven by the surrounding environment.

If Naruse was driven by the surrounding environment to shake off its old-fashioned image, one would not know it by the news coverage on Naruse, which made it seem as if Naruse had always been a forerunner in gender policy areas. Numerous articles in the press praise Naruse's initiatives.

Not coincidentally, Naruse's new initiatives were synchronized with the government's new direction towards encouraging a 'gender-free' society. Through the overlap of personnel, or through *amakudari* practices whereby government bureaucrats retire to executive positions in top firms, governmental policies are transmitted to the corporate level. A top member on Naruse's board of directors is also on the government's Council of Gender Equality (CGE) advisory council. This board member has decided that the firm should become a top leader in gender equality and 'family-friendly' measures. Naruse's policy initiatives align with the CGE's policy, and Naruse's achievements in creating a 'gender-free' environment have been the subject of numerous articles in major newspapers and publications of semi-governmental think-tanks. Since 2002 Naruse has published a 'gender-free' pamphlet that it uses in 'human rights training' sessions to help employees understand the firm's new policies on gender equality. A 'Group to Promote Gender Equality' was begun in 2002. In 2003, the firm hired a retired Chief of the Ministry of Health, Labour and Welfare's (MHLW) Employment Equality-Family and Children's Division to spearhead their new initiatives on work/family reconciliation, promotion and development of women managers, personnel reform, and employment diversification. She was made the head of the newly created Corporate Social Responsibility division, under which Work and Family Reconciliation Support policies reside. As part of CSR, the firm sees the goal of building gender equality *(danjo kyoudou sankaku*) as its social responsibility and social contribution, linking it explicitly to demographics as a 'low birth-rate strategy.' Although this former bureaucrat could not simply dictate government policy wholesale, she did have considerable influence. The connection with government agencies is also made through other employees of Naruse, who have spent time on loan to semi-governmental agencies such as the 21st Century Foundation, which promotes the dissemination of government policies in such areas as family-friendly initiatives. To the best of my knowledge, MNF, in contrast, has never explicitly linked flexible work arrangements, Childcare Leave or Childcare Time to governmental initiatives to spur the fertility rate. When I was studying MNF in 1999, the personnel department was initially unaware of the 'Family-Friendly' prize that the MHLW was offering to companies who exceeded the minimum policy standards for work and family reconciliation policies. Rather, and in keeping with US-based rationales for managing with flexibility, they emphasize that employees who have discretion over their own time are happier and more productive employees, and that policies to encourage this lead to better recruiting and retention of excellent staff.

Work/family reconciliation policies and firm environment

Another point of contrast between these two firms is the relative ease with which women took long childcare leaves at Naruse. Both firms offered Childcare Leave (CCL) at the beginning of the 1990s, but Naruse's package provided up to five years of unpaid leave, and a guaranteed job upon return to work as a regular employee, although not necessarily in her same position. While most women do not choose to take the full five years, the policy has benefited some. One year's leave seems most common, but it is not unusual for an employee who has taken one year to continue until three years, having become pregnant with her second child before the end of her first leave. Women sometimes calculated the intervals between births; and in that way, they could avoid commuting again to work in a packed train during the period of morning-sickness and then heavy pregnancy. One employee had extended her leave to have a second child when her husband was transferred to a distant city. She took a total of five years off before returning to Naruse in advance of her husband's transfer back. Although her job in basic research was not awaiting her, she still had a job. While she did not regret the time spent with her family, when I asked her if she had any advice for other women who might take CCL, she said, 'As one would think, it's best to return after a year.' Another person who was pregnant in 2003 with her second child, was thinking into the future when her first would be entering elementary school. She worried that her child would have difficulty making the transition without after-school childcare, which was not yet available in her neighbourhood. She contemplated the possibility of timing a third pregnancy and birth to coincide with elementary school entrance, so that she could extend her CCL and her oldest daughter would not have to come home alone. Although the company does not keep detailed data on average length of leave, the personnel director did note that there were two peaks, with most women taking either one- or three-year leaves.

In sum, one could characterize the Naruse firm environment (excepting retail sales) as accommodating female employees' desires to take time off for child-rearing. The firm initiated policies allowing CCL even before the enactment of the Childcare Leave Law. By now it has become standard practice at Naruse for women to use CCL and other related policies such as Childcare Time.

Women at MNF, on the other hand, did not have the option to take more than one year of consecutive CCL. They usually took at most one year's leave, and often took only several months' leave, because they feared they could not keep up with the rapidly changing financial sector if they stayed out longer. Hence, the nature of the industry affects employees' decisions. MNF's work environment was characterized by high pressure, heavy workload, regular short-term deadlines, global communications, and rapid change. At the same time, because many top expatriate managers at MNF were from the US, MNF employees sometimes had to deal with managers who held the home office's corporate cultural attitudes towards maternity leave, where frequently women took less than the maximum allowed three months stipulated in the US's Family and Medical Leave Act of 1993. In the theoretical framework utilized by Sue Durbin (in this volume), we could say that a few US managers brought with them to Japan 'embedded knowledge' of how maternity leave should be treated. Their embedded knowledge clashed with the legal framework of the corporation in its Japanese setting, sometimes causing stress for employees. At the same time, however, MNF, in recognition that a one-year CCL is often not sufficient to help workers cope with the myriad challenges that arise during the early child-bearing years, did introduce a policy that would allow employees to cut their normal ostensible 40-hour working week down to as little as 24 hours (a 40 per cent cut) for one year, without losing their status as a regular employee. It was not a blanket policy, but had to be approved case-by-case. At the time of my study, a few highly regarded women managers were taking advantage of this arrangement. MNF top managers saw this as a key policy to retain excellent female staff needing more time for childcare. A 2004 company report notes that this policy is by now well established, with some 44 employees having made use of it since its introduction in 2000, for reasons of childcare, postgraduate education, and elder care.

Workplace speed-ups and rationalization have also affected employees at Naruse, where managers reported to me that in the past 20–30 years, the firm has streamlined its staffing and increased its expectations of what full employees must accomplish, in terms of workload and quality.[13] Still, the employees I interviewed seemed more relaxed and secure about their jobs in the firm and less worried than MNF workers that leave would deleteriously affect their status. One reason may be that Naruse rarely hires mid-career managers from other firms. Another reason may be the absence of a cultural clash of differing expectations from managers who come into the firm from abroad. Everyone is not only aware of CCL and CCT policies, but they have lived with them at this firm for well over a decade. While some managers and employees may not be happy with these policies, according to my informants, they rarely voice their discontent. Especially in the current political environment, with heavy media coverage on the low birthrate, ageing society, and the problems that these conditions will cause for Japan's future competitiveness, it is difficult for managers to openly oppose the legitimacy of CCL policies. Naruse has positioned itself as a leader in this area, after all.

Another reason for the somewhat more relaxed attitude of Naruse women might be the firm's long-term position towards women's careers, and the women's relative lack of expectation of promotion. As I mentioned above, MNF does promote and financially reward able female employees quickly even if they have few years of service, and employees themselves are concerned about their relative standing to each other. Many express a desire to move up the job ladder. Furthermore, only a very few MNF employees belong to the union. They expect to make their own career at MNF for as long as it is mutually satisfying, and when it no longer works, to move on (and possibly up) to another foreign-owned firm. My MNF interviewees sometimes mentioned the possibility of leaving the firm, and a few indeed left for better opportunities in other foreign-owned firms. This attitude towards employment is more individualistic, less company-based, and more fluid than that at the large Japanese firm where the expectation of 'lifetime employment' exists. Japanese employees at MNF recognized this as a 'more American' approach to work.

At MNF, although employees recognized that their tenure with the firm would be connected to their productivity on the job, most still felt secure enough to take the standard one-year of childcare leave allowed by law. That is, there was no established 'culture of layoff', as Fried (1998) had found at a major US financial services firm. MNF employees seemed less anxious than their US counterparts who take the absolute minimum childcare leave and get back to work as soon as possible.[14] On the other hand, the employees at MNF Japan were aware of US and UK business culture, either from their experiences as MBA students abroad, or through upper-level managers at MNF Japan. One could see this awareness reflected in the great caution with which they approached marriage announcements, birth timing, and preparation for leave-taking.

Many women at MNF went to great lengths in planning their births to minimize interruptions at work and to demonstrate their commitment to work. Several women told me that they worked long hours of overtime in the period before going on maternity leave, in preparation to transfer their work to others in their departments. Ms Sato exemplifies this practice: (born 1966, age 35) she had four years of service at MNF and held the position of vice-president. She previously worked at a Japanese financial services firm straight out of college, but quit in order to go abroad to study for an MBA. When she returned to Japan, she had an internship in one foreign financial service firm before taking her job at MNF. She married in 1996 to a fellow Japanese man whom she had met in business school. Their child was born in 1999. She remarked:

> I, kind of waited, um, for three years after I started with this company to get pregnant, 'cause I thought maybe getting pregnant during first or second year may not be the best idea, so . . . I kind of waited, so that I [would] have . . . kind of more acceptable circumstances . . . but unfortunately [laughs] my boss left, so, um, it's almost like working in a new environment.

Later in the interview, I learned that not only did Ms Sato time the baby's year of birth, but also the month. She wanted him to be born in the late autumn, so that he would have a good chance of getting a spot in a government-run nursery by the time she returned to work. In preparation to take maternity leave, Ms. Sato worked from 9 a.m. to midnight every weekday of the month before she went on leave. She decided to take only four weeks rather than the standard six weeks of maternity leave prior to the birth, because she wanted to get to know her new boss before she went on leave. She also decided not to take childcare leave, but to return to work after slightly more than twelve weeks because her boss was new. That is, they had had little time to get to know each other before she took maternity leave, and she felt she needed to demonstrate her value to him as quickly as possible. In order to do this, she had to pay a babysitter service about $3500 a month for three months before a space became available in a nursery. It was obvious that Ms Sato was very committed to her career, and tried to plan as best she could to keep from inconveniencing her boss, so that he would see her as a valuable employee rather than a burden.

In contrast, Naruse women only recently have been encouraged to think of their jobs in terms of careers, and even male employees do not expect to become managers until their late thirties or early forties. While Naruse has changed their salary scheme in recent years towards more emphasis on results, the company still seems to be much more based on the lifetime employment, seniority-based pay scheme. MNF, in contrast, has a shorter-term, individual achievement-based perspective.

We can also discern the relatively relaxed work environment of Naruse in its Childcare Time policy, wherein workers with children up to first-grade of elementary school are allowed to take two hours of time off per day, rather than the one hour that was standard (and the legal requirement) at MNF. While Naruse women felt awkward about leaving early when others remained on-the-job, they also felt frustrated that they couldn't accomplish the same amount of work as they had before having a child. Still, many women made full use of CCT. At MNF, employees sometimes experienced harassment from managers or fellow employees who were disgruntled at seeing them leave early. This sometimes caused them to quit. The tension surrounding Childcare Time at MNF may have arisen from the peculiar requirements of the financial industry, where government regulations require certain reports at the end of each workday, and overtime in some sections was extensive and at times unpaid. On the other hand, Naruse employees also reported the existence of forced overtime that exceeded the legal limits (and was unpaid). So, part of the relative ease that Naruse women experienced in using CCT might be attributed to 'protection of motherhood' notions that were more entrenched in the Japanese firm than in the US firm.[15] I must stress that 'relative ease' occurred in a context where Naruse employees taking CCT knew that some colleagues resented being left with the extra work. Women on CCL or CCT made great efforts to show their appreciation so that personal relationships would not collapse. The same personal adjustments held true for MNF women, and for the female factory workers I studied in the early 1980s. Women had rights to childcare time, but unless they took great care to show their appreciation for any inconvenience their colleagues might experience, they could not carry on successfully at the firm. Ms Sato of MNF, whom I mentioneded above, finally quit and moved to another foreign firm due to consistent verbal harassment from her American boss, who expected her to stay until 9 or 10 p.m. every night. In a follow-up interview at her new place of employment in 2001, she remarked, 'My prior [American] boss used to leave the office at 6 p.m. every day. The new boss was an evening person – he would come to work at 10 a.m. By the time he felt his engine revving, I had to leave.' Even 7.30 p.m. was not late enough for him. This boss lowered her bonus even though she achieved her goal, and he requested that she move to another department. Instead, she began job hunting and found a better position elsewhere, though she took a cut in pay.

In 2003, Naruse opened a brand-new, fully equipped daycare facility at the main office in Tokyo. The facility, with capacity of 21 children, takes in children as young as three months, and operates Monday through Friday between 8 a.m. and 7 p.m., with the possibility of extension to 8 p.m. This on-site centre is part of the firm's efforts to showcase their commitment to gender equality. While many women may choose to place their children with facilities close to their homes or with grandparents rather than to face commuting from the suburbs to central Tokyo with an infant, some women are making use of flextime to avoid the worst of the rush hour when they have their children in tow. MNF Japan had seriously considered building a daycare centre, but ultimately decided against it for security reasons (This was shortly after 9/11.) Instead, in 2003 they contracted for emergency childcare services and sick-child services with a private daycare and babysitting service in the Tokyo area. The corporation subsidizes the employees' expenses. It is reportedly extremely popular.

As I mentioned earlier, since the late 1990s Naruse actively promoted women within the firm, and has grouped its efforts towards this goal under the rubric, 'Positive Action'. Within this policy initiative, they include support systems for reconciling work with childcare and family care, programmes to develop and promote women and programmes to improve the corporate environment and prevent sexual harassment. As a result of their efforts, fewer women quit work because of pregnancy or childcare, and the average rate of women's years of service has risen to 14.4 within the Naruse group and 18.5 years within Naruse, Inc. Furthermore, 63 per cent of female employees now feel that the firm trains and promotes both women and men, and women managers have increased their share from 5.3 per cent in 2000 to 10.4 per cent in 2004 for the Naruse group. This now exceeds the national average of 9.8 per cent (ILO *Yearbook of Labour Statistics* 2002).[16] In June 2004, a Naruse manager met with me to discuss these recent initiatives. She noted that the group as it now stands is composed of 70 per cent women, and that 40 per cent of the male employees will retire over the next seven years. Hence, she saw some urgency in training and promoting women now to assume more managerial roles as these men retire. She said that the Corporate Social Responsibility department had floated a proposal to make the goal of raising the share of female managers to 30 per cent by the end of 2004, and the company had said they would consider it. The executive board rejected the proposal. She was very disappointed, noting that they would not listen to her arguments that this is a global world and they should take the international scene as an example for gender equality. She did not elaborate further on her meaning, but my understanding is that she was trying to convince the board to raise women's share in management by appealing to the government's new target of 30 per cent for women's share in leadership positions in society by 2020 (Meguro 2004). She noted ruefully, 'Men don't want to have female bosses.'

In sum, in terms of policy transfer, MNF Japan was influenced by the organizational culture of its home office, combined with a results-oriented individual achievement ethos, and the US style of gender equality in corporations. Work/life balance and managing with flexibility were the themes of their efforts to support employees with time constraints, in particular, valuable female employees. In contrast, Naruse, playing catch-up, followed and enhanced upon Japanese government initiatives on gender equality, and 'family-friendliness'. These had been originally inspired by the international scene, Japanese feminists, and the low birth-rate and ageing society.

While MNF had a higher percentage of women in management, they did have a head-start of a decade. Perhaps Naruse will catch up before too long. Naruse's context as a large Japanese firm that still maintained many vestiges of the 'lifetime employment' package, in some ways fostered women's retention. Enhancing this is the fact that Naruse's business climate, while facing challenges and becoming more fast-paced, was not changing as rapidly as MNF's. One had the sense that the employees at Naruse had more leeway in their daily lives. In both firms, the creation of a normative environment favouring work/life balance is an ongoing, and challenging, project. Furthermore, through the accounts of my informants we can see that implementation of policy is not merely a matter of taking up contractual benefits. Employees invest a great deal of time and sometimes expense in preparations, in anticipation of the trouble they fear they will cause their co-workers and bosses. Even when the policy is in place and has a track record of use, employees worry about the affect their absence will have on their reputations as talented and diligent workers. Japanese culture is characterized by specific reciprocity. While Childcare Leave could be conceived of as a right granted to all workers by the government, in practice it is taken up by specific individuals who are situated within specific, ongoing gendered relationships in the workplace. Individuals who make use of flexibility hence feel they must do whatever they can to minimize the damage inevitably caused by their temporary absences. Sometimes even heroic efforts, as in Ms Sato's case, fail.

While there is much that firms can do to further gender equality and enhance the uptake of flexible work arrangements, some things are beyond their purview to change. Among these are social norms relating to the gendered division of labour. Are Japanese men willing to take on childcare and homemaking responsibilities in tandem with their partners? Although I cannot explore this issue thoroughly in this chapter, suffice it to say that many of the men I studied, while desiring to spend more time in caring for their children, were up against stiff, unwritten cultural norms about men's commitment to the workplace. Indeed, although it is now being called into question, a man's commitment to work has long been seen in Japan as his commitment to his family. While I heard from one man at Naruse who left work twice a week without doing overtime so that his spouse could do overtime while he picked up the baby from daycare, this man did not dare to take Childcare Leave. He felt he was pushing the limits of his team's understanding as it was. In fact, not a single man at either firm I studied had taken Childcare Leave. Nationally, men's uptake of CCL is low; well under 1 per cent of eligible men in 2002 (Sato and Takeishi, 2004: 15).

My impression from talking with male employees is that they are more interactive with their children and less authoritarian than their own fathers were, and they do quite a lot with their children, as well as performing household chores, on the weekends. This is confirmed by what I see out on the streets: one can now see fathers hanging out with their children in the parks without Mum, or taking them to the daycare centre in the morning, or shopping at the market with toddler in tow. It is also confirmed in the qualitative research of other researchers (see, for example, Ishii-Kunz 2003), and in the appearance of nappy-changing facilities in men's restrooms. Twenty years ago, such 'salarymen' would have been a rare sight in urban areas. Perhaps the man with a full-time career partner is pulling more of the load, and perhaps the companionate father will become more common than the authoritarian father, but I cannot predict it from this research.

Conclusion

In conclusion, work/life balance policies enable women to marry, have children, and stay on the job, even in very challenging circumstances where long commutes, expectations of overtime, and the demands of daycare and school district cut short their hours of sleep. These policies don't guarantee *balance*, since husbands usually do not have equal flexibility, so the burden of household care falls disproportionately on the wives. Even with these policies, if life intervenes with additional problems such as children's chronic illnesses, psychological, or other problems, or eldercare issues that take longer than three months to solve, women sometimes quit. But such policies offer women a way to stay working as regular employees, and that makes a tremendous difference in the household economy as well as in women's sense of identity as professionals.

The strategies women in both firms employed to balance their work with their family lives were similar. Men's opinions on childcare leave-taking and childrearing also seemed similar in the two firms. My impression is that MNF men had even more difficulty than Naruse men to make use of flextime for routine family matters such as childcare, although in family emergencies men felt free to take time off.

We could look at the example of policy transfer from four perspectives: the governmental policies, the firm, the household and the individual. At the governmental level, since 1986, many laws have been put in place to enhance gender equality at work as well as to foster 'family-friendly' work environments. This legislation was created first as a response to outside international pressure, but later in response to domestic demographic trends. On paper, the chances for Japanese families to enjoy the rewards of dual careers while rearing children look good. At the nationwide firm level, however, we see that implementation lagged, and many firms still fail to implement the governmental guidelines. Cultural norms of appropriate behaviour for men and women also affect the uptake of 'family-friendly' policies at the firm level, despite gender neutrality in policy itself. These cultural norms form the moral universe governing which gender should be given the leeway to take time off for care-giving activities, and determine how much commitment to work an employee should demonstrate. At the household level, workers make elaborate arrangements with co-workers, daycare institutions as well as extended kin in order to manage their responsibilities. Individuals go out of their way to minimize the damage they might create by causing inconvenience to fellow employees. In some households, women and men are forging new patterns of shared care-work and chores within the family, while in others, women are taking on both corporate and family duties without the assistance of spouses. Although many families manage to achieve some kind of balance, a closer look sometimes reveals the compromises individuals have had to make in arriving at this balance and the tensions that are created in the process. Some of these tensions may eventually lessen if the dual career lifestyle becomes normalized, if service overtime and solo-transfers are kept at the minimum, and if more extensive social support systems are created to assist families.

As I have noted, there were distinct differences between the two firms arising from the corporate cultural backgrounds, with MNF ready at an earlier stage to give women more opportunities for advancement, and Naruse lagging in this regard but more relaxed in terms of giving women time to rear their children. With provisions for paid CCL and a high quality of public daycare, Japanese employees could end up having better conditions for rearing children than employees in the US, especially if firms demand less service overtime. The question remains as to how successful the government will be in encouraging all firms to provide 'family-friendly' work environments and gender-equal opportunities. The current demographic trends will likely bring on a labour shortage in the future. Then firms may be impelled to respond more positively to these policy stances in order to attract and retain workers. Certainly the government will not cease to promote these directives as long as the birth-rate remains low. Some say the way out is migration, but Japan is unlikely to become a nation of large-scale migration in the near future.

Notes

1. I would like to thank Heidi Gottfried and James Nickum for their helpful comments on earlier drafts of this chapter.
2. I carried out the MNF research between 1999 and 2002, interviewing more than 79 people in various job positions in Tokyo and Osaka. MNF had a total of 1542 employees in Japan in 2001, and thousands of employees worldwide. I carried out the Naruse research between January 2003 and June 2004. I interviewed 25 people in the greater Tokyo metropolitan area, who work at the Research Centre, the Main Office, and Marketing/Business Operations, Naruse's workforce in Japan. In 2003, there were over 3500 regular employees in Naruse, Inc. Naruse Group encompassed 25 000 employees in 2001.
3. Itoh (1994: 247) offers two factors dampening mid-career movement among Japanese firms' employees. One is the 'loss of firm-specific human capital in which the worker has invested'. The other, which is the flipside of the coin, is 'to discourage mid-career separation (as well as to provide incentives), firms pay

workers compensation less than the value of their marginal product when they are young, and greater than their marginal product when they are old.'

4. For a discussion of the discourse surrounding the low birth-rate, see Roberts 2002.

5. For an in-depth, inside view of the policy-making process for the gender policy-making environment in the past decade, see Osawa 2000a; for more on the Angel Plans see Roberts 2002: esp. 57–75, 84–6.

6. In 1996, firms of 1–4 employees comprised 61.8 per cent, and those of under 30 employees comprised 33.0 per cent of all firms. 51.8 per cent of workers are employed in these small firms. An additional 4.2 per cent of firms had between 30 and 99 employees, and 0.8 of firms had 100–299 employees. Firms of 300 employees or more made up only 0.2 per cent of the total, employing 13.2 per cent of all workers. See Japan Institute of Labour 2000: 30.

7. Relations between large 'parent' firms and the multitude of small 'child' sub-contracting firms in the same industrial group tended to be hierarchical and interdependent, although this relationship has been changing towards more independence for the small firms since the 1980s as large firms increasingly seek lower costs overseas. Basically, small firms act as buffers for their parent clients. They change production at the larger firms' direction, and they bear the brunt of economic downturns. Hence, 'lifetime employment' cannot be guaranteed in these firms, and they are generally not unionized. For details, see Whittaker 1994.

8. The law stipulates 30 minutes each to be the minimum time off. Labour unions of some firms often negotiated increases in Childcare Time; at the manufacturing firm where I worked in the early 1980s, women generally took one hour per day at the end of the day, until the child was three years of age. Some firms allowed longer CCT hours. According to the Labour Standards Law, only women may take this leave. One website explaining these provisions notes, 'We can interpret this to mean that CCT is not only for childcare but also to protect the maternal body' (*botai*): http://tamagoya.ne.jp/roudou/094.htm.

9. Schoppa (2006) argues that young women who exit fail to lobby for improvements in the system and therefore act as impediments to progress.

10. This statistic is taken from the National Census, 2000, published by the Cabinet Office Statistics Bureau. It appears on page seven of the [Shinshin Enzeru Puran (kashou) Sakutei ni Mukete no Iken Koukan Kai] no Kaisai ni Tsuite (On convening the forum for the drafting of the 'New New Angel Plan' (tentative name): http://www.mhlw.go.jp/topics/bukyoku/seisaku/syousika/event/041026/1.html.

11. MNF had already been promoting women in its US offices for some years.

12. For more in-depth treatment of MNF's implementation of and rationales for work/life balance policies, see Roberts 2003.

13. According to Suzuki Fujitaku (2005: 89), currently Japanese firms are experiencing a corporate reorganization that is qualitatively different from other such changes in the corporate structures up to now. He labels the current period 'an unprecedented period' characterized by external challenges as international competition intensifies and the domestic market contracts amidst prolonged economic stagnation.

14. Fried notes that in the early 1990s, non-professional female staff took up to three months' childcare leave, while professionals took an average of five and a half months. By 1997, however, the professional staff had shortened their average leave time to an average of ten weeks, while non-professionals took an average of eight weeks (1998: 41). Fried notes that many employees at the firm she studied were haunted by past layoffs, fearing that a perception that they were not fully

committed to their jobs would work against them, if and when layoffs happened again (1998: 184–5).

15. According to Vera Mackie (2003: 181), one can distinguish between two types of protections under the 'protection of motherhood' rubric in Japan. First are 'maternity provisions' such as maternity leave and nursing leave policies, which are directed at the biological mother who is pregnant or in the parturitial period. The other category consists of 'protective provisions' such as those preventing women from working late at night, from working overtime, or from working in dangerous industries. The latter, inasmuch as they focus on all women and not only on mothers, address women's potentiality to become mothers.

Since the 1960s in the US, arguments towards equality in employment for women have been based on the similarity of women and men; equality with difference was not acknowledged. Hence, the notion that female employees have a legitimate right to utilize protective measures, especially those relating to maternity, is likely to be stronger in Japanese firms than in US firms.

16. The figure for Naruse, Inc. was 8.9 per cent in 2004.

Part III
Gendering New Employment
Forms

6
Self-Employment in Comparative Perspective: General Trends and the Case of New Media

Karin Gottschall and Daniela Kroos

Introduction

Self-employment is an increasingly prominent development within the context of the new economy and a feature of national labour markets. During the 1980s and 1990s most OECD countries saw a notable rise in self-employment outside of agriculture[1] both in absolute terms as well as a proportion of total employment (amounting to 6.7 per cent on average for the years 1995–9). This development can be considered as new in so far as it reverses the long-standing decline of traditional forms of self-employment associated with agriculture and small craft businesses and seems to re-establish a somehow 'pre-industrial' employment pattern in expanding modern service industries. Indeed, self-employment in the cultural industry and other growing sectors of the new economy seems to gain in importance when compared to the industrial sector (cf. among others European Commission 2001b; Serrano-Pascual and Mósesdóttir 2003). Another feature of new self-employment in some countries is the rapidly expanding incidence of solo self-employment or freelancing.[2] Both in the UK and the US self-employed workers without employees have traditionally predominated. In Germany it was the growth of this employment form, which led to the spike in overall self-employment (cf. Kim and Kurz 2001; OECD 2000a). But the incidence of solo self-employment fuels debate over the significance and meaning of the trend.

An optimistic version views the rise in solo self-employment as reflecting a change in work attitudes within the labour force, i.e. a trend towards a new spirit of entrepreneurialism and more autonomous concepts of work. This is claimed to have the potential to create new jobs and to increase the share of highly qualified forms of work. Furthermore, new self-employment seems to enable the development of more flexible arrangements between life and work (cf. Leicht 2000). Representatives of the pessimistic version, however, claim that higher self-employment rates should not be considered as a harbinger of job-growth, but rather as a result from the push effects of unemployment and rationalization processes. They predict a down-grading of job quality and the expansion of social risks as well as inequalities relative to workers in standard employment relationships, due to the low level of protection for the self-employed in labour law and social security schemes. According to this view, a substantial proportion of self-employment does not enjoy the advantages of free entrepreneurship, but rather can be understood as *labour-only contracting* or *false self-employment* (cf. Smeaton 2003; Gill 2002; Breen 1997; Meager and Bates 2001, 2002).

The impact of self-employment on gender relations is also the subject of controversy. Undoubtedly, women make up a rising share (about a quarter to one-third) of the self-employed, particularly in the category of solo self-employed in the service sector. On the one hand, this might indicate that gender barriers in this traditionally male form of work have been overcome. Moreover, there is evidence that women prefer self-employment due to career problems experienced in corporate hierarchies (the glass-ceiling effect) as well as difficulties combining work and family in dependent employment (Granger et al. 1995). On the other hand, self-employment obviously is not free of gender-specific segregation concerning industrial sectors, occupational positions, working hours, income and motivation (cf. Hughes 2003; McManus 2001a; Burchell et al. 1993). This raises two questions: To what extent does self-employment increase the market integration of women? Does the related tendency towards dual-earner households contribute to more gender-equal patterns of work and life?

The debate outlined above is based on highly generalized ideas of solo self-employment. The influence of globalization processes on national labour market developments, and the more or less pronounced growth of the service sector in all Western industrialized countries seem to justify such a general discussion. However, comparative studies on welfare capitalism as well as life course research rather suggest that even under conditions of globalization and individualization, employment and career patterns might be affected by regime differences (cf. Rieger and Leibfried 2003; Heinz and Marshall 2003). Especially the Variety of Capitalism (VoC) approach implies that wage determination and skill formation vary substantially across economies: while production regimes in liberal market economies are characterized by low wage regulation and a high importance of general education and professional schooling, coordinated economies like Germany dispose of collective bargaining and more firm-based vocational training schemes (Hall and Soskice 2001). The approach refers predominantly to the regulation of wage labour. Nevertheless, it might serve as a reference for the investigation of self-employment since we can assume that the institutional infrastructures, relevant actors and standards of employment set up by the respective regimes define the framework in which these new patterns of employment evolve. Moreover, the integration of feminist scholarship and the comparative welfare state debate provide a fruitful enlargement to overcome the shortcomings of the VoC approach in explaining gender differences in labour market integration (McCall and Orloff 2005).[3]

In this chapter, we take a closer look at the development of solo self-employment, labour market regulation and risk management[4] in Germany, the UK, the US and Japan. This allows for the comparison between two liberal market economies, the UK and the US, and two coordinated market economies, Germany and Japan. Whereas Germany, the UK and the US are examples of early industrialized economies, where traditional forms of dependent employment are in decline and new forms of self-employment gain in importance, the Japanese economy is marked by late industrialization and ongoing significance of traditional forms of self-employment. These factors constitute Japan as an interesting contrasting case. Furthermore, we focus on the cultural industries as an emblematic part of the new economy with high shares of self-employment. Drawing on an institution–actor approach we expect the degree of regulation of a national labour market and life course regime to affect the dynamics and qualitative features of solo self-employment. Additionally attention will be given to the question of whether and to what extent solo self-employment enhances gender equality and is accompanied by a transition from a male breadwinner model to a dual-earner concept.

In the next section, we describe the development of solo self-employment in all four countries using macro-level data. This includes a closer look at self-employment in the cultural sector, relating the dynamics of this sector to overall trends in self-employment. The third section brings the cultural industries of Germany, the UK and the US into particular view, focusing on the interaction of institutional regulation and agency in this field. Based on qualitative case studies and results from our own empirical research, individual and collective 'risk-management strategies' and their gender impact are highlighted.[5] Concluding remarks will try to reassess the different perspectives in order to understand the global character and regulatory challenges of self-employment as a new pattern of work.

Volume, structure and social risks of solo self-employment

Volume and structure

As already indicated above, a general expansion of self-employment in Western countries can be observed. Within Europe, Germany and the UK represent the countries with the most pronounced rise of self-employment over the last two decades (see Table 6.1). Indeed, the UK's self-employment rate increased from 6.6 per cent in 1979 to 12.4 per cent in 1990 and stabilized, after some fluctuations, at 11.4 per cent in 1998. Similarly, in Germany the number of self-employed workers inched upwards since the mid-1980s, even if initially at a much slower pace. Between 1990 and 1998, the German self-employment rate grew from 7.7 per cent to 9.4 per cent

Table 6.1:   Self-employment (SE) shares (outside agriculture, %)

	Germany	UK	US	Japan
Self-employment rate (in total employment)				
1979	8.2	6.6	7.1	14.0
1990	7.7	12.4	7.5	11.5
1998	9.4	11.4	7.0	9.7
Share of female self-employment (of total SE)				
1990–1997	28.3	24.8	37.0	33.9
Share of solo self-employment (of total SE)				
1990	40.2	68.9	–[1]	78.0
1997	47.0	74.2	78.9	74.4

1: no data available.
Source: OECD 2000a.

and is still increasing (OECD 2000a: 158). In the course of this development the role of women in self-employment has become more and more important; they make up at least a quarter of all self-employed in both countries (cf. Leicht and Lauxen-Ulbrich 2003; Weir 2003; OECD 2000a). Women are at the forefront of the increase in solo self-employment, to which the main part of self-employment growth in both Germany and the UK has to be attributed.

In the UK, 74.2 per cent of the self-employed had no employees in 1997, compared to 47.0 per cent in Germany, where this form of self-employment was less typical until the 1990s (OECD 2000a: 162). In contrast to these noticeable growth rates, self-employment in the US has changed little since the 1970s and stabilized at about 7 per cent by 1998 (OECD 2000a: 158; Luber and Gangl 1997).[6] Nonetheless, at a percentage of 78.9 per cent in 1997 (OECD 2000a: 162) the share of solo self-employed workers among all self-employed is even higher in the US than in Germany and the UK. Similarly, at 37.0 per cent the female share of self-employment is highest in the US as compared to the UK and Germany.

In contrast to these developments in Germany, the UK and the US, Japanese self-employment can be considered as a residual of late industrialization and is tied to the old economy rather than to new service sector jobs. Indeed, the share of the self-employed in the Japanese labour market has been continually decreasing for several decades now. In fact, it fell from a relative high level of 14.0 per cent in the 1970s to 9.7 per cent in 1998 (OECD 2000a: 158).[7] Additionally, the share of solo self-employed workers has declined. Japanese self-employment is also less marked by high accumulation of human capital or concentration in metropolitan areas (Ministry of Health, Labour and Welfare [Japan] 2003; Genda and Kambayashi 2002). Correspondingly, outside of the agricultural sector self-employment is mainly rooted in construction, manufacturing, retail and eating, and services (Japanese Labour Force Survey 2002; Dore 2000).

We found another sharp contrast between Japan and the other three countries in the declining rate of female self-employment. Whereas the conditions for female employment improved in the public sector, they did not change very much in private businesses, where they are still more closely tied to the concept of the male breadwinner. In the private sector, Japanese women are more likely to occupy positions in the form of family work than in the other forms of self-employment. Generally, women encounter a hostile environment to self-employment in Japan (Genda and Kambayashi 2002).

Despite the more pronounced similarities in self-employment volume and female participation in Germany, the UK and the US, we find substantial differences in the composition of solo self-employment in these countries. In the UK, shares of self-employed workers near parity between the industrial and the service sectors, even though the latter show much higher growth rates since the beginning of the 1990s. Key sectors of self-employment include: construction, real estate, financial and business services and personal services. British self-employment growth is only partly due to service sector growth, and must be understood as an element of diversification of employment forms in a flexible labour market. In Germany, however, the growth of the service sector is the main factor contributing to the rise in self-employment over the last decade. Business services, personal/social services and professional services in the fields of education, health, culture and entertainment have seen the most important influx of self-employed (cf. Bögenhold and Fachinger 2004; Weir 2003; Leicht and Luber 2000; Robinson 1999). These sectors have attracted newly self-employed women, many of whom have moved to previously male-dominated sectors. All in all, the service sector has been the driving force of German self-employment growth. This affects the qualification structure of self-employment: highly skilled self-employment in highly qualified sectors accounts for a larger share of overall self-employment in Germany than in the UK (cf. Luber 2003; Kim and Kurz 2001; Leicht 2000). Again, German self-employed women contribute to this development in an outstanding way, as the share of young university graduates among the female self-employed is very high (cf. Leicht and Lauxen-Ulbrich 2003). In contrast to the German experience, self-employed women in the US tend to be less educated than self-employed men. Generally, as in the UK, both the industrial sector and the service sector host a range of occupations showing substantial shares of self-employment (McManus 2000). However, according to McManus, it is female self-employment that has the most impact on the growth of low-end self-employment in the US. She links this to the commodification of household labour (childcare workers, housekeepers, janitors, etc.) in the self-employment sector, making up two-fifths of self-employed service workers. At the same time, female self-employed workers in the US also gained more access to high-end labour market positions than female employees. In combination with the predominant dual-earner model the liberal American market economy led to high levels of polarization in the self-employed workforce (McManus 2001b; Cohany 1998; Devine 1994) (Table 6.2).

Table 6.2:   Trends in the sectoral distribution of self-employment (outside agriculture)

	Germany[1]	UK[2]	US[3]	Japan[4]
Predominant economic sector of self-employment	New economy and service sector is predominant (influx of the 1990s mainly into services)	Shares are about similar in the old and the new economy as well as in the industrial sector (influx in the 1980s) and the service-sector (influx in the 1990s)	Both the industrial sector/the old economy and the service sector/the new economy	Old economy, industrial sector
Industries with high shares of self-employment	Retail, hotel and eating, business services, personal/ social services, professional services	Construction, real estate, financial and business services, personal services	Construction, real estate and insurances, retail, personal/social services	Construction, manufacturing, retail and eating, services
Level of qualifications in self-employment	Highly qualified occupations play a crucial role	Both highly qualified and less qualified occupations	Both highly qualified and less qualified occupations	Highly qualified occupations play a marginal role

Sources:
1: Bögenhold and Fachinger 2004; Kim and Kurz 2001; Leicht 2000; Leicht and Luber 2000.
2: Weir 2003; Kim and Kurz 2001; Leicht and Luber 2000; Robinson 1999.
3: McManus 2001b; McManus 2000; Cohany 1998.
4: Japanese LFS 2002; Dore 2000.

Working hours

Flexible working hours are another characteristic of self-employment with highly gender-specific working patterns. In contrast to the small minority of British self-employed men who work on a part-time basis, almost half of the self-employed women work part-time. British self-employed men work longer hours than dependent employees, whereas female working time patterns in self-employment seem to be closer to those of employed women.[8] These data refer to self-employment in general, but they suggest that a very large share of solo self-employed women work on a part-time basis, whereas solo self-employed men tend to work long hours (Lohmann 2001: 10). In Germany, working hours of self-employed men and women are similar, though both sexes work longer hours than in the UK and thereby correspond to a larger extent to the image of the independent entrepreneur. However, part-time shares of the solo self-employed are high. Again, part-time work is more significant for women, whereas male self-employment more often implies very long working hours (Leicht and Lauxen-Ulbrich 2003: 22). Unlike these working time patterns, the self-employed in Japan tend to work slightly less than dependent employees, but again women are more likely to work on a part-time basis (Japanese Labour Force Survey 2002). Generally speaking, these findings suggest that in terms of working time the self-employed in the UK and the US fit the image of the free entrepreneur less than in Germany. In all four countries however, and especially in the UK and the US, working time patterns of the self-employed are highly gendered, revealing higher shares of part-time self-employment among women than men.

Income and social security

Similar to their working time patterns, income of the self-employed seems to vary considerably due to fluctuating work intensity and their dependence on the cyclical demand for services. The income distribution of the self-employed displays high levels of polarization since the 1990s (and new data suggest that this trend holds on in the 2000s, Weir 2003). In Germany, the UK and the US the self-employed are strongly represented in both the lower and the upper end of the income distribution. Despite this similarity, two issues with regard to the income distribution of the solo self-employed stand out: first, the polarization of incomes tends to be stronger in the US and the UK than it is in Germany; second, this polarization turns out to be more pronounced for women than for men, even if the calculation is based on hourly wages (taking account of women's high share in part-time work). However, generally women, young workers, part-time workers and service sector workers face a high probability of low incomes. These groups of workers particularly characterized the influx in both British and German self-employment during the 1990s. We assume that, given the commonality of low and unsustainable incomes, the household context could be of special importance here. A large share of jobs in solo self-employment is no longer linked to the concept of male breadwinner income. So it is not surprising that income heterogeneity among the solo self-employed is even stronger than among the self-employed in general, and that they are more often subject to the risk of precarious income streams (cf. Leicht and Lauxen-Ulbrich 2003; Meager and Bates 2001; McManus 2001a, 2001b; Knight and McKay 2000; Jungbauer-Gans 1999; Devine 1994).

Japanese self-employed workers find themselves in precarious income conditions. A first look at the annual income distribution of the Japanese self-employed though indicates much less polarization than in the other three countries. Apart from a group of about 10 per cent of all self-employed in the second-lowest income group, which is probably related to part-time work, the self-employed are quite evenly spread over the different income categories. However, in general the self-employed tend to earn less than employees and occupy the middle- and high-income groups to less extent (Ministry of Health, Labour and Welfare [Japan] 2003). According to Genda and Kambayashi (2002) the decrease in self-employment income is a new development and is partly due to rising competition between small and large firms, which followed de-regulation measures in the 1990s. They suggest that this negative income trend motivates in part the shift away from self-employment in Japan.

The insecure income conditions of many of the solo self-employed can be intensified by a lack of social security provision. Whereas the British National Health Service provides health care services for all inhabitants and the majority of German self-employed pay either obligatory or voluntary contributions to a health insurance (cf. Fachinger 2002), the inability of the solo self-employed to provide for times of low work intensity or for old age is alarming. Although the British self-employed are integrated into the National Insurance and are entitled to a modest basic old age pension, Meager and Bates (2001) fear that the growth of new self-employment since the 1980s may lead to a growing number of self-employed workers who have to face insecurity and relative poverty in later life. This is due to the exclusion of the self-employed from the supplementary State Earnings Related Pension Scheme and to the low and unstable income in the labour market sector preventing the self-employed from saving. In Germany and Japan the situation is no better, since in both countries social security entitlements are linked to a large extent to dependent employment.

Although in Japan basic social security provisions, i.e. National Health Care and the National Pension Scheme, were made available to the self-employed in 1961, they are marked by such low benefit levels that additional private insurance or saving is crucial (Osawa 2001). Unlike employees, the self-employed cannot compensate for this lack of coverage through occupational benefits, and like most Japanese working households they can no longer count on an extended family to take care of basic needs. In

Germany the great majority of the self-employed are not integrated into the public Pension Insurance designed for dependent workers. Only the self-employed in the cultural professions have access to a special branch of the public Pension Insurance that was introduced in the 1980s. However, due to low and unstable income and to low benefits, additional private saving is necessary. All in all, at least one-third of the self-employed in Germany do not have the income necessary to make sufficient old-age provisions (Betzelt and Fachinger 2004). In the US the risk of being in poverty in later life seems to be even more pronounced (McManus 2001b) Additionally, due to their exclusion from occupational health and pension schemes and the lack of respective government schemes, self-employed workers in the US are less likely to have health insurance or pension insurance coverage than dependent workers (Ferber and Waldfogel 1998; Devine 1994).

Self-employment in the cultural sector

As we have seen in the previous paragraphs, the volume, structure and working conditions of overall self-employment – regardless of country-specific differences – do not necessarily fit the image of growing entrepreneurial success and new concepts of work. Does this picture change if we look at the dynamics of self-employment in the cultural sector[9] as the leading industry of the so-called new economy in the UK, US and Germany?

First, referring to growth dynamics we find that the proportion of self-employed workers amounted to 34 per cent (1999) in the UK (Walby 2001: 14) and 24 per cent (1997) in Germany (Rehberg et al. 2002: 81). In Europe, highly qualified workers account for 26.7 per cent of all workers in this sector, compared to 22.4 per cent of workers in non-cultural sectors (European Commission 2001b: 89).[10] For the US, we cannot present detailed figures, but studies indicate a pronounced increase in numbers of both highly qualified and low qualified self-employed (McManus 2001b).

This global growth trend is matched by some common features regarding working conditions. Thus, contrary to overall self-employment *working hours* are less gendered in the cultural sector. Despite heterogeneous working time patterns and in spite of childcare responsibilities more often curtailing women's hours (cf. Perrons 2003), long working hours of 45 to 60 hours per week are normal to earn one's living as a self-employed worker (Rehberg et al. 2002). Periods of hard work, sometimes on multiple jobs simultaneously, and long hours, including night and weekend shifts, alternate with slack periods when only a small job or none is at hand. Greater time autonomy and sovereignty claimed for self-employment with respect to working hours often becomes merely theoretical. Only a small, well-established elite of highly specialized professionals seems to really enjoy this privilege today. Additionally, Batt et al. (2001) found in their study on new media workers in New York City that they spend only about half of their working time on direct production, whereas the remainder is spent on search for new work, administrative tasks and unpaid vocational training. This underlines the effort that is necessary to maintain steady employment and future employability due to insecure working arrangements.

While long working hours are a uniform characteristic of freelance cultural work income structures seem to be polarized and gendered. Available studies indicate a polarization between low *earnings* particularly among freelancers in some branches and peak incomes for a privileged 'professional elite' (cf. Rehberg et al. 2002; Satzer 2001; Grass 1998: 74). Recent empirical studies in Germany and the European Union suggest that women in the media industry are working under even more unfavourable conditions than their male colleagues (cf. Gill 2002; Rehberg et al. 2002; Satzer 2001). For female self-employed cultural workers, the German data show lower incomes in spite of their average higher formal education levels, and hence they have to work longer hours to earn the same income as men. In a comparative study on new media workers in various European countries Rosalind Gill and her team (2002) found that women in comparison to men work on fewer jobs simultaneously and less lucrative jobs, resulting in such low incomes that they are pushed into other occupations to earn their living. Gill's study on this 'most modernized' group of media workers showed gender income disparities of 40 per cent.

Generally, even though the incomes of the solo self-employed in particular branches are quite high, this has to be valued against the exclusion from occupational benefits and state social security schemes reserved for dependent employees. In the US, for instance, new media workers tend to earn higher salaries if they are independent contractors than if they are dependent employees. However, this income advantage has to be reassessed in light of their exclusion from benefits such as paid vacation, paid sick leave, health insurance and pension schemes (Batt et al. 2001).

Overall, solo self-employment in the cultural industries of Germany, the UK and the US sector exhibits both the positive and the negative features of new self-employment. Regarding gender, the picture is not clear-cut either: while the income distribution of the self-employed in the cultural industries is as highly gendered as in overall self-employment, working time patterns are less gendered.

First results: understanding comparative macro-trends in solo self-employment

Summarizing, the overall growth of self-employment in Germany, the UK and the US reveals both similarities and differences in the structure and conditions of solo self-employment. In liberal market economies, as in the US and the UK, the growth of solo self-employment does not reflect an increase in non-standard work but rather indicates a diversification of weakly regulated standard work. In fact the exact employment status plays a minor role in these labour markets: there is no clear-cut distinction between workers in insecure dependent employment relationships and solo self-employed workers clawing for jobs. This absence of regulations or weak regulations for dependent employment in the US probably accounts for the stagnating US self-employment rate. Whereas weak employment regulation might therefore repress self-employment growth, a low degree of regulation of industrial branches and low access conditions to particular occupations rather push self-employment development. As the example of the British construction industry shows, weak regulation can open up self-employment to a large share of the workforce in all economic sectors and increase its appeal to employers. Yet the diversification of standard work implies a deterioration of working conditions and social risks in both the US and the UK not least since the production regime in both countries goes hand in hand with a liberal welfare regime (Estévez-Abe 2005). Indeed, the solo self-employed in both countries seem to display a larger variety of working arrangements as well as being more heavily exposed to market risks than dependent employees. Therefore, we find strong polarization among different groups of the self-employed regarding occupations and incomes as well as high levels of social risks. Whereas social risks affect a large part of the workforce in liberal market economies (McManus 2000), we find that gender segregation is higher in the sector of self-employment than in dependent employment, and women make up a disproportionate share of low-end solo self-employment. At the end of this chapter we will come back to this coincidence of high wage polarization and high gender inequality which cannot easily be explained by the Varieties of Capitalism approach.

While the wage polarization trends in solo self-employment in the UK and the US are in line with the governing principles of liberal economies, self-employment dynamics in Germany do not follow the blueprint of coordinated market regulation. They can rather be understood as a tendency towards increased flexibility within a coordinated market economy. On the one hand, the highly regulated standard employment relationship still predominates in large parts of the labour market. On the other hand, the German labour market currently displays new dynamic features and is marked by de-regulation tendencies both from within the economy and politics. In the policy field we can observe new active labour market policies and new paradigms regarding the provision of social security which seem to imply an individualization of labour. These developments also impact the characteristics of self-employment, since a subsidized form of solo self-employment was introduced in 2003, the so-called 'Ich-AG' ('Self-Corporation'). First evaluations of the new tool indicate that while growing in absolute terms, 'Ich-AGs' seem to be linked to the most precarious forms of solo self-employment and imply high risks of business closure (Bach et al. 2004). Figures of these subsidized forms of self-employment are expanding heavily (Schulze Buschoff 2005) and the fact that this employment form is on the political agenda indicates that public understanding of employment and work is no longer exclusively tied to the notion of dependent employment and the standard employment relationship including a high level of social security provided by a breadwinner income.

At the same time, market driven self-employment is very much shaped by its gains in the low-regulated, highly qualified new services during the 1990s. In comparison to 'classical' employment relationships in Germany, solo self-employment has indeed established a new form of non-standard work on the German labour market, being linked to ambiguous working conditions and poorer social security. However, income polarization among the solo self-employed is slightly weaker in Germany than in the UK and the US and might still reflect the generally more compressed labour market hierarchy. Moreover, the social risks faced by German self-employed workers are mainly linked to the inability to save enough to cushion poverty risks in old age, deriving from the fact that they are excluded from the general social security scheme (cf. Gottschall 2002). Thus compared to dependent workers they profit less from the benefits of the conservative welfare regime. Regarding gender, we observe the reverse gender dynamics found in British and US self-employment. Gender differences in solo self-employment are less strong in Germany, as female solo self-employment in Germany is based to a larger extent on service sector occupations requiring high qualifications. Though the German labour market in general is strongly gender-segregated and is still marked by a male breadwinner model, this seems to be less the case in self-employment than in dependent employment.

Regardless of differences self-employment dynamics in the three Western countries can be linked to the expansion of service industries in highly industrialized economies. The case of Japan, however, is different. Due to belated industrialization, self-employment rates are still decreasing and Japanese self-employed do not necessarily conform to the image of mobile 'portfolio' workers in the new economy. One reason for declining self-employment in Japan can be found in the deteriorating conditions for female self-employment.[11] On the one hand, female employment is growing in the strongly segregated sector of dependent employment and is to a still high extent found in family businesses. On the other hand, the Japanese labour market regulation and social security regime still support a strong male breadwinner model and create incentives for women to work part-time rather than full-time (Osawa 2001, 2003; Gottfried and O'Reilly 2002; Shire and Imai 2000). Last but not least, the worsening economic conditions of self-employment led to a decline in the returns of self-employment, i.e. the self-employed have to cope with lower incomes and more modest social protection than employees (Genda and Kambayashi 2002).

Risk management in cultural industries: globalized and degendered?

The previous paragraphs tried to take stock of the growth dynamics and work characteristics of self-employment on the macro-level highlighting that even in branches with a highly qualified workforce like the cultural industries working conditions entail social risks and are to some extent gender-biased. We will now turn to the meso- and micro-level and apply an institution–actor approach in order to identify the social practices which constitute the specific profile of self-employment. Drawing on the insights of comparative studies on the modern life course special emphasis will be given to labour market and life course regulation. Here we will argue that weak market regulation contributes to a flexibilization of the so-called standard biography with an ambivalent impact on gender relations in the labour market and private lives.

A closer look at labour market regulation reveals as a common feature in Germany, the UK and the US that the occupational labour markets in cultural industries lack or only have weak institutions regulating entry and career building, like skill certificates and career ladders. At the same time, established collective bargaining bodies are rare. While in the German case the training and career structure in the media production industry deviates from the national blueprint characterized by vocational training and formalized career ladders, the British and the US case seem to be more in line with their national characteristic of absence of comprehensive and standardized occupational labour market institutions. Second, the employment pattern of the whole workforce is characterized by a relatively young workforce, high interfirm mobility, patterns of short-term employment and ubiquitous freelancing (Baumann 2002; Batt et al. 2001). High professional standards go hand in hand with working time depending on customer needs and varied income structures. Social differentiation is a function of gender as well as variables like age, work experience, skill level and sector (see Betzelt and Gottschall 2004 for Germany; Batt et al. 2001 for the US).

These characteristics, including the tendency of growing social polarization, can be attributed to strong impact of globalization and modernization on the labour market in the cultural industries lessening the impact of national labour market and social regulations during the 1990s in most Western countries. Despite booming demand and economic expansion, technological changes (like digitization and replacement of in-house employment by a freelance workforce on a large scale) were used to cut costs and stay competitive in the old and new media industries. With respect to the supply side, increasing numbers of well-qualified university and college graduates, among them many women, entered the external labour markets, leading to increased competition among employees (Unesco 2000). In turn, market conditions for media professionals in the globalized and digitized new century became highly competitive and risky for the individual, demanding high and specialized skill levels, while at the same time material rewards for many freelancers appear to be rather modest.

We can now assume that the weak labour market regulation in cultural industries has an effect on the life course since in all capitalistic societies the life course is organized predominantly around the occupational career (Kohli 1986) and thus generates gendered standard biographies (Krüger 2003). Within this framework we find nation-specific patterns of life course regimes with Germany characterized by high regulation, curb-on-wage labour and inequality structured by status and gender, while the UK and the US as liberal market regimes dispose of low regulation, enhancement of wage labour and an inequality structure mainly defined by market success or failure (Leisering 2003).[12] The weak labour market regulation in cultural industries implies that transitions in the life course (like the transition from training to work or climbing a career ladder) and situations of work-related risks (like disability, unemployment and retirement or illness) are not well defined and taken care of by specific institutions. Thus they pose special challenges to the workforce and the question arises how the self-employed deal with the special risk profile of their work.

A growing body of Anglo-American case studies including our own empirical work on Germany allows for a closer look at individual and collective risk management strategies.[13] And here again a comparison seems useful, because while working conditions might be globalized, infrastructures and competencies arising in response to these risks might still be linked to national labour market and national social security schemes as well as different gender regimes.

Our conceptual framework for analysing risk management strategies in occupational labour markets and welfare regimes refers to temporalities, both short-term as well as long-term (life course) dimensions of employment. Risk management involves synchronic and diachronic dimensions: getting work, acquiring and maintaining skills, securing the quality of work by control over income, time and copyright, and social security, including employment security, compensation and social benefits. Furthermore we refer to agency on the level of individual as well as collective social practice. The term 'risk management strategies' in this context refers to distinct social practices which are actively pursued in order to cope with actual or potential risk situations.

Individual risk management: negotiation in network structures and safeguarding household forms

As stated above, manifest and established labour market institutions, like certificates and well-defined career paths, are weak or absent from the occupational labour market of cultural and new media workers. This makes labour market transactions insecure and gives way to the generation of informal governance. The most prominent social mechanism capturing the informality of market transactions in this field is negotiation in network structures which allow for control of communication, trust and reputation (Haak and Schmid 1999).

Based on the interviews in our study we identified different patterns of networking with customers and other professionals in the field. All interviewees judged establishing and cultivating dyadic relationships with one or several customers as crucial for market success. They problematize this as a time-consuming task, since they usually experience that client networks are highly vulnerable due to changes of market or corporate conditions, new technologies and newcomers in the field with fresh ideas. Additionally, most of the freelancers in our study relied on so-called professional networks, that is job-related contacts to other professionals in the field, for communicating about quality and price standards, securing new jobs, and looking for a partner for larger projects or somebody to step in in case of illness. For both cases, however, the freelancers also identified ambiguities as a result of strong network integration. Long-term client relationships might result in dependency, as they lead to identification with a certain client, rendering business with competitors and changing the field of specialization more difficult. And given that a position in a client's network is never guaranteed, contacts to other freelancers are not only based on cooperation but also on competition (Gottschall and Henninger 2004).

Corresponding with these results, other studies for the US, UK and Germany show that market success in media industries is indeed predicated primarily on individual cultural and social capital (Blair 2001; Gill 2002; Baumann 2002; Krätke 2002). For New York media workers, Batt et al. find that, despite the rapid growth of on-line job selection and internet-based recruiting, personal networks (contact to clients and other professionals) continue to be the primary source of finding a job. Moreover the availability of personal networks not only affects getting a job, but also might determine what professionals can demand in wages. The key role of personal networks for obtaining jobs and sustaining employability is facilitated by the spatial concentration of new media industries in urban centres and certain districts where professionals live and work and potential employers can be met on an informal basis (Batt et al. 2001: 21). A study comparing labour market transactions in the German and British media production industries demonstrates that for getting a job and achieving employment security, freelancers in both countries primarily rely on connections through so-called intermediaries, i.e. personal contacts (colleagues, university friends) and industry insiders, who might be in the position of employers, too (Baumann 2002: 40).[14]

While the importance of personal networks for freelancers in maintaining their market position is widely supported, empirical evidence for the gender effect of this integration scheme is less clear. Following the literature on female corporate career prospects, informal ways of governance disadvantage rather than promote women since the relevant networks are often male-biased (cf. Allmendinger and Hackman 1995). As the importance of social capital in freelancing is even higher than in corporate bodies it is not surprising that a comparative study of freelance new media workers in six European countries identified the informality of labour market structures as one reason for emerging gender inequality. Apart from sexist assumptions, the existence of 'old boys' networks and their significance for getting projects created problems for women (Gill 2002: 82). In our study, however, there are also indicators, at least for Germany, that the extent to which gender is important differs with respect to occupation and branches: female freelancers in journalism perceived their situation more disadvantaged than their counterparts in new media like web design, where interviewees (men and women) interpreted the minority status of women as an advantage, since it renders them more visible thus facilitating personal contacts to clients. One issue arising in this context, called the 'post-feminist problem' by Gill, is the reluctance of new media workers (men and women) to understand their experiences as having anything to do with gender. Due to prevailing individualistic and meritocratic discourses in this field, irritating or even discriminatory experiences tend to be understood rather as personal failures or random events (Gill 2002: 85).[15]

This line of research highlights the role of informal contacts as a substitute for standardized skills and as a means to secure a long-term employment relationship. Research drawing on the concept of 'portfolio work' complements and contrasts the above-named results in showing that the availability of transferable professional skills is a prerequisite for taking up and keeping a freelancing position. As Handy argues, freelancers can build up 'a collection of different bits and pieces of work for different clients' (Handy 1994: 175), thus organizing their career paths more around the acquisition of a marketable portfolio of specialized skills and prestige projects than on long-term tenure with one employer. The capacity to use this market position to exert control over working conditions like pay and deadlines differs depending on the supply of special skills and relations to clients. So Fraser and Gold show that freelance translators in the UK enjoy higher levels of autonomy and control over their working conditions than freelance editors and proofreaders (Fraser and Gold 2001). Results for Germany also show that new media and IT professionals with highly specialized and scarce skills are more likely to opt out of dependent employment and enjoy better working conditions as freelancers than their less qualified in-house colleagues (Henninger 2004; Mayer-Ahuja and Wolf 2005). Nevertheless the portfolio concept draws on a distinction between freelancing and dependent work that, especially in the case of new media industries in uncoordinated market economies, might no longer apply. As Batt et al. (2001: 8) report for new media workers in New York, the vast majority move from one employer to the next in a much shorter time span than the typical American worker, diminishing the meaningfulness of different employment statuses like 'individual contractor' or 'employee'.

Another feature of risk management is the safeguarding function of special *household forms*. This might cause surprise since usually the household forms of workers are seen as independent variables of the social structure. Though, as welfare state theory and gender-sensitive labour market research show, the dominant employment patterns in Western societies, that is the standard employment relationship as well as the classical professional one, are combined with a special household form and are gendered at the same time. Especially in Germany and the UK, postwar employment patterns in terms of income, working time, career perspectives and their corporate regulation as well as the social security provisions constituted a male breadwinner model with a corresponding female housewife position (see Esping-Andersen 1990; Lewis and Ostner 1994 and Gottfried and O'Reilly 2002). The decline of this model due to the erosion of a family wage over the past decades is more pronounced in the US than in the UK and Germany. This has led to a dual-earner model especially in the US, whereas a 'one and a half breadwinner model' with a predictable gender divide has emerged in the UK and Germany. Departures from this model, however, can be found with highly qualified women – as the growing body of dual-career research shows, though this does not necessarily include equal sharing of household work and parenting (Blossfeld and Drobnic 2001; Crompton and Birkelund 2000; Hochschild 2000). As our secondary data analysis on the social structure of freelancers in old and new media industries in Germany indicates, the household forms of a single household and dual-earner households seem to prevail in this group, even if there are children living in the household. A dominance of childless households is reported for freelancers in the media industries. This might be due to the relatively young age of this occupational group in Germany as well as other Western countries (Rehberg et al. 2002; Brasse 2002). Nevertheless, there are also indicators that especially female freelancers in the new media might choose not to have children because of the working conditions in this field, e.g. intense stop-and-go work patterns and long hours as well as instability of income (Gill 2002: 84; Batt et al. 2001). On the other hand, available data on freelancers in Germany who are parents support the view that freelancing is more favourable for combining work and family duties than dependent work, since it allows for more flexibility in working time and space.[16] Our interview findings show that the household form, i.e. the existence of a partner with either a stable income and/or flexible working hours like part-time work, often serves as a cushion for the incalculable aspects and risks faced by the partner in the marketplace. This holds true for male as well as female freelancers. A weakening of the gender division of labour circumscribed by the male breadwinner model can also be found with regard to childcare. A small but still remarkable group of freelancers in our interview sample reported a reversed role taking. In cases where women had higher incomes, be it as a media free-lancer or as a dependent employee, the male partners took over childcare while working part-time. Another functional fit of 'work and life' can be found in partnerships where both partners are working as media freelancers, supporting each other in professional terms as well as with regard to domes-tic tasks. While these examples support the view that freelancing provides high options for work-life choices, our sample also provides evidence for the destructive potential of media freelancing. Some interviewees expressed concern that short-term contracting, intensive workloads, long working hours and low incomes endanger their partnerships and in the long run might not allow for setting up a family. While men reflected on their inabil-ity to provide a family wage, women problematized the missing work–life balance and reinforced conflicts about sharing housework (Gottschall and Henninger 2004).

Collective risk management

Turning to collective representation in the field of freelancing first of all recalls the 'falling-in-between-status' of this employment form. Neither con-stituting a classical profession with access to professional organizations safe-guarding monopolistic market positions (like in Germany, for example, the doctors' associations) nor being secured by corporate regulations and more or less strong unions which workers can rely on, freelancers in the cultural and new media industry as a 'postmodern workforce' (gender mixed, highly qualified, individualized) seem to have no model for collective action at hand. At the same time, there is a need for some sort of lobby for this new constituency, although the support for trade unions is generally fading. Empirical findings from the UK, US and Germany show that in the face of expanding market risks freelancers call for professional advice and further training, networking support and legal aid in order to meet the needs of a more and more tight and competitive market.

Interestingly, innovative approaches to these changing requirements can be found, though more in Germany than in the UK and the US. In Germany, especially in the field of new media and graphic design, new associations arose within the last decade, which can be described as hybrid in the sense that they combine elements of traditional trade unions as well as of pro-fessional organizations. One example of an innovative union structure is a special task force called 'Connexx-AV'. Established in 1999 within the large services trade union 'Ver.di',[17] Connexx-AV tries to reach journalistic free-lancers in private broadcasting, film, audiovisual media and the internet. Another example is the rise of a new designers' association successfully com-peting with the traditional elitist clubs (who require a university diploma for admission), attracting new and young members. Both organizations are socially inclusive, open to newcomers in the field, including part-timers, employees and freelancers, and both offer services especially tailored for freelancers. Based on electronic as well as face-to-face communication (especially in urban areas) they support networking among freelancers as a way of succeeding in the market and they pursue at the same time more traditional strategies such as trying to set standards for quality and prices for knowledge-based services. As our research shows, these new organizational players are well accepted, attracting a rising number of members and making progress in getting established as professional representation bodies by the market counterparts, although in the light of cut-throat price competition their bargaining power is limited (Betzelt and Gottschall 2004). The two examples also show that the organizational feature of innovation in collective action tends to be path-dependent. Journalism in Germany represents a field with a longstanding and relatively dense union tradition and the transition from dependent work to freelance work is a well-established career track. This seems to contribute to the willingness of freelance journalists to join a union initiative. The field of architecture and design, on the other hand, is more characterized by small businesses and freelance work with guild-like professional bodies. Thus freelancers in this field might be attracted by renewed but nevertheless professional-type organizations rather than union initiatives.

Compared to this story of relative success[18] the potential for and outcome of collective action in the US and UK media industries seem to be more restricted. In both countries traditional forms of collective representation have been weakened over a long period of time. This applies especially to the large-scale old media companies which are more likely to be unionized than the new media companies. The increase of the latter probably added to the erosion of traditional forms of collective action since as small and volatile firms they impede rather than enhance worker solidarity. At the same time, the more commodified character of media work, especially in the US in comparison to Germany and other continental countries such as Sweden, has made new media workers more dependent on some kind of collective constituency for sustaining employment and career, as Christopherson argues in a comparative case study for the US (Christopherson 2004: 19). However, this crucial need for professional organizations capable of serving as a labour market intermediary to help media workers reduce transaction costs is not well met. Christopherson argues that corporate actors in the US media industries, given the flexibilization of employment regulations, undermine collective voice options, forcing workers, especially those whose skills are in high demand, into a competitive entrepreneurial route. Thus, it seems plausible that the dynamics of uncoordinated market economies contribute to a strong individualized perception of options in the face of market risks. In a study of a fast-growing new media market region in the south-east of England, Perrons finds that freelancers tended to accept the frequent market fluctuations as a characteristic of the sector and considered themselves personally responsible for maintaining marketability by constantly updating their skills. While her interviewees saw little role for trade unions, there was evidence that the prospects of unions reaching these workers relies more and more on innovative communication forms like the use of websites, providing information and advice (Perrons 2004a: 15).

How does gender enter this picture? It seems as if women in media industries rely more on and have easier access to associations in obtaining jobs and building a career than on personal networks, especially if the latter are male biased (Batt et al. 2001). The new collective associations in German cultural industries that we took a look at indeed seem to offer equal opportunities for integration. They reflect the more or less equal gender-mix of the labour force in the sense that they are equally open to male and female professionals. The implicit normative professional ideal carries no overt male connotation; instead the ideal member – the *individualized autonomous freelancer* – seems to be gender neutral. However, this normative orientation also contains the idea that a professional worker is not a parent and does not care for family members. Parenthood as well as questions of work–life balance are not in the scope of the associations' policies, rather they are taken as a member's private matter. While such an expectation marks a boundary between the private and the public and seems to meet the individualistic attitude of the workforce, there is another side of the coin where this border dissolves. As a necessary precondition, the image of the autonomous self-employed worker is based on a particular model of dual-earner partnership in the household, whereby one partner must cushion the incalculable aspects and risks faced by the other in the marketplace. As mentioned before, the dual-earner or adult-worker model indeed seems to be a widespread individual choice, enabling social risks in this field to be minimized. The collective actors we interviewed in Germany take these private solutions for granted; the risks are implicitly seen as a natural element of working as a media professional and hence are usually not envisioned as a field of collective responsibility. This perception works in favour of men rather than women and adds to other internal discriminatory practices (e.g. pay inequities) within the cultural industries and new media. Whether these unfavourable conditions also might give rise to 'voice' instead of 'exit' options for women within the collective bodies remains an open question. A single initiative of freelance women in the media section of Ver.di in Germany to put the situation of female freelancers on the agenda of the trade union has not been very successful so far. They are struggling with the double burden of being a marginalized group in the membership of the union of predominantly employees and the gender blindness of traditional union policy.[19] For effective future work they need a basic infrastructure and more political support within the union. Nevertheless, the resonance of the initiative among female freelancers shows that this action is meeting a need (Betzelt 2003).

Conclusion

Our final remarks will reassess the merits of a comparative perspective for investigating self-employment dynamics and resume the controversial debate on self-employment in the new economy.

As we have seen the profile of solo self-employment varies across Germany, the UK, the US and Japan. It is marked by different growth dynamics and different sectoral distribution. Additionally, solo self-employment in the UK and the US is characterized by income polarization and gendered working conditions to a far larger extent than in Germany. Especially the differences in growth dynamics, sectoral distribution and income polarization seem to follow the Varieties of Capitalism and Welfare Regime approaches (Hall and Soskice 2001; Esping-Andersen 1990) which imply that in liberal market economies the so-called standard employment relationship providing a family income and a basic social security provision is far less pronounced than in cooperative market economies. However, these approaches do not seem to be able to account for the observed differences in gender. Contrary to the argument that liberal market economies (with wage flexibility and general skills) dispose of high class inequality and less gender inequality, we find marked gender differences in self-employment in the UK and the US. At the same time Germany stands out in that gender differences in self-employment seem to be less pronounced than in dependent employment although coordinated market economies are thought to produce more gender inequality and less class inequality (Soskice 2005). What at first sight seems a puzzle can be solved by an argument linking class and gender effects and taking into account the cross-national differences in the structure of self-employment. In the UK and the US a low degree of regulation of industrial branches and low access conditions to particular occupations opened self-employment to a large share of the workforce in all economic sectors, whereas in Germany – against the background of a declining but still remarkable dominance of the standard employment relationship – self-employment is more concentrated in the expansive and highly qualified services with a substantial share of female professionals. So we find income polarization in overall self-employment in Germany to a lesser degree than in the UK and the US. Additionally we might assume that gender gaps in earnings within the qualified services are less pronounced though not missing. Thus in the German case of self-employment high qualification (that is a class effect) seems to override a gender effect while in the case of the US and the UK the relative weight of and the concentration of women in low-end jobs (that is a combined gender and class effect) do not allow for a meritocratic remedy of gender discrimination. These results might also indicate that the above-named political economy approaches can claim explanatory power mainly for the field of standard dependent work, but that understanding the current dynamics of the increasing non-standard employment patterns demands for a broader analytical framework.

If we look at cultural industries the long shadow of different labour market regulations seems to fade even more. The findings on risk management strategies in the cultural industries in Western countries, though still incomplete, bear evidence of a globalized pattern of risk management. Individual risk strategies predominate, which is not surprising given the high education and ability of this workforce to represent its own interests. These strategies, however, not only refer to market communication but also to household form, thus crossing the border between private and public spheres and restructuring the work–family nexus inherent to the traditional (weak or strong) standard employment relationship. Collective strategies are gaining importance only with rising competition in media markets. They are obviously more likely to evolve in the more coordinated German market which still provides a significant infrastructure of unions and professional associations more capable of acting than in the UK where the Thatcher decades disempowered collective bodies. Interestingly, the emerging collective bodies of representation for freelancers in Germany do not follow either the traditional model of a professional association with its exclusive character or the pure unionist model disregarding individual differences of workers. Instead the new associations are hybrid, referring to collective practices without questioning individual market success as the basis of freelance work. Gender seems to make a difference as women are disadvantaged by informal governance structures of the labour market such as networking and the higher price they have to pay for a professional career following the adult worker model – at least as long as male partners are less available for equal parenting or cushioning the market risks of freelancing.

This leads to the conclusion that self-employment indeed might represent a *new paradigm of employment* which does not fit the well-known traditional type of (male) self-employment like 'entrepreneur/employer' or 'professional'. Two aspects can be highlighted here. From a legal point of view some forms of self-employment (like 'contracting only') represent new forms of employment relationships that do not conform to the standard legal definition of who is an 'employee' and who is an 'employer' (Dickens 2004: 605). From a sociological perspective self-employment in cultural industries can be characterized by the coexistence of basic opportunities, i.e. highly qualified and autonomous work, and basic risks, i.e. unpredictable income streams given the fluctuation of demand, modest material rewards and uncertain career paths. Thus this employment pattern is cross-cutting analytical categories like 'profession' and 'job' with their implications of stable social structure and standardized life course.

Obviously the results of this study cannot unanimously sustain the pessimistic or optimistic interpretations of self-employment cited in the introduction. Rather the ambivalent structure and the cross-national differences in volume and structure of this pattern of employment suggest a demand for further investigation in this dynamic field. This quest can be underlined by the fact that self-employment seems to become a stable part of the employment systems. Most freelancers remain independent and others try to start an independent career. This rising number of freelance workers cannot simply be attributed to push factors like outsourcing or tightening labour markets. There is strong evidence that even the originally involuntarily self-employed prefer freelancing to dependent employment after some time (Fraser and Gold 2001; Hughes 2003; Perrons 2003). This holds true for women and men. It appears that the autonomous nature of the work as well as the achievement of high and specialized qualifications, which reinforce intrinsic motivation and high identification with the work, is contributing to the attraction of freelancing in this field. These new forms of work are yet to be matched by the development of a new gender order and work–life balance securing 'sustainable' working conditions and mechanisms to prevent self-exploitation in globalized, highly competitive markets.

Notes

1. In the following we solely refer to self-employment outside the agricultural sector.
2. For the purpose of this contribution the terms *solo self-employed* and *freelancers* are defined as independent workers without employees. Whereas solo self-employed is more generally used, freelancer applies predominantly to workers in the cultural sector.
3. See different contributions in the special issue of *Social Politics*: 'Gender, Class, and Capitalism', *Social Politics*, Summer 2005, 12.
4. The term refers to the way workers address market-related risks that lack institutional regulation.
5. Focusing on 'new self-employment' from a macro-perspective entails methodological problems similar to the deficiencies of the conceptualization of the 'new economy' (see Shire in Part I of this volume). In order to concentrate on self-employment outside of agriculture and to some extent on solo employment, we rely on older macro-level data from the late 1990s (OECD 2000a). However, these data on self-employment volume will be complemented by recent quantitative data on general self-employment structure and features and by insights from available secondary sources and our own empirical research. Whereas quantitative data on Germany are mainly based on the German Census Study, the UK data are derived from the British Labour Force Survey and from smaller work-related surveys. Data on self-employment in the US and Japan are derived from the Current Population Survey, the Panel Study of Income Dynamics (both for the US) and the Japanese Labour Force Survey.
6. Data from the Current Population Survey suggest a pronounced rise to 9.7 per cent in 1990 (Devine 1994: 20). This discrepancy might be due to the exclusion of owner-managers of incorporated businesses from the OECD data.
7. The Japanese Labour Force Survey, however, indicates much higher rates of self-employment: according to these data, the self-employment rate fell from 14.1 per cent in 1990 to 11.3 per cent in 2000. Differences are also evident in the share of self-employment among women. Whereas the OECD data overrate the share at almost 34 per cent during 1990 and 1997 (OECD 2000a: 161), the LFS data designate shares of 10.7 per cent in 1990 and of 7.8 per cent in 2000. These

discrepancies are due to differing definitions of the self-employed (concerning owner-managers of incorporated businesses and family workers) and to differing thresholds with regard to working hours. The Japanese LFS includes all workers who worked for at least one hour in the preceding week. However, both data sources indicate a steady decline in self-employment in general.

8. Working time patterns in the US, however, seem to be slightly less gendered.

9. The term 'cultural sector' refers to all cultural industries as classified by the International Standard Classification of Occupations (ISCO88), including occupations in old and new media industries. Some of the studies cited here apply to the media industry in a more narrow sense (Rehberg et al. 2002; Satzer 2001; Grass 1998) or to new media, i.e. parts of the media industries, which have undergone substantial change through new technologies (Perrons 2003; Gill 2002; Batt et al. 2001). In the following we refer to the UK, US and Germany only, since industry-specific figures for Japan are not available.

10. In contrast, high levels of qualifications are not characteristic of Japanese self-employment. However, at least in the metropolitan regions, the share of self-employed workers equipped with high levels of human capital seems to be rising (Ministry of Health, Labour and Welfare [Japan] 2003; Genda and Kambayashi 2002).

11. Another reason for the diminishing role of self-employment lies in changes in the Japanese labour market regime especially since the late 1980s. Whereas the owners of small businesses have been a crucial support group for successive conservative governments for a long time and were highly protected against internal competition, politico-economic strategies of the recent past changed the status of the self-employed to a considerable extent. The attention of economic policies has become more and more centred on large-scale enterprises. The introduction of a large-scale retail store law and other de-regulation measures alongside the collapse of the bubble economy have increased the number of competitors the self-employed have to face (Genda and Kambayashi 2002; Pempel 1998).

12. This results in a higher level of class inequality and a less marked gender inequality, but does not erase the latter (Estévez-Abe 2005; England 2005).

13. Our own cross-sectional analysis of freelancing in publishing and new media professions carried out since 2001 in four larger German cities encompasses journalists, graphic and web designers, editorial freelancers, translators, and software developers. A review of secondary data and a standardized online survey of cultural and new media workers (focusing on the social structure, market position and household situation) allowed for an estimate of the social structure of these groups in Germany as well as for the sampling of the interview group. A second step included about thirty expert interviews with key representatives of professional organizations and unions in the field. Last, over forty guided in-depth interviews with freelancers in the cultural industries were carried out, focusing on professional identity, individual strategies of risk-management and work and life patterns (for findings see Gottschall 2002; Betzelt and Gottschall 2004; and Gottschall and Henninger 2004).

14. As the author points out, it makes a difference whether these intermediaries communicate an individual's reputation for doing his or her job or whether they serve as purely societal intermediaries who act as guarantors for an individual's social standing. Whilst the first networking function works as a substitute for skill standards the latter may promote social exclusion (Baumann 2002).

15. Martin and Wajcman (2003) find similar results in a study of the changing role of emotions for managerial performance. In the past, women were at a disadvantage in managerial career tracks since gender displays coded as emotionality remained out of place in the 'rational' world of work. As positive emotions gained importance for managerial performance de-gendering effects as well as gender recoding might occur. However, the male and female managers investigated in the study tended to interpret experiences with the importance of this symbolic resource in terms of individual biographies and rarely as a result of gender-specific discrimination.

16. This is in line with existing representative data for Germany that show that single and childless households are not overrepresented among self-employed workers compared to employees (Leicht and Lauxen-Ulbrich 2003).

17. Ver.di is the German acronym for 'united service workers' union', now the largest trade union in Europe (2.8 million members) which resulted from a merger of five unions representing various services in 2001.

18. Membership in these professional organizations varies with a relatively high coverage in the field of journalism and with substantially lower rates in the field of graphic design.

19. For a detailed account of the slow and ambiguous change of gender relations in German trade unions see Koch-Baumgarten 2002 and Klenner and Lindecke 2003.

7
Living and Working Patterns in the New Knowledge Economy: New Opportunities and Old Social Divisions in the Case of New Media and Care-Work

Diane Perrons

This chapter develops a theoretical understanding of the widening social divisions, characteristic of the new knowledge economy. To do so, it builds upon the traditional conceptualization of the knowledge economy linked to the expansion of work in and with new information and communication technologies, but goes further by theorizing the differential economic properties of knowledge and caring goods, which have similarly expanded, in order to explain why old social divisions by class and gender are reproduced albeit in new forms in the contemporary era. As the chapter focuses on two sectors at opposite poles of the economy, knowledge workers in new media and childcare workers, the term 'new economy' rather than 'knowledge economy' is used. The original empirical material comes from one local labour market (Brighton and Hove in the United Kingdom), but the discussion is contextualized within the UK and to a lesser extent the EU.

New media is an archetypal sector of the knowledge economy, characterized by work with ICTs, and new working patterns in terms of working times and employment contracts. These entrepreneurs, freelancers and employees generally fall in the upper deciles of the pay distribution, but are not immune from some of the adverse changes and risks in working practices characteristic of the new economy. Even though this is a new sector, involving a wide range of skills, gender divisions and social inequalities remain. By contrast, care-work is not in itself new, yet collective provision of care through the market (commodification) or by the state has increased in recent years as a response to the feminization of paid employment. Care-workers in the UK differ in their age and skill composition: younger people with diverse qualifications being involved in childcare while elder care especially home elder care, similar to Japan (Nishikawa and Tanaka in this volume) is characterized by middle-aged and older women with few formal qualifications. The precise nature of working conditions also varies depending on whether care-workers are employed in either the public sector or private sector.

Theorizing the new economy

There are many contrasting conceptualizations of the new economy (Gadrey 2003; Daniels 2004). A narrow definition connects the new economy to the dot.com boom, whereas a slightly wider view extends the period to the rapid inflation-free growth at the end of the 1990s (Greenspan 1998).[1] More broadly and perhaps more conventionally, the new economy is linked to the expansion of information and communication technologies with specific reference to the internet (Freeman 2003; Shire in this volume). Even though some of the more optimistic expectations associated with rising productivity and inflation-free growth have become more muted following the collapse of the dot.com bubble in 2000, the idea that ICTs create new possibilities for growth, a potentially more affluent future and a new phase of capitalist development remains. Indeed, new ICTs, which combine advanced computing and communication technologies with high quality networking infrastructure and continuously falling costs, have been heralded as the 'first global technological transformation' (Soete 2001: 143). Correspondingly, ICTs have been said to exert a more significant impact on socio-economic patterns of development, organizations, products, services and work than the steam engine, railways or motorized transport. Though as many writers emphasize, how ICTs shape outcomes depends on the specific institutional or socio-economic frameworks prevailing in different countries (see for example Castells 1996; Rubery and Grimshaw 2001).

Social theorists, such as Richard Sennett (1998) and Ulrich Beck (1992, 2002), also have advanced the idea of a new era. In contrast to the techno-optimists, their rather bleak scenarios focus on social changes corresponding in part to new more flexible working relationships characteristic of the new economy.[2] Richard Sennett refers to the corrosion of character linked to the contrast in values between those required by the mobile flexible worker and those necessary for the stability of families and communities. Ulrich Beck (1992, 2000) refers to increasing risks and opportunities associated with growing individualization in the 'Brave New World of Work'. Richard Florida (2002) similarly portrays dramatic social changes, but like the economists, he offers a more optimistic view of human ingenuity and the rise of a creative class. While Florida (2002) recognizes the increase in inequality in the contemporary era, he focuses much more on the creative class itself and how cities and regions can create the conditions in which this class can flourish.

My understanding of the new economy differs from the above, by recognizing the significance of new technologies, but also the deteriorating working conditions and widening social divisions. In this respect it is more similar to analyses of Danny Quah (1996) and Robert Reich (2001) who in different ways link these positive and negative dimensions analytically and argue that these diverging characteristics form part of an emerging digital divide. Indeed, nowhere is this starker than in the United States when the ninety-third consecutive month of growth recorded in December 1998 (the cornerstone of one interpretation of the new economy) was simultaneously the record year for redundancies (Benner 2002). Moreover, as the incomes of the elite expanded dramatically, those of ordinary workers stagnated. In Silicon Valley, perhaps the iconic instance of the new economy, the average earnings of corporate executives increased by 2000 per cent between 1991 and 2000 while production workers experienced a 7 per cent decline; the earnings ratio moving from 41:1 to 956:1 (Benner 2002; see also Krugman 2002).

In this chapter I consider the new economy to be something of a new era whose effects are pervasive but also differentiated. By building on the work of Danny Quah (1996, 2003) I foreground and try to explain widening income inequalities (Atkinson 2003; Piketty and Saez 2003) and social divisions characteristic of the new era, but take Quah's analysis further by exploring how these social divisions are also gendered. This perspective, on which I have elaborated elsewhere (Perrons 2004a), is briefly summarized because it differs somewhat from the understanding of the knowledge economy in this volume. It does not contradict these other approaches; centred on ICT and knowledge intensity (Walby and Shire in this volume), or the focus on knowledge creation (Nishikawa and Tanaka in this volume), but uses the term 'new economy' to refer to the whole economy and its increasingly divided character.

For Quah (1996, 2003) the hallmark of the new economy is the increasing significance of knowledge, weightless or dematerialized goods. This definition is technical and based on economists' conceptualization of knowledge work. It does not imply any assessment of the complexity or skill involved, and thus differs from the more sociological understandings of knowledge work developed by Nonaka and Takeuchi (1995) and built upon by Makiko Nishikawa and Kazuko Tanaka (in this volume) in the context of care-work. To avoid this confusion or the value connotations associated with the term 'knowledge', in later work Quah refers to knowledge goods as 'bit-strings', that is, anything that can in principle be digitized. Thus, pop and rock singers as well as architects, to the extent that their music and designs can be digitized, are knowledge workers as well as those working more directly with ICTs.

Quah argues that given their economic properties, the rising proportion of knowledge goods in any economy should lead to greater overall equality but in practice the opposite happens. The reasoning is as follows: knowledge goods/bitstrings are infinitely expansible, that is they can be replicated at very low costs, and they are non-rival; thus one person's consumption does not prevent another's. For example, many people can simultaneously use PowerPoint but cannot eat the same chocolate biscuit. These properties should tend to generate greater equality. However, as Quah (1996) explains, knowledge goods are also characterized by increasing economies of scale; although they can be replicated and thus have very low marginal costs, the cost of the first product, e.g. a new computer game, can be very high. As a result, large firms tend to dominate the market and having done so, they create a range of related products locking consumers into their particular brand – Microsoft would be a good example. A further property is the superstar effect, which refers to consumers' preferences for products of greater brand recognition even though they may be barely distinguishable from competitors. Given their weightless nature there are few constraints on market size so these producers/workers capture an increasing share of the market.[3] As knowledge goods and knowledge workers become more important in the economy therefore, social inequalities correspondingly increase.

Quah (1996) suggests that people accept widening inequalities because of higher levels of social mobility in the new economy, which raise individual expectations of becoming rich. By contrast, I argue that in practice, work is typically coded by ethnicity, sexual orientation, class and gender, the last forming the main focus of this chapter. Thus rather than being random, the predicted widening social divisions are likely to reinforce existing structural inequalities in the labour force, in this case gender inequalities.

In addition to the expansion of knowledge work, there has also been an expansion in low paid jobs in what can be described as care-work or activities that are more people-related and in which women and ethnic minorities tend to be overrepresented. These goods exhibit opposite technical or economic properties than the knowledge goods/bitstrings as outlined above. In general, these services are not infinitely expansible or non-rival but are inherently technologically unprogressive; productivity increases are difficult to achieve and wages tend to be low (Baumol 1967). For example, although a professional childcare worker can care for more than one child simultaneously there is a fixed and relatively small limit to the number of children each carer can supervise, thereby constraining productivity, income and earnings (Folbre and Nelson 2000). Hilary Land (2003) has pointed out that some private nurseries in the UK try to transcend this limit through electronic tagging, and productivity could be increased by new technologies such as replacing home visits by text message reminders to the elderly to take their medicine (Coyle 2004). But in general productivity is constrained unless, as noted above, the nature of the service is profoundly, and many would consider adversely, changed.

Some of the fast growing occupations during the 1990s in the UK were in the caring services such as nursery nurses, hairdressing and housekeeping as well as in sectors linked to the knowledge economy such as professional and managerial jobs, including software engineers and computer programmers (Nolan and Slater 2002). As Maarten Goos and Alan Manning (2003) find, both 'good jobs' with earnings in the top two deciles (predominantly knowledge workers) and 'bad jobs' with earnings in the lowest decile (generic caring-related work) have increased between 1979 and 1999, especially in the former.[4] Thus the changing composition of employment can account for a large part of the earnings inequality in the UK.

Indeed the combined expansion of these two areas of work is not surprising as they are in some respects interrelated. Employers of high level knowledge workers are beginning to provide concierge services to facilitate long working hours. Moreover, as female employment has increased, and this has been especially noticeable among mothers with young children (see Harkness 2003), and as more people work long hours or believe they do so, then they become more dependent on marketized services either because they no longer have time to do this work themselves or because they choose to spend their spare time in other ways. People earning high salaries can afford these services because they are so relatively cheap. Thus this demand also reflects the widening inequality of which it is a part. As compared to the past when workers in an industry like automobiles could aspire to buy their own car, childcare workers often cannot afford the weekly fee to use private nurseries and cannot take out loans for services of this kind.[5]

The arguments in this section have been abstract and largely reflect market logic, but all markets operate within social and political frameworks and correspondingly are open to modification by prevailing cultural norms, political and social pressures, including state legislation and action by trade unions and employees. And therefore, the impact of these processes will be mediated by the prevailing socio-economic framework or welfare regime of different states. The remainder of this chapter relates mainly to the UK.

Despite introducing new employment regulation to enact EU Directives in relation to equalities issues and working time, the UK has tended to prioritize market logic and encouraged de-regulation and flexible working practices. As a consequence, income inequalities have been rising more rapidly than in continental Europe, but similar to trends in the United States (Atkinson 2003). The gender gap in earnings remains and is especially high among high earners. However, the UK differentiates its position from the US by seeking to combine 'flexibility and fairness' (Brown 2003: para 277) and demonstrates partial commitment to the European Social Model by extending maternity, paternity and parental leave while retaining its opt-out from the Working Time Directive. In practical terms this means that living standards for many people, especially low-income families in the UK, are higher than in the US (Ehrenreich 2005; Toynbee 2005) but lower than those of other EU countries with similar levels of GDP (see Perrons et al. 2006).

The analytical framework highlights the dual nature of the new economy and to some extent reconciles the optimistic accounts that stress the potential economic and social benefits arising from new technologies and the more pessimistic social theorists who emphasize deteriorating working conditions, increasing insecurity, and individualization. The next sections explore the working conditions of new media workers and childcare workers in one local labour market in the UK (see Gottschall in this volume for a discussion of the German case).

IT and care-workers in the UK

IT workers

The dot.com boom was based on the rapid increase in the number of companies set up specifically to run on the web. These companies were primarily 'e-tailors' with few material foundations and little history of trading and so were particularly vulnerable to stock market fluctuations. While many disappeared when the bubble burst in 2000 some, such as Lastminute and Amazon, have survived and are now beginning to make profits. These companies were very much at the tip of an iceberg and the more enduring influence of new ICT technologies is the way that they have become generalized throughout the economy – in communications between firms, between firms and customers, in designing working patterns, sales, advertising, marketing and public relations – alongside more conventional practices. These developments have been expanding as the scale and quality of internet use has advanced. In 1999 only 13.2 per cent of households (3.2 million) could access the internet from home, but by 2004, 49 per cent (12.1 million) could do so. Furthermore, the proportion of households with higher quality broadband connections reached 3 million homes by 2004. Indeed, as internet use in general expands and the quality of access increases, then people are increasingly likely to make purchases on-line.

This expansion contributed to the growth of employment in IT and IT-related sectors including new media. Calculating numbers of employees is complex (see Shire in this volume) because firms categorized as Information Technology also employ a wide range of non-IT-related people and likewise firms throughout the economy employ IT professionals (see Panteli et al. 2001). While these workers are nevertheless considerably better educated and better paid than the average, with over half being graduates, they are still subject to market fluctuations and temporary and insecure contracts.

Despite being a new sector, gender imbalance remains stark. About one-third of the IT workforce is estimated to be female but a considerably lower proportion is in professional IT jobs; only just over one-tenth of computer programmers and analysts are women (E-Skills 2004). Indeed when present, women are more likely to be concerned with customer support or help desks, areas which generally have lower levels of pay (E-Skills 2004). The sector is also currently losing more women than it is recruiting (George 2003) and further even when women have science, engineering and technology (SET) degrees they are less likely than men to end up in SET occupations. Indeed, their most likely occupational group is personal and protective services (DTI 2004). This inequality is also found in the new media sector but in both cases the imbalance is not as stark as in caring work discussed below.

Childcare

There has been considerable expansion of all forms of care-work in the UK and in the number of people working in this field, ranging from 'social care' (with around 1 million workers) including people working in residential homes, and childcare (around 400000 workers) including people working in nurseries, as childminders and in after-school clubs. The extent of childcare provision should continue to rise with the revised National Childcare Strategy 2005, largely through the private sector.[6]

Expanding childcare is associated with the government's strategy of increasing employment and creating the ideal citizen for the new economy – the autonomous, independent, self-regulating citizen who is responsible for managing risks and their own individual and family well-being (Cameron et al. 2002; Rose 1999). Even so, childcare provision is often patchy, inflexible and expensive, which either prevents carers from returning to work or forces them to work fewer hours to fit around their childcare (Land 2004).

Less attention has focused on the terms and conditions of employment among social care and childcare workers themselves. In the first National Childcare Strategy, reference was made to the career progression but the minimum wage was cited as their main form of protection, and yet the minimum wage in the UK is only 30 per cent of average wages, the lowest level in the EU apart from Spain (at 28 per cent) (see Stewart 2005). Indeed the government does not want to 'over-professionalize' the profession but rather to seek people who '*have a way with kids*' (House of Commons 2000 cited by Cameron et al. 2002: 585, my emphasis). This comment reflects the attribution of childcare to 'mothering' rather than education in the UK. Thus, childcare is taken to be a natural talent rather than a skill or based on knowledge that requires education, training and correspondingly monetary reward. This view contrasts considerably with childcare development in other European countries, in particular the Nordic countries and Spain, where people working with children 0–6 years are more likely to have a relatively high level of education with at least three years of training at post-18 level in order to provide what is recognized as a complex, multiskilled, demanding and professional job (Cameron et al. 2002).

For children between three and five years old, childcare and education have to some extent merged in the UK as the government now covers the cost of 2.5 hours a day education whether provided by a state nursery school, whose staff include formally qualified teachers on the national pay scale or by private nurseries whose staff typically have taken additional training but receive pay lower than teachers. Given the responsibility of the work involved, low pay can only be explained by characteristics of care-work, outlined in the first section, the association between childcare work and mothering and the gender composition of the workforce in a society that systematically undervalues women's work.

Despite expanding childcare provision and the need for increasing amounts of elder care given demographic trends, this work continues to be highly gendered (98 per cent women), low paid, insufficient to allow people to live independently or pay for a pension and with a low social value. Younger people are more prevalent in childcare and older people in social care. In the study below and in wider national surveys in the UK and the US childcare workers nevertheless report above-average levels of job satisfaction, leading some people to argue that the job is a reward in itself, a comment which overlooks the inherent satisfaction derived from interesting and rewarding work that is also higher paid. People working in elder care express lower levels of job satisfaction but in a survey of such workers in Brighton and Hove workers expressed responsibility towards the people they cared for as one reason for not being tempted away towards similarly low qualified but higher paying work in the supermarkets (Prism Research 2000).

New media and care-workers in Brighton and Hove

Brighton and Hove is a city on the south coast of England and markets itself as one of the fastest growing new media clusters in the EU and more extravagantly as 'Silicon Beach' or the 'cyber capital of Europe' owing to the presence of between 200 and 300 new media firms. While portraying itself as 'the creative capital of Europe', the Brighton and Hove Council also applies for funding from the European Social Fund and the UK government's social exclusion unit, which highlights the divided nature of the city. Overall it is an area of comparatively high unemployment and low wages especially in relation to the south-east region and to the UK as a whole. The council has also been pursuing the government's strategy of privatizing many public sector services such as care homes for the elderly. The major recent expansion of childcare provision in the city has been in the private sector. However, given the continuing importance of public sector administration and the presence of two major universities in the city some public sector crèches and nurseries remain.

The public–private sector mix, together with the fusion between childcare and education provision for the 3–5-year-olds, means that the care sector overall is extremely complex and the terms and conditions of employment correspondingly varied. Likewise, defining new media and the number of new media workers is complex as it involves a wide range of rather different skills including art, design and computing and does not fit well with the occupational categories designed for an earlier epoch. In both cases aggregate statistics do not adequately portray the complex and varied nature of the working conditions and work performed. Thus to get a more comprehensive picture the findings below come from qualitative research.

The findings are based on a purposive and largely administered structured survey of 100 employees in new media, care-work and garbage collection (not referred to in this study) (see Perrons 2004b) carried out in 2002, together with 30 follow-up in-depth interviews. Additionally material is drawn from in-depth interviews with 55 new media entrepreneurs, managers and freelancers first carried out in 2000 and updated in 2003.[7]

In the discussion below some of the contrasting experiences of people working in these sectors are discussed paying particular attention to gender bias, insecurity, and the lack of formal representation, which to varying degrees are common to both sectors, reflecting the way that the new economy is associated with increased individualization alongside old social divisions.

Gender bias

Nationally childcare workers are 98 per cent female and this pattern was reflected in the interviewees in Brighton and Hove. Although the national government has tried to widen the gender, age and ability composition of childcare workers, childcare work remains predominantly young and female, with the older workers more likely to be the formally qualified teachers working in nursery schools at the local level.

The new media sector is more varied. Defining new media as a sector concerned with 'the range of interactive and digital products and services that offer new ways to trade, market, educate and entertain, delivered through the Internet, CD Rom, DVD, interactive TV and intranets' (Copeland 2000: 7), we find more than the stereotypically masculine skills linked to writing code and fixing hardware but even so women continue to be underrepresented (Panteli et al. 2001). Indeed, in Brighton and Hove people with the latter skills were generally referred to as 'techies' who in this study were all male but were by no means seen as the leading-edge. Nevertheless women were underrepresented in terms of numbers, status and earnings for entrepreneurs, mangers and employees alike. Taken together, the two sectors exhibit continuing segregation according to the traditional gender stereotypes.

Focusing on new media, results from the 2000 survey indicate that only 30 per cent of firms were owned or managed by women and in the subsequent employee survey 32.6 per cent were women. Similar to national trends, women were more likely to be involved in customer support or when in management dealing with human resource issues. Moreover, the firms owned or managed by women were much smaller in terms of turnover and the number of employees, and two of the women owners of larger companies were in partnership with their husbands. Women who owned firms with employees were in general older and drew on resources and contacts that they had made during their previous working lives. Being older and female, however, did not fit the image of the dot.com entrepreneur and several women recounted difficulties in acquiring capital from banks to expand their organizations. Similarly, female employees earned less on average than men.[8] This survey is not representative but these figures parallel overall trends in the UK.

To address the gender bias in new media the local promotion agency has hosted breakfasts for new media women and held speed networking events (similar to speed dating) (Wiredsussex 2004) designed to raise the profile of and opportunities for women in the sector and to allow those with less time or inclination to socialize in more traditional ways to promote their ideas, companies and skills.

Nevertheless, the introduction of ICTs widened the temporal and spatial boundaries of work and created new opportunities especially for women to develop new careers and combine careers with caring, though as discussed below there are varied experiences and costs as well as benefits.

The relatively low capital costs enabled people to set up small businesses from home. Some consciously chose to work in new media, while others almost stumbled upon the option as a consequence of other changes in their lives. Clare (ID 1/46),[9] for example, established her own firm following her divorce. When married she had commuted to London for fairly specialized work involving databases. Once she assumed sole responsibility for the children she wanted to live and work in Brighton and Hove. She found it difficult to find a job partly because she lacked formal qualifications in computing, but she also sensed discrimination in relation to her age (midthirties) and gender. As a result, she decided to 'go it alone'. She comments that despite the difficult beginning, now 'It's wonderful! As I own and run my own business from home my work/life balance could not really be improved. I have the flexibility I need.' Similar to other women with young children in this sector Clare works during the children's school hours and resumes work when they have gone to sleep, which of course leads to a long overall working day. Indeed, Clare embodies many features of the new age worker: working from home, at times of her own choosing, and yet she is fully connected to the global economy, subcontracting programming work to India and selling on world markets.

The ability to determine working hours and stay close to home was mentioned by all of the female respondents with caring commitments. Setting up independently or freelancing was therefore a way of controlling the hours of work as Janice explains: 'The internet – this is just what I was waiting for. I can now run my own business from home and have much more flexibility and control over work than when I was a freelancer' (ID 1/12).

Janice recalled some bad experiences as a freelancer: being called up at short notice to work on projects away from home, never being certain about their duration and on occasions having real difficulty getting home in time to pick up her daughter. Janice also commented on the way her new business gave her independence and control over work and was pleased to be away from 'office politics' and the male world where she felt she was never taken seriously: 'The IT world is still a very male world and some men have difficulty in treating women as equal.'

At the same time, working from home created as well as resolved tensions: 'homework does create tensions with the children' (ID 1/31), 'if she cries and my partner is looking after her it's difficult to concentrate' (ID 1/28) or 'I am continually kicked out of the office and accused of ignoring my family and preferring the computer to real people . . . It's too easy to just go in for 30 minutes and spend 3 or 4 hours without noticing the time slipping away.' (ID 1/12). Other problems arose from working from home, including isolation, 'not having people to bounce ideas off' (ID 1/1) and the continual presence of work 'you are constantly reminded of work – you can never escape it' (ID 1/18) . . . there is 'the to-do list always beckoning' (ID 1/34). In this respect, the widening of temporal and spatial boundaries eroded traditional work rhythms and indeed any boundaries around the working day, much more so for the entrepreneurs and freelancers than regular new media employees for larger firms who were more likely to have set working hours.

In some respects, the lack of boundaries around work reflects the inherent intellectual nature of knowledge work which in principle can take place anywhere at any time. People also enjoyed the work and the blurring of boundaries between work and life was often voluntary: 'work and life merge – work is my hobby, work is a myth' (ID 1/9). A man with no caring responsibilities made this last comment, but even so only a tiny minority expressed any dissatisfaction with work content.

At the same time, besides intrinsic satisfaction there are specific features of the sector and people's status within it, which tend towards long hours especially for the entrepreneurs and freelancers. The flow and nature of work is unpredictable and all start-ups face uncertainty (Baines and Wheelock 2000). In addition, time has to be set aside for 'training', that is to check for new ideas and innovations and update skills. Whether voluntary or not this tendency towards long hours is a further source of gender bias given the traditional division of labour between women and men over caring work.

Many firms were start-ups and establishing an even flow of work is always difficult. There was a tendency to take on work whenever it was available, given no certainty about future contracts. Although there are many freelancers in the city, it was not always possible to expand a workforce at short notice, given the varied skills required, as Janice explains:

> I took on a project that required more phone lines and people to run them at very short notice. Besides the logistics, purchasing more equipment and software – the staff had to be briefed, databases created and deadlines were extremely tight. At the same time I had to continue servicing other clients and it was the school holidays – I only managed to take one day off with my daughter during the whole period. (ID 1/12)

Ironically, one of Janice's new projects is to develop a virtual lifestyle and work–life adviser. Similarly, as Liz remarked, the 'timing and scheduling of work makes it difficult to subcontract . . . one of the problems with the internet is that there are no standards and qualifications . . . you cannot be sure of who you are hiring – there is no proper accreditation. It's important to build a network of trustworthy people' (ID 1/17).

For dependent employees in larger companies, working hours were more regular as people could be switched between projects in accordance with fluctuations in the volume of work. Nonetheless employees were expected to respond to deadline crises, whenever necessary. One company, for example, required workers to voluntarily opt out of the EU's Working Time Directive, but rewarded excessive hours with bonuses such as 'stress busters' at a local luxury hotel or bottles of champagne. Such measures reflect a more general pattern of paternalism within the sector, where 'treats' arc substituted for higher pay. In other cases, people are paid in terms of time-off at a future date, but these time deficits often remain unpaid. By contrast, childcare workers employed in nurseries worked regular working hours and did not take 'work' home. Some of the problems relating to uncertain hours and uncertain patterns of work could apply to childminders, who are effectively independent entrepreneurs.

Insecurity

Given the uneven flow of work freelancers play an important role, as Ed explained:

> I would like to recruit but the nature of the business is very volatile. If large projects come off then I will need to recruit but you can never tell where the business is coming from so I cannot employ people on permanent contracts so I employ people on a contractual basis – fixed term contracts. (ID 1/13)

Firms also used freelancers to expand their skill base and keep up-to-date by learning from their experiences in other companies. Thus in Phil's company:

Two men are employed on a permanent full-time basis but seven free-lancers used on a regular basis, six of them men and one woman. The freelancers are regularly employed but on a part-time basis . . . these are grey ghost employees – i.e. in a hierarchy they are closer to the company than agency, sub-contractors or freelance employees but the company cannot employ them on full-time contracts because the flow of work is uneven and also because the type of skills required will differ from job to job – so being able to draw on a labour market which has a pool of skills within it which are being developed also through their work for other companies is very important. (ID 1/7)

When demand is high, freelancing enables people to build their career profiles and can provide greater autonomy over working times and work content. As indicated above, people enjoy doing the work and freelancing. Working for a small company or setting up independently was one way of retaining control. Freelancers, for example, had internalized many of the ideas associated with individualization. They tended to accept market fluc-tuations as a characteristic of the sector and considered themselves person-ally responsible for maintaining their marketability by constantly updating their skills. In this way, they enacted the part of the ideal citizens in the new age (Rose 1999). Furthermore, in the short term the rates of pay are far higher than among dependent employees. But employment can also be extremely precarious. Contracts are normally short-term, and based around specific projects which contributes to the unpredictability of working hours and rates of pay.

Work in larger new media organizations generally follows a more even paced tempo, but the content can become 'formulaic' (ID 1/29) as design-ing one system can be similar to another, even though the clients can be as varied as the health service or a designer clothes firm. Dependent employ-ees in general expressed lower levels of work satisfaction than entrepreneurs and freelancers. People often trade off control over work and working hours with employment regularity and income, though being an employee by no means guarantees job security. While freelancers bore the brunt of fluctua-tions, employees were not immune from the threat of downsizing. For example, one of the larger companies in the city expanded rapidly follow-ing the success of a TV programme and subsequently let go half of its staff. Then within two days they advertised for freelancers. Indeed, this company has had a wildly fluctuating workforce despite its national and international success. A multinational acquired a 50 per cent equity stake in 2000 and has now bought out the company completely, making its future in Brighton somewhat unclear.

This section has demonstrated the insecure working arrangements that typify the new media sector and make the application of any form of employment regulations difficult. Good equal opportunities policies on paper are no protection even for people on permanent contracts if they cannot establish a work history. A further source of insecurity, financial insecurity, especially for firms, arises from buyers defaulting on agreements or from hiring employees who are less capable than they may appear from their résumés. The novelty of many of the skills and the lack of formal accreditation in the new media sector create vulnerability for both employees and employers alike.

Childcare workers enjoy greater job and income security, especially those employed by the public sector. Some child and elder care workers, though none in this particular research, are employed by temporary employment agencies, where the terms and conditions of employment are variable, but generally less advantageous than those working in the public sector. Childminders, not included in the survey, would, like the new media workers, obtain some benefits by working from home. They are, however, also likely to experience income fluctuations as a result of changing demand.

Regulation and representation

New media workers almost universally saw little role for trade unions. They expressed more or less incredulity when responding to my questions about trade unions. A typical response indicated that unions, 'They were something we learned about at school' (ID 5) or 'You mean *trade* unions? – No, I can honestly say that those two words have never been mentioned all the time I have been here. I suppose trade unions are there to represent the workforce independently of the company but it makes me think about miners and things' (ID 2/512).

Even those sympathetic to the idea of trade unions thought they were irrelevant to this particular sector. In small firms, lines of communication between employees and managers (often the directors) were generally direct so employees saw no need for more formal mediation mechanisms. Furthermore, the sector, firms within it, and the city as a whole have the reputation of being 'laid back', 'cool' and flexible, so 'everyone is accepted', 'we employ all sorts here' – 'if I have an issue I take it up with my line manager'. Indeed, the smaller new media companies did not have formal equality policies and they were generally considered unnecessary, as 'discrimination was not an issue'. Nevertheless, others noted the desirability of such policies. Joe commented that 'things were a bit more organized' when they became part of a larger group and 'now we have all the equalities policies but it is not really an issue in Brighton – people are very broadminded – it's not really an issue here' (ID 2/5). Despite the 'laid back' and apparently egalitarian working atmosphere, gendered patterns of vertical and horizontal segregation are clearly evident, suggesting that informality may not be the best way of addressing inequalities (see Gill 2002).

While equality issues were not perceived to be of high priority, employees were concerned by the high 'churn factor' especially in one of the larger organizations which had a reputation for 'hiring loads of people when there is an upturn and then getting rid of them in a downturn' (ID 2/5). After one particular downturn in 2002, the company let go around 50 employees. According to a local trade union official, contacted after the event, the employees were simply 'called in one afternoon – called into a room, were given an envelope that said "Please don't open this, open it when you get home. By the way we have turned your computer off and you're all sacked."'(ID 2/907). Subsequently the employees organized with assistance from the union and working conditions improved for those who remained.[10] So far this is a rare incidence of worker organization in this sector but as the work of new media workers becomes more routine, their receptiveness to union organizing may increase. At the same time larger firms can be very resistant to union organization and undermine worker demands by threatening to move elsewhere as the case below (this time relating to IT workers) demonstrates.

One of the major employers of IT workers in the finance sector was sub-contracting some of the PC-related work to India and required the Brighton and Hove workers to train the Indian workers, which as Helen pointed out is quite difficult, 'because it's blatantly obvious that you are training people to do your job, you know . . . However hard they try and fudge the discussion' (ID 52). Initially it was just supposed to be the routine side of the work but Helen thought it would only be a matter of time before 'they displace the whole team'.

As time passes, IT and new media work become more routine especially in the larger firms so employees are 'less like pioneers at the technological frontier and more like routine white-collar workers' (ID 46). As a consequence, new media jobs are more likely to be subjected to global competition, which in turn weakens the power of employees to obtain more secure working conditions and ensure that equal opportunities policies exist in practice as well as on paper. By contrast, work in personal services and care is always place- and person-dependent, so there is less chance of these jobs going offshore, though migrant workers are frequently employed in these sectors, especially in care homes to supplement the ageing local employees.

At the time of the survey, childcare employees were not very confident that unions would help resolve their key concern, which was low pay. The level of unionization varied, however, between the public and private sectors. All of the teachers and nurses working in crèches and nurseries linked to public institutions, such as the local authority or the university, were union members. The learning support assistants, who are generally people with few if any formal qualifications, were not, arguing they could not afford the subscriptions. None of the nursery workers or assistants in private sector nurseries belonged to the union.

One key reason that employees joined unions was for legal protection. Employees were concerned about potential litigation from parents in the event of any kind of accident or accusation and the unions were considered a vital support. However, even supporters, including those with a history of trade union membership, viewed unions as rather distant or 'remote'. Similar to the IT and new media workers, care-workers felt that unions would not address their specific concerns, and that there was too much rivalry between unions and competition for their 'subs' (subscriptions).

In both the public and private sectors, there are people with different qualifications and varied terms and conditions of employment 'caring' for children in the same workplace. As with all activities involving caring, it is difficult to fragment the work actually done between employees on the basis of skills, as conceded by a nursery manager: 'they have an equal say in planning and in contact with the children, *there is no difference in the work they do*' (ID 4) (My emphasis). Indeed, one of the key concerns of employees is the growing gap between the responsibilities and pay of childcare assistants. The assistants earn between £5 and £6 per hour (at the time marginally above the minimum wage) for work involving being with and talking to children, some of whom have quite complex social problems. As a teaching support assistant commented, 'It's not just picking up the paint pots any more. It's a skilled job on an unskilled wage' (Kelso 2002).[11] Indeed national data confirm that childcare work is one of the lowest paid jobs in the UK, with average gross annual pay of less than £11,000, which is lower than for people working as gardeners or cleaners (Daycare Trust 2001).[12]

Despite these concerns, childcare workers expressed a high degree of satisfaction with the nature of work, their sense of achievement and their work–life balance. Low pay, however, remains a key issue making it very difficult if not impossible to buy housing or even pay an independent rent in the Brighton and Hove area. Indeed, one of the employees, who had worked for over twenty years and inherited her parents' apartment, contemplated moving out because she couldn't afford the annual maintenance charges.

Overall the care sector is characterized by quite profound differences in pay and working contracts, probably more so than in the nature of the work and work context, with further differences between those working in or connected to public sector institutions and those in the private sector (see Prism Research 2000). Given the responsibility of the work involved, low pay can only be explained by the technical characteristics of care-work, and the gender composition of the workforce in a society in which women's work is of low social value. These factors are compounded by the difficulty of organizing workers in small workplaces. Individual nurseries are generally small, caring for between 20 and 40 children, and employing ten or fewer employees even though large companies with multiple branches sometimes own them.

Some months after the first survey, public sector workers took part in a one-day strike (July 2002) as part of the national council workers' pay dispute. The result was a three-year pay deal, with a guaranteed minimum wage rate of £5 per hour. The strength of action and degree of membership commitment was viewed with surprise by the press and delight among union leaders, with newspaper headlines reading: 'Angry women find a voice over pay that doesn't add up' and 'First strike for most of mums' army' (Kelso 2002). A variety of employees including classroom assistants, social workers, carers, librarians and housing officers took part in the strike to high-light the problem of low pay, especially given high housing costs. This action illustrates that even with a fragmented and individualized workforce, col-lective action is possible and the existence of regulations at a national and supra-national level are useful by providing benchmarks and a framework for local negotiations. The private sector nursery workers are not covered by the agreement but they might benefit indirectly if local wages rise as a consequence.

Conclusion

This chapter has developed a conceptualization of the new economy that helps to explain why widening social divisions take a gendered form, despite the growing number of equal opportunities policies that have been implemented by national and supra-national institutions. This perspective has been illustrated by qualitative research on the new media and childcare sectors in Brighton and Hove. One of the key findings is that work remains highly segregated in the new economy with childcare work almost exclusively performed by women. While the employment composition of new media is more varied it too is profoundly segregated.

In both occupations workers reported high levels of job satisfaction. Their concerns varied, with new media workers, especially the freelancers and the small-scale entrepreneurs experiencing job uncertainty while the prime concern for the childcare workers was low pay. Both groups of workers had to varying degrees internalized the philosophy of the autonomous, inde-pendent, self-regulating citizen who is responsible for managing risks and their own individual and family well-being and thus took it upon them-selves rather than to the unions to resolve their problems. Even so, the survey period coincided with the first recorded collective action by both groups. Workers in one of the larger new media firms joined a trade union and the low-paid care support workers went on strike.

Finally, returning to the broader questions relating to the new economy and gender divisions, all technologies are introduced within specific socio-economic frameworks but it takes time for these frameworks to adjust and for their full potential to be realized. When Fordist labour processes were

combined with Taylorist scientific management in the early part of the twentieth century it was not until Keynesian demand management policies and
the welfare state introduced more equitable ways of dividing the social
product between capital and labour that the working classes reaped any benefits from the productivity increases. With the heightened competitive pressure of globalization, redistribution between social groups is more complex
so at present the new economy is associated with rising economic inequality as the productivity increases have yet to be shared. This inequality is
especially marked between those involved in knowledge work and those
more directly associated with care and these divisions are profoundly
gendered. Thus despite the new 'knowledge' economy old gender divisions
remain.

Acknowledgements

The author would like to thank the Leverhulme Trust for financing some of
the research; the firms, employees and union officials who contributed their
time to the study; Lotte Dunford and Róisín Ryan Flood for arranging the
interviews; Paul Dinnen, who transcribed the tapes and Heidi Gottfried and
Sylvia Walby for their editorial advice.

Notes

1. Daniels (2004) notes that there were 3000 references to the term 'new economy'
   in the US business press in 1999 and 20 000 in 2000.
2. See Rubery and Grimshaw (2001) for a table that documents optimistic and pessimistic scenarios about the impact of ICTs on the scale and quality of work.
3. Another example would be the *Harry Potter* books; although the end product has
   a physical form, it can be distributed virtually to printers throughout the globe,
   thus making J. K. Rowling a global superstar. The difference in earnings between
   herself and other authors is probably far greater than between those of Charles
   Dickens and his contemporaries.
4. Goos and Manning (2003) develop their own categorization of 'good and bad
   jobs' from occupational and industry/sectoral categories and differentiate them
   by pay decile.
5. In London, private nurseries can cost as much as £17,500 each year while the
   annual average pay of a childcare worker is £11,000. The usual cost is in the order
   of £8,700 and while the government provides support for childcare costs of low-
   income families this only amounts to around 30 per cent of the total cost.
6. The employment rate of mothers with pre-school children doubled between 1984
   and 2000; the majority (66 per cent) is part-time employment (see Harkness 2003
   and Cameron et al. 2002).
7. For small micro enterprises the difference between small entrepreneurs and freelancers is often fuzzy (see Gottschall this volume).
8. The survey findings are presented in more detail in Perrons 2004b.
9. IDn/n refers to the respondents: the first number indicates whether the quotation comes from the first or second set of interviews and the second number refers
   to the individual identification number.
10. See Perrons 2004b for further details.

11. This quotation comes from a worker taking part in the strike discussed below (see Kelso 2002).
12. The average in the survey Table 3 was higher because some of those interviewed were teachers, and half of them were in nurseries attached to the public sector but the care assistants in the private nurseries were mainly on the minimum wage.

8
Are Care-Workers Knowledge Workers?

Makiko Nishikawa and Kazuko Tanaka

Introduction

In all developed societies, the phenomenon of the ageing of society, in conjunction with the feminization of the labour force, calls for formal arrangements of elderly care. Japan is no exception in this regard, with care services for the elderly being the fastest growing sector in the economy. When compared to 1996, the numbers of organizations and workers engaging in care services for the elderly had nearly doubled in 2001 (Ministry of Health, Labour and Welfare 2002). The introduction of the Long-Term Care Insurance Law (LCIL) in 2000 has further accelerated the growth, de-regulation and privatization of services that have traditionally been provided by local governments. The rationale behind the LCIL was to promote cost-efficiency, innovation and high quality care. Accordingly, a number of formal educational institutions, qualification systems and training courses have since been introduced. On the other hand, with the increasing trend towards flexibilization of the labour market in general, and with the privatization of service providers since the introduction of the LCIL in particular, the number of Japanese homecare service workers who are employed as part-time or on-call (*Toroku*) workers has been increasing rapidly. These are workers who seldom visit their official place of employment and, instead, spend most of their working hours at clients' homes as needed, thereby working under new arrangements of work time and space.

In terms of the technology used, care-work belongs to the old economy that relies heavily on human labour, and in this sense, we should draw a line between care-work and other new types of work representing the new economy.[1] However, care-work is an integral part of the new economy in two senses: Firstly, as Perrons highlighted in this volume, the new economy is characterized by the rise of high-risk, unpredictable, long-hour work, and by the increasing number of women who work under these conditions. This requires formal care services that substitute informal care traditionally provided by family members. Secondly, and more importantly, the new economy is characterized by knowledge workers who produce values through their knowledge (Drucker 1993b). According to Kokuryo (1999), knowledge adds its values by combining with other knowledge, and ICT contributes greatly in this process of infinite expansion of knowledge creation. However, to be transferred through ICT, knowledge must be digitized. Perrons in this volume actually defines knowledge workers as those producing goods that can be 'digitized'.

Knowledge has both explicit and tacit dimensions, however, and it is explicit knowledge which can be digitized and successfully transferred through ICT. On the other hand, for tacit knowledge to be transferred, we need dialogue or collective reflection (Nonaka 1990) which requires the old 'technology': direct human interaction. Thus, ICT enhances our capacity to deal efficiently with the explicit or *quantitative* dimension of knowledge and information, but for the tacit or *qualitative* dimension of knowledge to be transferred, we still need rich communication through human interaction. It is true that those workers who effectively utilize ICT have enjoyed the advantages in the new economy, but what ICT actually brings to us and to the knowledge-based economy in general, in this sense, is limited. Nonaka (2005), in fact, argues that the development of ICT has decreased rather than increased the values of explicit knowledge and digitized information, but the key to success in the fierce competition in the knowledge-based economy is the creation and accumulation of tacit knowledge that is not replicated easily.

What care-workers produce is a service, which is a deed, a performance, and efforts (Rathmell 1966), and their service outcome is basically measured not by *quantity* but by *quality*, which is 'an elusive concept in abstract terms, and is best defined in terms of people's experiences' (Henderson and Atkinson 2003: 162). This emphasis on *quality* in care-work seems to accord with the nature of work in the knowledge-based economy suggested above. Moreover, it is true that care-workers continuously update and modify their knowledge and know-how in practice settings in an ongoing effort to develop frameworks and options and to raise the quality of their services that can be applied to as yet unknown clients and situations in the future (Nishikawa 2004), and in this sense, their work is certainly knowledge-intensive. However, to become fully-fledged knowledge workers, they must share their individual and often idiosyncratic knowledge with others, make collective efforts to externalize it, combine the externalized knowledge, and internalize it again, in order to create greater knowledge and values.

In this chapter, we argue that while care-work is an integral part of the new economy, the increasing flexibilization of employment makes it difficult for care-work to be identified with the knowledge work that is said to occupy a central position in the new economy. We investigate the extent of the influence of employment flexibilization on care-workers' knowledge, and address such questions as how flexibilization affects the acquisition and accumulation of knowledge by care-workers and in what ways flexibilization prevents them from becoming fully-fledged knowledge workers.

This chapter begins by examining the trend towards flexibilization of the labour market and the need for and development of formal care services in Japan as well as in other countries. It then goes on to investigate how flexibilization affects homecare workers' knowledge acquisition by looking at the relevant literature as well as by analysing data from a survey conducted by the authors. The survey was carried out during the summer of 2003, using a sample of 595 homecare workers affiliated to homecare service organizations in the Tokyo metropolitan area.

Homecare work as flexibilized gendered work

Trends towards flexibilization of labour

During the postwar period, the concept of the male breadwinner became firmly entrenched as the predominant employment model. According to this model, men were supposed to earn sufficient income to support their families, while women were to take responsibility for domestic affairs and family care at home. As a result of the intense competition spawned by the era of economic globalization, however, employment practices that had protected the male breadwinner came to be perceived in advanced economies as an extra cost. In addition, the shift towards the service economy created expanding demand for flexible labour (OECD 2001a). Since it is not possible to 'stock' a product in the service sector, service workers should readily respond to fluctuating demand (Scrinzi 2003). Women, primarily taking responsibility for the family at home, have tended to 'choose' flexible modes of employment in order to combine work with domestic obligations. The subsequent increase in women's paid employment associated with the development of flexibilization of the labour market has resulted in the erosion of the male breadwinner model in advanced societies (Crompton 2002; Perrons 1999; Gottfried and O'Reilly 2002).

Japan is no exception in this regard. The male breadwinner model, which had been deeply ingrained in Japanese employment practice, has been gradually eroded under the pressure of increasing global competition. During this era of intense global competition, accompanied with a prolonged recession during the 1990s, the flexibilization of the labour market has continued apace (Tanaka 1999; Nakano 1999). For men, non-standard modes of employment have seen an increase among both younger and older age groups, while employment practices for the supposed breadwinners in the middle age group remain relatively standard. While the former two groups typically offer numerical flexibility to their employers, the middle age group, who have traditionally provided functional flexibility to their employers, also adjusted their work-time to market fluctuations by doing overtime work or by giving up their holiday. For women, however, non-standard employment has increased among all working age groups. If they are relatively young, they tend to work as dispatched workers, and if they are married and have children, they tend to work as part-timers. Many married women now choose to work part-time in order to earn supplemental income for their households, as they can no longer expect the steady rise of their husband wage due to the ongoing changes in the traditional employment practices. These wives often adjust their working hours and their income so as to remain dependent on their husband, so that they can take advantage of the current social security systems.[2] This has helped to preserve the male bread-winner model, albeit in a modified way (Nishikawa 2003a).

The speed of flexibilization has accelerated during the 1990s. These days, among paid women employees, non-standard workers are more numerous than their standard counterparts. Among the various types of non-standard employment, part-time work is the largest category for women workers, constituting more than 70 per cent of non-standard paid work. Women continue to earn less than men, but the relative rates are gradually improving for full-time workers. On the other hand, among women, part-timers earn significantly less in terms of hourly wage than full-timers, and, moreover, the gap is widening (Ministry of Health, Labour and Welfare 2004). Flexibilization of labour has had a much greater impact on the way women work than on the way men work.

What is more, the Japanese government has taken steps to de-regulate labour protection to the particular detriment of women workers. The Part-time Law, established in 1993, only stipulates the minimum level of standard labour protection measures. The issues of unequal treatment and indirect discrimination remain unresolved. The Dispatched Worker Law, which was established in 1985, enabled private companies to engage in dispatching activities, albeit only for certain occupations. During the 1990s, the list of allowed occupations became longer, and restrictions were ultimately removed altogether when the law was revised in 1998. In reality, this revision was something of a rubber stamp that merely endorsed what was already happening in the labour market. As a result of the revision, replacement of regular full-time employees with part-time and dispatched workers has been accelerated (Nakano 1999). Both part-time and dispatched work are typically engaged in by women, though the former tend to be occupied by middle-aged, married women and the latter by younger women, and their working conditions in particular have steadily deteriorated as a result of government policy in this area.

In sum, the trend towards flexibilization of labour has become a mainstream current in advanced economies, as a result of the increase in global competition since the 1970s. This has meant that, in conjunction with a concomitant trend towards de-regulation, increasing numbers of women have been pulled into the labour market as non-standard workers. In Japan, too, married women are the typical targets of non-standard employment practice. Full-time workers increasingly are replaced by part-time and other non-standard workers. This process of non-standardization can also be seen in care-work in Japan, which is discussed below.

Care-work: expanding flexible and gendered work

Growth in women's labour force participation has caused significant reductions in informal family care (Badgett and Folbre 1999). Demand for care-work has consequently increased steadily, and in OECD countries today, care-work for children and the elderly is the subject of considerable attention. Due to recent social and demographic changes, such as low birth rates, increasing longevity, high divorce rates, and weakened informal networks of social support, the demand for care of the elderly is growing in all advanced societies.

As the number of older persons in need of long-term care increases, home-care continues to be the predominant care setting for the majority of households. Care for the elderly at home is typically flexibly organized as a 'female-type' service occupation, placed at the lower end of the occupational scale with low status and low wages. Elderly care, moreover, has traditionally been carried out by women at home without formal training or qualifications. Structural barriers to the acceptance of such care-work as a professional occupation can be seen in conflicting perceptions as neither fully constituting paid nor unpaid work.

In a number of OECD countries, long-term care policies have been reformed to allow users more choice among care providers and flexibility with regards to the way care is provided (Lundsgaard 2005). The cash benefits system was widely introduced in many European countries during the late 1990s (Ungerson 2003). This system offers care users a choice between cash and services. If cash is chosen, however, the amount received is insufficient to pay for the services that are provided in response to the latter choice. In most cases, care beneficiaries who choose cash opt to pay the relatives who care for them. In these cases, the labour is not fully exchanged for a wage, so that the carer does not enter into a formal employment relationship with her 'client', thus preserving the semi-commodified nature of care-work. Women of lower economic means tend to receive cash to become informal carers at home or to work casually as low-wage carers in the grey market, while women of the middle class tend to choose care services instead of cash and purchase additional services from the market when necessary (Theobald 2003). In most advanced economies, the quality and substance of care-work for the elderly vary significantly, ranging from, for example, unpaid care-work by family members, to paid informal carers, unqualified care-workers, and qualified care-workers. In many Western industrialized countries, however, homecare work has not yet been firmly established as a professional occupation.

Homecare work in Japan: flexibilized gendered work

Among advanced societies, the greying of society in Japan has proceeded the fastest, mirroring rapid social and demographic change such as delayed marriage, a declining fertility rate, and prolonged longevity, with the result that adequate homecare services have constantly been in short supply. Since the late 1980s, the Japanese government has introduced various measures to cope with this problem, but these measures are far from gender-neutral.

The Japanese homecare service system was launched at the national level in 1963 when the Geriatric Welfare Law was passed. Initially, services were limited to low income households, but the income restriction was abolished in 1982. While the Japanese government consistently asserted the primary responsibility of the family to care for the elderly, it finally accepted during the late 1980s that families were no longer capable of supplying sufficient care for the elderly at home. The government's successive implementation of the Gold Plan (1989), the New Gold Plan (1995) and Gold Plan 21 (1999) rapidly increased the number of homecare workers by means of setting concrete goals.

There was an urgent need for the Japanese government to meet the goals of the successive Gold Plans by promptly recruiting homecare workers via the training and qualification systems. The Japanese government mainly targeted the middle-aged, married women who have left the labour market upon marriage or childbirth as the potential sources of labour. At the beginning, no particular qualification was required but personal experiences of care, such as raising children or taking care of old parents were the important selection criteria, but eventually, various qualification systems were introduced to standardize the quality of care (Nishikawa 2003b).

Qualification systems for care-workers were institutionalized first by the establishment of the 'certified care-worker' (*Kaigofukushishi*) system as a national qualification in 1987, and then of homecare worker training systems in 1992. Training for homecare workers is conducted by local governments or by agencies designated thereby. Compared to the certified care-worker qualification, homecare workers' trainings last for much shorter periods of time. There are three levels of certificate obtained from homecare worker trainings, from the first to the third grade, and the second grade is the standard among Japanese homecare workers. The second-grade certificate is obtained after 130-hour trainings. This relatively short period of training time fits with the expectation of married women who want to re-start working as 'respectable' workers, while combining with domestic responsibilities. Standardization of homecare services can be seen as the first step towards according professional status to care-work.

During the 1990s, however, both the national and local governments increasingly came to perceive the expansion of homecare provision as a superfluous financial burden in the midst of severe and prolonged recession.

In fact, local governments rapidly shifted from being direct providers of homecare services to being indirect providers via social welfare councils (Ito 2001). Eventually, the Japanese government opted for marketization of homecare services to promote cost efficiencies, and introduced the Long-Term Care Insurance System (LTCI) in 2000. The LTCI is a social insurance scheme which provides both home and institutional care for the elderly. In Japan, informal care by family members still plays a large role, but it is not supported financially by public programmes. Under the LTCI, the benefits are given by local governments on condition that the services are provided by formally trained care-workers.[3]

With the launch of the LTCI, various types of agencies emerged to offer homecare service on the market, such as private firms, cooperatives, medical hospitals and NPOs, other than the traditional service providers, such as local governments, social welfare councils and other social welfare foundations. As a result, the homecare service market has become more competitive, and under pressure to reduce costs and due to the labour-intensive nature of the services provided, homecare agencies in the private sector have become more dependent on irregular, non-standard forms of employment.

The Japanese care service system is divided into institutional care and homecare. In the consecutive Gold Plans, the Japanese government attempted to increase the latter type of care services, mainly because of perceived cost efficiency compared to the institutional option. The care-workers engaged in these two types of care services work according to different systems of flexible work-time: those working as institutional care-workers engage in shift work and night work, providing 24-hour 365-day services, while those working as homecare workers respond to fluctuating demand from clients, with work more often than not concentrated during the daytime. As a result, the former category tends to feature relatively young single workers according to the standard employment model, while the latter is dominated by middle-aged, married women with non-standard modes of employment. According to a national survey conducted in 2002, eight out of ten institutional care-workers worked as full-time regular workers, while the same proportion of homecare workers worked as non-regular workers. The majority of the former group were in their twenties or thirties, while the majority of the latter were in their forties and fifties. Care-workers were predominantly female, but the gender composition differed between institutional care and homecare: while 20 per cent of institutional care-workers were male, the corresponding figure for homecare workers was only 5 per cent (Kaigo Rodo Antei Senta 2002).

For homecare workers, about half were *Toroku* workers (Kaigo Rodo Antei Senta 2002). *Toroku* workers register their names with agencies (this is the literal meaning of 'Toroku'), who assign homecare service jobs according to their clients' demands and workers' schedules. According to the same 2002 survey, average weekly working hours for *Toroku* workers were 14 hours, less than half the figure for regular full-time care-workers, who worked 40 hours a week on average. *Toroku* workers are paid for hours spent at clients' homes that often fluctuate each month, while regular full-time care-workers earn monthly, stable salary. The average monthly income of *Toroku* workers was 68 000 yen, less than a third of their regular full-time counterparts, who earned on average 222 000 yen per month (Kaigo Rodo Antei Senta 2002).

It is generally assumed that homecare workers, who visit clients' homes and provide care services on an individual basis, require a higher skill level than institutional care-workers in order to cope independently with the varying needs of clients. In addition, because they work within the context of the clients' ordinary life settings, they presumably need both technical flexibility and mental flexibility to provide quality care. Furthermore, as they work independently, they require advanced information-handling skills and risk management skills. Time management is also important for these workers. On the other hand, in institutional settings, care-workers are basically given direct instructions from their supervisors or seniors. Division of labour is found, and their job is more or less standardized by the organizational rules and procedures. However, the non-standard modes of employment and the corresponding low income and low social recognition of homecare workers are hardly attractive to workers with higher qualifications, such as the holders of the certified care-worker qualification. While relatively many institutional care-workers have obtained the certified care-worker qualification, the majority of homecare workers hold the homecare second-grade certificate, and due to unstable work condition, their turnover rate is relatively high. This, in turn, prevents employers from investing in human capital.

In sum, social and demographic changes in Japan have caused a rapid shift towards an ageing society, which has in turn stimulated increasing demand for care-work for the elderly. Flexibilization of homecare workers accelerated after the introduction of the LTCI. Intense competition in the market for care-work has encouraged increasingly fragmented provision of services and modes of employment. Although moves were made towards establishing homecare work as a professional occupation during the 1990s, the introduction of the LTCI has reversed or at least discontinued this trend, resulting in irregular and non-standard fragmented work undertaken mainly by middle-aged women with comparatively less training.

Homecare work as knowledge work

Care-workers and their knowledge

There is a considerable body of literature which suggests that information technology (IT) has changed the way people work, and that knowledge workers now play a major role in the new knowledge-based economy (Burton-Jones 1999; Drucker 2002). IT has dramatically improved our ability to access and use data and information, and those with the capacity to generate knowledge through the processing and management of information are said to have become vastly more important actors in the new economy (Castells 2000b, 2001).

While the definition of knowledge workers varies considerably according to author, the term is generally used for people with considerable theoretical knowledge gained through formal education, and with regard to continuous knowledge acquisition and updating within a specific field (Burton-Jones 1999; Drucker 2002). Another important characteristic of knowledge workers is that they regard and identify themselves as professionals, and thus feel more affinity with those engaged in the same specialized field in other institutions than with colleagues at their own institution who work in a different knowledge area. Workplace relations among knowledge workers in the same field, therefore, are more aptly characterized as those between senior and junior colleagues rather than as those between bosses and subordinates (Drucker 2002). Ensuring a high standard of product is more effectively achieved by monitoring one another's work, rather than by top-down control, and the organizations they work for tend to be small and narrowly focused, rather than large and diverse in the range of services offered (Burton-Jones 1999).

Does care-work, then, constitute a part of knowledge work in the new economy? While it is well known that care-work has existed for decades, the theoretical knowledge or 'technical rationality' (Schon 1983, 1987) of this field has not developed as fully as that of traditional knowledge workers such as doctors or engineers. In Japan, as mentioned above, it has only been since the late 1980s that formal educational institutions have been established to certify care-workers, and that various formal training courses, in the field of physical care in particular, have been introduced. However, while such measures have been devised mainly with a view to the provision of entry-level certificates or qualifications, learning and training opportunities for those already engaged in care service remain limited (Nishikawa 2003b). After initial entry, therefore, continued learning and updating of knowledge is left to the efforts of individual care-workers and their organizations. As the size of these organizations tends to be small, however, the training provision has been rather limited.

The under-development of theoretical knowledge, formal education and training systems seem, however, to be partly related to knowledge content. As the subject of care service is people, and because providing good quality care depends on developing relationships between a carer and the person cared for (Himmelweit 1999), care-workers' knowledge tends to be idiosyncratic, backed up by continuous acquisition of local and client- or situation-specific knowledge, such as a client's habits and preferences, or family and community backgrounds. This is particularly the case for homecare workers. Their major style of learning is inductive, rather than deductive, involving the construction of 'particularized theory', which is 'what an individual practitioner with an individual style and unique set of strengths and weaknesses has found effective with particular clients in particular settings' (Evans 1999). As a result, homecare workers are hardly motivated to transfer and share knowledge with others in the same profession globally, let alone locally. Thus, the bulk of their knowledge tends to remain either tacit or embodied in individual care-workers.

This tacit nature of care-workers' knowledge is also reflected in the fact that, traditionally, education and training for caring professions has been conducted by means of apprenticeship. As Evans has noted, the most critical method of learning in caring professions is through practical experience, where practice teachers and other staff help students to understand what is going on in the practice setting and how to perform appropriately as professional carers. Academic teachers, whose main role is to draw connections with theoretical knowledge, are comparatively peripheral to this process of learning (Evans 1999).

Tacit knowledge is not easily acquired through the use of technology (Nonaka and Takeuchi 1995; Kokuryo 1999), but rather it often involves interaction with other people. Nonaka's model of knowledge conversion (Figure 8.1) demonstrates how tacit knowledge is transferred and generated through human interactions (Nonaka 1990).

In this model, there are four different modes of knowledge conversion: (1) from tacit to tacit, which is called 'socialization'; (2) from tacit to explicit, called 'externalization'; (3) from explicit to explicit, or 'combination'; and (4) from explicit to tacit, called 'internalization'. An individual can acquire tacit knowledge directly from others by sharing experiences without using language. Socialization can be seen between masters and students, as in apprenticeship, or between fellow workers or workers and clients. Externalization is a process of articulating tacit knowledge as explicit concepts. This involves the use of metaphors, analogies, concepts, hypotheses or models. This process also requires dialogue or collective reflection. Combination represents the process of organizing concepts into a knowledge system, combining different bodies of explicit knowledge. Lastly, internalization is the

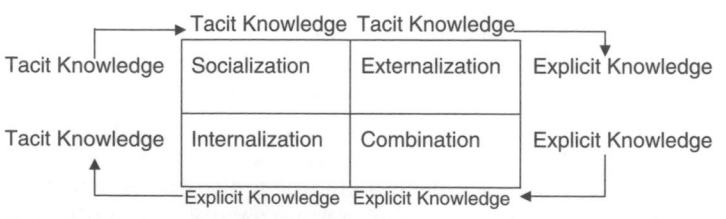

Source: Nonaka and Takeuchi (1995: 62).

Figure 8.1:   Four modes of knowledge conversion

process of embodying explicit knowledge into tacit knowledge through 'learning by doing'. Each mode of knowledge conversion produces different knowledge types: socialization creating 'sympathized knowledge' such as shared mental models and technical skills, externalization creating 'conceptual knowledge' such as metaphor and analogy, combination creating 'systemic knowledge' such as prototypes and new component technologies, and internalization producing 'operational knowledge' about, for example, project management, production processes, new-product usage, and policy implementation. Nonaka's model suggests that tacit to tacit transfer and tacit to explicit transfer require collaborative effort, that is, physical face-to-face contact, among workers (Nonaka 1990; Nonaka and Takeuchi 1995).

Burton-Jones, moreover, suggests that as far as the explicit to tacit and tacit to tacit knowledge permutations are concerned, IT has limited use, although the explicit to tacit dimension can be partly addressed by using a case-based system, and the tacit to tacit dimension may also be partially assisted by a more context-sensitive approach to providing information. However, most sharing of tacit knowledge occurs through physical face-to-face interaction among people, and 'IT systems have some way to go before they can simulate the real world immediacy' (Burton-Jones 1999: 12).

As mentioned above, since the greater part of care-workers' knowledge is embodied in individual care-workers, face-to-face contact with senior colleagues and fellow workers seems to play a crucial role in the transfer and generation of knowledge. In terms of homecare workers, this might take place either at the office or at a client's home; however, the knowledge transferred and generated at each site is assumed to be different. At the office, homecare workers can consult with their seniors and fellow workers after or before visiting a client's home. They can thereby either exchange explicit knowledge or generate explicit knowledge out of tacit knowledge, which can later be internalized. They might also engage in socialization, but knowledge gained and transferred at the office by means of socialization is limited to the tasks experienced at the office. As discussed above, practical experience is the most critical method of learning for care-workers, and in terms of homecare workers, it is at the client's home that they practise their work. There, they are supposed to engage in both internalization and socialization. The explicit knowledge learned through formal education and at the office becomes embodied as tacit knowledge through learning by doing (or internalization) at the client's home. Socialization can occur through interaction with senior and fellow workers if they visit a client's home together, and also through interaction with clients and their families. The latter kind of interaction is supposed to transfer and generate client-specific, and therefore idiosyncratic, local knowledge, while knowledge created by the former interaction has a larger scope, such as mental models and technical skills that can be shared among those working in the same occupation.

In sum, care-workers' knowledge cannot be made fully explicit or shared and combined globally, but rather is local and idiosyncratic. Consequently, theoretical knowledge and formal training have not yet been adequately developed. With the accumulation of explicit knowledge remaining insufficient, internalization (or learning by doing) also seems to have limited use in the generation of knowledge. Workers can neither learn effectively from the accumulated experiences of others nor from systemic knowledge derived from the accumulation thereof. The bulk of their knowledge, therefore, remains tacit, and the sharing and acquisition of knowledge is most effectively carried out, as in fact it has traditionally been done, by physical face-to-face interactions either in practice settings with seniors, fellow workers and clients or on the job. Thus, the key method for care-workers to become knowledge workers is through face-to-face interaction.

Flexibilization and homecare workers' knowledge

As mentioned above, since the enactment of the Long-Term Care Insurance Law, the share of the private agencies providing care services in Japan has increased, as have the proportions of part-time care-workers and *Toroku* care-workers, particularly among homecare workers, as compared to institutional care-workers. Then, how does this type of flexibilization affects homecare workers' knowledge?

In Japanese homecare service agencies, non-standard modes of employment are so prevalent that most of the front-line homecare workers (HH) work on a part-time or *Toroku* basis. It often happens that even chief homecare workers, who are responsible for supervising the front-line homecare workers and managing their clients, are not employed on a permanent basis, but work under fixed contracts.

How then, does this type of flexibilization affect homecare workers' knowledge acquisition? Firstly, it can limit the opportunities for face-to-face interaction between junior workers and senior workers. As they basically work in their clients' homes, they have relatively short time to spend at the office. When juniors workers work full-time, however, they have both adequate time and opportunities for face-to-face communication, consulting with senior workers at the office before and/or after visiting clients, but if they work part-time, and especially if they work as *Toroku* workers, their opportunities for face-to-face interaction with seniors are limited, as they are basically paid for time spent at clients' homes and, therefore, have a lower incentive to visit the office at which they are employed. They do communicate with their chief homecare worker after and/or before visiting clients, but this often takes the form of either written documentation or a telephone conversation. In such cases, it is difficult to transfer tacit knowledge. This also means that the tacit knowledge gained by each front-line worker through interaction with clients cannot be effectively transferred to their colleagues and thus shared collectively.

Secondly, flexibilization not only limits opportunities for face-to-face contact between junior and senior workers, but also restricts the opportunities for communication between fellow workers. For example, in a few major private firms interviewed by the authors that own many homecare service branches throughout the Tokyo metropolitan area, it is quite common for non-regular part-time workers and *Toroku* workers to gather together at their office for a meeting no more than once a month. For these part-time workers and *Toroku* workers, the opportunity to mutually transfer and generate knowledge, whether tacit or explicit, is thus very limited. This also contrasts to the characteristic of knowledge workers mentioned above, whereby monitoring one another, as opposed to top-down supervision and control, is the standard mode of generating and updating collective, professional knowledge.

Finally, for non-regular part-time workers or *Toroku* workers, communication (or socialization) is quite likely to be more involved with their clients than with their supervisors and fellow workers such that communication in the former setting, therefore, can be more influential in their knowledge acquisition and accumulation. This may well enhance the idiosyncratic and local nature of their knowledge, thus further hindering the accumulation of collective, professional knowledge.

In the following section, we analyse survey data, and examine how Japanese homecare workers acquire and accumulate their knowledge, and in what ways flexibilization affects their knowledge acquisition and accumulation.

Data analysis

Data

The following results are based on the analysis of data collected in a survey conducted by the authors during the summer of 2003. The sample was drawn from 130 homecare service establishments in the Tokyo metropolitan area owned by three of the major private firms providing homecare services in Japan. We asked the firms and establishments to select front-line homecare workers with a balanced mix of experience, including junior and senior workers, and employment type. The survey was conducted in the form of face-to-face interviews using a structured questionnaire. The overall sample size was 595. Table 8.1 shows the distribution of respondents by experience and type of employment.

Knowledge acquisition and accumulation by Japanese homecare workers

In our survey, we asked the respondents 'How important are the following factors with a view to doing your job well?' Fourteen items for response were listed, and the answers were scaled with five ratings from 'important' to

Table 8.1:   Distribution of respondents by experience and employment type (N = 595)

Experience	%	Employment type	%
Up to 1 year	30	Regular full-time	21
1 to 3 years	37	Non-regular full-time	24
3 years and more	31	Part-time	40
NA	2	*Toroku*	15

Table 8.2:   Important factors in successful homecare work (M.A.)

	% important	*% somewhat important*
Doko-homon	81	17
Instruction by supervisors/ seniors at the office	71	27
Feedback from clients	67	31
Advice from colleagues at the office	64	33
Off-the-job training at the office	64	33
Formal education	59	34

'unimportant'. Table 8.2 shows the items for which more than half of the respondents answered 'important'.

As can be seen in Table 8.2, *Doko-homon* was chosen as the most important factor in terms of Japanese homecare workers doing their job well. *Doko-homon* is a custom in the Japanese homecare services whereby junior workers are accompanied by senior workers when visiting a client's home for the first time, so that the senior worker can help the junior worker to establish good relations with the client, and can instruct the junior worker in the basic knowledge and skills needed to deal effectively with the particular client.[4] Instruction by supervisors or seniors at the office came next to *Doko-homon*, then feedback from clients, followed by advice from colleagues at the office. All four of these items involve human interaction, and, therefore, imply the importance of tacit knowledge. Although off-the-job training (off-JT) at the office and learning at formal educational institutions are also important factors in the acquisition of explicit knowledge, these were perceived as less important than the previous four items. This suggests that tacit knowledge is perceived as more important than explicit knowledge in terms of homecare workers doing their job successfully.

We also asked respondents who had more than one-year experience in homecare work, and who felt that their own knowledge and skills had increased compared to a year previously, to choose from among ten items

Table 8.3: Effective ways to develop knowledge and skills (M.A.)

	% chosen
Exchanging information with fellow workers	78
Learning from supervisors/seniors	73
Trial and error	70
Learning from clients and their families	60
Off-JT at the office	54

those that they thought were effective methods for developing their knowledge and skills. Table 8.3 shows the items chosen by more than half of the respondents.

For those who had worked as homecare workers for more than a year, communicating with fellow workers was perceived as the most effective method of accumulating knowledge and skills, followed by learning from supervisors and seniors. Learning by trial and error came next, followed by learning from clients and their families. While the first two items relate to experiences at the office, the last two items relate to experiences at clients' homes. All four items suggest that face-to-face interaction is the most effective way for homecare workers to develop their skills and acquire knowledge. Again, compared to these four items, off-JT at the office was less popular, suggesting that explicit knowledge is perceived as not as important, when compared to tacit knowledge, with regard to accumulating professional knowledge.

Thus, from the results shown in Tables 8.2 and 8.3, we can see that interaction with seniors, fellow workers and clients, which enables the exchange of tacit knowledge, is crucial to the acquisition and accumulation of knowledge by homecare workers. Formal training, which facilitates the learning of explicit knowledge, is also important, although it is less important to homecare workers than human interaction.

Flexibilization and the acquisition and accumulation of knowledge

How, then, does flexibilization affect the acquisition and accumulation of knowledge by homecare workers? Does it, as we discussed in the previous section, limit opportunities for interaction with seniors and fellow workers, and if so, to what extent? Also, does flexibilization have the effect of enhancing the idiosyncratic nature of homecare workers' knowledge, thereby hampering the generation of collective knowledge?

To answer these questions, we first look at the time spent by homecare workers at the office. Table 8.4 shows the average hours spent at the office for different types of homecare worker. We have four types of workers: regular full-time workers are those working full-time on a permanent basis, non-regular full-time workers are those working full-time but under a fixed-term contract, part-time workers are those working shorter hours than full-timers under a fixed-term contract, and *Toroku* workers are those who register their names with agencies and provide services as needed.

On average, regular full-time workers spend 25 hours a week in their office, and the corresponding figure for non-regular full-time workers is 18 hours a week. Full-time workers, therefore, whether regular or non-regular, would seem to have sufficient time to communicate face-to-face with their seniors and fellow workers. However, for part-time and *Toroku* workers, the average time spent at the office is significantly shorter: for part-time workers, three hours a week, and for *Toroku* workers, two hours a week. Among the *Toroku* workers we interviewed, 28 per cent indicated that they had not visited their office even once during the week previous to the interview. Their opportunities for face-to-face interaction with seniors and fellow workers, therefore, are clearly extremely limited.

This situation is reflected in the items *Toroku* workers see as important to doing their job well (Table 8.5), and in the ways they develop their skills and knowledge (Table 8.6).

Table 8.4:   Average hours per week spent at the office by employment status

Types of employment	Average hours spent at the office per week
Regular full-time workers	24.8
Non-regular full-time workers	18.1
Part-time workers	3.1
Toroku workers	2.2

Table 8.5:   Important factors in successful homecare work by employment status (M.A.)

	Reg. FT (%)	Non Reg. FT (%)	PT (%)	Toroku (%)
Doko-homon	80	89	83	61
Instruction by supervisors/ seniors at the office	75	77	73	47
Feedback from clients	61	70	69	66
Advice from colleagues at the office	69	71	62	52
Off-JT at the office	62	65	66	57
Formal education	55	57	60	63

Table 8.6: Effective ways to develop knowledge and skills by employment status (M.A.)

	Reg. FT (%)	Non Reg. FT (%)	PT (%)	Toroku (%)
Exchanging information with fellow workers	90	85	73	50
Learning from supervisors/ seniors	76	69	81	59
Trial and error	62	79	65	77
Learning from clients and their families	56	69	57	52
Off-JT at the office	50	55	54	55

For regular full-time workers, non-regular full-time workers, and part-time workers, the factor perceived as the most important in successful homecare work is *Doko-homon*, followed by instruction by supervisors or seniors at the office. However, for *Toroku* workers, the most important factor is feedback from clients. Further, feedback from clients was the third most popular response for both non-regular full-time workers and part-time workers, with a greater percentage of these groups seeing it as important when compared to regular full-time workers. Another interesting feature to note is that advice from colleagues at the office was more important for both regular and non-regular full-time workers than for part-time workers and *Toroku* workers. This seems to reflect the fact that the former two types of workers spend more time at the office than the latter two, as we have seen in Table 8.4.

Table 8.6 shows the items chosen by homecare workers as effective methods for developing their individual knowledge and skills. For both regular and non-regular full-time workers, the most popular method was exchanging information with fellow workers. However, differences can be seen between these two types of workers in that a greater percentage of regular workers indicated learning from supervisors and seniors as an effective method compared to their non-regular counterparts, while a larger proportion of non-regular workers viewed trial and error and learning from clients and their families as important. For part-time workers, the most popular choice was learning from supervisors or seniors, while for *Toroku* workers, it was trial and error, with the perceived effectiveness of the other items on the list relatively low.

The results from Tables 8.4 to 8.6 suggest that because regular and non-regular full-time workers spend relatively more time at the office, they have greater opportunities for interacting face-to-face with supervisors, seniors and fellow workers, and can utilize these opportunities to develop their knowledge and skills. However, part-time workers and *Toroku* workers spent less time at the office, and therefore, had fewer opportunities to interact face-to-face with supervisors, seniors, and fellow workers. This is particularly true for *Toroku* workers, who consequently rely on their clients or on a process of trial and error at their clients' homes to acquire and accumulate knowledge. Although part-time workers also spend comparatively little time at the office, they do seem to have some channels available to them for communication with their supervisors and seniors, whom they regard as important and effective sources for acquiring knowledge. However, part-time workers' opportunities for interaction with fellow workers are nonetheless limited compared to full-time workers.

To what extent, then, are opportunities to interact with fellow workers restricted by employment types? In our survey, we asked respondents whether or not they agreed with various statements about their job. These statements included 'I often discuss problematic issues with my colleagues', and 'I would like to discuss problematic issues with my colleagues but do not have time to do so'. The answers were scaled with five ratings from agreement to disagreement. Table 8.7 shows the percentage of respondents who agreed with these statements, by their employment status.

From Table 8.7, we can see that full-time workers, whether regular or non-regular, were much more likely to answer that they often discuss things they do not understand with their colleagues than part-time and *Toroku* workers. On the other hand, part-time workers and *Toroku* workers were slightly more likely than regular or non-regular full-time workers to reply that they would like to discuss problematic issues with their colleagues but do not have time to do so. However, it is worth noting that even among full-time workers, between one-fifth and one-quarter of respondents replied that they did not have time to communicate with colleagues about problematic issues.

Finally, we looked at the criteria by which homecare workers assess the quality of their work. In our survey, we asked the respondents, 'Which criterion do you use to assess whether or not you are doing your job well?' As can be seen in Table 8.8, for all employment types, the most popular criterion chosen was assessment based on feedback from clients. However, this was more the case for *Toroku* workers than for other types of workers. On the other hand, full-time workers, whether regular or non-regular, were more

Table 8.7:   Opportunity to discuss with colleagues by employment status

	Reg. FT (%)	Non Reg. FT (%)	PT (%)	Toroku (%)
Often discuss with colleagues	57	59	27	15
Want to discuss but have no time	20	24	29	34

Table 8.8: Criteria used to judge quality of work (S.A.)

	Reg. FT (%)	*Non Reg. FT (%)*	*PT (%)*	*Toroku (%)*
The objectives of service for the particular client	39	37	28	23
Feedback from clients	48	55	55	67
Others	13	8	18	10

likely than part-time or *Toroku* workers to assess their work according to the service objectives for a particular client. These results suggest that full-time workers are more likely than part-time and *Toroku* workers to reflect on collective knowledge in their job performance, while part-time workers and especially *Toroku* workers are more likely to reflect on local knowledge.

In summary, firstly, compared to full-time workers, part-time workers and *Toroku* workers spend much less time at the office, and, therefore, have little opportunity for face-to-face interaction with their supervisors, seniors and fellow workers. This limits the possibility of transferring tacit knowledge and generating explicit, collective knowledge. Although part-time workers seldom visit the office, they appear to have access to channels for communication with their supervisors and seniors, as reflected in the fact that they regard these people as important sources for acquiring knowledge and skills. However, for *Toroku* workers, the problem of alienation seems to be serious. These workers heavily rely on their own process of trial and error to develop their knowledge and skills, and their work tends to reflect feedback from their clients more than instructions from their supervisors or seniors. Consequently, they are more likely to develop idiosyncratic knowledge and skills than the other types of workers.

Secondly, we found that interaction with fellow workers and mutual exchange of information are indispensable to homecare workers' acquisition and development of knowledge. This is consistent with the feature of knowledge workers mentioned above, where mutual monitoring constitutes the fundamental mode of updating knowledge. However, part-time workers and particularly *Toroku* workers have far fewer opportunities to interact with their fellow workers than their full-time counterparts. Even many full-timers feel that they lack sufficient time for such interaction.

Thus, we can see a divide between full-time workers and part-time/*Toroku* workers, whereby the former have relatively greater opportunities to acquire and generate collective, professional knowledge, while the latter, in particular *Toroku* workers, have fewer such opportunities, and are more likely to develop idiosyncratic knowledge that is rarely shared with or utilized by other workers.

Conclusion

Care has traditionally been provided by family and relatives, and the scope and provision of public care has been limited in many advanced societies until quite recently. However, recent social and demographic changes have made increases in both the number and quality of paid care services inevitable. Japan has been no exception here, and since the late 1980s, the government has introduced measures to rapidly increase the number of care-workers, and has introduced various qualification systems to establish care-work as a profession. Accordingly, care-work has been increasingly standardized and professionalized.

On the other hand, the Japanese government's de-regulation of care service providers has not only encouraged competition for service quality as intended, but has also reduced labour costs. This has resulted in increased numbers of non-regular part-time workers and *Toroku* workers. While home-care work ought to be a highly skilled vocation, flexible and unstable work schedules, together with low income and poor social recognition due to the gendered nature of work, rarely attract skilled labour, with the result that homecare workers are predominantly relatively low-skilled, middle-aged, married women, working to earn supplementary income for their household. In turn, the composition of the workforce further devalues care-work.

Under these opposing trends of standardization in quality and flexibilization in quantity, polarization of employment circumstances has developed among homecare workers. Full-time homecare workers, who are able to come and go between their office and their clients' homes, have opportunities for transferring, sharing and developing the knowledge gained from their experiences at clients' homes as well as at the office through face-to-face interaction with their seniors and fellow workers. On the other hand, part-time workers and *Toroku* workers are largely restricted to comparatively limited experiences of work at clients' homes, with little opportunity to immerse themselves in the professional world. They either work under the direction of their supervisors in the manner of unskilled labour, or deal with their clients using their limited idiosyncratic and local knowledge, often developed by a process of trial and error in interactions with their particular clients, but not with collective assurance.

As part-time workers and *Toroku* workers now constitute the majority of homecare workers, and with the proportion thereof continuing to rise, it is a great loss to the profession of care-work as a whole that the knowledge gained by these workers is not shared and fully utilized, in spite of the fact that it is collective knowledge that has been valued and respected in our society.[5]

Our findings in this chapter suggest that unlike other knowledge-intensive work, the bulk of care-workers' knowledge remains tacit and embodied in individual care-workers. Therefore, for care-workers to become knowledge workers, sharing knowledge through face-to-face interaction with seniors and fellow workers is crucial. Face-to-face interaction not only makes it possible to transfer the tacit knowledge embodied in individual care-workers, but also enables the conversion of tacit knowledge into explicit knowledge. Once knowledge is externalized, it can then be used for effective internalization on an individual level, as well as for developing theoretical knowledge that can be shared and learned collectively. However, what can be seen is that flexibilization has adversely affected the process of knowledge creation, restricting effective accumulation of both tacit and explicit knowledge among care-workers. As a result, collective knowledge among care-workers has not been developed sufficiently to regard them as knowledge workers.

So far, the winners of the new economy seem to be those who successfully digitize their knowledge and enjoy the process of knowledge creation by utilizing ICT. ICT surely has a potential for knowledge-intensive work that is expanding rapidly in our society, as it enables transferring information without much cost and without sharing time and space. However, ICT has limited use for work that deals heavily with tacit knowledge such as care-work. In order for care-workers to become fully-fledged knowledge workers, therefore, it is necessary to introduce means for care-workers to share and develop collective knowledge, regardless of their working sites and employment forms. Given that much tacit knowledge has not been made explicit and accumulated among care-workers, what they really need at the moment is face-to-face rich communications with senior and fellow workers. In this sense, it is necessary to reintroduce regulation aimed at curtailing excessive flexibilization of care-workers' employment.

Notes

1. See Shire in this volume for details.
2. See Osawa in this volume for details.
3. Formally trained workers are those who obtained the certified care-worker qualification or those who have successfully finished homecare worker trainings and gained the corresponding certificate (from the first grade to the third grade).
4. The frequency of such paired visits varies by agency and by the junior worker's capability, but is generally limited to one to three times for each new client.
5. See also Durbin in this volume for collective knowledge.

9
Who Gets to be a Knowledge Worker? The Case of UK Call Centres

Susan Durbin

Introduction

Call centres have become an established part of the UK economy, since their inception in the late 1980s. They are a product of complex, competitively driven spatial and organizational change within corporate structures (Bristow et al. 2002). This chapter situates call centres in the context of a knowledge-based economy and explores the relationship between 'knowledge', the core product of a knowledge economy, and gender. The focal point for knowledge creation in call centres is the interaction that takes place between humans (advisers and customers) and technologies. These technologies have the capacity to create a wealth of knowledge and enable the sharing of knowledge and information within the organizational system. This chapter considers the gender implications of a knowledge-based economy by exploring the extent to which women are involved in the generation, management and sharing of knowledge and revealing the exclusive (male) nature of the knowledge process and its outputs.

Call centres are not a sector in their own right but a business methodology that has been adopted by organizations operating in both the public and private sectors. They fit best with the OECD definition of 'knowledge work', although there are also overlaps with EU and UN definitions (see Karen Shire in this volume). Call centres represent a new form of work in which women are employed under a new set of conditions, including flatter organizational structures, broader spans of control (which lead to limited career progression) and new forms of spatial and temporal flexibility that have been facilitated by the information technology revolution and the availability of flexible female labour. This has led to the emergence of 'new' forms of work that contain 'old' practices, such as women constituting the majority of those who work flexibly and practise their so-called 'soft' skills.

This chapter challenges the representations of the knowledge economy that is presented as a gender-free concept. The creation, accumulation

228

and diffusion of knowledge has now become an important source of production in the knowledge economy, the very 'creation of knowledge from knowledge' becoming the main source of economic productivity, being a key stimulus for growth, enabled by information technologies (Castells 2000a; David and Foray 2002; Drucker 1993a; European Commission 2001a; OECD 2002a; Reich 2001). Given the increasing significance of the knowledge economy and the number of women active in the labour market, it is important to ask, to what extent are women involved in the collection, sharing and application of knowledge? What are the specific implications of this for women who are employed in call centres?

Methodology

This chapter is based upon fieldwork analysis at four call centres that form a part of two of the UK's largest financial services organizations, referred to throughout as Bankco and Finco. Call centres within this industry dominate the UK call centre sector, with a market share of 21.2 per cent (Datamonitor 2004) and within this sector, women comprise approximately 70 per cent of adviser and team manager populations (IDS 2001). Bankco has approximately 15 million customers and just under 80000 employees, of which 4000 are employed in its call centres. Finco is smaller with approximately 10 million customers and 15000 employees, of which 700 are employed in its call centre operations. The Bankco sites are located in the west and north and Finco's, the south and east, in the UK.

Both organizations operate their call centres using 'third generation' technology, with calls being handled in a seamless fashion across multiple networked locations. Their call centres are identical in terms of gender composition (75 per cent female at adviser and team manager levels) management structures and technology systems. Both fieldwork sites were selected and access negotiated through a key gatekeeper in the call centre industry who identified both organizations' call centres as members of a call centre 'best practice' group. Two call centres from each organization were offered and accepted as case study research sites.

The fieldwork was conducted between 1999 and 2001 and involved the use of semi-structured interviews with senior and team managers and questionnaires with team managers. Non-participant observation of advisers and team managers, during their routine work practices with customers, was carried out on an ongoing basis over a period of twelve months. This included 'sitting in' and listening to advisers receiving and dealing with customer calls. A total of 114 interviews were conducted and this chapter draws upon 61 of these interviews with team managers and 27 with senior managers.

What is a knowledge-based economy?

The knowledge-based economy emerged in the 1990s, in the USA, predominantly in the information technology and finance industries. Knowledge-type organizations within these sectors all share common features: their key role as providers and/or users of new information technologies; networked organizations; innovation-driven businesses; and high investors in research and development and/or computer-related equipment (Castells 2000a). Call centres are emblematic of these networked firms which are themselves a key feature of the new economy, this being organized around global networks of capital and information. Access to technological know-how is at the root of productivity and competitiveness. Castells (2000a) postulates that the new economy is networked because under the new historical conditions, productivity is generated through and competitiveness played out in a global network of interaction between business networks. Financial markets are the strategic, dominant network of the new economy and within the overall model, call centres give these organizations the opportunity to operate across multiple sites in a seamless fashion, with flatter organizational hierarchies. Actors within the system are linked through technology and within this system, call centres have become pivotal points for the integration of different channels, through the internet, telephone and information technologies. This enables these businesses to integrate service and sales channels through a 24-hour, seven-day-a-week operation.

Knowledge-based economies are characterized by substantial reliance on new information technologies, not only for communication but also for the creation of new knowledge (Foray 2002). Communities geared towards knowledge production have the following characteristics: extensive knowledge creation and reproduction; mechanisms for exchanging and disseminating the resulting knowledge; and an intensive use of new technologies. The knowledge economy is also divisive, producing 'winners' and 'losers' as it becomes the main source of wealth and inequalities (Carnoy 2000; Castells 1997, 1998, 2000a; Gill 2002; Liff et al. 1999; Liff 2000; Liff et al. 2000; Liff and Steward 2001a, 2001b; Liff et al. 2002; Lindley 2002; Lisbon European Council 2000; Perrons 2003; Quah 1996; Reich 2001; Rodrigues 2002).

Karen Shire (in this volume) identifies the different (and partially overlapping) approaches to the measurement of a knowledge economy, using the metrics developed by the United Nations (UN), European Union (EU) and the Organization for Economic Co-operation and Development (OECD), illustrating the absence of an agreed, universal definition. Call centres do not fully meet the criteria in any of these definitions due to their ubiquitous nature but their closest match is with the OECD definition, as it includes ICT as a key sector in its classification. There is a partial match with the UN and EU definitions, the former encompassing all forms of media, including telecommunications, software and data processing, the latter financial services.

What is knowledge?

Knowledge is the accumulation of facts, experiences and learning from which we make reasoned judgements that are used to constantly improve the production of knowledge process in the organizational context. In the call centre environment, the emphasis is upon gathering, reviewing and applying information about customers to develop value-added services. What makes knowledge more than simply a body of information is that it involves the ability to extend, extrapolate and infer new information (the creation of knowledge from knowledge) – in other words, we transform information into an intangible product that adds value (Steinmueller 2002). Information is a necessary medium or 'raw' material for eliciting and constructing knowledge and is affected by adding something to or restructuring it. It is a flow of messages, while knowledge is created by that very flow of information, anchored in the beliefs and commitment of its holders (Nonaka and Takeuchi 1995).

One way to 'unpack' the concept of knowledge is to distinguish between different knowledge types and to apply these to different types of organizations (Blackler 1995; Lam 2002). Lam (2002) has typologized knowledge into four 'types': embrained, embodied, encoded and embedded, and claims that all organizations contain a mixture of these knowledge types but that some organizations may be dominated by one type more than another. The categories of explicit-tacit and individual-collective forms of knowledge give rise to these four types of knowledge:

- Embrained knowledge (individual and explicit) is dependent on the individual's conceptual skills and cognitive abilities and is represented by formal, abstract or theoretical knowledge, which is learned through reading books and in formal education. Embrained knowledge enjoys a privileged social status within Western culture and is most likely to be found in the 'ideal typical organizational form' of a professional bureaucracy (based upon individual and standardized knowledge).
- Embodied knowledge (individual and tacit) is action-orientated and learned through experience and training based on apprenticeship relations. It is particular knowledge which becomes relevant in the light of the practical problem-solving experience. Embodied knowledge is most likely to be found in an 'operating adhocracy' (a highly organic form of organization with little standardization of knowledge or work process).
- Encoded knowledge (collective and explicit) is shared within organizations through written rules and procedures and formal information

systems. It is formed in making explicit as much as possible of tacit knowledge. This is well illustrated by the principles of scientific management which attempts to codify worker experiences and skills into objective scientific knowledge. Encoded knowledge is to be found in the 'ideal typical organizational form' of a machine bureaucracy, which has a collective and standardized knowledge base where the dominating principles are specialization, standardization and control. This is a mass production environment, with Fordist production and Taylorist management predominating: 'the managers are the key agents responsible for translating individual knowledge into rules and procedures and for filtering information up and down the organisational hierarchy' (Lam 2002: 71).

- Embedded knowledge (collective and tacit) is built into routines, habits and norms that cannot easily be transformed into information systems. It is produced through social interaction among different members of the organization and supported by its shared cultural norms. Embedded knowledge is relation-specific and dispersed. It is an emergent form of knowledge capable of supporting complex patterns of interaction in the absence of written rules. Embedded knowledge is most likely to be found in the J-form organisation (with a collective and non-standardized knowledge base) (Lam 2002: 69).

Lam's knowledge types are useful for determining who has access to knowledge and how this is created. Nonaka and Takeuchi (1995) and Nonaka and Nishiguchi (2001) concentrate on knowledge forms rather than types, focusing upon how knowledge is created in Japanese organizations through articulation of the categories of explicit and tacit forms of knowledge. Explicit knowledge is defined as being articulated in formal language, including grammatical statements, mathematical expression, specification manuals, etc. and can be transmitted across individuals, formally and easily. Tacit knowledge, on the other hand, is difficult to articulate in formal language and remains personal knowledge that is embedded in individual experience, involving intangible factors such as personal belief, perspective and the value system. Nonaka et al. claim that tacit knowledge has been overlooked as a critical component of collective human behaviour that is an important source of competitiveness in Japanese companies, these companies becoming successful because of their skills and expertise at organizational knowledge creation. Crucially, organizational knowledge is created during the cyclical conversion of tacit to explicit to tacit knowledge.

According to this perspective, key players in knowledge creation are frontline employees, middle and senior managers. A knowledge spiral is created, involving interaction between tacit and explicit knowledge, which becomes larger in scale as it moves up the ontological levels. Thus, organizational knowledge creation is a spiral process, starting at the individual level and moving up through expanding communities of interaction that crosses sectional departments, divisional and organizational boundaries (Nonaka und Takeuchi 1995; Nonaka and Nishiguchi 2001). But what form does the knowledge spiral take when interaction fails to take place among key workers in call centres, who create knowledge through their interaction with the customer and information technologies? If, as Nonaka et al. claim, knowledge begins with the individual, then what happens when the tacit knowledge of key employees in call centres is not drawn upon? In the call centre context, information technologies play a crucial role in the gathering, dissemination and creation of knowledge.

While Nonaka et al. demonstrate, through case material, how knowledge is created through the cyclical interaction between tacit and explicit knowledge, this is further developed by Lam, through the four knowledge types. When a gender lens is applied, it becomes clear how access to knowledge is gendered at different levels and amongst different workers in the organizational structure. Crucially, neither Lam nor Nonaka et al. consider the gendering of knowledge. It is therefore significant to identify the presence of Lam's four knowledge types in call centres, the levels in the organizational structure in which they are present and women's involvement with and accessibility to these knowledge types.

Lam (2002) argues that tacit knowledge, which is difficult to create and transfer in the absence of social interaction and labour mobility, constitutes the most important source of learning and sustainable competitive advantage in the knowledge economy and institutions that are able to harness it are more likely to demonstrate strong innovative capabilities. Tacit knowledge denotes all intellectual or corporeal capabilities and skills that the individual cannot fully articulate, represent or codify (Styhre 2004). Once tacit knowledge is harnessed and captured, it becomes encoded into the organization's knowledge system. The encoding of knowledge is a crucial stage in the creation and sharing of knowledge.

The encoding of knowledge provides the architecture through which organizations transfer an understanding of key objectives and priorities and whether or not these have been met during the annual business cycle. It forms a single body of knowledge that is contributed to and shared explicity. Tacit knowledge, on the other hand, is the product of informal exchanges and observations which may not be converted into explicit understanding, without a formal process for sharing this form of knowledge (e.g. through quality circles). Tacit knowledge may be equally valuable but its value is a function of the efficiency of an organization to convert learning at all levels into meaningful and relevant knowledge.

In order for knowledge-type organizations to optimize the use and application of knowledge in the workplace, knowledge should be transparent, understandable and freely shared, both explicitly and collectively (Blackler 1995; Foray 2002). Knowledge-intensive firms need to share knowledge held by employees if they are to gain the most from their intellectual (symbolic) capital and compete effectively in the marketplace (Swart and Kinnie 2003). This chapter demonstrates that whilst women are more likely to share in and have access to knowledge types that are individual, men retain the monopoly on collective forms of knowledge and as a consequence, continue to set the framework for the routines, habits and norms (culture) in organizations. In terms of call centres, encoded and embedded knowledge have the greatest importance, as the latter sets the cultural framework for the business and the former its priorities/focus and women do not have full access to either. In contrast, women have much greater access to valuable tacit knowledge, which they share readily and informally but this invariably is not accessed by senior managers. The willingness to listen to customers and employees is a function of management style, there being some evidence that those with power attempt to limit access to formal knowledge (encoded and embedded) and disregard informal, experiential learning (embodied knowledge).

The specific forms of knowledge that have been identified by Lam (2002) (embrained, embodied, encoded and embedded) may continue to be male-controlled, thereby perpetuating knowledge as a gendered concept. Lam's four knowledge types are useful in categorizing sources of knowledge in organizations but when considered from a gender perspective, it becomes evident that women have a different relationship with knowledge production and distribution, when compared to men.

The knowledge economy and call centres

Call centres epitomize knowledge-type organizations (see also Ursula Holtgrewe, in this volume, who places call centres at the 'less skilled' end of the labour continuum). They are focal points for the creative use of knowledge to develop new, intangible products, facilitated by the revolutionary use of technology (David and Foray 2002). Call centres gather customer and employee information and knowledge to create encoded knowledge within an overall knowledge system, where it becomes shared and externalized. This is combined/integrated with new waves of technological innovation to enhance customer service and improve the capability to monitor the workforce.

Call centres are engaged in information processing activities, and in certain circumstances are used to actively manage the organization's relationship with its customers, supported by an extensive and sophisticated information management capability. The pioneering nature of the call centre concept has meant that many have been developed from 'greenfield sites' with totally new structures, practices, processes and work environments. Fundamental to this approach was the development of an information gathering capability that not only ensured the efficient delivery of services but also drove their continuous improvement.

The growth and development of call centres has been attributed to four factors: outsourcing (to lower costs, for example, through partial closure of the branch network); the collapse of barriers to the financial services and telecommunications industries (de-regulation); developments in technology; and socio-demographic factors, such as the availability of flexible, qualified labour (Market Assessment International 1999). A fifth factor is the globalization of production and consumption, which has led to spatial and temporal flexibility within the call centre sector.

Call centres represent an emergent knowledge industry built upon a different way of working, technology being used for both process and performance management of telephone enabled services, with a strong emphasis upon the individual operator's ability to manage customer relations. Call centre working is a relatively new form of employment in the UK economy; First Direct Bank pioneered the concept in the late 1980s. By 2001, there were more than 5000 call centres in the UK, employing around 1.5 per cent of the workforce, women being overwhelmingly represented at the adviser and team manager levels (around 70 per cent) (IDS 2001).

The UK banking industry and call centres

The UK banking industry has been pivotal in the development and expansion of call centre working, its phenomenal growth being attributable to its early adoption of this new channel for service delivery, which was implemented in parallel with the reduction in the size of branch networks. Financial institutions increasingly utilized information and communication technologies in their day-to-day, centralized, customer servicing operations, long before the widespread investment in call centres took place in virtually every other industry since the mid-1990s (Bain and Taylor 2002: 44). This shift in channel delivery was inspired by the banking sector's desire to reduce costs and offer a more time flexible service to customers, in an increasingly competitive market (Storey et al. 1999).

In 1990, 500000 people were employed by commercial banks (banks that undertake a mixture of personal retailing and services and commercial lending). The 'big four' (Lloyds/TSB, Barclays, Midland and National Westminster) employed more than half of all those in the banking industry at this time, 62 per cent of all bank employees being women (Storey et al. 1999). Information technologies have changed the face of UK banking and first attracted bankers because they enabled administrative work to be performed more quickly and accurately; and because the development of customer relationship databases permitted the development of cross-selling strategies and the expansion of business activities (Baethge et al. 1999). Storey et al. (1999) argue that, in the late 1990s, there were two technological strategies in the UK banking industry: (1) the devolution of processing work to branch level; or (2) the removal of processing work to regional centres (call centres). New technology presages a future in which software and hardware companies in computing and technologies will become both direct competitors and architects of a radical reshaping of the industry. There is now also the added dimension of the offshoring of call centre work (both processing and customer service orientated) to locations such as India and Africa.

Bankco and Finco have both developed their call centre capability to a point whereby they can flex processing capacity between their branches and call centres and between call centres themselves. They have also developed the concept of 'sales through service', this entailing treating customer service activities as an opportunity/prompt to sell. In the case of both organizations, there has been a widening of the working window of both service and sales to the point where they operate a 24-hour, seven-day-a-week availability. Consequently, this increased spatial flexibility has required call centres to review their temporal and contractual arrangements.

The re-gendering of flexibility in call centres

The nature and delivery window for work undertaken within call centres and the sophisticated information technology systems that set and manage the operational framework, offer increased scope for spatial, temporal and contractual flexibility. Cultural nuances and/or differences, as well as growing customer dissatisfaction, may constitute limits to spatial flexibility, as an increasing number of UK organizations offshore their call centre operations to Asia, Africa and Eastern Europe, in order to capitalize upon the availability of cheap, flexible and well educated labour. Within these cultural constraints, call centres are networked to create a 'virtual' capability, enabling the organization to optimize its available capacity by transcending geographical constraints. This spatial capability is critical for high volume, low margin businesses such as financial services. The corollary to this increased spatial flexibility is the development of the necessary temporal and contractual flexibility required to operate the networked model over time and space.

Bankco's and Finco's call centres utilize just over 100 working parameters to cover their 24-hour, seven-day-a-week operations, providing a wide range of opportunities for flexible working, which are mainly taken up by female front-line advisers. Working parameters to cover these hours comprise a wide range of flexible hours: full-time (37 hours per week); reduced hours (25, 20, 16 hours per week); zero hours (where employees are called upon if needed); annualized hours (where employees commit to work a particular number of hours per year with no fixed hours); fixed hour contracts; fixed rotating (alternate weekends); and flexible contracts (which must include twenty-five core and ten unsociable hours). Full-time working incorporates flexibility through the application of working 'parameters' which operate on the principle of alternating start and finish times over a two-weekly cycle. These possibilities for differential flexible engagement in the workplace can be both employer- and employee-led (Perrons 2000) and are specific to call centres, being enabled by the operating technologies, management information outputs and capacity planning tools.

This increased flexibility has been a catalyst for the re-gendering of service work, providing women with greater opportunities to enter into employment arrangements with work patterns that allow them to continue to meet their domestic commitments. These changes have meant that women have increasingly moved from the confines of the home into the arena of paid work but this is still often segregated into employment with lower status and pay (e.g. part-time work). Walby (1997) has argued that this change derives from the winning of political citizenship by first-wave feminism in the early twentieth century, in the context of an increasing demand for women's labour in a developing economy and women's access to education at all levels. Women's increased participation in the UK labour market is associated with the shift from a manufacturing to a service industry, this coinciding with the specific requirement in call centres for the social and technical skills that are most commonly associated with women and often described as 'soft' skills, namely relationship management and functional (keyboard) dexterity.

The high proportion of women and the limited use of students in UK call centre employment (Table 9.1) contrasts with the findings of Ursula Holtgrewe's (in this volume) who has found non-standard forms of flexibility operating in German call centres in the banking sector. Holtgrewe argues that banks in Germany hire students regardless of their gender and that this is an 'undoing' of gender, a process of de-gendering flexibility. The combination of longer university courses and a cut in student grants has meant

Table 9.1: Employment status (advisers, team managers and senior managers)

Gender composition (advisers and team managers	75% female
Full-time employment (advisers)	57%
Part-time employment (advisers)	43%
Full-time employment (team managers)	93%
Part-time employment (team managers)	7%
Temporary workers (agency)	2%
Number of students employed	6
Number of senior managers	27 (all male)
Female team managers	
Age profile	68% aged 25–35 years
Marital status	46% married, 24% living with partner
Dependent children	46% (13% aged under 5 years)

that German students seek longer working hours. By contrast, the cut in grants in the UK has not resulted in a corresponding increase in students taking up work in the case study call centres. Location could be a factor as both Bankco and Finco are situated away from main university campuses and in low unemployment areas. This analysis of UK call centres reveals a process of re-gendering through the hiring of women and the very limited hiring of students. This occurs predominantly on a part-time basis but within new working parameters.

At the adviser level, in all four call centres, flexible hours are overwhelmingly worked by women, as their availability provides a closer match to the flexibility profile required by these organizations (e.g. they are not out-flexibilized as in the German model where the hiring of students is occurring regardless of their gender). Amongst the team manager population, there is a narrower range of flexible working in evidence, which is not unusual at this level. The majority of this group work full-time flexible hours (76 per cent of men and 52 per cent of women).

Organizational knowledge

Although the accumulation and application of knowledge has always been a key ingredient in the development of human societies, what is significantly different in the modern era is the speed of its accumulation and diffusion, through information and telecommunication technologies (Lisbon European Council 2000). This growth in the production, dissemination and use of knowledge means that there will be much greater scope for the encoding of knowledge, making it potentially more accessible and marketable. The relationship between explicit and tacit knowledge is therefore important, as organizations sharing knowledge are likely to be more effective in the creation of knowledge from knowledge (Lindley 2002).

Frenkel et al. (1999) postulate that 'front-line' call centre work involves the use of different levels of contextual knowledge. It also demands different levels of skill (Belt 2003; Belt and Richardson 2000; Callaghan and Thompson 2002; Korczynski 2001; Thompson et al. 2004). Call centre work has also been defined as routine, boring and repetitive (Bain et al. 2002; Belt 1999; Fernie and Metcalf 1997; Kinnie et al. 2000a, 2000b; Knights et al. 1999; Taylor and Bain 1998). Frenkel et al. usefully draw out the complexities of call centre employment and the varying levels of skills required. Call centre work invariably involves a fusion of complex knowledge working and the execution of repetitive, routine tasks, the variation between the two depending upon the context within which the centre operates.

In contrast to back office activities, front-line customer operations are less routinized, with employees having some discretion over the management of the interaction with customers. Variations in demand for products and services directly impact upon front-line workers and challenge their ability to demonstrate emotional resilience and operational flexibility. Front-line work is invariably strategically important, with employees providing the key interface which enables the business to develop its customer knowledge base. Consequently, call centres have developed a sophisticated recruitment and selection process with employers looking for specific social and technical skills (Belt 2003, 2004; Thompson et al. 2004).

Customer requirements vary enormously, from simple account information to the sale of a new product or service. Advisers must manage the interaction with the customer whilst simultaneously operating the information systems which facilitate the gathering of knowledge. Advisers are required to demonstrate a wide array of technology skills (up to eight software packages combined with the use of the telephone, computer and internet) as well as technical knowledge of the product range which is constantly changing. High standards of keyboard skills (speed and accuracy), numeracy, literacy, the use of appropriate grammar, spelling and product knowledge are vital for this role.

Call centre advisers therefore fit in between what Frenkel et al. (1999) have described as users of 'lower-order' contextual knowledge (knowledge about company-specific products and procedures) and higher-order forms (conceptual understanding of different products, the market and the industry generally). Advisers are largely dependent on lower-order contextual knowledge for the routine aspects of their role but also display a degree of creativity and social and organizational skills in their execution of more complex tasks. Advisers sit at the 'entry' point of the flow of customer knowledge into the call centre, where knowledge is created, captured and diffused. However, not all of this knowledge is encoded and used and thus remains embodied as an untapped resource.

The team manager group has close day-to-day contact with the adviser population, this group having primary responsibility for people management. Team managers have the social and technology skills required by knowledge workers (proficiency in the use of information technologies, teamwork, communication, learning skills and the need to keep up with incessant change) and apply these in the call centre to achieve an extensive and increasingly technically complex range of tasks. Team managers utilize encoded knowledge (where they are given access) to monitor the performance of advisers to support the adviser coaching process, further enhancing knowledge extraction and relationship-building. Some of the coaching content is derived from the embodied knowledge captured by the advisers and shared with team managers, though this tends to be shared locally and informally.

The adviser population is the primary source of knowledge generation, the credibility and value of this depending upon their willingness and ability to successfully obtain relevant information from customers. It is apparent that the aggregated, encoded knowledge is not then shared with advisers who operate the system, as access is restricted by senior managers. These advisers also hold substantial embodied (tacit and individual) knowledge, which could contribute to the knowledge system but is not utilized. The creation and access to embedded knowledge would appear to remain the almost exclusive preserve of male employees, who occupy positions at the highest levels in the business, where power is concentrated. This sets the cultural tone for the exclusion of women in the business. Exclusion from this 'culture making' process is therefore denied to anyone outside these levels of the business (predominantly women).

Call centres are a primary example of a networked, knowledge-enabled operation in which content and system efficiency are rigorously and continuously under scrutiny, using the power of information technologies to disaggregate and re-aggregate information to produce productive knowledge. In a real sense, call centres are sites where the opportunities for sharing embrained, embodied and encoded knowledge are at their greatest. Accepting for a moment that the development and dissemination of embedded knowledge are inextricably linked to the distribution of power, there is within the call centre itself the ability to more easily and readily distribute that embedded knowledge. Despite women having these knowledge capabilities (embrained and embodied), employers still value women primarily for their ability to manage customer relations, through the use and application of their 'soft' (emotional) skills; in a sense, their emotional knowledge. Call centres are networked organizations with the potential of a networking knowledge capability.

The term 'adviser' is applied generically to groups of employees in call centres in financial services, irrespective of their product knowledge and/or their skills to deal with particular types of customer service/sales issues, some of which are highly regulated. The title 'adviser' creates an impression that the employee is both qualified to provide service/sales advice and is acting in an independent capacity, regardless of their employment arrangements. The reality is that only employees with particular qualifications can offer 'with advice' services, the level of regulation being such that these transactions are regularly tape recorded and scanned for irregularities internally and sometimes externally, when audited by the compliance authority.

Finco and Bankco: a case of gendered knowledge

The team manager populations at Bankco and Finco possess a relatively high level of educational qualifications (Table 9.2) and thus share in the acquisition of embrained knowledge, which is individual and explicit and can be gained at both a societal and institutional level. This is important because education is central to the knowledge economy (Bell 1973; Castells 2000a;

Table 9.2: Educational qualifications (team managers)

	Male (%)	Female (%)
Degree	32*	33*
General Certificate of Education ('A' Level)	29**	18**
Combined 'post-school' qualifications (degree and 'A' Level)	61***	52***
Management qualification	14	12
Call centre management qualification	7	15

Notes:
* Compared with 17% of men and 14% of women having attained a degree or equivalent qualification in the UK population as a whole.
** Compared with 30% of men and 17% of women having attained GCE 'A' Levels in the UK population as a whole.
*** Compared with 47% of men and 34% of women having attained post-school qualifications in the UK population as a whole.
Source: Social Trends 2002.

Drucker 1993a; Foray 2002) as embrained knowledge enjoys a 'privileged' position in society, being linked to the 'professional-type organization' (Lam 2002).

Table 9.2 suggests a relatively well-educated group of workers where access to embrained knowledge is no longer restricted for women, although the subjects studied by men and women remain gendered. Women share in this knowledge type, which is both explicit and individual in form.

The second knowledge type (embodied) relies on the formal, embrained knowledge of its members but also draws its capability from the diverse 'know-how' and practical problem solving skills embodied in the individual, for example, during the adviser–technology–customer interaction. This knowledge type takes on a tacit and individual form and is broadly gender-neutral, in that all men and women are capable of 'embodying' knowledge. Partial gendering occurs because of its reliance upon embrained knowledge. Advisers constantly develop embodied knowledge through the process of dealing with customer queries and problems and socializing with peers and team managers. Team managers' involvement in problem-solving sometimes occurs through active involvement in team meetings and associated activities, where the exchange of ideas and solution building are commonplace.

A large proportion of accumulated, embodied customer and employee knowledge remains tacit and only becomes explicit in particular circumstances. Advisers spend between 80 per cent and 90 per cent of their time dealing with customers using information technologies and use these interactions as an opportunity to gather tacit knowledge. The creation of value from this tacit knowledge is a function of the system's ability to organize it for future use by other advisers and other parts of the organization. Ninety per cent of team managers are dependent upon the information systems to do their job, though 84 per cent said that they would change the technology to improve speed and accessibility, primarily through a reduction in the number of systems to navigate. Many team managers felt that if there was a greater opportunity to share tacit knowledge, it could be used to improve the quality of service and increase sales to customers.

Significantly, 75 per cent of team managers had never been consulted about the technologies they were using, nor about the introduction of new technologies, although there were opportunities for designers to consult with users through usability centres and meetings. This exclusion of key users of technologies means that important tacit knowledge remains an untapped resource in design networks. Many team managers specifically complained about the lack of consultation and highlighted that knowledge accumulated about customers and system users was not being made explicit and shared. Makiko Nishikawa (in this volume) has established that the sharing of embodied knowledge is limited among Japanese homecare workers, as upward and horizontal information flows are inhibited by limited socialization and externalization of knowledge. In the case of Bankco and Finco, socialization occurs between advisers and team managers informally. The potential for embodied knowledge to become explicit and shared within the knowledge network has not been realized despite evidence from the case studies of the positive effects of knowledge sharing.

The third knowledge type (encoded) is shared within organizations through written rules and procedures and formal information systems (Lam 2002) and takes on a collective and explicit form. This 'formal' information system is enabled through sophisticated information technologies. The very information and knowledge that becomes encoded could be gendered through the application of an encoding approach that is usually the result of a male decision-making process. Encoded knowledge plays a central role in the knowledge economy (David and Foray 2002) and this is also the case in call centres. This information is shared within the organization through written rules and procedures, using formal information systems that often reflect the bureaucratic nature of the organization. Worker experiences and skills become codified into objective scientific management within the machine bureaucracy, which has a collective and standardized knowledge base, where the dominating principles are specialization, standardization and control (Lam 2002). Customer interactions and employee performance become shared knowledge that can be written and codified into the information system (e.g. scripted) and standardized (e.g. how to deal with the customer).

Advisers have no access to encoded knowledge, this being limited to regular displayed printouts of their performance. Whilst advisers are able to access and use systems for customer queries and transactions, they are unable to access data on either individual or overall call centre performance. Team managers have restricted access to this information, after it has been gathered, encoded and re-formatted by management information analysts. This information allows team managers to assess individual and team performance, who is (and isn't) dealing with customers, length of calls and number of calls queuing into the call centre. Senior managers enjoy full and unrestricted access to encoded knowledge and make decisions in terms of which groups of employees will have access to certain types of information. Women, although enjoying restricted access at the team manager level, are not sharing in the encoding process, which represents an explicit and collective form of knowledge.

The fourth knowledge type (embedded) has strong links with organizational culture, reflecting the shared values of the organization, this taking on a collective and tacit form amongst male senior managers. This knowledge type is gendered as embedded in the top of organizations, where culture (and strategy) is formulated and made explicit to those 'in the know'. Since women are under-represented in senior management, embedded knowledge is itself gendered. Embedded knowledge is, in many ways, at the edge of understanding and the most important type of knowledge needed to 'get on' in otherwise male-dominated organizations. There is little evidence of embedded knowledge in the call centres studied, except at senior management level. Embedded knowledge is relation-specific, dispersed and operates in the absence of written rules, which contrasts with the highly structured environment of a call centre, where knowledge becomes codified, explicit and shared. Embedded knowledge is highly gendered and the importance of this should not be underestimated when assessing women's place in the knowledge economy, as it could be argued that it is the most important knowledge in any organization, being cultural and strategic in nature.

Different groups of workers have access to knowledge in the call centre model, depending on their position in the organizational hierarchy, which is predominantly female at the bottom and almost exclusively male at the top. Advisers, when simultaneously interacting with customers and operating the IT system, collect and process information, developing new knowledge about the customer and the effectiveness of the process and systems. Advisers use their embrained knowledge in this process, acquired during formal and business training, and is then applied in the context of the culture of the organization – the adviser must follow a 'script' when selling services. Advisers are thus predominantly gatherers of knowledge that is ultimately encoded but a great deal of this remains embodied, tacit and uncollected.

Team managers represent the level at which the first aggregation of performance information and knowledge takes place. Encoded knowledge at this level allows them to manage individual and team performance, as well as to identify potential improvements to the operating system itself. Team managers use their encoded knowledge to inform adviser coaching[1] and training, measure the effectiveness of the process (methodology and technology) and gauge the overall impact on the customer through sales and satisfaction levels. These team managers also possess high levels of embrained knowledge, as discussed earlier. Embodied knowledge is often informally shared at this level, through group sessions with individuals and groups of advisers, as well as peer groups, although these sessions are infrequent. In terms of embedded knowledge, team managers are often agents for cultural transfer in their role as teachers and monitors of key behaviours in advisers. They are the pivotal link between advisers and senior managers and are gatherers of tacit knowledge. To create knowledge, the best management style is neither top-down nor bottom-up but is, according to Nonaka and Takeuchi (1995) 'middle-up-down', where middle managers form a bridge between the ideals of top management and the chaotic realities of the front-line. Middle managers are at the centre of knowledge management, at the intersection of the vertical and horizontal flows of information within the company (Nonaka and Takeuchi 1995; Mintzberg 1983).

Senior managers are a key source of encoded and embedded knowledge, in terms of the gathering of knowledge on the call centre industry and specific call centre trends. This knowledge is shared at a high level. Knowledge gathered in the call centre is aggregated in one place and this is used, along with external information, to set the call centre strategy, for example, whether the call centre uses 'talk time' as its key adviser performance measure (advisers should spend at least 65 per cent of their day talking to customers) or 'grade of service' (advisers should answer 80 per cent of calls within 20 seconds). Senior managers gather embodied knowledge by talking to other organizations and are at the pinnacle of encoded knowledge as they can generate knowledge about almost anything.

The relationship between hierarchical job position and knowledge types is such that individual forms of knowledge (embrained and embodied) are present at the lower end of the hierarchy whilst collective forms of knowledge (encoded and embedded) are present at the higher end of the hierarchy. All knowledge types are used to develop the next generation of call centres. Embrained knowledge is linked to coaching/training and recruitment, at all levels in the call centre. Encoded knowledge is used to review particular trends around process and the IT system which determine the IT equipment and how the call centre is laid out and organized. Embodied knowledge is accumulated through quality circles and embedded knowledge (for strategy formulation) by looking both inside and outside the business to identify new trends. All information becomes knowledge when it becomes a catalyst for some change in action.

Individual knowledge (embrained and embodied) is knowledge owned by the individual, learned and experienced at both a societal and organizational level, which can be applied independently to specific types of tasks or problems. It is transferable but also moves with the person and is therefore capable of being lost to the organization. In contrast, collective knowledge is distributed and shared in the organization as a whole, being accumulated, organized and stored in accordance with specific rules, procedures, routines, habits and shared norms, either as shared data or in a state of flow from interaction (Lam 2002). Generally, where knowledge is 'collective' (embedded and encoded), women are excluded from knowledge-sharing but where it is individual (embrained and embodied), women fare a little better. The key point is that tacit knowledge has to become explicit in order for it to be of any use in the call centre context. Where women have access to tacit knowledge, this tends to be on an individual basis and not where it counts most (e.g. embedded knowledge) at the senior managerial level. Knowledge thus constitutes an important element of the patriarchal structure of paid work in the context of the knowledge economy.

Given the dearth of female representation at the senior, decision-making and strategy formulating levels in the call centres and parent organizations, it is not possible to hypothesize how encoded or embedded knowledge would be shared differently if more women were present at these levels. If women's representation at these levels improved, would increased representation lead to a different style of management and an increased willingness to listen to customers and employees? Judy Wajcman (1998) provided a thorough analysis of exactly what 'gains' women do make when they achieve managerial positions and in the process dispelled a range of myths about the impact of women becoming managers on organizations and the masculine nature of management itself. These and other findings demonstrate that there is much more to 'equality' than simply allowing women access to organizational positions once monopolized by men, though it is apparent that access to and involvement in development of the embedded forms of knowledge, which shape the values and culture of the organization itself, is critical if women are to have any chance of changing the nature of the organization.

Conclusions

Call centres were originally developed to simultaneously facilitate organizational cost-cutting and manage the growth in demand from customers for improved access to services via the telephone, often outside normal business hours. This original concept has been enabled and developed by the application of sophisticated information technologies, which have themselves increased the potential for new forms of flexibility and, as a consequence, the re-gendering of service work. Changes in the gender regime and the shift from manufacturing to services in the UK economy, has meant an increase in the number of women participating in the paid labour market, some of whom may have been attracted by the new forms of temporal flexibility offered by call centres and the relational nature of the work itself.

Although flexible working previously existed in the UK, the emergence of the call centre has led to new forms of spatial and temporal flexibility. Call centres are being used to create a 'virtual' capability, whether networked locally, nationally or globally, to provide a seamless service to customers through sophisticated routeing, regardless of spatial constraints. New forms of temporal flexibility are enabled through the adoption of a multiplicity of working parameters, which have potential benefits for employees, customers and the organization alike, although employees tend to be recruited to fit with the predetermined work (service) patterns. This 'virtual' network enables organizations to optimize the utilization of their building stock, readily transfer workload within the system, extend the customer service window and increase its capability to generate sales.

In Castells' (2000a) terms, the knowledge economy produces 'winners' and 'losers' and this applies in call centres, where women are 'losing out' because men have maintained their positions of power through their dominance within the management structure, control of the design and operation of the processes and information architecture and, most importantly, control of the primary knowledge types (encoded and embedded). This analysis of the relationship between gender and knowledge production and utilization, demonstrates how knowledge types are gendered, thereby adding a further dimension to Lam's (2002) knowledge types.

David and Foray (2002) postulate that encoded knowledge is the most important type, because it is shared organizational knowledge, and whilst women play a part in its generation, they do not enjoy full access because of their position in the hierarchy. In contrast, Lam (2002) argues that tacit knowledge is the most important, as it constitutes the richest source of learning and is the root for sustainable competitive advantage. However, whilst women may be able to freely share this type of knowledge, the evidence is that the organization infrequently draws upon this and, as a consequence, fails to convert it into encoded (explicit) knowledge. The embedded knowledge (tacit and explicit) which invariably shapes the routines, habits and norms that underpin the organizational culture, remains the preserve of those in the dominant positions of power, namely men.

Call centres add a strategic flexibility dimension to organizational activities and notwithstanding that the nature and structure of the work content best suit female 'soft' skills, women, as knowledge workers, continue to lose out because of their exclusion from the networks that underpin the knowledge types referred to above.

Note

1. Use of pre-recorded transactions between individual employees and customers to highlight compliance issues and improve relationship and call management techniques.

10
Restructuring Gendered Flexibility in Organizations: a Comparative Analysis of Call Centres in Germany

Ursula Holtgrewe

Introduction

Telephone call centres are represented as the less skilled and externally flexible segment of the new economy. They are frequently cited as an exemplary case for neo-Taylorist standardization and automation of service work, where tasks are simplified and jobs are poorly paid and insecure. Through such a downgrading of working conditions, companies achieve numerical flexibility. This pattern has often been gendered, especially in computerized service and clerical work. A gendered segmentation of tasks and workforces has been a way for companies to legitimately become more numerically flexible. Especially in coordinated economies, part-time work plays a crucial part in the gendering of flexibility (cf. Nishikawa and Tanaka in this volume). The equation of downgrading, de-skilling and feminization may possibly be reiterated in call centres, another instance of ICT-supported flexible information work. Yet empirical findings suggest that call centres do not simply re-enact a Taylorist logic of rationalization and that in this new field heterogeneous patterns of gendering apply.[1]

Call centres are companies or organizational units which specialize in customer contact over the phone supported by networked information and communication technology. Call centres embody both a logic of standardization and a logic of service quality and customer orientation, in which rationalization is both enhanced and limited by the flexibility and indeterminacy of communications. While historically (starting with the early telephone operators) women have often been employed in jobs that were new, rationalized and concerned with compensating the limitations of new technology, this chapter argues that with the use of call centres, companies restructure the traditional arrangements of gendered flexibility, recombining diverse workforces and human resource practices.

In German call centres, we observe a differentiation of gendering processes. In lower-skilled call centres such as mail order the neo-Taylorist patterns of de-skilling and feminization are continued. In small and medium

248

enterprises (SMEs) we find a different, more functionally flexible pattern of women's employment, which has been typical of clerical work. In small marketing call centres, skilled women part-timers accept flexible working time schedules and fairly low remuneration, but take over a range of enriched tasks ranging from call handling to project management. In the male-dominated areas of call centre work such as technical hotlines and financial services, traditionally masculine notions of skill are being recast – in opposition to the feminized and emotional labour image of call centre work. A new pattern in which gender loses its relevance is found in banks in Germany. In the banking industry students are hired regardless of gender and in the place of skilled female part-timers. Thus, flexibility comes to be redefined in terms of dynamism and knowledge work.

This differentiation suggests that business organizations in certain industries face the tension between an increasingly market- and knowledge-driven 'new economy' and a changing gender regime and seek to increase and extend their strategic options in and through these changes. Theoretically this chapter aims to emphasize and explore the role of organizations in between both emergent and strategic, path-dependent and transformational changes in economies and gender regimes.

Gender, restructuring and organizations

Call centres and the new economy

Call centres can be regarded as part of the new economy for several reasons. To begin with, call centres make intensive use of ICTs, connecting telecommunications and computer technology, and technology is used to relocate work in time and space. Call centre operations may be outsourced, shifted to greenfield sites outside the purview of established industrial relations institutions and collective agreements, and routed through networks of call centres connected by phone and data lines. As in other networked industries, this does not mean that space becomes irrelevant but that the 'delocalising potential of new ICT . . . makes the characteristics of locations even more important' (Huws 2003: 58; cf. Castells 1996, passim). Call centres tend to be located where a suitable workforce for their respective service can be found. In Germany as elsewhere (Belt et al. 2002), that is often in metropolitan, but de-industrialized areas such as Bremen, Hamburg, Berlin/Brandenburg or the Ruhr area with a high availability of students, or in the case of simpler services, in the East German regions where the lack of alternative employment keeps labour turnover down (Arzbächer et al. 2002; Arnold and Ptaszek 2003).

Call centres also represent a general reshaping of customer relations and modes of consumption. Organizations using call centres do not just offer an additional channel of communication, but try to generate new knowledge and operate strategically upon the information they have and can gather.

Computerized data mining, for example, searches for actual and potential patterns of consumption in customer databases and thus generates knowledge about possible customers and sales prospects. Such prospects can then be pursued by outbound calling. Part of a CSR's (customer service representative) interactive work in such cases is to get a customer to cooperate with and tie herself into an organization's routines, and even to take over some of the work which had previously been done in the organization. Technical hotlines and customer information services operate recursively on the limitations and consequences of ICT use. Computer technology enables products, services and prices to be differentiated and customized in such a way that self-service over the internet must be complemented or supported by the more flexible articulation of IT, communication and expertise that call centres provide.

In terms of temporal reorganization, the flexibility that call centres provide is clearly market-driven. The interactive character of call centre work requires working times to be closely tied to customer demand. Call centres are used to increase service times up to 'round the clock' availability, though in some cases 24-hour, seven-days-a-week operating times were found to be exaggerated in relation to customer demand. Staff shortages or overstaffing become immediately visible through the data generated by automated call distribution systems which note idle times and 'calls lost'. Consequently, shift patterns and working time arrangements tend to be highly sophisticated, often supported by computerized planning and scheduling systems. In addition, the willingness of CSRs to change their working schedules at short notice is often included as a performance measure in appraisal systems. Employment contracts (and also collective agreements, where they exist) increasingly cover flexible 'working time accounts' based on a corridor of hours per week or month to eliminate overtime pay. On the other hand, within the parameters of a company's forecasting of call volumes, many employees can exercise considerable discretion to choose their own schedules – even where working conditions are otherwise tightly regimented. As will be demonstrated below, particular types of call centre services place different demands on workers' temporal flexibility, which in turn plays an important part in the gendering of call centre workforces.

As regards knowledge work, call centre workers are found at the boundaries of types of knowledge – 'on the front line' as Frenkel et al. have aptly put it (1999). Interacting with customers, they translate contextualized demands and problems into encoded knowledge bases and vice versa – indeed, they do the encoding and embraining of knowledge (cf. Durbin in this volume; Lam 2002) on behalf of the organization. Since speech is the tool of their trade, they represent an interesting contrast with Nishikawa and Tanaka's care-workers (in this volume): a certain explication of knowledge is essential, and this is work performed by both customers and CSRs. Yet this does not necessarily lead to CSRs' professionalization (i.e. a codification of their skills), but rather to a combination of intense use of information technology to both support and control work, an intense use but not necessarily a recognition of skill, and considerable efforts that call centres put into training. Thus, call centres illustrate the need to consider not just knowledge types but the shifts and translations between types of knowledge in analysing knowledge work and organization.

In sum, call centres are representative of a key aspect of the 'new economy': how 'modern ICTs widen the range of organizational options available to companies' (Huws 2003: 65) and open up space for organizations to strategically act upon a number of aspects of the firm's environment: labour markets, customer relations, competition, institutional regulation, etc. However, the increased strategic options also make it necessary for companies to act upon them. These options may be structured by the path-dependencies of specific varieties of capitalism (Hall and Soskice 2001), but they may also offer opportunities for change.

Yet call centres do not fit comfortably into the knowledge-based *sectors* of the economy, since they are established in various organizational configurations and in various industries and sectors. They range from specialized service firms to in-house departments, and from public administration and health through retail, financial services and telecommunications to manufacturing. So far, there is no internationally viable way of counting call centres and call centre jobs, though a large segment of call centres belongs to the OECD's 'knowledge-intensive service sector' (Shire in this volume).

Obviously, the discussions of the new economy, the network or knowledge society do not just address changes in social structure and work organization. Like gender (Acker 2003) or social relations in general (Giddens 1984), they also have a strong symbolic and legitimatory dimension. On the symbolic level, call centres draw on the semantics of the new economy which describes itself as constitutively innovative, knowledge-based and immaterial. As new, recently established organizations, they present themselves as innovative and are generally perceived in this way. Norms and expectations of innovation in turn legitimize change.

The dimensions of signification and legitimation, however, do not just mirror and legitimize structural changes. Neither can structural changes be explained through the performativity of discourses exclusively. Indeed, empirically, we observe some differentiation between 'talk' about and structural changes of gender relations in call centres. In order to account for such loose couplings and differentiations between the discursive and the structural, I borrow the concept of semantics from the tradition of German systems theory (Luhmann 1980). Semantics mean generalized repositories of meaning which social systems draw upon to describe themselves and to ascribe actions and decisions. For gender relations, equality and difference present semantic fields which are of interest here. In work organizations, rationality, market demands, performance and skill are important. For call centres specifically, service and knowledge, expertise and customer-orientation come to mind. In the systemic view, both social structures and semantics evolve separately but are interrelated. In most cases, the evolution of social structures takes historical and analytical precedence (Stäheli 1998) because a structure needs to be in place in order to be made sense of. Stichweh (2000) argues, however, that changing semantic fields and concepts may precede or facilitate structural changes. At any rate, the concept keeps the actual relationship of the structural and the symbolic open to empirical investigation. From a feminist point of view, however, it is important to bear the inherently conflictual character of social self-descriptions in mind, which is somewhat alien to the orthodox Luhmannian terminology. Viewed in terms of semantics, 'knowledge' in its diverse forms is not just a resource for organizations and individuals. Its recognition and valuation in organizational talk and action become the site of both discursive and material struggles between workers and organizations, between management factions, professional groups, and also between men and women (cf. Durbin in this volume).

Call centres as specifically flexible organizations

From an organizational perspective the establishment of call centres is part of organizational strategies to comprehensively design their relations and communications with customers. Call centres are boundary-spanning units, i.e. units specializing in communicating with an organization's environment. Their specific environment is customers or clients who are strategically central for any business organization. The needs and demands of customers are processed and articulated with a company's offerings, and the point of selling and marketing strategies is to influence customers' demands and preferences to fit with products and services. Here, connections between information and communication technology are used to both standardize and diversify products and services, to flexibly bundle and segment customer groups, to gather information about customers and influence them to cooperate with the organization. All of these functions tie in with one another, and organizational and technological means are put to work by and through CSRs' communicative skills and flexibility in customer interactions. This boundary-spanning function is the reason why call centres cannot follow an unambiguously (neo-) Taylorist logic of rationalization. Such a logic is counter-balanced by the logic of organizational flexibility and the capacity to react to market and customer changes. At the boundaries of organizations this balancing act takes place both in management and in everyday work (Frenkel et al. 1999; Korczynski 2001, 2002; Holtgrewe and Kerst 2002a, 2002b; Kerst and Holtgrewe 2003).

Hence in call centres we observe the 'construction of flexibility' (Arzbächer et al. 2002) on multiple levels. Institutionally, call centres are often established outside of traditional collective agreements, regulations and traditional HRM policies. Workforces and human resource practices are recombined and temporal and interactive flexibility is managed on an everyday level. As we shall see, this comprehensive and multilayered flexibility addresses gender relations as well, flexibly articulating 'old' and 'new' patterns of flexibility.

Gender, skill and organizational flexibility

Traditionally, organizational flexibility has been centrally, but not deterministically structured by gender regimes while structuring gender regimes and gendered institutions in turn. This view would suggest the development of path-dependent patterns of flexibility in which institutionally and culturally embedded gender contracts are reproduced or changed incrementally (Smith and Gottfried 1998; Gottfried 2000; Pfau-Effinger 2000).

At first glance, call centres draw on women's work in a pattern that is familiar and almost traditional in service and clerical work (Game and Pringle 1984; Gottschall et al. 1985; Gottschall et al. 1989; Webster 1996): starting with telephone exchanges, then typing, data entry, typesetting or clerical work, the routinization and rationalization of work has been linked historically with its feminization. Women in such jobs, however, are mostly not unskilled, but rather have some level of general education and/or occupational training. Thus, the feminization of routinized work combines the advantages of numerical and functional flexibility. If routinized work is done by skilled women with limited labour market options, their skills need not be recognized but are kept in reserve to compensate for the very problems and side-effects of rationalization. Organizational flexibility is achieved through women workers' skill reserves and downward flexibility. Juliet Webster for example points to the continuity in the supposedly new patterns of flexibility:

> There is strong evidence that forms of employment now being hailed as flexible are in fact long-established patterns of labour market exploitation with which women workers are all too familiar. Institutionalised and legitimated as flexibility they may simply serve to confirm and extend the appalling working conditions of millions of working women, with the low pay, lack of employment protection, lack of equal opportunities and career prospects and insecurity which is commonplace in women's work. (Webster 1996: 84)

Most recent research addressing gender relations in call centres also sees a reproduction of the pattern of flexibility as the devaluation of women's work (Belt et al. 2002; Krenn et al. 2003; Durbin in this volume).

Other authors, however, argue more generally that changes in gender and in employment relations are not or no longer unidirectional. The gendered and gendering effects of skill, security, standard employment and labour market segmentation are beginning to differentiate with women acquiring improved qualifications and attempting to participate continuously in the labour market. These interrelations depend all the more on a society's respective institutional context, as various authors pointed out throughout the 1990s, as well as on women's culturally and biographically embedded decisions (Rubery and Fagan 1994; Flecker 2000; Pfau-Effinger 2000).

De-regulation thus does not necessarily lead to a coherent pattern of flexibility, nor is the feminization of the labour force by any means naturally connected to labour market flexibility. Sylvia Walby (2002a, and in this volume) argues that taking gender relations into account, increasing flexibility should not be mistaken for wall-to-wall de-regulation. While market forces are gaining ground in processes of globalization, gender regimes are changing in the direction of increased regulation by nation-states and the European Union – so that institutional changes often operate in tense and contradictory relations. The question of path-dependency (Gottfried 2000) versus the transformation of previous paths thus needs to be addressed empirically.

The case of call centres suggests that in certain contexts, organizations may strategically break away from such path dependencies. Call centres represent a genuinely 'new economy' widening of organizational options, a possible escape[2] for companies from traditional labour relations. We shall see that the recruitment and HRM practices of call centres in Germany do not simply reiterate the traditional pattern of downwardly flexible women's work. Flexibility itself is being restructured – and the mode of flexibility is not just shaped by national and transnational institutions but also by the contexts of particular industries and organizations. Especially the case of German banks points to the construction of a flexible relationship of organizations and specific industries with society-wide institutional gender regimes. Flexible organizations flexibilize work beside and beyond the established gendered patterns of flexibility. Flexibility is decoupled from gender when new transitory workforces become available – while, as we shall see, the semantics of skill and dynamism reiterate fairly traditional gender distinctions.

Flexibility and organizations

All these lines of argument suggest that flexibility addresses gender relations and regimes and that it can be expected to move in contradictory patterns. I argue that in such processes of institutional change, the actual development of these contradictions, inequalities and temporal imbalances is best explored on the level of industries and organizations.

Theoretically, the concepts of gender regimes and contracts structuring the gendering of work and employment patterns often imply a neo-institutionalist outlook with a focus on organizations following norms and expectations, isomorphically adapting to regulations, norms or professional standards (Powell and DiMaggio 1991; Scott 1995). On the other hand, organizations, especially business organizations, are the collective actors who centrally articulate and shape the work and employment side of gender regimes. Organizations design jobs and hierarchies (Acker 2003), employment relations and HRM strategies and they utilize particular labour forces (Jenkins 2004). Doing this, they do not just enact gendered labour markets, societal institutions and cultural images. Rather, they actively act upon them, both strategically and by default (Jepperson 1991). It is thus on the level of work organizations that the described tensions between market-led de-regulation and flexibility on the one hand, political regulations and social norms of equality on the other, are being processed, and this processing happens in a strategic way. For example, organizations implement equal opportunity policies, select among available 'tools' and aims, or seek to escape or avoid such expectations and demands. Evidently, however, they are neither totally adaptive to their environment nor omnipotently rational and strategic. Both enactment of and strategic action upon gender regimes and gender relations take place in organizations' respective contexts and environments: labour markets, welfare states, cultural expectations, regions, industries, networks, etc. (Tienari et al. 1998; Quack and Morgan 2000a, 2000b).

Conceiving of both aspects, adaptation and strategy, as parts of a recursive loop results in a structurationist (Giddens 1984) model of institutions, cultures and societies both enabling and restricting actors' capacity to act, i.e. to reproduce and/or transform social relations (Ortmann and Sydow 2001). And in this model the organizational fields, the actors, rules and resources in the field and the actors' strategies mutually constitute one another (Friedberg 1995). Where and when gender (or age, ethnicity, experience) matter, what service, quality and skill actually *are* – all of this is enacted and may be negotiated in the organizational field in question.

Call centres should thus be explored as an organizational field in which new and old features combine and articulate. On the 'new' and transformative side of these changes are the strategic centrality of knowledge, customer relations and flexibility, the interlaced organizational design of customers, products, services and structures, and the semantics of the new economy and innovation. These new features are nonetheless met with the persistence and/or path-dependent development of traditionally gendered labour markets and careers and of gendered constructions of skill and expertise.

Re- and de-gendering work in call centres

Call centres in Germany: managing flexibility

The German call centre sector has been expanding beyond operator services, mail ordering and direct marketing since the mid-1990s with some consolidation since 2000. The first direct bank (the former Bank24) started operations in autumn 1995. The development was triggered by interrelated technological and institutional factors which converged in the mid-1990s. The liberalization of telecommunication and energy markets, the strong growth of mobile telecommunication and the diffusion of internet access into private households led to the emergence of new markets, new packages of goods and services, new types of customers and new information needs (Arzbächer et al. 2002; Bain and Taylor 2002). Currently (in March 2006), there are roughly 280000 people employed in German call centres. The question of gender relations in call centres has only begun to be addressed (Bialucha-Rhazouani 2002; Holtgrewe 2003; Kutzner 2003), possibly because gender researchers have expected to simply reconfirm the all-too-familiar processes of de-skilling and downgrading.[3]

In call centres, the overall majority of workers are women, yet call centre work is not exclusively women's work. Most studies find that on average two-thirds of call centre agents are women, with the degree of feminization varying from 90 per cent in direct marketing and mail ordering services to 50 per cent in technical hotlines across different national contexts (Belt et al. 2002; Bittner et al. 2002). Part-time employment rates in German call centres are generally put between 40 and 50 per cent with wide variation between types of call centres. Higher-skilled and in-house call centres rely on higher proportions of full-time employees.[4] Apart from women returning to work who work part-time, university students and both male and female full-time workers also make up the workforce in call centres (Bittner et al. 2002). Workforces tend to be young with at least a third of all CSRs under 30 years of age and three-quarters under 40. In the sample of our own call centre survey (five call centres, 491 agents), 28.1 per cent of all agents worked full-time, 46 per cent of whom were women. Part-time workers who were not students comprised 27.9 per cent of the surveyed workforces with 86 per cent of such part-timers being female. University students comprised 44 per cent of call centre workers. Among the students, women and men were equally represented. The proportion of students in our study is higher than in other studies, because students are concentrated in banking call centres. Full-time workers were chiefly found in in-house call centres, which had typically taken over workers from other functions of the company organizations. Women part-timers mainly worked in outsourced call centres and in call centres where tasks with lower skill requirements were common. Part-time work in call centres overall, however, was fairly extensive, with an average working time of 20 hours per week.[5]

Call centre workforces

Call centre labour markets are segmented along both old and new lines, which are related to working time and availability rather than directly to gender. The norm of flexibility is central since the deployment of workers in call centres is connected as tightly as possible to shifts in call volumes.

In our study we found three distinct types of workforces (cf. Kerst and Holtgrewe 2003) where processes of gendering and undoing gender can be observed. These types will be illustrated here with evidence from our case studies.

(1) In lower-skilled call centre work such as mail ordering, the neo-Taylorist pattern was retained. These call centres favoured women part-timers with unspecific service qualifications, with the expectation that these women would comply with restrictive working conditions and emotional labour demands.
(2) We also found a pattern of women's employment which has been typical of clerical work in small and medium enterprises. In small marketing call centres, skilled women part-timers accepted flexible working time and fairly low remuneration, but took over a range of tasks reaching from call handling work to project management.
(3) Banks have moved away from the traditional pattern of routinizing clerical work by employing skilled women part-timers. Instead they hired students regardless of gender, thus decoupling flexibility from gender and recasting it in terms of knowledge work and the need for a dynamic workforce.

While both of the first two workforce patterns reiterate traditional patterns of gendered employment in Germany, the third pattern found in the banking industry is new. Here flexibility has indeed been redefined. Whereas traditionally, numerical and functional flexibility have been optimized by recruiting skilled women for deskilled part-time work (Gottschall et al. 1985; Jenkins 2004), what we currently find in German banking call centres is a de-gendered articulation of functional and numerical flexibility guaranteed by the transitory status of students.

Neo-Taylorism in mail ordering

The mail order call centre we studied handled orders and enquiries from private customers of a teleshopping TV channel. Of the 500 CSRs, all worked part-time and 75 per cent were women, most of whom had previous occupational training and experience in customer-contact jobs. The centre had fairly restrictive working conditions, low wages and a very flexible shift system according to which CSRs were employed in three groups corresponding with different planning horizons (Holtgrewe and Kerst 2002b). The recruitment of female part-timers had been the result of a homogenization of the workforce over time. A works council member reported that the share of students had been decreased from around 90 per cent to 40 per cent at the time of our research since students were harder to discipline.

When we started here [in 1998, U.H.] there were almost only students, 90 per cent. Meanwhile they don't really want them anymore. They don't take so much nonsense. They don't care . . . (mail order1, works council member, translation U.H.)

This call centre complemented its neo-Tayloristic standardization of work with nostalgic attempts to reconstruct the friendliness and closeness to the customer of traditional retailing businesses. Agents reported receiving much appreciation from their customers, who tended to be elderly people from lower income groups: 'you don't get that friendliness in department stores nowadays' (mail order1, agent, translation U.H.). While customer interactions were scripted and strictly supervised, friendliness and empathy were inculcated in communication trainings. Workers also drew on previous experience in service jobs which were often close to the working-class *habitus* of their customers, for example as taxi drivers, part-time pub landladies or sales workers in the small corner shops typical of the region.

In this type of call centre employment, the combination of normative appeals and restrictive working conditions continued the alliance between rationalization and emotional labour which has been recurrently observed in retailing by authors such as Siegfried Kracauer in the 1920s, C. Wright Mills in the 1950s, and most recently by Barbara Ehrenreich (Kracauer 1929/1971; Mills 1953/1971; Ehrenreich 2001).

Job enrichment in marketing

The second pattern of women's work which is specific to SMEs in Germany (cf. Gottschall et al. 1989) is represented in the example of a small marketing call centre with 26 agents which specialized in supporting business-to-business sales. The job in this centre typically consisted of identifying prospective buyers of investment goods and making appointments for the sales staff of the call centre's clients. The enterprise pursued a clear quality approach, emphasizing the reliability of pre-sales research. At the time of our interviews, the workforce was exclusively female and part-time, although occasionally men were employed. Working times mostly fell into the nine-to-five range since prospective customers were contacted during normal office hours. The owner preferred to employ mature people returning to work with experience in clerical or sales occupations. One of the team leaders we encountered held a pre-1991 East German engineering degree, a qualification specifically devalued since reunification. In this call centre, CSRs also took over project management tasks. This configuration of the work and employment structure falls in line with the practices of other small and medium enterprises. We found a profile of a skilled female workforce who were not supposed to turn up their noses at simpler call handling tasks, yet at the same time were capable of and encouraged to take up more complex work. From the workers' point of view, the comparatively low wages were compensated by interesting work and by the cooperative and familiar relationships with co-workers and supervisors.

Banks I: decoupling gender and flexibility

Banking call centres are the type that departs from established gendered (and gendering) patterns of employment. At the start of our study, we expected banking call centres to continue patterns of de-skilling the work of women returning to work part-time. Yet we found that the demand for flexibility by the banking industry outpaced the flexibility supplied by female part-time workers. Women returning to work part-time tend to be mothers, and their preference for working times that suit school hours (half-day in Germany) places limits on their working time flexibility. Banks have responded to these limitations by employing fewer female part-time workers over time. Also in terms of *habitus*, students appear more mentally agile to personnel managers as indicated by one general manager:

> In the beginning, we had many housewives and mothers in there . . . but with increasingly complex tasks in the call centre it gets difficult. The longer the working time, the better the knowledge is present for us, and mental flexibility – there's nothing wrong with housewives, but students are of course quite differently involved and are better able to react in this fast-moving industry we're in and to attune to that. That has had the effect that now we hardly hire anyone who is not studying. (Bank3, CC general manager, quoted from Bialucha-Rhazouani 2002: 63f.)

Banks are thus departing from the traditional divisions of labour in cases where temporally and habitually more and differently flexible workers are available. According to some accounts, for some time banking call centres practised a norm of mixing together diverse groups of workers (cf. Belt 2002), but as soon as flexibility took on the semantic connotations of the 'new economy' and its dynamism, women with banking qualifications became perceived as housewives and mothers. The interpersonal skills they had ascribed to them fell into disregard. Students working part-time offered a new and attractive type of skilled transitory workforce. Students have skills which are not yet certified, they have practice in the rapid acquisition of knowledge and also in impression management, i.e. sounding competent even if they are not. They are also able to work at unusual hours, and they can afford to have limited aspirations in their current jobs. Plus, importantly, they perceive call centre work as a learning opportunity to acquire the kind of service and communication skills that are not taught in universities.

Banks II: asserting masculinity

While the recruitment of the general CSR workforce became increasingly gender-blind in banks, and the ascription of interpersonal skills to women was rendered irrelevant, hegemonic masculinity was asserted both in terms of management and technical expertise. In recruiting for supervisory and management positions, banking call centres favour full-time workers. These recruitment patterns have less to do with functional necessities, since supervisors are not in charge of fixed groups and teams, and more to do with the norms and the semantics of flexibility:

> Managers are on principle expected to be endlessly flexible. That's just a matter of attitude. If I say as a manager, I can only come to work three days a week and I have to motivate people to be flexible and to actually live the capacity planning – that's leadership by example. (Bank1, general manager, translation U.H.)

'Endless' flexibility addresses availability for work rather than gender directly – but the statement represents a closure of career options for the less-than-endlessly flexible worker. Yet in supervisor and management positions in call centres there is a considerable share of women – figures range from 11 per cent in the study by Kutzner (2003) to 31 per cent (Bittner et al. 2002: 69).[6]

A more explicit reassertion of masculinity is found in those call centres which are dominated by men, i.e. technical hotlines, sales in service call centres and private banking. Here, managers eagerly redefine gender ascriptions by shifting the meaning of skills and competencies. In the field in general, there is a widespread consensus among managers, also reflected in training handbooks, that recruitment needs to focus on employees' social and communicative skills and personality traits. Expert knowledge in contrast can be acquired through learning (Frenkel et al. 1999). Yet in the hotlines, this technical expertise is rated higher (cf. Belt et al. 2002):

> It's different with us, and with the colleagues in the hotline it may be even more so. There, you have real computer geeks, and in part, these guys just aren't nice. It's not in their nature. They don't look nice, they aren't nice. But they are brilliant in their field . . . That's probably different in other services and certainly in outbound. There, the largest part is friendliness, communicative skills. But in the areas where expertise matters, that's less important. (supervisor Bank1)

This image appears to be slightly overstated. In tasks involving technical problem-solving over the phone, communicative skills are certainly more important than purely technical brilliance, and it is socially quite possible for men to be both friendly and competent. From this supervisor's point of view, however, such friendliness would appear almost unprofessional. In a field which is often perceived as feminized and de-skilled, this manager (and others interviewed) defended 'their' men against possible demands for 'unnatural' social skills in the name of technical expertise and a stereotypical image of masculine geek culture. Bialucha-Rhazouani (2002) reports that in sales as well, managers framed social skills in masculine ways, emphasizing assertiveness and tenacity rather than empathy. Hotlines and sales incidentally are those areas in call centre work which pay the highest wages.

While it is not new, but always interesting to observe just how flexible, ambiguous and even contradictory gendered ascriptions and definitions of skill are (Game and Pringle 1984), the question which remains concerns understanding the effects of such articulations of expertise and friendliness. Assigning certain skills to some sectors of call centre work may legitimate social closure against women (Cyba 1998), but it is also possible that women in the field profit from claims to expertise and professionalism as well (and indeed, women working in technical hotlines do claim such expertise).

Recomposing workforces

In all three cases we find evidence of call centres increasingly identifying their 'ideal' labour forces along the lines of the task structure, the customer market structure and the demands on working time and flexibility of the respective call centre business.[7] The pattern of employing women part-timers with limited aspirations and options on the labour market and with skills being kept in reserve is thus differentiated. Mail order and other low-end call centres continue, in the Taylorist tradition of combining regimented work and emotional labour, to employ female part-time workers in the established way. The SME model where skilled women are employed 'elastically' in between call handling work and complex project tasks is also continued in the context of call centre work in smaller organizations – leading to a combination of interesting and enriched work with limited remuneration. Both mail ordering services and small call centre businesses continue the paths of labour utilization which their industries of origin have pursued, a consistency reinforced by perceptions of customers' expectations. Banks, however, have discontinued the gendered employment patterns at a time when other flexible groups of workers have emerged and the strategic emphasis is being placed on dynamism and innovation. Notably, bank call centres mostly have comparably favourable working conditions.

The variety of gendering of call centres thus appears to be contingent upon the respective industry and type of service, on the size of the company and – not least – on the degree and focus of a company's strategy shaping the use of call centres. In the cases of the mail ordering and the small business service call centres, traditional gendered employment patterns are retained. They fit with both their industries of origin and with customer expectations. Retailing in Germany in general is characterized by a reduction of personnel cost, staffing shortages and increasingly pressurized working conditions in which the contradictory demands of market performance and customer orientation are addressed to employees directly (Voss-Dahm 2003). Service innovation in our case is restricted to the communication channels employed (teleshopping), and this service can be best performed by (a reconstruction of) 'traditional' empathy and friendliness under tight temporal restrictions. The quality-orientation and personalized style of small business marketing is aimed at strategically shaping the market and educating customers about the service quality they require. Such call centres distinguish their service from cheaper, low-end marketing outfits by building trust in their high-quality knowledge of sales prospects gathered on the phone and fed into customers' sales activity records. Workers' low wages are compensated by friendly working relationships and some job enrichment and discretion at work.

Banks pursue the most comprehensively strategic approach to the utilization of call centres: a deliberate escape from traditional industrial relations, organizational hierarchies and customer relations. Greenfield sites are established (frequently remote from traditional banking locations), hierarchies flattened and customers offered fundamentally new services and delivery channels – and in the process, new transitory workforces are discovered.

In sum, in line with the 'optional' concept of the knowledge economy, call centres, ICTs and gendered patterns of flexibility offer companies an increased range of strategic options, which are utilized with varying degrees of path-dependency and transformation of traditional patterns. The more strategic and comprehensive a company's and an industry's approach to call centres, the more flexibly they will draw on specific labour forces and gender regimes, and the more options they will discover in turn. In relation to gendered employment patterns in banking in general, however, these findings are specific to call centres and do not mean that gender is becoming less relevant throughout the industry.

Re-engineering skill in call centres

Across the cases, call centres with their specifically flexible demands, their non-standard employment patterns and their newness in the employment system represent a departure from the established German system of occupational training. In Germany, clerical and service occupations are to a large extent included in the densely regulated occupational training system with institutionalized apprenticeships combining school and workplace training (Hillmert 2002). Training for clerical and secretarial skills also takes place in upper secondary schools with an occupational rather than academic focus, in which case formal qualifications are regulated by the chambers of commerce. Women participate in the 'dual system' (to a lesser extent than men, Rabe-Kleberg 1993), but tend to be concentrated in clerical and service occupations. Institutional arrangements in Germany tend to force women into discontinuous careers, and it is often occupationally trained women whose skills become devalued on the labour market by the likelihood of career interruptions. For example, half-day schools and childcare facilities exert considerable institutional pressure on the working time needs of mothers, in turn limiting their labour market options. A look at the private service sector thus requires a modification of Estévez-Abe's (2005) argument that vocational training in coordinated market economies tends to segment occupations and to encourage firm-specific skills to the disadvantage of women. Training in clerical and service occupations tends to be more industry- than firm-specific. Through women's discontinuous careers, their qualifications are then utilized in a more generalized way. Institutional influences and the labour market thus devalue women's skills, and cultural perceptions confound skills with naturally feminine traits. Thus, skilled women represent the traditional source of 'downwardly elastic' flexibility which goes beyond purely numerical flexibility.

Yet call centres represent a re-engineering of skill. Internationally, personnel managers in call centres often claim that, 'particular formal qualifications don't matter'. For recruitment, they rely on tests of interpersonal and communicative skills rather than on training certificates, and subsequently offer extensive training to new CSRs internally (cf. Thompson et al. 2000).

In Germany, CSR skills have only selectively been integrated into vocational training for clerical occupations (Arzbächer et al. 2002), and chambers of commerce offer training courses and certifications. Yet these have mostly been established to guide unemployed workers into call centre jobs. Training here is tied to the changing, post-welfarist management of labour-market policy and the new rhetorical emphasis on employability rather than to the established system of vocational training (cf. Larner 2002).

A statement of a personnel manager in banking is typical of the changing meaning of both training and skill: 'Qualification comes second, first we need the enthusiasm. The knowledge and all the rest we do internally and then we make this person a very, very tiny, slimmed-down banker' (Manager Personnel, Bank3).

Within a densely regulated system of vocational training such an orientation departs from established definitions of qualifications. Banks indeed try to escape from the careers and expectations connected with their industry-specific vocational training (cf. Vitols 2003). The specific demands of customer contact in the context of changing sales strategies are a lever for this escape. Institutionalized, industry-specific learning and experience is replaced by supposed 'personality' traits and shorter, ad hoc, company-specific training related to specific products and strategies.

Yet in the call centres in our sample, more than 80 per cent of the CSRs who were not students had completed two or three years of vocational training, mostly in clerical and service occupations. The companies' re-engineering of skill was thus still based on workers' previous qualifications and experience. Prior qualifications do not disappear and can still be utilized, but they are both devalued and rendered invisible through the new semantics of personality. The aspect of invisibility points to changes in the training system and its institutionalization. The long-term career and mobility promises of a regulated training system based on industry-specific skills (Estévez-Abe et al. 2001) have traditionally been gendered (Smith and Gottfried 1998; Estévez-Abe 2005). If qualification in call centres (and probably other fields of the knowledge economy, cf. Thompson et al. 2000) is de-institutionalized and turned into portfolios of firm-specific, short-term skills and ascribed personality traits, the gender implications for this skill regime are less predictable and will be differentiated according to industry as well as company strategies and contexts. Again, with regard to skill, we may expect increased optionality for companies and thus, increased varieties within and across varieties of capitalism.

Gendered employment and reorganization in banking

Since banking has been regarded as the 'heartland of gendered bureaucracy' (Tienari et al. 1998: 24), a comparison is worthwhile of the de-gendered flexibility pattern of German banking call centres to other instances of gendered/gendering organizational change in banking. While in both the UK and Germany, traditional careers in banking have been male-dominated, women have gained considerable ground. In Germany, 50 per cent of banking apprentices, and in recent years also half of the graduates of the further occupational training courses and banking academies have been women. Their share in graduate trainee programmes has increased to just below 50 per cent in the 1990s (Tienari et al. 1998: 29).

During the same period, banking has been an area of major organizational change (Regini et al. 1999). The influence of institutional and regulatory change and the use of information technology have led both to a cross-national convergence of management models and orientations (*Leitbilder*) such as 'lean banking', and to a persistence of nationally specific actual patterns and practices of reorganization (Tienari et al. 1998; Hildebrandt 1999; Quack and Morgan 2000a). In most countries, reorganization has been characterized by decentralization, internal marketization, a flattening of hierarchies, a diffusion of team working and interdisciplinary project work. Centrally, customer relationships have been recast with a focus on sales and on segmenting customer groups according to their respective value and potential for comprehensive financial services (Batt 2000). These developments led to a differentiation of sales channels. Banks focused their face-to-face contact and advisory capacity on promising customers and products while expanding self-service, electronic and telephone banking for others.

The German banking system has traditionally been based on universal banks offering a comprehensive range of services to different customers (Baethge et al. 1999b; Quack 1999; Morgan and Quack 2000; Quack and Morgan 2000a). Qualification has been based on the German dual system of apprenticeship, with further institutionalized steps of occupational training and strong internal labour markets. In recent years, the recruitment of university graduates and the establishment of trainee programmes has increased. In the 1990s, gradual downsizing and cost-cutting strategies of automation were complemented by a redirection of resources towards investment banking.

In Germany, which lagged behind other countries in these developments, reorganization strategies have often been employed in tentative and contradictory ways. Towards the end of the 1980s, for example, it was received wisdom that the Citibank approach of standardized products and self-service would not be accepted in Germany (Arzbächer et al. 2002). In the 1990s, direct banks were established nevertheless and mass-market banking was outsourced to call centre and internet-based subsidiaries, only to be reintegrated into full-service banks a few years later. The separation and segmentation of service and sales channels has been followed by the establishment of 'multi-channel services'.

Especially the segmentation of customers has led to considerable changes in the product structure, the skills required, and gendered careers in banking. While a traditional German banking clerk developed a deep general knowledge of the business through her apprenticeship, increasingly the training has focused on the selling of standardized products to 'average' private customers with an emphasis on soft and interpersonal skills (Vitols 2003). Karen Shire (2005) reports that – contrary to our call centre findings – face-to-face selling managers still draw on gendered images of deskilling. One manager in a branch office told her, the ideal person for this would be a cosmetics saleswoman rather than a banking clerk: he regarded looks and friendliness as sufficient for selling standardized banking products.

Advising wealthier customers (*Vermögenskunden*) meanwhile has become the job of financial advisers, either university graduates or graduates of the banking academies. Notably, the shift towards selling has also led to an increase in women's share of branch manager posts and lower and middle management positions (Quack 1997, 1999; Tienari et al. 1998).

Banks' strategies of customer segmentation and diversifying communication channels thus have a variety of gendered outcomes. The downward flexibility of skilled women doing downgraded jobs still features in German banking, but in middle management it has been translated to a higher level than with the routinized clerking of the 1980s. With increasing downsizing and back-office automation in banks, women have improved their skills and moved on to management positions, but to somewhat devalued ones under tighter controls. The demands on selling banking services have also increased. Data mining and the standardization of products, which is complemented by continuous innovation, generate computerized sales proposals for specific customers which sales clerks are expected to sell. Sales clerks thus need to communicate and make interactive sense of sales strategies generated elsewhere in the organization (Bienzeisler and Tünte 2003). The traditional banking clerks' expertise and advising capacity is thus replaced, or rather rendered invisible, by a combination of knowledge generated in databases and the supposedly 'interpersonal' skills of convincing a customer of the company's offer. In face-to-face customer contact, managers interpret these demands in a gendered way, drawing on specifically feminine aesthetic and emotional labour (cf. Witz et al. 2003), while in call centres new labour forces come into view.

In this context then, call centres have functioned as experimentation sites for a redefinition of skill and a recomposition of workforces. With the shift towards multi-channel sales, deskilled banking clerks in the branches and socially skilled students and people with non-banking qualifications in the call centres face similarly contradictory demands at work. They compete over the definition of skill and expertise, and indeed, over jobs.

Comparing call centre work and gender in Germany and the UK

Call centres play distinct parts in the respective economies of Britain and Germany:

> With an earlier establishment of call centres Britain is frequently seen as an example for the successful expansion of service employment. In Germany, white-collar work has traditionally been embedded in the specific traditions of occupational training and co-operative industrial relations which define the German model. Call centres represent a strategic challenge to that model. Their expansion has been at the forefront of changes aiming at making employment more flexible in Germany. (Shire, Holtgrewe and Kerst 2002: 2)

A fairly similar gendered employment structure is thus situated in a distinct societal context, and this context helps explain the earlier adoption and wider diffusion of call centres in the UK and US (Bain and Taylor 2002). 'Varieties of capitalism' research (Hall and Soskice 2001) has frequently pointed out how liberal-capitalist societies offer a favourable and enabling institutional context for market-oriented reorganization and process innovation (cf. Lehrer 2001), while such strategies take longer and take a different shape in regulated capitalist societies.

While both the general labour force participation rate of women and their share of part-time work in Germany are lower than in Britain,[8] call centres are similarly feminized with two-thirds to 70 per cent women. The actual proportion of women in each call centre varies depending on the business: up to 90 per cent in mail order and outsourced businesses, around 50 per cent in technical hotlines (Bittner et al. 2002; Belt et al. 2002). Especially in outsourced call centres, gender may even vary with the particular campaign or project. The share of female part-timers in German call centres is higher than in Britain (40–50 per cent vs. 27 per cent respectively, according to Belt et al. 2002), though Durbin (in this volume) finds 43 per cent of part-timers in her case studies.

However, British research on gender in call centres predominantly finds a reiteration of traditional gender divisions. Women fill the de-skilled and devalued new service jobs (Jenkins 2004), and they are recruited for their supposed social skills – which often enough turn out to be coping skills (Webster 1996; Tyler and Taylor 2001; Belt 2002; Belt et al. 2002; Thompson and Callaghan 2002), misrecognized as 'natural' or as personality traits. Call centres across industries seem to be comfortable with fairly traditional gendered and gendering ascriptions (Durbin in this volume), while, as we have seen, in Germany gender loses some relevance especially in banks, the most strategically ambitious industry using call centres.

A tentative explanation in line with varieties of capitalism *and* gender regime could be the following. It is possible that the combination of a market-led gender regime and a commodified female workforce (in the sense of Esping-Andersen 1990) in a liberal market economy still offers enough flexibility even for new, knowledge- and ICT-based organizational forms – leaving gendered ascriptions of skill intact. In the context of a regulated economy, however, with a modernized male-breadwinner gender regime, women's limited labour market participation presents dysfunctional limitations when firms aspire to market-driven flexibility. Thus, firms seek to avoid or escape the regulated institutional ensemble and gender regime if and when their market requires patterns of flexibility which are incompatible with the gender regime. While the shift to a public gender regime in a liberal economy typically means an expansion of the flexible female workforce, the case of German banking call centres demonstrates the tensions between the gender regime and the 'new economy' market orientation of firms in a regulated economy.

A complementary explanation hinges on the specificity of the 'new' workforces which supply German banks with a de-gendered type of flexibility (cf. Arzbächer et al. 2002). In Germany, university education generally takes longer than in the UK and courses tend to be less regulated. In recent years, with cuts in state-sponsored grants to students, it has become quite common for students to work long-hour part-time jobs even during the semesters, especially in metropolitan areas with higher costs of living. Due to the length of a university education in Germany students present a workforce with just the right combination of retention and volatility – plus they have communicative skills which now can be ascribed to age and lifestyle rather than gender.

In the German banking case, the commodification of students' labour as a potential workforce has overtaken that of women – at least in terms of flexible working times and schedules. The availability of this new workforce may in turn have enhanced firms' perceptions of wider options in the composition of workforces. Thus both reasons, the limited flexibility of women and the increased flexibility of students, are likely interrelated and mutually reinforcing. The restructuring of flexibility in this case emphasizes the tensions and contradictions inherent to a regulated variety of capitalism with a modernized-conservative gender regime faced with the increased strategic options which the new economy offers firms.

Conclusions: gendered banking and de-gendered call centres

While in other industries, call centres indeed reiterate the gendered paths of Fordist rationalization, the case of banks is the most complex. Theoretically the banking case points to an increasing flexibility in the relationship of organizations and specific industries and the society-wide gender regimes through the utilization of new organizational forms.

In Germany, the established gendered pattern of flexibility consisted of a devaluation of *skilled* women's work and limited labour market opportunities. Yet, in the case of German banking call centres, the restructuring of organizational flexibility and an increasing market orientation have devalued the capacity for flexibility supplied by women workers in a modernized breadwinner gender regime and shown up its limitations. The traditional forms of gendered working times and labour supply in this new and strategically implemented organizational form become a restriction rather than a resource. The escape of banking call centres from previous regulations through the establishment of independent call centre subsidiaries is also a move away from the previous patterns of gendered and gendering flexibility. Hence, the establishment of a new organizational form de-genders divisions of labour by replacing one flexible but immobile workforce with another even more transitory one.

Both women working part-time and students are workforces whose labour market participation is strongly influenced by the institutions of the welfare state and by culturally embedded norms of appropriate lifestyles and commitments within and outside work. Drawing on gender regimes and gender relations to generate flexibility thus becomes one option among others; organizations and industries can make use of this increased range of options according to their strategic outlook. However, on the symbolic level, the semantics of skill and dynamism reiterate the established gender distinctions. We might say that ascriptions and meanings of femininity lose 'practical' relevance while the connotation of masculinity with management and technical expertise is reasserted, only becoming slightly more accessible for women without care responsibilities.

The possibilities of making gender relevant or not (cf. Wilz 2002) then appear to be contingent upon a gender regime's 'fit' with companies' and industries' strategic range and strategic alternatives. Path dependencies and breakaways are both possible within the same industry, and organizations' orientation towards the market leads them to recombine them in the face of perceived options and restrictions. A focus on organizations and their strategies towards their (actual and potential) markets thus adds a promising level of analysis to the effects of changing interrelations between transforming gender regimes and economies.

Notes

1. The findings presented in this chapter are based on the DFG research project 'Call Centres in between Neo-Taylorism and Customer Orientation' which was conducted by the author as a principal researcher (together with Julia Althoff, Sandra Arzbächer, Hanns-Georg Brose and Christian Kerst) at Duisburg University from 2000–2. Thanks are due to these collaborators, to our interviewees and to the editors and authors of this volume who intensively discussed previous versions and helped to draw out the conclusions presented here. Karen Shire's help with the language and many other things is especially much appreciated. The author is responsible for any remaining errors.

   The DFG project involved case studies of seven German call centres (with expert interviews, workplace observations and a survey of 491 call centre agents), plus shorter visits in four additional call centres. Sites were selected in order to cover the range of relevant industries, functions and skill levels. In the sample of call centres there were three banks, three outsourcing/marketing call centres, two call centres in telecommunications and one each in the fields of transport, mail order and health. The type of organization studied ranged from a telephone bank with 700 agents at three sites to a small telemarketing agency with 26 agents. All except for one telecommunications call centre were German-based companies.

2. The notion of escape (Oliver 1991) means a possible response strategy of organizations to institutional pressures. While classic neo-institutionalism focuses on organizations adapting their structures and routines to institutionalized expectations, Oliver explores a variety of strategic responses ranging from escape, avoidance or defiance to strategies of manipulation, influence and control over the environment.

3. For the same reason, the question in our own study was not chiefly gender-related. We thought about call centres as boundary-spanning units in an organizational and functional perspective first. Under conditions of organizational flexibility on the one hand, of a de-standardization of life-courses and gender regimes on the other, we expected the gendered pattern of skill deployment to extend to other segments of the workforce (Gundtoft and Holtgrewe 2000: 197).

4. Representative figures for national call centre 'industries' do not exist yet.
5. We did not find any short-hours part-time work (*geringfügige Beschäftigung*, which is subsidized through lower taxes and social insurance in Germany), and were told by personnel managers that the cost for training CSRs was too high to make it effective.
6. This is roughly in line with recent German microcensus data in which women are found in 33 per cent of management positions and 21 per cent of top management positions (Statistisches Bundesamt 2005: 53).
7. Since the study did not cover long-term developments, I cannot prove that such a homogenization of workforces is indeed a general trend, but managements' interpretations need to be taken at face value.
8. Labour force participation of women aged 15–64 years: 64.5 per cent in Germany, 69.2 per cent in the UK; part-time employment as a proportion of total employment for women: 36.6 per cent in Germany, 40.1 per cent in the UK (OECD 2004a).

Appendix to Chapter 3

Mari Osawa

Table 3.A1: Public pension schemes in the four countries (from perspective of women's lifestyle choice)

	Japan	United States	United Kingdom	Germany
Historical backgrounds for public pension schemes	1942: Workers' pension scheme was introduced for male blue-collar workers 1961: Public pension schemes covered all the Japanese citizens 1973: Price slide and income slide were introduced 1985: National pension scheme was reformed to a comprehensive Basic Pension scheme 1994: Income slide was reformed to net income slide. It has been enacted that pension eligibility age would be gradually raised from 60 to 65 by 2030 2000: income slide was abolished	1935: Pension scheme was established for employees in commercial/industrial enterprises Pension scheme coverage has been gradually expanding thereafter 1972: Price slide was abolished 1983: it has been enacted that the pension eligibility age would be gradually 67 by the year 2007	1946: Comprehensive National Insurance scheme started 1975: Wage or price slide was introduced, and State Earnings Related Pension (SERPS) has been established 1980: Wage slide was abolished 1986: Benefit level of SERPS was reduced, shift to occupational pension and/or individual pension schemes was encouraged 1999: Stakeholder pension was introduced 2000: SERPS would be replaced from April 2002 by the State Second Pension (S2P) which favours low income earners	1889: Old-age pension scheme was introduced 1957: Wage slide was introduced 1992: Wage slide was reformed to net income slide 1999: Rates of contributions of both employees and employer were reduced with subsidy from the tax revenue 2000: Benefit level was reduced (net income replacement rate was reduced from 70% to 67%). The upper limit of the contribution rate in future was reduced from 26% to 22.5%. Individual funded pension scheme has been introduced

Table 3.A1: Continued

	Japan	United States	United Kingdom	Germany
Relationship with occupational/private pension schemes	Many people join occupational/private pension plans (as the 3rd tier)	Many people join defined-benefit/ contribution-type occupational/private pension plans	Many people join occupational/private pension plans to contract out of state 2nd tier pension	Occupational pension schemes are widely available for workers in the private sector
(Contributions) Who pays the pension contribution?	Non-employees other than dependent spouses of full-time employees (Class 1): Individual-base Full-time employees (Class 2): Individual-base (Class 3 status mitigates pension contribution payments for married couples)	Individual-base	Individual-base	Individual-base
Criteria for requiring pension contribution	Class 2: to satisfy the three-quarter criteria Class 1: not to meet the three-quarter criteria but would satisfy the ¥1.3 million criteria if his/her spouse is an employee	Employees: to earn some income Self-employed: to earn $400 or more in a year Non-working: no eligible for membership	Employees: to earn £67 or more in a week Self-employed: to earn £3,825 or more in a year Low income earner: on the optional basis	Employees who work for 15 hours or less in a week or earn 620 DM or less in a month are able to join the public pension scheme on the optional basis Other workers are required to join the public pension scheme Self-employed are able to join the scheme on the optional basis (some are compulsory)

level points (bend-point system)

Pension-splitting between husband and wife (at divorce)	The pension scheme does not provide the pension-splitting option. At divorce after April 2007 income related portion might be split on the optional basis, and for Class 3 period after April 2008 the income related portion have to be split half and half (mandatory)	If they have been married for 10 years or longer, a divorced person receives the necessary documents division of their pension rights, or a division of pension benefits under judicial court's order or their mutually agreed splitting-ratio. If not remarried, a divorced person is also able to receive the spouse benefit (60% of the basic pension benefit for the ex-spouse) based on the ex-spouse's contribution (50% of his/her ex-spouse's pension benefits)	A divorcing couple jointly turns into necessary documents and divides their 2nd tier pension benefits under judicial court's order or their mutually agreed splitting-ratio. If not remarried, a divorced person is also able to receive the spouse benefit (60% of the basic pension benefit for the ex-spouse) based on the ex-spouse's contribution	A divorcing couple are able to choose either a division of their pension rights, or a division of pension benefits as a kind of credit, or a division at mutually agreed splitting rate (in the latter two cases, a divorced person is not able to gain independent pension right from his/her ex-spouse)
(Reference) Replacement rate gap among households (numbers in the parenthesis are an example of estimation)	(Basic pension + 2nd tier portion) male breadwinner households > double-income households [male breadwinner household: 64.6%; double-income households: 50.5%; male single households: 46.5%; female single households: 56.9%]	Male breadwinner households > double-income income households [male breadwinner household: 65.0%; double-income households: 44.9%; male single households: 43.3%; and female single households: 47.1%]	Male breadwinner households > double-income income households [male breadwinner household: 42.9%; double-income households: 36.2%; male single households: 34.8%; female single households: 38.2%]	Male breadwinner households = double-income households = male-single households = female-single households: 43.0%

Table 3.A1: *Continued*

	Japan	United States	United Kingdom	Germany
Pension eligibility age	Basic pension: 65 Employees' pension: 60 (will be gradually 65 by 2025 for men and 2030 for women)	65 (will be gradually 67 by 2007)	Men: 65 Women: 60 (will be gradually raised to 65 between 2010 and 2020)	Men: 65 (will be raised to 65 by 2009) Women: 60 (will be raised to 65 by 2018)
(Reference) How much pension benefits is dependent on tax revenues	A third of basic pension benefits is financed with tax revenues	The government levies taxes on high-income people's pension benefits and fund it in the pension account	None	The federal government grants subsidies for pension expenditures

Notes: 1. This table is made based on Kosei-nenkin Kikin Rengokai (Employees' Pension Fund Association) (1999) 'Kaigai no Nenkinseido (Overseas Pension Schemes)', Toyo Keizai Shimposha; Shakaihoken Kenkyusho (Institute of Social Insurance) (2002) 'Josei to Nenkin – Josei no Lifestyle no Henkato ni Taioshita Nenkin no Arikata ni Kansuru Kentokai Hokokusho' (Women and Pension, Report from the Working Group on Pension Schemes to Respond to Changing Lifestyles of Women); Discussion papers for the Pension Group in Social Security Council.

2. 'Three-quarter criteria' means that, in terms of daily/weekly working hours and monthly working days, a worker works for three-quarters or more of normal full-time workers. ¥1.3 million criteria' means that worker's annual income is ¥1.3 million or more.

3. Japan's pension scheme has the following pensioner statuses:

Class 1 insured: does not meet the three-quarter criteria but would satisfy the ¥1.3 million criteria if his/her spouse is an employee (self-employed and unemployed belong to this category).

Class 2 insured: satisfies the three-quarter criteria (full-time employees, i.e., members of employee's pension schemes).

Class 3 insured: falls short both of the three-quarter criteria and the ¥1.3 million criteria (dependent spouses of employees).

Calculation base for collecting contribution?	Income	Income	Income	Income
Relationship between pension contribution and calculation base	Class 2: proportional to income Class 1: flat rate	Proportional to income	Employees: proportional to income Self-employed: flat rate, if the income exceeds a certain level, income proportional contribution is applicable (without corresponding benefit)	Proportional to income
Preferential measure(s) for childcare	Employees (not temporary): contribution reduced, but regarded themselves as paying full contribution during the childcare leave Temporary employees and self-employed: no preferential measures	None	Home responsibility protection: if the income becomes smaller than lower earnings limit due to childcare (for a child under age 16), the required number of years of contribution (qualifying years) for full pension is reduced	If a person raises a child under age 3, he/she is regarded him/herself as paying the pension contribution at the same amount as the average pension insured person. Preferential measures are also applicable if the income falls short of the average wage while raising a child under age 10
Income-splitting between a husband and wife	None	None	None	A married couple who have been married longer than 25 years are able to divide their pension benefits (= income-splitting) on the optional basis

Table 3.A1: *Continued*

	Japan	United States	United Kingdom	Germany
(Public pension benefits) Who receives the pension benefits?	Individual-based (however, the pension scheme also has Class 3 status as well as the survivor's pension benefits for senior spouses)	Individual-based (however, the pension scheme also has the spouse benefit for wife/ husband based on the spouse's contribution)	Individual-based (however, the pension scheme also has the survivor's pension benefits for senior spouses)	Individual-based (however, the pension scheme also has the survivor's pension benefits for senior spouses)
Class 3 insured person status, or spouse's pension schemes	Class 3 status guarantees basic pension benefits for homemakers even if they didn't pay their own pension contributions	The pensioner's spouse who is 65 years or older receives pensioner's spouse benefit (50% of the pensioner's pension benefits)	A pensioner's spouse over pension age is able to receive a spouse benefit (60% of the pensioner's basic pension benefit)	None
Survivor's pension for senior spouses	Class 2 insured must be applied survivor's pension programme (the basic pension scheme does not include survivor's programme for senior spouses). The survivor receives the three-quarter of the employees' old age benefit (the 2nd tier) of the deceased spouse,	The insured must be applied survivor's pension programme. A widow(er) is entitled to survivor's benefit (100% of the old age benefit of the deceased), over age 60 (50 for disabled persons), and unmarried after bereavement. The	For a bereavement on or after 9 April 2001, a widow(er) may be able to receive a basic pension benefit based on the contribution of the deceased (mandatory). A man who was widowered before 8 April 2001 can claim only widowed parent's	A widow(er) is able to receive a survivor's pension benefit (income-tested) if he/she is over age 45 and not remarried (mandatory)

Survivor's pension benefits for young bereaved spouse or his/her child

Basic pension: a widow receives survivor's basic pension if she has a child who is under age 18 (mandatory). Employees' pension: a widow receives survivor's benefit (three quarter of the 2nd tier benefit of the deceased) irrespective of her age or having child (mandatory). A widower under age 55 at bereavement is not entitled as a survivor, and can not claim survivor's benefit while he is under age 60 if the survivor is unmarried after bereavement. The options for the survivor are her/his own employees' old age benefit or the survivor's benefit, or half of the sum of both benefits

A widow(er) receives mother's/father's benefit (75% of pension benefit of the deceased) if (s)he is unmarried after bereavement and raises a child who is either under age 16 or disabled (mandatory). survivor's benefits may be able to inherit 2nd tier pension (50–100% of the 2nd tier pension of the deceased depending on when the deceased (would) reach(ed) the pension age)

A widow(er) receives the widowed parent's allowance as well as the 2nd tier pension right of the deceased, if he/she is raising at least a child who is under age 16 or a student at ages of 16 to 18, or if she is expecting her husband's baby (mandatory). A widow(er) who was aged over 45 and under pension age at the bereavement, and not raising children can receive bereavement allowance (rate depending on the age at the bereavement) for allowance. A widow(er)

A widow(er) who is raising a child under age 18 and not remarried receives the same benefit as mentioned above (mandatory). A widow(er) under age 45 who has no child and not remarried receives a survivor's pension benefit at a reduced level (income-tested) (mandatory)

Table 3.A1: *Continued*

	Japan	United States	United Kingdom	Germany
		52 weeks from the date of bereavement (mandatory). Bereavement allowance stops at remarriage		
Pension benefit structure	'Minimum' + income related portion (2nd tier portion is only applicable to Class 2 insured)	Income related portion only	'Minimum' + income related portion (2nd tier portion is only applicable to employees)	Income related portion only
Structure of 'minimum' portion	Flat rate (same for all pensioners)	None (livelihood subsidy is provided to low-income people)	The same benefit amount is applicable to all pensioners (the basic pension benefit)	None (livelihood subsidy is provided to low-income people)
(Public pension benefits)				
Relationship between contribution and pension benefits	Basic pension: flat rate (however, the duration of contribution is also taken into consideration) Employees' pension (2nd tier): proportional to income	Proportional to income	Basic pension: flat rate (however, the duration of contribution is also taken into consideration) Employees' pension plans (2nd tier): Proportional to income	Proportional to income
Redistribution	Redistribution via the basic pension scheme	Applicable multipliers for income level will be lowered at two different income-	Redistribution via the basic pension scheme	None

Bibliography

Acker, Joan (1990) 'Hierarchies, jobs, bodies: a theory of gendered organizations', *Gender & Society*, 4 (2): 139–58.

Acker, Joan (2003) 'Hierarchies, jobs, bodies: a theory of gendered organizations', in Robin J. Ely, Erica Gabrielle Foldy and Maureen Scully (eds), *Reader in Gender, Work and Organization* (Oxford: Blackwell): 49–61.

Ajia josei shiryô sentâ (1997) *Peijing hatsu, Nihon no onnatachi e. Sekai josei kaigi o dô ikasu ka* (Tokyo: Meiseki shoten).

Allmendinger, Jutta and J. Richard Hackman (1995) 'The more, the better? On the inclusion of women in professional organizations', *Social Forces*, 74 (2): 423–60.

Alvarez, Sonia (1999) 'Advocating feminism: the Latin American feminist NGO "boom"', *International Feminist Journal of Politics*, 1 (2): 181–209.

Altvater, Elmar and Birgit Mahnkopf (1996/2000) *Grenzen der Globalisierung. Ökonomie, Ökologie und Politik in der Weltgesellschaft* (Münster: Westfälisches Dampfboot).

Anker, Richard (1998) *Gender and Jobs: Sex Segregation of Occupations in the World* (Geneva: International Labour Office).

Annacker, M. (2005) 'Die Hartz-Reformen des Arbeitsmarkts unter Geschlechterperspektiven', Diploma thesis (Ruhr University Bochum: Faculty of Social Science).

Arnold, Katrin and Mariusz Ptaszek (2003) 'Die deutsche Call-Center-Landschaft: Regionale Disparitäten und Arbeitsmarktstrukturen', in Frank Kleemann and Ingo Matuschek (eds), *Immer Anschluss unter dieser Nummer – rationalisierte Dienstleistung und subjektivierte Arbeit in Call Centern* (Berlin: Edition Sigma): 31–48.

Arntz, Melanie, Michael Feil and Alexander Spermann (2003) 'Die Arbeitsangebotseffekte der neuen Mini- und Midijobs – eine ex-ante Evaluation', *Mitteilungen aus der Arbeitsmarkt- und Berufsforschung*, 36 (3): 271–90.

Arzbächer, Sandra, Ursula Holtgrewe and Christian Kerst (2002) 'Call centres: constructing flexibility', in Ursula Holtgrewe, Christian Kerst and Karen A. Shire (eds), *Re-organizing Service Work. Call Centres in Germany and Britain* (Aldershot: Ashgate): 19–41.

Asahi Shimbun (2005) *Nihongata Keiei Dou Naru: Nihon no kigyoushakai wo kenkyuu suru Ronarudo Do-a shi Mirai wo Kataru* ('What will become of the "Japanese style of management"'), Ronald Dore, researcher of Japan's corporate society, speaks of the future' (5 January).

Atkinson, Anthony (2003) *Top Incomes in the United Kingdom over the Twentieth Century*, http://www.nuff.ox.ac.uk/users/atkinson/TopIncomes20033.pdf, accessed 25 June 2005.

Bach, Hans-Uwe, Christian Gaggermeier, Anja Kettner, Sabine Klinger, Thomas Rothe, Eugen Spitznagel and Susanne Wanger (2004) 'Entwicklung des Arbeitsmarktes im Jahr 2005', *IAB-Kurzbericht*, 17 (12 November).

Badgett, M.V. Lee and Nancy Folbre (1999) 'Assigning care: gender norms and economic outcomes', *International Labour Review*, 138 (3): 311–26.

Baethge, Martin, Jim Kitay and Ida Regalia (1999a) 'Managerial strategies, human resource practices, and labour relations in banks: a comparative view', in Martin Baethge, Jim Kitay and Ida Regalia (eds), *From Tellers to Sellers: Changing Employment Relations in Banks* (Cambridge, Mass.: MIT Press).

Baethge, Martin, Nestor D'Alessio and Herbert Oberbeck (1999b) 'The end of institutional stability? The German banking industry in transition', in Marino Regini, Jim Kitay and Martin Baethge (eds), *From Tellers to Sellers. Changing Employment Relations in Banks* (Cambridge, Mass.: MIT Press): 287–315.

Baier, M. (2004) 'The working women's (international) network in Ōsaka', MA thesis (Vienna University).

Bain, Peter and Phil Taylor (2002) 'Consolidation, "cowboys" and the developing employment relationship in British, Dutch and US call centres', in Ursula Holtgrewe, Christian Kerst and Karen A. Shire (eds), *Re-organizing Service Work. Call Centres in Germany and Britain* (Aldershot: Ashgate): 42–62.

Bain, Peter, Aileen Watson, Gareth Mulvey, Phil Taylor and Gregor Gall (2002) 'Taylorism, targets and the pursuit of quantity and quality by call centre management', *New Technology, Work and Employment*, 17 (3): 170–85.

Baines, Susan and Jane Wheelock (2000) 'Work and employment in small businesses: perpetuating and challenging gender traditions', *Gender, Work and Organisation*, 7 (1): 45–56.

Bakker, Isabella (1998) *Unpaid Work and Macroeconomics: New Decisions, New Tools for Action* (Ottawa, Canada: Status of Women Canada).

Barker, Kathleen and Kathleen Christensen (eds) (1998) *Contingent Work* (Ithaca: Cornell University Press).

Batt, Rosemary (2000) 'Strategic segmentation in front-line services: matching customers, employees and human resource systems', *International Journal of Human Resource Management*, 11 (3): 540–61.

Batt, Rosemary, Susan Christopherson, Ned Rightor and Danielle D. van Jaarsveld (2001) *Net Working. Work Patterns and Workforce Policies for the New Media Industry* (Washington DC: Economic Policy Institute).

Baumann, Arne (2002) 'Informal labour market governance: the case of the British and German media production industries', *Work, Employment & Society*, 16 (1): 27–46.

Baumol, William J. (1967) 'Macroeconomics of unbalanced growth: the anatomy of the urban crisis', *American Economic Review*, 57 (2): 415–26.

Beck, Ulrich (1992) *Risk Society: Towards a New Modernity* (London: Sage).

Beck, Ulrich (2000) *Schöne neue Arbeitswelt* (published in English as *The Brave New World of Work*) (Frankfurt: Campus).

Beck, Ulrich (2002) 'Zombie categories: interview with Ulrich Beck', in Ulrich Beck and Elisabeth Beck-Gernsheim (eds), *Individualization* (London: Sage).

Bell, Daniel (1973) *The Coming of Post-industrial Society* (New York: Basic Books).

Belt, Vicky (1999) 'Are call centres the new sweatshops?', *The Thursday Review, Independent*, 14 January: 4.

Belt, Vicky (2002) 'Capitalising on femininity: gender and the utilisation of social skills in telephone call centres', in Ursula Holtgrewe, Christian Kerst and Karen A. Shire (eds), *Re-organizing Service Work. Call Centres in Germany and Britain* (Aldershot: Ashgate): 123–45.

Belt, Vicky (2003) 'Work, employment and skill in the New Economy: training for call centre work in the North East of England', 21st Annual International Labour Process Conference, University of the West of England, Bristol, UK, 14–16 April.

Belt, Vicky (2004) 'A female ghetto? Women's careers in telephone call centres', in Stephen Deery and Nick Kinnie (eds), *Call Centres and Human Resource Management: a Cross-national Perspective* (Basingstoke: Palgrave Macmillan).

Belt, Vicky and Ranald Richardson (2000) 'Women's work in the information economy: the case of telephone call centres', Centre for Social and Policy Research, University of Teeside, *Occasional Paper No. 1*: 7–22.

Belt, Vicky, Ranald Richardson and Juliet Webster (2002) 'Women, social skill and interactive service work in telephone call centres', *New Technology, Work and Employment*, 17 (1): 20–34.

Benner, Chris (2002) *Work in the New Economy. Flexible Labour Markets in Silicon Valley* (Oxford: Blackwell).

Berkovitch, Nitza (1999) *From Motherhood to Citizenship. Women's Rights and International Organizations* (Baltimore: Johns Hopkins University Press).

Betzelt, Sigrid (2003) 'Trade unions between innovation and gender-blindness. Evidence from the cultural industries in Germany', IIRA 13th World Congress, Berlin, 8–12 September, http://www.zes.uni-bremen.de/~sbetzelt/vortraege.htm.

Betzelt, Sigrid and Uwe Fachinger (2004) 'Jenseits des "Normalunternehmers": Selbständige Erwerbsformen und ihre soziale Absicherung', *Zeitschrift für Sozialreform*, 50 (3): 312–43.

Betzelt, Sigrid and Karin Gottschall (2004) 'Publishing and the new media professions as forerunners of pioneer work and life patterns', in Janet Zollinger Giele and Elke Holst (eds), *Changing Life Patterns in Western Industrial Societies* (London: Elsevier): 257–80.

Bialucha-Rhazouani, K. (2002) 'Erwerbstätigkeit von Frauen in Callcentern. Eine Untersuchung zur Bedeutung von Geschlecht in einer neuen Organisationsform', Diploma thesis in sociology (Duisburg: Duisburg University).

Bienzeisler, Bernd and Markus Tünte (2003) 'Parallelwelten: Telefongestützte Rationalisierung im Finanzdienstleistungssektor', in Frank Kleemann and Ingo Matuschek (eds), *Immer Anschluss unter dieser Nummer – Rationalisierte Dienstleistung und subjektivierte Arbeit in Call Centern* (Berlin: Sigma): 109–26.

Bittner, Susanne, Marc Schietinger, Jochen Schroth and Claudia Weinkopf (2002) 'Call centres in Germany: employment, training and job design', in Ursula Holtgrewe, Christian Kerst and Karen A. Shire (eds), *Re-organising Service Work. Call Centres in Germany and Britain* (Aldershot: Ashgate): 63–85.

Blackler, Frank (1995) 'Knowledge, knowledge work and organisations: an overview and interpretation', *Organization Studies*, 16 (6): 1021–46.

Blair, Helen (2001) 'You're only as good as your last job: the labour market in the British film industry', *Work, Employment and Society*, 15 (1): 149–69.

Blossfeld, Hans-Peter and Sonja Drobnic (2001) *Careers of Couples in Contemporary Societies. From Breadwinner to Dual Earner Families* (Oxford: Oxford University Press).

Bögenhold, Dieter and Uwe Fachinger (2004) 'Struktureller Wandel selbständiger Erwerbsarbeit: Analysen auf der Grundlage der Scientific Use Files der Mikrozensen', *ZeS-Arbeitspapier* 3 (Universität Bremen: Zentrum für Sozialpolitik).

Bonoli, Giuliano (2003) 'Social policy through labour markets: understanding national differences in the provision of economic security to wage earners', *Comparative Political Studies*, 36 (9): 1007–31.

Boyer, Robert and Jean-Pierre Durand (1997) *After Fordism* (Basingstoke: Palgrave Macmillan).

Brasse, Claudia (2002) 'Zusatzauswertungen der "Connexx-Studie"' (unpublished tables) (Dortmund: Prospektiv GmbH).

Breen, Richard (1997) 'Risk, recommodification and stratification', *Sociology*, 31 (3): 473–89.

Brinton, Mary (1993) *Women of the Economic Miracle. Gender and Work in Postwar Japan* (Berkeley: University of California Press).

Bristow, Gillian, Peter Gripaios, S. Keast and Max Munday (2002) 'Call centre growth and the distribution of financial services activity in the UK', *The Service Industries Journal*, 22 (3): 117–34.

Broadbent, Kaye (2003) *Women in Japanese Services* (London: Routledge).

Broadbent, Kaye (2005) 'Pawaa Appu! Women only unions in Japan', *Electronic Journal of Contemporary Japanese Studies*, Article 8 (31 October), http://www.japanesestudies.org.uk/articles/2005/Broadbent.html, accessed 23 February 2006.

Brown, Gordon (2003) *Hansard Columns 277 and 281*, http://www.publications.parliament.uk/pa/cm200203/cmhansrd/vo030409/debtext/30409-04.htm#30409-04_spmin1, accessed 9 April 2005.

Brush, Lisa D. (2002) 'Changing the subject: gender and welfare regime studies', *Social Politics*, 9 (2): 161–86.

Burchell, Brendan, Jill Earnshaw and Jill Rubery (1993) New *Forms and Patterns of Self-Employment in Britain* (Baden-Baden: Nomos).

Burgoon, Brian and Phineas Baxandall (2004) 'Three worlds of working time: the partisan and welfare politics of work hours in industrialized countries', *Politics & Society*, 32 (4): 439–73.

Burton-Jones, Alan (1999) *Knowledge Capitalism. Business, Work, and Learning in the New Economy* (Oxford: Oxford University Press).

Butler, Judith (2004) *Undoing Gender* (London and New York: Routledge).

Cabinet Decision (2002) *Kongo no Keizai Zaisei Un-ei oyobi Keizai Shakai no Kozo Kaikaku ni Kansuru Kihon Hoshin*.

Cabinet Office (2003) *FY2002 Annual Report on the State of Formation of a Gender-Equal Society and Policies to be Implemented in FY2003 to Promote the Formation of a Gender-Equal Society* (Tokyo: Cabinet Office, June).

Cabinet Office (2004) *FY2003 Annual Report on the State of Formation of a Gender-Equal Society and Policies to be Implemented in FY2004 to Promote the Formation of a Gender-Equal Society* (Tokyo: Cabinet Office, June).

Callaghan, George and Paul Thompson (2002) 'We recruit attitude: the selection and shaping of routine call centre labour', *Journal of Management Studies*, 39 (2): 233–54.

Cameron, Claire, Ann Mooney and Peter Moss (2002) 'The child care workforce: current conditions and future directions', *Critical Social Policy*, 22 (4): 572–95.

Campbell, John Creighton (2002) 'Japanese social policy in comparative perspective', *World Bank Institute Working Papers*, Stock No. 37197.

Carnoy, Martin (2000) *Sustaining the New Economy* (New York: Russell Sage Foundation).

Casey, Catherine (2004) 'Knowledge-based economies: organisations and sociocultural regulation of work', *Economic and Industrial Democracy*, 25 (4): 607–27.

Castells, Manuel (1996) *The Rise of the Network Society. The Information Age: Economy, Society and Culture*, Volume I (Massachusetts: Blackwell Publishers).

Castells, Manuel (1997) *The Power of Identity. The Information Age: Economy, Society and Culture*, Volume II (Oxford: Blackwell).

Castells, Manuel (1998) *End of Millennium. The Information Age: Economy, Society and Culture*, Volume III (Oxford: Blackwell).

Castells, Manuel (2000a) *The Rise of the Network Society. The Information Age: Economy, Society and Culture*, Volume I, 2nd edition (Oxford: Blackwell).

Castells, Manuel (2000b) 'Materials for an exploratory theory of the network society', *British Journal of Sociology*, 51 (1): 5–24.

Castells, Manuel (2001) *The Internet Galaxy: Reflection on the Internet, Business, and Society* (Oxford: Oxford University Press).

Cerny, Philip G. (1996) 'International finance and the erosion of state policy capacity', in Philip Gummett (ed.), *Globalization and Public Policy* (Cheltenham: Edward Elgar).

Charles, Maria (2004) 'Skill profiles, gender ideology, and sex segregation: structural and cultural constraints on occupational choice', paper prepared for presentation at the Conference of Europeanists, Chicago, 13 March.

Charles, Maria (2005) 'Skill profiles, gender ideology, and sex segregation: structural and cultural constraints on occupational choice', *Social Politics*, 12 (3): 289–316.

Chase-Dunn, Christopher, Yukio Kawano and Benjamin D. Brewer (2000) 'Trade globalization since 1795: waves of integration in the world-system', *American Sociological Review*, 65 (1): 77–95.

Christopherson, Susan (2004) *The Divergent Worlds of New Media. How Policy Shapes Work in the Creative Economy* (Ithaca: Cornell University Press).

Cohany, Sharon R. (1998) 'Workers in alternative employment arrangements: a second look', *Monthly Labour Review*, 121 (11): 3–21.

Congregation for the Doctrine of the Faith (2004) *Letter to the Bishops of the Catholic Church on the Collaboration of Men and Women in the Church and in the World*, http://www.vatican.va/roman_curia/congregations/cfaith/documents/rc_con_cfaith_doc_20040731_collaboration_en.html, accessed 24 December 2005.

Connell, Robert W. (1987) *Gender and Power: Society, the Person, Sexual Politics* (Cambridge: Polity Press).

Connell, Robert W. (2002) *Gender* (Cambridge: Polity Press).

Convention on the Elimination of All Forms of Discrimination against Women (CEDAW) (1979), http://www.un.org/womenwatch/daw/cedaw/text/econvetion.htm, accessed 11 October 2005.

Cook, Alice and Hiroko Hayashi (1980) *Working Women in Japan: Discrimination, Resistance, and Reform* (Ithaca and New York: Cornell University Press).

Copeland, P. (2000) *New Media Factfile* (Brighton: Wiredsussex).

Coyle, Diane (2004) 'Getting the measure of the new economy', presentation at the Social Study of Information Technology Workshop, London School of Economics Information Systems Department, 24 April.

Crompton, Rosemary (2002) 'Employment, flexible working and the family', *British Journal of Sociology*, 53 (4) (December): 537–58.

Crompton, Rosemary and Gunn Elisabeth Birkelund (2000) 'Employment and caring in British and Norwegian banking: an exploration through individual careers', *Work, Employment and Society*, 14 (2): 331–52.

Crouch, Colin (1982) *Trade Unions. The Logic of Collective Action* (London: Fontana).

Crouch, Colin (1993) *Industrial Relations and European State Traditions* (Oxford: Clarendon Press).

Crouch, Colin and Wolfgang Streeck (eds) (1997) *Political Economy of Modern Capitalism. Mapping Convergence and Diversity* (London: Sage).

Cyba, Eva (1998) 'Geschlechtsspezifische Arbeitsmarktsegregation: Von den Theorien des Arbeitsmarktes zur Analyse sozialer Ungleichheiten am Arbeitsmarkt', in Birgit Geissler, Friederike Maier and Birgit Pfau-Effinger (eds), *Frauenarbeitsmarkt. Der Beitrag der Frauenforschung zur sozioökonomischen Theorieentwicklung* (Berlin: Sigma): 37–61.

Dackweiler, Regina (2000) 'Wir sind der Nukleus der globalen Zivilgesellschaft – Zusammenspiel und Wechselverhältnis der internationalen und nationalen Frauenbewegungen am Beispiel des österreichischen Gewaltschutzgesetzes', in Ilse Lenz and Michiko Mae (eds), *Frauenbewegungen weltweit. Aufbrüche, Kontinuitäten, Veränderungen* (Opladen): 167–99.

Daniels, P. (2004) 'Reflections on the "old" economy, "new" economy and services', *Growth and Change*, 35 (2): 115–38.

Danjo Kyodo Sankaku Kaigi Eikyo Chosa Senmon Chosakai (2002) 'Raifusutairu no Sentaku to Zeisei, Shakaihosho seido, Koyo shisutemu' ni kansuru Hokoku' (Tokyo: Danjo Kyodo Sankaku Kaigi Eikyo Chosa Senmon Chosakai).

Danjo Kyodo Sankaku Kaigi Eikyo Chosa Senmon Chosakai (2004) 'Raifusutairu no Sentaku to Koyo Shugyo ni kansuru Seido/Kanko ni tsuitenoi Hokoku' (Tokyo: Danjo Kyodo Sankaku Kaigi Eikyo Chosa Senmon Chosakai).

Datamonitor (2004) *Call Centres in the United Kingdom: Industry Profile*.

David, Paul A. and Dominique Foray (2002) 'An introduction to the economy of the knowledge society', *International Social Science Journal*, 54 (171): 9–23.

Davis, Flora (1999) *Moving the Mountain. The Women's Movement in America since 1960*, 2nd edition (Urbana: University of Illinois Press).

Daycare Trust (2001) *Who Will Care? Recruiting the Next Generation of the Childcare Workforce*, policy paper 4 (London: Daycare Trust).

Devine, Theresa. J. (1994) 'Characteristics of self-employed women in the United States', *Monthly Labour Review*, 117 (3): 20–34.

Dex, Shirley and Andrew McCulloch (1997) *Flexible Employment. The Future of Britain's Jobs* (Basingstoke: Palgrave Macmillan).

Dex, Shirley, Janet Willis, Richard Paterson and Elaine Sheppard (2000) 'Freelance workers and contract uncertainty: the effects of contractual changes in the television industry', *Work, Employment and Society*, 14 (2): 283–305.

Dickens, Linda (2004) 'Problems of fit: changing employment and labour regulation', *British Journal of Industrial Relations*, 42 (4): 595–616.

Dore, Ronald (1973) *British Factory-Japanese Factory. The Origins of National Diversity in Industrial Relations* (Berkeley: University of California Press).

Dore, Ronald (2000) *Stock Market Capitalism: Welfare Capitalism* (Oxford: Oxford University Press).

Dostal, Werner (1996) 'Arbeitsmarkt für Computerberufe leicht erholt', *Materialien aus der Arbeitsmarkt- und Berufsforschung (MatAB)*, 2.

Drucker, Peter F. (1993a) *Post-Capitalist Society* (New York: HarperCollins).

Drucker, Peter F. (1993b) *Post-Capitalist Society* (Oxford: Butterworth Heinemann).

Drucker, Peter (2002) *Managing in the Next Society* (New York: St. Martin's Griffin).

DTI (2004) *Gender and Innovation*, http://www.setwomenstats.org.uk/set4statistics/index.htm, accessed 11 October 2005.

Durbin, Susan (2004) 'Is the knowledge economy gendered?' Unpublished PhD, School of Sociology and Social Policy, University of Leeds.

Dyson, Kenneth (1992) 'Theories of regulation and the case of Germany: a model of regulatory change', in Kenneth Dyson (ed.), *The Politics of German Regulation* (Aldershot: Dartmouth Publishing): 1–28.

Ebbinghaus, Bernhard (2001) 'When labour and capital collude: the political economy of early retirement in Europe, Japan and the USA', in Bernhard Ebbinghaus and Philip Manow (eds), *Comparing Welfare Capitalism. Social Policy and Political Economy in Europe, Japan and the United States* (London: Routledge): 76–101.

Ebbinghaus, Bernhard and Phillip Manow (eds) (2001) *Comparing Welfare Capitalism. Social Policy and Political Economy in Europe, Japan and the United States* (London: Routledge).

Economist, The (2005) 'Japan's economy: reading the tea leaves', 6 August: 32.

Ehrenreich, Barbara (2001) *Nickel and Dimed. On (Not) Getting By in America* (New York: Metropolitan).

Ehrenreich, Barbara (2005) 'Gender inequality: old patterns, new challenges', *Ralph Miliband Lectures on Inequalities: Dimensions and Challenges*, LSE, 3 February.

England, Paula (2005) 'Gender inequality in labour markets: the role of motherhood and segregation', *Social Politics*, 12 (2): 264–88.

E-Skills UK (2004) *Quarterly Review of the ICT Labour Market*, E-Skills Bulletin, Quarter 1, http://www.e-skills.com/public/downloads/bulletin_1_2004.pdf, accessed 10 October 2005.

Esping-Andersen, Gøsta (1990) *The Three Worlds of Welfare Capitalism* (Cambridge: Polity Press) (Okazawa Norio and Miyamoto Taro (trans.) (2001) *Fukushi Shihon Shugi no Mittsu no Sekai* (Kyoto: Minerva Shobo)).

Esping-Andersen, Gøsta (ed.) (1996) *Welfare States in Transition: National Adaptations in Global Economies* (London: Sage).

Esping-Andersen, Gøsta (1997a) 'Hybrid or unique? The Japanese welfare state between Europe and America', *Journal of European Social Policy*, 7 (3): 179–89.

Esping-Andersen, Gøsta (1997b) *Welfare States in Transition: National Adaptations in Global Economies* (London: Sage).

Esping-Andersen, Gøsta (1999) *Social Foundations of Postindustrial Economies* (Oxford: Oxford University Press).

Esping-Andersen, Gøsta (2001) (Okazawa Norio and Miyamoto Taro (trans.) *Fukushi Shihon Shugi no Mittsu no Sekai* (*The Three Worlds of Welfare Capitalism*) (Kyoto: Minerva Shobo).

Esping-Andersen, Gøsta, Duncan Gallie, Anton Hemerijck and John Myles (2002) *Why We Need a New Welfare State* (Oxford: Oxford University Press).

Estévez-Abe, Margarita (1999) 'Comparative political economy of female labour force participation', paper prepared for the 95th American Political Science Association Meeting at the Atlanta Hilton and the Marriott Marquis, 2–5 September.

Estévez-Abe, Margarita (2002) 'Gendering the varieties of capitalism', unpublished manuscript delivered to the Conference on Female Employment and Fertility, Yale University, July.

Estévez-Abe, Margarita (2005) 'Gender bias in skills and social policies: the varieties of capitalism perspective on sex segregation', *Social Politics*, 12 (2): 180–215.

Estévez-Abe, Margarita, Torben Iversen and David Soskice (2001) 'Social protection and the formation of skills: a reinterpretation of the welfare state', in Peter A. Hall and David Soskice (eds), *Varieties of Capitalism. The Institutional Foundations of Comparative Advantage* (Oxford and New York: Oxford University Press): 145–83.

European Commission (2000a) *Communication from the Commission to the Council, the European Parliament, the Economic and Social Committee and the Committee of the Regions. Towards a Community Framework Strategy on Gender Equality (2001–2005)*, Brussels, 7 June 2000, COM (2000) 335 final, 2000/0143 (CNS).

European Commission (2000b) *The Lisbon Special European Council (March 2000). Towards a Europe of Innovation and Knowledge*, http://europa.eu.int/scadplus/leg/en/cha/c10241.htm, accessed 2 March 2006.

European Commission (2001a) *Employment in Europe 2001. Recent Trends and Prospects* (Brussels: European Commission DGV).

European Commission (2001b) *Exploitation and Development of the Job Potential in the Cultural Sector*, DG Employment and Social Affairs (München: MKW Wirtschaftsforschung GmbH).

European Commission (2002) *Employment in Europe 2002. Recent Trends and Prospects*, DG Employment and Social Affairs (Luxembourg: European Commission Directorate-General for Employment and Social Affairs).

European Commission (2003) *Building the Knowledge Society. Social and Human Capital Interactions*, Commission Staff Working Paper, Brussels, 28 May.

European Industrial Relations Observatory On-Line (EIRO) (2004) *Trade Union Membership 1993–2003*, http://www.eiro.eurofound.eu.int/2004/03/update/tn0403105u.html, accessed 15 January 2006.

Eurostat (2005) *Technology and Knowledge Intensive Sectors*, http://europa.eu.int/estatref/info/sdds/en/hrst/hrst_sectors.pdf, accessed 8 December 2005.

Evans, Dave (1999) *Practice Learning in the Caring Professions* (Ashgate: Aldershot).

Evans, Mary (1997) *Introducing Contemporary Feminist Thought* (Cambridge: Cambridge University Press).

Ezawa, Aya and Fujiwara Chisa (2003) 'Lone mothers and welfare-to-work policies in Japan and the United States: towards an alternative', paper presented at the annual conference of ISA Research Committee No. 19, University of Toronto, 21–24 August, Toronto.

Fachinger, Uwe (2002) *Sparfähigkeit und Vorsorge gegenüber sozialen Risiken bei Selbständigen: Einige Informationen auf der Basis der Einkommens- und Verbrauchsstichprobe 1998*, ZeS-Arbeitspapier No. 1 (Universität Bremen: Zentrum für Sozialpolitik).

Fachinger, Uwe, Dieter Bögenhold and René Leicht (2001) 'Self-employment and wealth creation: observations on the German case', *International Journal of Entrepreneurship and Innovation*, 2 (2): 81–91.

Felski, Rita (1997) 'The doxa of difference', *Signs*, 23 (1): 1–22.

Ferber, Marianne A. and Jane Waldfogel (1998) 'The long-term consequences of non-traditional employment', *Monthly Labour Review*, 121 (5): 3–12.

Fernie, Sue and David Metcalfe (1997) *(Not) Hanging on the Telephone: Payment Systems in the New Sweat Shops*, Centre for Economic Performance (London: London School of Economics).

Ferree, Myra Marx (1995) 'Making equality: the women's affairs offices in the federal republic of Germany', in Dorothy Stetson and Amy Mazur (eds), *Comparative State Feminism* (London: Sage): 95–114.

Ferree, Myra Marx (2004) 'The framework of gender politics: race, class and gender discourses in the context of European integration', paper presented to ESRC Gender Mainstreaming Seminar, Leeds, May.

Ferree, Myra Marx and Beth Hess (1994) *Controversy and Coalition: the New Feminist Movement across Three Decades of Change* (New York: Twayne.).

Ferree, Myra Marx, Carol Mueller and Carol McClurg (2004) 'Feminism and the women's movement: a global perspective', in David Snow, Sarah A. Boule and Hanspeter Kriesi (eds), *The Blackwell Companion to Social Movements* (London: Blackwell).

Flecker, Joerg (2000) '"Sachzwang Flexibilisierung"? Unternehmensreorganisation und flexible Beschäftigungsformen', in Heiner Minssen (ed.), *Begrenzte Entgrenzungen. Wandlungen von Organisation und Arbeit* (Berlin: Sigma): 269–91.

Florida, Richard (2002) *The Rise of the Creative Class and How it's Transforming Work, Leisure, Community and Everyday Life* (New York: Basic Books).

Folbre, Nancy and Julie A. Nelson (2000) 'For love or money – or both?', *Journal of Economic Perspectives*, 14 (4): 123–40.

Foote, Daniel (2001) 'Deregulation and labour law: the United States', *Bulletin of Comparative Labour Relations*, 38: 147–68.

Foray, Dominique (2002) 'Introduction and general perspectives', *International Social Science Journal*, 54 (171): 5–7.

Fraser, Janet and Michael Gold (2001) ' "Portfolio workers": autonomy and control amongst freelance translators', *Work, Employment & Society*, 15 (4): 679–97.

Freeman, Richard B. (2003) 'The labour market in the new information economy', *Oxford Review of Economic Policy*, 18 (3): 288–305.

Frenkel, Stephen J., Marek Korczynski, Karen A. Shire and May Tam (1999) *On the Front Line: Organisation of Work in the Information Economy* (Ithaca: Cornell University Press).

Fried, Mindy (1998) *Taking Time: Parental Leave Policy and Corporate Culture* (Philadelphia: Temple University Press).

Friedberg, Erhard (1995) *Ordnung und Macht. Dynamiken organisierten Handelns* (Frankfurt/Main, New York: Campus).

Fuente, Angel de la and Antonio Ciccone (2002) *Human Capital in a Global and Knowledge-Based Economy* (Brussels: European Commission Employment and Social Affairs Directorate).

Gadrey, Jean (2003) *New Economy, New Myth* (London: Routledge).

Gagnon, Suzanne and Sue Ledwith (eds) (2000) *Women, Diversity and Democracy in Trade Unions* (Oxford: Oxford Brookes University).

Game, Ann and Rosemary Pringle (1984) *Gender at Work* (London: Pluto Press).

Gamson, William A. (1975) *The Strategy of Social Protest* (Homewood, Ill.: Dorsey Press).

Geissler, Birgit, Friederike Maier and Birgit Pfau-Effinger (eds) (1998) *Frauenarbeitsmarkt. Der Beitrag der Frauenforschung zur sozioökonomischen Theorieentwicklung* (Berlin: Sigma).

Gelb, Joyce (2003a) *Gender Policies in Japan and the United States. Comparing Women's Movements, Rights and Politics* (New York: Palgrave).

Gelb, Joyce (2003b) *Gender and Politics. Comparing Women's Movements, Rights and Policies in Japan and the United States* (New York: Palgrave).

Genda, Yuki and Ryo Kambayashi (2002) 'Declining self-employment in Japan', *Journal of the Japanese and International Economies*, 16 (1): 73–91.

George, Rebecca (2003) 'Achieving workforce diversity in the e-business on demand era', *IBM Global Solutions*, http://www.e-skills.com/pdfs/ITchampions_03.pdf, accessed October 2005.

Giddens, Anthony (1984) *The Constitution of Society* (Cambridge: Polity Press).

Giddens, Anthony (2001) *Sociology*, 4th edition (Cambridge: Polity Press).

Gill, Rosalind (2002) 'Cool, creative and egalitarian? Exploring gender in project-based new media work in Europe', *Information Communication and Society*, 5 (1): 70–89.

Goos, Maarten and Alan Manning (2003) 'McJobs and MacJobs: the growing polarisation of jobs in the UK', in Richard Dickens, Paul Gregg and Jonathan Wadsworth (eds), *The Labour Market Under New Labour* (Basingstoke: Palgrave Macmillan): 70–85.

Gottfried, Heidi (2000) 'Compromising positions: emergent neo-Fordisms and embedded gender contracts', *British Journal of Sociology*, 52 (2): 235–59.

Gottfried, Heidi (2002) 'Comments on "atypical" and "irregular" labour in contemporary Japan', *Social Science Japan Journal*, 5 (2) (October): 247–50.

Gottfried, Heidi (2003) 'Temp(t)ing bodies: shaping gender at work in Japan', *Sociology*, 37 (2): 257–76.

Gottfried, Heidi and Lina Beydoun (2002) 'Women and the new economy in the US', unpublished manuscript presented to the GLOW workshop at the University of Tokyo, September.

Gottfried, Heidi and Kato Nagisa Hayashi (1998) 'Gendering work: deconstructing the narrative of the Japanese economic miracle', *Work, Employment and Society*, 12 (1): 25–46.

Gottfried, Heidi and Keiko Aiba (2002) 'Women and the new economy in the UK', unpublished manuscript presented to the GLOW workshop at the University of Tokyo, September.

Gottfried, Heidi and Jacqueline O'Reilly (2002) 'Re-regulating breadwinner models in socially conservative welfare regimes: comparing Germany and Japan', *Social Politics*, 9 (1): 29–59.

Gottfried, Heidi and Laura Reese (2003) 'Gender, policy, politics and work: feminist comparative and transnational research', *Review of Policy Research*, 20 (1) (Spring): 3–20.

Gottfried, Heidi, Steve Rose, Heidi Hartmann and David Fasenfest (2004) 'Autonomy and insecurity: the status of women workers in the United States', *Josei Roundou Kenkyu* (*Bulletin of the Society for the Study of Working Women*), 46: 17–39.

Gottschall, Karin (2000) *Soziale Ungleichheit und Geschlecht: Kontinuität und Brüche, Sackgassen und Erkenntnispotentiale im deutschen soziologischen Diskurs* (Opladen: Leske & Budrich).

Gottschall, Karin (2002) 'New forms of employment in Germany: labour market regulation and its gendered implications', *Occasional Paper Series No. 8*, March (Detroit: Wayne State University, College of Urban, Labor and Metropolitan Affairs).

Gottschall, Karin and Katherine Bird (2003) 'Family leave policies and labor market segregation in Germany: reinvention or reform of the male breadwinner model?', *Review of Policy Research*, 20 (1): 115–34.

Gottschall, Karin and Annette Henninger (2004) 'Freelancers in the German new media industry: beyond standard patterns of work and life', paper presented at the international workshop 'Studying New Forms of Work: Concepts and Practices in Cultural Industries and Beyond', Berlin, 26–27 March, http://www.zes.uni-bremen.de/~ahenni/paper_ah_kgs.pdf.

Gottschall, Karin, Otfried Mickler and Jürgen Neubert (1985) *Computerunterstützte Verwaltung* (Frankfurt/Main, New York: Campus).

Gottschall, Karin, Heike Jacobsen and Ilse Schütte (1989) *Weibliche Angestellte im Zentrum betrieblicher Innovation. Die Bedeutung neuer Bürotechnologien für Beschäftigungssituation und Berufsperspektiven weiblicher Angestellter in Klein- und Mittelbetrieben* (Stuttgart: Kohlhammer).

Granger, Bill, John Stanworth and Celia Stanworth (1995) 'Self-employment career dynamics: the case of "unemployment push" in UK book publishing', *Work, Employment and Society*, 9 (3): 499–516.

Grass, Bernd (1998) 'Arbeitsbedingungen freier Journalisten. Bericht zu einer Umfrage unter Mitgliedern des DJV', *Journalist*, 11: 65–80.

Greenspan, Alan (1998) 'Is there a new economy?', *California Management Review*, 41 (1): 74–85.

Gundtoft, Lars and Ursula Holtgrewe (2000) 'Call-Center – Rationalisierung im Dilemma', in Hanns-Georg Brose (ed.), *Die Reorganisation der Arbeitsgesellschaft* (Frankfurt/Main, New York: Campus): 173–203.

Haak, Carroll and Günther Schmid (1999) *Arbeitsmärkte für Künstler und Publizisten – Modelle einer zukünftigen Arbeitswelt*, Arbeitspapier, Wissenschaftszentrum Berlin (WZB), Querschnittsgruppe Arbeit und Ökologie.

Hall, Peter and David Soskice (eds) (2001) *Varieties of Capitalism: the Institutional Foundations of Comparative Advantage* (Oxford: Oxford University Press).

Hanami, Tadashi (1991) 'Nihon-teki Sabetsu no Kozou' (The Structure of Japanese-Style Discrimination), *Jurisuto*, 988 (15 October).

Hanami, Tadashi (2000) 'Equal employment revisited', *Japan Institute of Labour Bulletin*, 39, Special Topic V. 1 January, W1: 1–8.

Handy, Charles (1994) *The Empty Raincoat. Making Sense of the Future* (London: Hutchinson).

Hara, Hiroko and Mari Osawa (1996) 'Joseigaku to josei seisaku', in Hiroko Hara and Mari Ôsawa (eds), *Ajia – Taiheiyô chiki no joseiseisaku to joseigaku* (Tokyo): 1–25.

Harkness, Susan (2003) 'The household division of labour: changes in families' allocation of paid and unpaid work, 1992–2002', in Richard Dickens, Paul Gregg and Jonathan Wadsworth (eds), *The Labour Market Under New Labour* (Basingstoke: Palgrave Macmillan): 150–69.

Hassel, Anke (2001) 'The governance of the employment–welfare relationship in Britain and Germany', in Bernd Ebbinghausm and Philip Manow (eds), *Comparing Welfare Capitalism* (London and New York: Routledge): 146–68.

Heinz, Walter R. and Victor W. Marshall (2003) *Social Dynamics of the Life Course. Transitions, Institutions, and Interrelations* (New York: Walter de Gruyter).

Helfferich, Barbara and Felix Kolb (2001) 'Multilevel action coordination in European contentious politics: the case of the European women's lobby', in Doug Imig and Sidney Tarrow (eds), *Contentious Europeans. Protest and Politics in an Emerging Polity* (Lanham: Rowman & Littlefield).

Henderson, Jeanette and Dorothy Atkinson (eds) (2003) *Managing Care in Context* (London: Routledge).

Henninger, Annette (2004) 'Freelancer in den Neuen Medien: Jenseits standardisierter Muster von Arbeit und Leben?', in Heike Kahlert and Claudia Kajatin (eds), *Arbeit und Vernetzung im Informationszeitalter. Wie neue Technologien die Geschlechterverhältnisse verändern?* (Frankfurt a.M./New York: Campus): 143–65.

Hicks, Stephen and Tom Palmer (2004) 'Trade union membership: estimates from the autumn 2003 Labour Force Survey', *Labour Market Trends*, 112 (3) (March): 99–101.

Higuchi, Yukio (2004) 'Employment strategies required in an aging society with fewer children', *Japan Labour Review*, 1 (1) (Winter): 17–28.

Hildebrandt, Swen (1999) *Lean Banking als Reorganisationsmuster für deutsche und französische Kreditinistitute? Anmerkungen zur Tragfähigkeit eines leitbildorientierten Managementkonzepts*, FS I 99–101 (Berlin: WZB).

Hillmert, Steffen (2002) 'Labour market integration and institutions: an Anglo-German comparison', *Work, Employment & Society*, 16 (4): 675–701.

Himmelweit, Susan (1999) 'Caring labour', in Ronnie J. Steinberg and Deborah M. Figart (eds), *Emotional Labour in the Service Economy, the Annals of the American Academy of Political and Social Science* (London: Sage).

Hirowatari, Seigo (1990) *Futatsuno Sengoshakai to Ho no Aida, Nihon to Doitsu* (Between Two Post-war Societies and Laws: Japan and Germany) (Tokyo: Ministry of Finance Printing Bureau).

Hirst, Paul and Jonathan Zeitlin (1997) 'Flexible specialization: theory and evidence in the analysis of industrial change', in J. Rogers Hollingsworth and Robert Boyer (eds), *Contemporary Capitalism. The Embeddedness of Institutions* (Cambridge: Cambridge University Press): 220–39.

Hobson, Barbara (1994) 'Solo mothers, social policy regimes, and the logics of gender', in Diane Sainsbury (ed.), *Gendering Welfare States* (London: Sage).

Hochschild, Arlie (1990) *The Second Shift* (New York: Avon Books).

Hochschild, Arlie Russel (2000) 'Global care chains and emotional surplus value', in William Hutton and Anthony Giddens (eds), *On the Edge. Living with Global Capitalism* (London: Jonathan Cape): 130–46.

Hochschild, Arlie (2001) *The Time Bind. When Work becomes Home and Home Becomes Work* (New York: Owl Books).

Hollingsworth, J. Rogers (1997) 'Continuities and change in social systems of production: the cases of Japan, Germany, and the United States', in J. Rogers Hollingsworth and Robert Boyer (eds), *Contemporary Capitalism. The Embeddedness of Institutions* (Cambridge: Cambridge University Press): 265–310.

Hollingsworth, J. Rogers and Robert Boyer (1997a) 'Coordination of economic actors and social systems of production', in J. Rogers Hollingsworth and Robert Boyer (eds), *Contemporary Capitalism. The Embeddedness of Institutions* (Cambridge: Cambridge University Press): 1–47.

Hollingsworth, J. Rogers and Robert Boyer (eds) (1997b) *Contemporary Capitalism. The Embeddedness of Institutions* (Cambridge: Cambridge University Press).

Holtgrewe, Ursula (2003) 'Geschlechtergrenzen in der Dienstleistungsarbeit: Aufgelöst und neu gezogen. Das Beispiel Callcenter', in Ellen Kuhlmann, and Sigrid Betzelt (eds), *Geschlechterverhältnisse im Dienstleistungssektor – Dynamiken, Differenzierungen und neue Horizonte* (Baden-Baden: Nomos): 147–60.

Holtgrewe, Ursula and Christian Kerst (2002a) 'Call Center: Die Institutionalisierung von Flexibilität', *Industrielle Beziehungen*, 9 (2): 186–208.

Holtgrewe, Ursula and Christian Kerst (2002b) 'Zwischen Kundenorientierung und organisatorischer Effizienz – Callcenter als Grenzstellen', *Soziale Welt*, 53 (2): 141–60.

Holtgrewe, Ursula, Christian Kerst and Karen A. Shire (eds) (2002) *Re-organizing Service Work. Call Centers in Germany and Britain* (Aldershot: Ashgate).

Hoskyns, Catherine (1996) *Integrating Gender. Women, Law and Politics in the European Union* (London: Verso).

Houseman, Susan and Machiko Osawa (eds) (2003) *Non-standard Work in Developed Economies* (Michigan: W. E. Upjohn Institute for Employment Research).

Huber, Evelyne and John D. Stephens (2000) 'Partisan governance, women's employment, and the social democratic service state', *American Sociological Review*, 65: 323–42.

Huber, Evelyne and John D. Stephens (2001a) *Development and Crisis of the Welfare State. Parties and Policies in Global Markets* (Chicago: Chicago University Press).

Huber, Evelyne and John Stephens (2001b) 'Welfare state and production regimes in the era of retrenchment', in Paul Pierson (ed.), *The New Politics of the Welfare State* (Oxford: Oxford University Press).

Hughes, Karen D. (2003) 'Pushed or pulled? Women's entry into self-employment and small business ownership', *Gender, Work and Organization*, 10: 433–54.

Huws, Ursula (2003) *When Work takes Flight. Research Results from the EMERGENCE Project*, IES-report 397 (Brighton: Institute for Employment Studies).

Huws, Ursula, Nick Jager and Siobhan O'Regan (1999) *Teleworking and Globalisation*, Institute of Employment Studies, report number 358 (London: IES).

ILO (2002) *Yearbook of Labour Statistics* (Geneva: International Labour Organization).

Imidas (2005) (Tokyo: Shuueisha).

Incomes Data Services Limited (IDS) (2001) *Pay and Conditions in Call Centres* (London).

Ishii-Kunz, Masako (2003) 'Balancing fatherhood and work: emergence of diverse masculinities in contemporary Japan', in James Roberson, and Nobue Suzuki (eds), *Men and Masculinities in Contemporary Japan. Beyond the Urban Salaryman Model* (London: Routledge Curzon).

Ito, Shuhei (2001) 'Kaigo Hoken wo Toinaosu' (Questioning the Long-Term-Care Insurance), *Chikuma-shobo*.

Itoh, Hideshi (1994) 'Japanese human resource management from the viewpoint of incentive theory', in Masahiko Aoki and Ronald Dore (eds), *The Japanese Firm. The Sources of Competitive Strength* (Oxford: Oxford University Press): 233–64.

Jahn, Werner and Kai Wegrich (2003) 'Phasenmodelle und Politikprozesse: Der Policy Cycle', in Klaus Schubert and Nils Bandelow (eds), *Lehrbuch der Politikfeldanalyse* (München, Wien: Oldenbourg Verlag): 71–107.

Japan Institute of Labour (2000) *Japanese Working Life Profile 2000 – Labour Statistics* (Tokyo: Japan Institute of Labour): 30.

Japanese Labour Force Survey (2002) *Japanese Statistics Bureau Online Tables*, http://www.stat.go.jp, accessed 1 June 2004.

Jenkins, Sarah (2004) 'Restructuring flexibility: case studies of part-time female workers in six workplaces', *Gender, Work and Organization*, 11 (3): 307–33.

Jenson, Jane (1997) 'Who cares? Gender and welfare regimes', *Social Politics*, 4 (2): 182–7.

Jepperson, Ronald L. (1991) 'Institutions, institutional effects and institutionalism', in Walter W. Powell and Paul J. DiMaggio (eds), *The New Institutionalism in Organizational Analysis* (Chicago and London: Chicago University Press): 204–31.

Jessop, Bob (2002) *The Future of the Capitalist State* (Cambridge: Polity).

Jungbauer-Gans, Monika (1999) 'Der Lohnunterschied zwischen Frauen und Männern in selbständiger und abhängiger Beschäftigung', *Kölner Zeitschrift für Soziologie und Sozialpsychologie*, 51: 364–90.

Kaigo Rodo Antei Senta (2002) *Jigyosho ni okeru Kaigo Rodo Jittai Chosa* (Survey on Work Conditions at the Care Service Establishments).

Keck, Margaret and Kathryn Sikkink (1998) *Activists Beyond Borders. Advocacy Networks in International Politics* (Ithaca and New York: Cornell University Press).

Kelsky, Karen (2001) *Women on the Verge. Japanese Women, Western Dreams* (Durham and London: Duke University Press).

Kelso, Paul (2002) 'Angry women find voice over pay that doesn't add up', *The Guardian*, 18 July.

Kerst, Christian and Ursula Holtgrewe (2003) 'Interne oder externe Flexibilität? Call Center als kundenorientierte Organisationen', in Frank Kleemann, and Ingo Matuschek (eds), *Immer Anschluss unter dieser Nummer – Rationalisierte Dienstleistung und subjektivierte Arbeit in Callcentern* (Berlin: Sigma): 85–108.

Kezuka, Katsutoshi (2000) 'Legal problems concerning part-time work in Japan', *Japan Labour Bulletin*, 39 (9): 5–10.

Khor, Diana (1999) 'Organizing for change: women's grassroots activism in Japan', *Feminist Studies*, 25 (3): 633–61.

Kilkey, Majella (2000) *Lone Mothers between Paid Work and Care* (Aldershot: Ashgate).

Kim, Anna and Karin Kurz (2001) 'Precarious employment, education and gender: a comparison of Germany and the United Kingdom', *Arbeitspapier* 39 (Mannheim: Zentrum für europäische Sozialforschung).

Kinnie, Nick, Sue Hutchinson and John Purcell (2000a) 'Fun and surveillance: the paradox of high commitment management in call centres', *International Journal of Human Resource Management*, 11 (5): 967–85.

Kinnie, Nick, Sue Hutchinson and John Purcell (2000b) 'Managing the employment relationship in telephone call centres', in Kate Purcell (ed.), *Changing Boundaries in Employment* (Bristol: Bristol Academic Press).

Kleemann, Frank and Ingo Matuschek (eds) (2003) *Immer Anschluss unter dieser Nummer – Rationalisierte Dienstleistung und subjektivierte Arbeit in Call Centern* (Berlin: Sigma).

Klenner, Christina and Christiane Lindecke (2003) 'Representation of women in works councils and equal treatment of men and women at company level', *WSI Mitteilungen*, 56 (00) (Special Issue): 66–73.

Knight, Genevieve and Stephen McKay (2000) 'Lifetime experiences of self-employment', *DSS Research Report*, 120 (London: Department of Social Security).

Knights, David, David Calvey and Pamela Odih (1999) 'Social managerialism and the time-disciplined subject: quality-quantity conflicts in a call centre', paper presented to the 17th Annual International Labour Process Conference, 29–31 March, School of Management, Royal Holloway University of London, UK.

Koch, Angelika and Gerhard Bäcker (2004) 'Mini- und Midi-Jobs – Frauenerwerbstätigkeit und Niedrigeinkommensstrategien in der Arbeitsmarktpolitik', in Dagmar Baatz, Clarissa Rudolph and Ayla Satilmis (eds), *Hauptsache Arbeit? Feministische Perspektiven auf den Wandel von Arbeit* (Münster: Verlag Westphälisches Dampfboot): 85–102.

Koch-Baumgarten, Sigrid (2002) 'Changing gender relations in German trade unions', in Fiona Colgan and Sue Ledwith (eds), *Gender, Diversity and Trade Unions. International Perspectives* (London: Routledge): 132–53.

Kôdô suru kai kirokshû henshû iinkai (ed.) (1999) *Kôdô suru onnatachi ga hiraita michi. Mekishiko kara Nyû Yôku e* (Tokyo: Miraisha).

Kohli, Martin (1986) 'The world we forgot: a historical review of the life course', in Victor W. Marshall (ed.), *Later Life. The Social Psychology of Aging* (Beverly Hills, CA: Sage): 271–303.

Kojima, Noriaki and Keiko Fujikawa (2000) 'Non-standard work arrangements in the US and Japan from a legal perspective', paper presented at the Non-Standard Work Arrangements in Japan, Europe, and the United States, sponsored by the W. E. Upjohn Institute, the Japan Foundation and Japan Women's University.

Kokuryo J. (1999) *O-pun A-kitekucha- Senryaku* (Open Architecture Strategies), (Diamond-sha: Tokyo).

Kokusai fujinnen Nihon taikai no ketsugi o jitsugen suru tame no renrakukai (ed.) (1989) *Rentai to kôdô. Kokusai fujinnen renrakukai no kiroku* (Tokyo).

Kolb, David (1984) *Experiential Learning* (New Jersey: Prentice-Hall).

Korczynski, Marek (2001) 'The contradictions of service work: call centre as customer-oriented bureaucracy', in Andrew Sturdy, Irena Grugulis and Hugh Willmott (eds), *Customer Service. Empowerment and Entrapment* (Basingstoke: Palgrave Macmillan): 79–101.

Korczynski, Marek (2002) 'Call centre consumption and the enchanting myth of customer sovereignty', in Ursula Holtgrewe, Christian Kerst and Karen A. Shire (eds), *Re-organising Service Work. Call Centres in Germany and Britain* (Aldershot: Ashgate): 163–82.

Korpi, Walter (2000) 'Faces of inequality: gender, class and patterns of inequalities in different types of welfare states', *Social Politics on Class and Gender*, 7 (2): 127–91.

Kotamraju, Nalini P. (2002) 'Keeping up: web design skill and the reinvented worker information', *Communication and Society*, 5 (1): 1–26.

Kouseiroudoushou, Koyoukintou/jidoukateikyokuhen (2003) (EEOL/Children and Family Bureau, Ministry of Health, Labour and Welfare (eds)) *Heisei 15 Nenkan Josei Roudou Hakusho* (White Paper on Women Workers) (Tokyo: Zaidan Houjin 21 Seiki Shokugyou Zaidan).

Kracauer, Siegfried (1929/1971) *Die Angestellten. Reportagen aus dem Neuesten Deutschland* (Frankfurt/Main: Suhrkamp).

Kramerae, Cheris and Dale Spender (eds) (2000) *Routledge International Encyclopedia of Women. Global Women's Issues and Knowledge* (New York and London: Routledge).

Krätke, Stefan (2002) 'Global media cities in a worldwide urban network, GAWC-globalization and world cities study group and network', *Research Bulletin*, 80, 15 March, http://www.lboro.ac.uk/gawc/rb/rb80.html, accessed 11 October 2005.

Krenn, Manfred, Jörg Flecker and Christian Stary (2003) *Die informationstechnische Revolution – Fortschritte und Rückschritte für die Arbeit. Zum Zusammenhang von Informations- und Kommunikationstechnologien und neuen Formen der Arbeitsorganisation* (Wien: FORBA).

Krüger, Helga (2003) 'The life-course regime: ambiguities between interrelatedness and individualization', in Walter R. Heinz, and Victor W. Marshall (eds), *Social Dynamics of the Life Course. Transitions, Institutions, and Interrelations* (New York: Aldine de Gruyter): 33–56.

Krugman, Paul (2002) 'For Richer', *New York Times*, 20 October.

Kuhlmann, Ellen and Sigrid Betzelt (eds) (2003) *Geschlechterverhältnisse im Dienstleistungssektor – Dynamiken, Differenzierungen und neue Horizonte* (Baden-Baden: Nomos).

Kutzner, Edelgard (2003) 'Arbeitsbeziehungen in Callcentern – Irritationen der Geschlechterordnung', in Ellen Kuhlmann and Sigrid Betzelt (eds), *Geschlechterverhältnisse im Dienstleistungssektor – Dynamiken, Differenzierungen und neue Horizonte* (Baden-Baden: Nomos): 161–74.

Laafia, Ibrahim (2002) 'National and regional employment in high tech and knowledge intensive sectors in the EU 1995–2000', *Eurostat Statistics in Focus*, Theme 9 – 3.

Labour Market Trends (UK) (1988) Table 1, p. 595 (December).

Lam, Alice (1992) *Women and Japanese Management: Discrimination and Reform* (London and New York: Routledge).

Lam, Alice (2002) 'Alternative societal models of learning and innovation in the knowledge economy', *International Social Science Journal*, 54 (171): 67–82.

Land, Hilary (2003) 'Leaving care to the market and the courts', European Social Policy Association Conference, Copenhagen, http://www.sfi.dk/graphics/ESPAnet/papers/Land.pdf, accessed 28 June 2005.

Land, Hilary (2004) *Women, Child Poverty and Childcare. Making the Links* (London: Daycare Trust).

Larner, Wendy (2002) 'Globalization, governmentality and expertise: creating a call centre labour force', *Review of International Political Economy*, 9 (4): 650–74.

Lash, Scott and John Urry (1987) *The End of Organized Capitalism* (Cambridge: Polity Press).

Lash, Scott and John Urry (1994) *Economies of Signs and Space* (London: Sage).

Leadbeater, Charles and Kate Oakley (1999) *The Independents. Britain's New Cultural Entrepreneurs* (London: Demos).

Lehmbruch, Gerhard (2001) 'The institutional embedding of market economies: the German "model" and its impact on Japan', in Wolfgang Streeck and Kozo Yamamura (eds), *The Origins of Nonliberal Capitalism* (Ithaca: Cornell University Press): 39–93.

Lehrer, Mark (2001) 'Macro-varieties of capitalism and micro-varieties of strategic management in European airlines', in Peter A. Hall and David Soskice (eds), *Varieties of Capitalism. The Institutional Foundations of Comparative Advantage* (Oxford and New York: Oxford University Press): 361–86.

Leicht, Rene (2000) ' "Die neuen Selbständigen" arbeiten alleine. Wachstum und Struktur der solo-selbständigen in Deutschland', *Internationales Gewerbearchiv*, 48 (2): 75–90.

Leicht, Rene and Maria Lauxen-Ulbrich (2003) *Soloselbständige Frauen in Deutschland: Entwicklung, wirtschaftliche Orientierung und Ressourcen*, Download-Paper No. 3 (Universität Mannheim: Institut für Mittelstandsforschung (IFM)).

Leicht, Rene and Silvia Luber (2000) 'Growing self-employment in Western Europe: an effect of modernization?', *International Review of Sociology*, 10 (1): 101–23.

Leisering, Lutz (2003) 'Government and the life course', in Jeylan T. Mortimer and Michael J. Shanahan (eds), *Handbook of the Life Course* (New York: Kluwer): 205–25.

Leitner, Sigrid, Ilona Ostner and Margit Schratzenstaller (2004) *Wohlfahrtsstaat und Geschlechterverhältnis im Umbruch. Was kommt nach dem Ernährermodell?* (Wiesbaden: Verlag für Sozialwissenschaften).

Lenz, Ilse (1997) 'Neue Wege, alte Barrieren? Veränderungen für Frauen in der japanischen Betriebsgesellschaft', in Ilse Lenz and Michiko Mae (eds), *Getrennte Welten, gemeinsame Moderne? Geschlechterverhältnisse in Japan* (Opladen): 179–210.

Lenz, Ilse (2000) 'What does the women's movement do, when it moves? Subjektivität, Organisation und Kommunikation in der neuen japanischen Frauenbewegung', in Ilse Lenz, Michiko Mae and Karin Klose (eds), *Frauenbewegungen weltweit. Aufbrüche, Kontinuitäten, Veränderungen* (Opladen: Leske and Budrich): 95–133.

Lenz, Ilse (2001a) 'Globalisierung, Frauenbewegungen und internationale Regulierung', *Zeitschrift für Frauenforschung und Geschlechterstudien*, 19 (1 and 2): 8–29.

Lenz, Ilse (2001b) 'Bewegungen und Veränderungen. Frauenforschung und Neue Frauenbewegungen in Deutschland', in Ursula Hornung, Sedef Gümen and Sabine Weilandt (eds), *Zwischen Emanzipationsvisionen und Gesellschaftskritik. (Re)Konstruktionen der Geschlechterordnungen in Frauenforschung – Frauenbewegung – Frauenpolitik*, Forum Frauenforschung Band 14 (Münster: Westfälisches Dampfboot): 188–220.

Lenz, Ilse (2002) 'Geschlechtsspezifische Auswirkungen der Globalisierung in den Bereichen Global Governance, Arbeitsmärkte und Ressourcen', *Gutachten für die Enquete-Kommission 'Globalisierung der Weltwirtschaft – Herausforderungen und Antworten' des Deutschen Bundestags*.

Lenz, Ilse (2003a) 'Globalisation, gender and work: perspectives on global regulation', *Review of Policy Research*, 20 (1): 21–43.

Lenz, Ilse (2003b) 'Aufbruch ins Reich der Sinne nach dem Überdruss im Käfig der Anforderungen? Der Wandel der Thematisierungen von Sexualität und Körpern in der Entwicklung der Neuen Frauenbewegung in Deutschland', in Ilse Lenz, Lisa Mense and Charlotte Ullrich (eds), *Reflexive Körper? Zur Modernisierung von Sexualität und Reproduktion* (Opladen: Leske and Budrich): 17–51.

Lenz, Ilse and Michiko Mae (eds) (1997) *Getrennte Welten, gemeinsame Moderne? Geschlechterverhältnisse in Japan* (Opladen: Leske and Budrich).

Lenz, Ilse, Michiko Mae and Karin Klose (eds) (2000) *Frauenbewegungen weltweit. Aufbrüche, Kontinuitäten, Veränderungen* (Opladen: Leske and Budrich).

Lenz, Ilse et al. (eds) (2005) *Die Neue Frauenbewegung in Deutschland* (Wiesbaden: Verlag für Sozialwissenschaften).

Levi-Faur, David (2005) 'The global diffusion of regulatory capitalism', *Annals of the American Academy of Political and Social Science*, 598: 12–32.

Levi-Faur, David and Jacint Jordana (2005) 'Preface – the making of a new regulatory order', *Annals of the American Academy of Political and Social Science*, 598: 6–9.

Lewis, Jane (1992) 'Gender and the development of welfare regime', *Journal of European Social Policy*, 2 (3): 159–73.

Lewis, Jane (ed.) (1993) *Women and Social Policies in Europe. Work, Family and the State* (Aldershot: Edward Elgar).

Lewis, Jane (1997) 'Gender and welfare regimes: further thoughts', *Social Politics*, 4 (2): 160–77.

Lewis, Jane and Ilona Ostner (1994) 'Gender and the evolution of European social policy', *ZeS-Arbeitspapier*, No. 4 (Universität Bremen: Zentrum für Sozialpolitik).

Liff, Sonia (1993) 'Information technology and occupational restructuring in the office', in Eileen Green, Jenny Owen and Den Pain (eds), *Gendered by Design? Information Technology and Office Systems* (London: Taylor & Francis).

Liff, Sonia (2000) 'Consumer e-commerce: potential for social inclusion?', *Consumer Policy Review*, 10 (5): 162–6.

Liff, Sonia and Fred Steward (2001a) 'Communities and community e-gateways: networking for social inclusion', in Leigh Keeble and Brian D. Loader (eds), *Community Informatics: Shaping Computer-mediated Social Relations* (London: Routledge).

Liff, Sonia and Fred Steward (2001b) 'Community e-gateways: locating networks and learning for social inclusion', *Information, Communication and Society*, 4 (3): 317–40.

Liff, Sonia, Fred Steward and Peter Watts (2002) 'New public places for internet access: networks for practice-based learning and social inclusion', in Steve Woolgar (ed.), *Virtual Society? Technology, Cyberbole, Reality* (Oxford: Oxford University Press).

Liff, Sonia, Peter Watts and Fred Steward (1999) 'Routes to inclusion in the information society: the contribution of e-gateways', in Claire Milne and Sean Creighton (eds), *Universal Community Service: Access For All to Internet Services at Community Level* (General Report, Malta Conference, 2–3 November): 57–68.

Liff, Sonia, Peter Watts and Fred Steward (2000) 'Inclusion in the information society: the distinctive role of e-gateways', *Teleworker*, 7 (1): 13–16.

Lindley, Robert (2002) 'Knowledge-based economies: the European employment debate in a new context', in Maria Joao Rodrigues (ed.), *The New Knowledge Economy in Europe. A Strategy for International Competitiveness and Social Cohesion* (Aldershot: Edward Elgar): 95–145.

Lisbon European Council (2000) *Presidency Conclusions*, 23 and 24 March 2000, http://www.bologna-berlin2003.de/pdf/PRESIDENCY_CONCLUSIONS_Lissabon.pdf.

Lohmann, Henning (2001) 'Self-employed or employee, full-time or part-time? Gender differences in the determinants and conditions for self-employment in four European countries and the US', *Arbeitspapier* 38 (Mannheim: Zentrum für Europäische Sozialforschung).

Lovenduski, Joni (1995) 'An emerging advocate: the equal opportunities commission in Great Britain', in Dorothy Stetson and Amy Mazur (eds), *Comparative State Feminism* (London: Sage): 114–32.

Lovenduski, Joni (ed.) (2005) *State Feminism and Political Representation* (Cambridge: Cambridge University Press).

Luber, Silvia (2003) *Berufliche Selbständigkeit im Wandel* (Frankfurt/Main: Peter Lang).

Luber, Silvia and Markus Gangl (1997) 'Die Entwicklung selbständiger Erwerbstätigkeit in Westeuropa und den USA 1960–1995', *Arbeitspapier Nr. 1/16* (Mannheim: Mannheimer Zentrum für Europäische Sozialforschung (MZES)).

Luhmann, Niklas (1980) *Gesellschaftsstruktur und Semantik. Studien zur Wissenssoziologie der modernen Gesellschaft,* Vol. 1 (Frankfurt/Main: Suhrkamp).

Lundsgaard, Jens (2005) 'Consumer direction and choice in long-term care for older persons, including payments for informal care: how can it help improve care outcomes, employment and fiscal sustainability?', *OECD Health Working Papers,* 20.

Mackie, Vera (2003) *Feminism in Japan* (Cambridge: Cambridge University Press).

Mae, Michiko (2000) 'Wege zu einer neuen Subjektivität. Die neue japanische Frauenbewegung als Suche nach einer anderen Moderne', in Ilse Lenz, Michiko Mae and Karin Klose (eds), *Frauenbewegungen weltweit. Aufbrüche, Kontinuitäten, Veränderungen* (Opladen): 95–133.

Manning, Stephan and Jörg Sydow (2005) 'Transforming creative potential in project networks: how TV movies are produced under network-based control', *Critical Sociology,* 31 (4).

Manza, Jeff and Clem Brooks (1999) *Social Cleavages and Political Change. Voter Alignments and US Party Coalitions* (Oxford: Oxford University Press).

Market Assessment International (1999) *Call Centres 1999: Strategic Market Intelligence for the Professional* (London: Market Assessment International).

Marshall, Victor W., Walter R. Heinz, Helga Krüger and Abil Verma (2001) *Restructuring Work and the Life Course* (Toronto: University of Toronto Press).

Martin, Hans-Peter and Harald Schumann (1997) *The Global Trap. Globalization and the Assault on Democracy and Prosperity* (London: Zed Press).

Martin, Bill and Judy Wajcman (2003) 'Fun, excitement and passion: positive emotions amongst men and women managers', unpublished paper, presented at the 98th Annual Meeting of the American Sociological Association, Atlanta, Georgia, 16–19 August.

Mathews, Gordon (2004) 'Seeking a career, finding a job: how young people enter and resist the Japanese world of work', in Gordon Mathews and Bruce White (eds), *Japan's Changing Generations. Are Young People Creating A New Society?* (London and New York: Routledge Curzon).

Maurice, Marc, François Sellier and Jean-Jacques Silvestre (1986) *The Social Foundations of Industrial Power. A Comparison of France and Germany* (Cambridge, Mass.: MIT Press).

Maurice, Marc and Arndt Sorge (eds) (2000) *Embedding Organizations. Societal Analysis of Actors, Organizations and Socio-Economic Context* (Amsterdam/Philadelphia: John Benjamins Publishing Company).

Mayer-Ahuja, Nicole and Harald Wolf (2005) 'Beyond the hype: working in the German internet industry', *Critical Sociology,* 31 (4).

Mazur, Amy (2001a) 'Introduction', in Amy Mazur (ed.), *State Feminism, Women's Movements and Job Training. Making Democracies Work in a Global Economy* (New York: Routledge).

Mazur, Amy (ed.) (2001b) *State Feminism, Women's Movements and Job Training. Making Democracies Work in a Global Economy* (New York: Routledge).

Mazur, Amy (2002) *Theorizing Feminist Policy* (Oxford: Oxford University Press).

McBride, Dorothy E. (2001) *Abortion Politics, Women's Movements and the Democratic State. A Comparative Study of State Feminism* (Oxford: Oxford University Press).

McCall, Leslie (2001) *Complex Inequality. Gender, Class and Race in the New Economy* (New York and London: Routledge).

McCall, Leslie and Ann Orloff (2005) 'Introduction to special issue of social politics: gender, class and capitalism', *Social Politics*, 12 (3) (Summer): 159–69.

McManus, Patricia (2000) 'Market, state, and the quality of new self-employment jobs among men in the US and Western Germany', *Social Forces*, 78 (3): 865–905.

McManus, Patricia (2001a) 'Women's participation in self-employment in Western industrialized nations', *International Journal of Sociology*, 31 (2): 70–97.

McManus, Patricia (2001b) 'Autonomy and dependency in the self-employment careers of men and women in the United States and Germany', paper presented at the Annual Meeting of the American Sociological Association.

Meager, Nigel (1994) 'Self-employment schemes for the unemployment in the European Community', in Günter Schmidt (ed.), *Labour Market Institutions in Europe* (Armonk, New York: M. E. Sharpe): 183–242.

Meager, Nigel and Peter Bates (2001) 'The self-employed and lifetime incomes: some UK evidence', *International Journal of Sociology*, 31 (1): 27–58.

Meager, Nigel and Peter Bates (2002) 'From salary workers to entrepreneurial workers?', in Günter Schmidt and Bernard Gazier (eds), *The Dynamics of Full Employment. Social Integration through Transnational Labour Markets* (Cheltenham: Edward Elgar): 298–339.

Meguro, Yoriko (2004) *Statement by Dr. Yoriko Meguro Representative of Japan*, 3 March, http://www.mofa.go.jp/announce/speech/un2004/un0403.html, accessed 12 October 2005.

Messner, Dirk and Franz Nuscheler (1996) 'Global governance. Organisationselemente und Säulen einer Weltordnungspolitik', in Dirk Messner and Franz Nuscheler (eds), *Weltkonferenzen und Weltberichte. Ein Wegweiser durch die internationale Diskussion* (Bonn: Dietz Verlag): 12–37.

Meyer, Mary and Elisabeth Prügl (1999) *Gender Politics in Global Governance* (Lanham: Rowman & Littlefield).

Mills, C. Wright (1953/1971) *White Collar. The American Middle Classes* (New York: Oxford University Press).

Millward, Neil, Alex Bryson and John Forth (2000) *All Change at Work? British Employment Relations 1980–1998, as Portrayed by the Workplace Industrial Relations Survey Series* (London: Routledge).

Ministry of Health, Labour and Welfare [MHLW, Japan] (2002) *Rodo Keizai Hakusho* (White Paper on the Labour Economy) (Tokyo).

Ministry of Health, Labour and Welfare [Japan] (2003) *Rodo Keizai Hakusho* (White Paper on the Labour Economy) (Tokyo).

Ministry of Health, Labour and Welfare [Japan] (2003) *White Paper on the Labour Economy: Economic and Social Change and Diversification of Working Styles*, http://www.mhlw.go.jp/english/wp/wp-l/index.html, accessed 13 October 2005.

Ministry of Health, Labour and Welfare [Japan] (2004) *Rodo Keizai Hakusho* (White Paper on the Labour Economy) (Tokyo).

Mintzberg, Henry (1983) *Structure in Fives. Designing Effective Organisations* (New Jersey, USA: Prentice Hall).

Miura, Mari (2001) 'Globalisation and reforms of labour market institutions: Japan and major OECD countries', *Discussion Paper F-94* (Institute of Social Science: University of Tokyo).

Miyama, Masako (2001) 'Japanese female part-time workers in the era of great competition', in Emiko Takenaka (ed.), *Labour and Gender* (Akashi-Shoten): 169–89.

Moghadam, Valentine M. (2000) 'Transnational feminist networks: collective action in an era of globalization', *International Sociology*, 15 (1): 57–85.

Molony, Barbara (1995) 'Japan's 1986 equal employment law and the changing discourse on gender', *Signs*, 20 (2) (Winter): 268–301.

Monthly Labor Review Editor's Desk (2004) *Union Membership Declines Again in 2003*, http://www.bls.gov/opub/ted/2004/jan/wk3/art03.htm, accessed 2 January 2006.

Morgan, Glenn und Sigrid Quack (2000) 'Confidence and confidentiality: the social construction of performance standards in banking', in Glenn Morgan, Sigrid Quack and Richard Whitley (eds), *National Capitalisms, Global Competition and Economic Performance* (Amsterdam, Philadelphia: John Benjamins): 131–57.

Müller, Ursula et al. (1991) 'Sexuelle Belästigung am Arbeitsplatz', *Schriftenreihe des BMJFFG* (Stuttgart: Kohlhammer Verlag).

Nakajima, Michiko, Yamada Shozou and Nakashita Yuko (1994) *Danjo Doitsu Chingin* (Equal pay for women and men) (Tokyo: Yuhikaku Sensho).

Nakano, Mami (1999) 'Kiki ni Tatsu Jyosei no Koyo' (Women's Employment Facing at the Crisis), *Women's Studies*, 7: 80–93.

National Institute of Population and Social Security Research (1998) *The Cost of Social Security in Japan. FY 1997* (Tokyo: NIPSSR).

National Institute of Population and Social Security Research (2000) *The Second National Survey on Family in Japan 1998* (Tokyo: National Institute of Population and Social Security Research).

National Institute of Population and Social Security Research (2001) *The Cost of Social Security in Japan. FY 2000* (Tokyo: NIPSSR).

National Institute of Population and Social Security Research (2002) *The Cost of Social Security in Japan. FY 2001* (Tokyo: NIPSSR).

National Institute of Population and Social Security Research (2003) *Child Related Policies in Japan* (Tokyo: NIPSSR).

National Women's Education Center (2003) *Danjyo Kyodo Sankaku Toukei Deita Bukku* (Gender Equal Society, Statistic Data Book) (Gyousei).

Nelson, Barbara J. and Nalma Chowdhury (eds) (1994) *Women and Politics Worldwide* (New Haven: Yale University Press).

Nikkeiren (Japan Federation of Employers Associations) (1994) *Shin-nihon-teki keiei shisutemu to kenkyu purojekuto. Chukan hokoku* (a research project on new Japanese-style management systems and practices: the interim report) (Tokyo: Nikkeiren).

Nimura, Kazuo (1987) 'Nihon roshikankei no rekishiteki tokushitsu' (The historical background of labour relations in Japan), *Shakai-seisaku Gakkai Nenpo* (Annals of the Society for the Study of Social Policy), 31: 77–95.

Nishiguchi, Toshihiro (2001) 'Coevolution of interorganizational relations', in Ikujiro Nonaka and Hirotaka Takeuchi (eds), *Knowledge Emergence. Social, Technical and Evolutionary Dimensions of Knowledge Creation* (New York: Oxford University Press): 197–222.

Nishikawa, Makiko (2003a) '1990 nendai no Nihonjosei no Rodokyokyu nikansuru Kousatu' (A study on the labour supply of Japanese women in the 1990s), *Journal of Social Science*, 54 (6): 5 (Institute of Social Science: Tokyo University).

Nishikawa, Makiko (2003b) 'Homuherupa no Sigoto nikansuru Kosatu' (A study on the Japanese homecare worker's job), *The Hosei Journal of Business*, 40 (3): 10, 15.

Nishikawa Makiko (2004) 'Kaigoshoku no Gino to Gakushu' (Knowledge, skills, and learning of the Japanese homecare workers), *The Hosei Journal of Business*, 40 (4): 3.

Nolan, Peter and Gary Slater (2002) 'The labour market: history, structure and prospects', in Paul Edwards (ed.), *Industrial Relations. Theory and Practice* (Oxford: Blackwell).

Nonaka, Ikujiro (1990) *Chishiki Sozo no Keiei* (A theory of organisational knowledge creation) (Nihon Keizai Shinbunsha: Tokyo).

Nonaka, Ikujiro (2005) 'Chishikishakai to Kigyo' (Knowledge-based society and the firms), *Nikkei*, 27 January–3 February.

Nonaka, Ikujiro and Hirotaka Takeuchi (1995) *The Knowledge Creation Company. How Japanese Companies Create the Dynamics of Innovation* (Oxford: Oxford University Press).

Nonaka, Ikujiro and Toshihiro Nishiguchi (eds) (2001) *Knowledge Emergence. Social, Technical and Evolutionary Dimensions of Knowledge Creation* (New York: Oxford University Press).

Nussbaum, Martha C. (2000) *Women and Human Development. The Capabilities Approach* (Cambridge: Cambridge University Press).

O'Connor, Julia, Ann Shola Orloff and Sheila Shaver (1999) *States, Markets, Families. Gender, Liberalism and Social Policy in Australia, Canada, Great Britain and the United States* (Cambridge: Cambridge University Press).

OECD (1976) *The 1974–5 Recession and the Employment of Women* (Paris: OECD).

OECD (1993) *Employment Outlook* (Paris: OECD).

OECD (1996) *Employment Outlook* (Paris: OECD).

OECD (1997) *Employment Outlook* (Paris: OECD).

OECD (1999) *Employment Outlook* (Paris: OECD).

OECD (2000a) *Employment Outlook* (Paris: OECD).

OECD (2000b) *Labour Force Statistics 1979–1999* (Paris: OECD).

OECD (2001a) *Employment Outlook. The Characteristics and Quality of Service Sector Jobs*, Chapter 3, http://www.oecd.org/dataoecd/11/15/2079411.pdf, accessed 13 October 2005.

OECD (2001b) *OECD Science, Technology and Industry Scoreboard 2001*, www1. oecd.org/publications/e-book/92-2001-04-1-2987/, accessed 13 October 2005.

OECD (2002a) *Measuring the Information Economy* (Paris: OECD).

OECD (2002b) *OECD Employment Outlook* (Paris: OECD).

OECD (2003) *OECD Science, Technology and Industry Scoreboard 2003*, www1.oecd.org/ publications/e-book/92-2003-04-1-7294/, accessed 13 October 2005.

OECD (2004a) *OECD Employment Outlook* (Paris: OECD).

OECD (2004b) *Education at a Glance* (Paris: OECD).

OECD (2005a) *Statistics Data and Indicators*, http://www.oecd.org/ findDocument/0,2350,en_2649_33703_1_119656_1_1_1,00.html, accessed 30 November 2005.

OECD (2005b) *OECD Science, Technology and Industry Scoreboard*, http://www. oecd.org/document/43/0,2340,en_2649_33703_35455595_1_1_1_1,00.html, accessed 6 December 2005.

OECD (2005c) *OECD Communications Outlook*, http://www.oecd.org/document/15/ 0,2340,en_2649_33703_35269391_1_1_1_1,00.html, accessed 6 December 2005.

OECD (2005d) *Biotechnology Statistics in OECD Member Countries*, http://www. oecd.org/countrylist/0,2578,en_2649_33703_1794151_1_1_1_1,00.html accessed 6 December 2005.

OECD (2005e) *Main Science and Technology Indicators*, http://www.oecd.org/document/26/0,2340,en_2649_33703_1901082_1_1_1_1,00.html, accessed 6 December 2005.

OECD (2005f) 'OECD in figures: statistics on the member countries', *OECD Observer/Supplement 1* (Paris: OECD).

OECD (2005g) *Income Distribution and Poverty in OECD Countries in the Second Half of the 1990s. OECD Social, Employment and Migration Working Paper No. 22*, by M. Foerster and M. d'Ercode, http://papers.ssrn.com/sol3/papers.cfm?abstract_id= 671783, accessed 13 October 2005.

Ogasawara, Yuko (1998) *Office Ladies and Salaried Men: Power, Gender and Work in Japanese Companies* (Berkeley: University of California Press).

Ogasawara, Yuko (2001) 'Women's solidarity: company policies and Japanese office ladies', in Mary Brinton (ed.), *Women's Working Lives in East Asia* (Stanford: Stanford University Press): 151–79.

Oliver, Christine (1991) 'Strategic responses to institutional processes', *Academy of Management Review*, 16 (1): 145–79.

Olson, Mancur (1982) *The Rise and Decline of Nations. Economic Growth, Stagflation and Social Rigidities* (New Haven: Yale University Press).

O'Reilly, Jacqueline (2000) 'Is it time to gender the societal effect?', in Marc Maurice and Arndt Sorge (eds), *Embedding Organizations. Societal Analysis of Actors, Organizations and Socio-Economic Context* (Amsterdam/Philadelphia: John Benjamins Publishing Company): 343–56.

O'Reilly, Jacqueline and Colette Fagan (eds) (1998) *Part-Time Prospects. An International Comparison of Part-Time Work in Europe, North America, and the Pacific Rim* (London: Routledge).

Orloff, Ann Shola (1993) 'Gender and the social rights of citizenship: state policies and gender relations in comparative perspective', *American Sociological Review*, 58 (3): 303–28.

Orloff, Ann Shola (2002) 'Gender equality, women's employment: cross-national patterns of policy and politics', presented at the Workshop on Welfare, Work and Family: Southern Europe in Comparative Perspective, European University Institute.

Ortmann, Günther and Jörg Sydow (eds) (2001) *Strategie und Strukturation. Strategisches Management von Unternehmen, Netzwerken und Konzernen* (Wiesbaden: Gabler).

Osano, Hiroshi and Mami Kobayashi (2005) 'Reforming corporate governance and employment relations', *Japan Labour Review*, 2 (1) (Winter): 58–80.

Osawa Mari (1993) *Kigyo Shakai wo Koete* (Go Beyond the Corporate-Centred Society).

Osawa, Mari (1994) 'Bye-bye corporate warriors: the formation of a corporate-centered society and gender-biased social policies in Japan', *Annals of the Institute of Social Science*, 35 (March): 157–94.

Osawa Mari (1996) 'Will the Japanese style system change? Employment, gender and the welfare state', *Journal of Pacific Asia*, 3.

Osawa Mari (1998) 'The feminisation of the labour market', in Banno Junji (ed.), *The Political Economy of Japanese Society. Internationalisation and Domestic Issues*, Volume 2 (Oxford: Oxford University Press): 143–74.

Osawa, Mari (2000a) 'Government approaches to gender equality in the mid-1990s', *Social Science Japan Journal*, 3 (1): 3–21.

Osawa, Mari (ed.) (2000b) *Danjo kyôdô sankaku shakai kihon-hô* (Tokyo: Kyôsei).

Osawa, Mari (2001) 'People in irregular modes of employment: are they really subject to discrimination?', *Social Science Japan Journal*, 4 (2): 183–99.

Osawa, Mari (2002) 'Twelve million full-time housewives: the gender consequences of Japan's post-war social contract', in Olivier Zunz, Leonard Schoppa and Nobo-hiro Hiwatori (eds), *Social Contracts under Stress. The Middle Classes of America, Europe, and Japan at the Turn of the Century* (New York: Russell Sage Foundation): 255–77.

Osawa, Mari (2003) 'Japanese government approaches to gender equality since the mid-1990s', *Wayne State University, Occasional Paper Series*, 9.

Ostner, Ilona and Jane Lewis (1995) 'Gender and the evolution of European social policies', in Stephan Leibfried and Paul Pierson (eds), *European Social Policy Between Fragmentation and Integration* (Washington: Brookings Institution): 159–94.

Outshoorn, Joyce (ed.) (2004) *The Politics of Prostitution. Women's Movements, Democratic States and the Globalisation of Sex Commerce* (Cambridge: Cambridge University Press).

Panteli, Niki, Janet Stack and Harvie Ramsay (2001) 'Gendered patterns in computing work in the late 1990s', *New Technology, Work and Employment*, 16 (1): 3–17.

Pascall, Gillian and Jane Lewis (2004) 'Emerging gender regimes and policies for gender equality in a wider Europe', *Journal of Social Policy*, 33 (3): 373–94.

Pempel, T. J. (1998) *Regime Shift. Comparative Dynamics of the Japanese Political Economy* (Ithaca: Cornell University Press).

Peng, Ito (2004) 'Post-industrial pressure, political regime shifts, and social policy reform in Japan and South Korea', *Journal of East Asian Studies*, 4 (3): 389–425.

Perlow, Leslie (1997) *Finding Time: How Corporations, Individuals and Families Can Benefit from New Work Practices* (Ithaca: Cornell University Press).

Perrons, Diane (1999) 'Flexible working patterns and equal opportunities in the European Union – conflict or compatibility?', *European Journal of Women's Studies*, 6 (4): 391–418.

Perrons, Diane (2000) 'Flexible working and equal opportunities in the United Kingdom: a case study from retail', *Environment and Planning A*, 32 (10): 1719–34.

Perrons, Diane (2003) 'The new economy and the work-life balance: conceptual explorations and a case study of new media', *Gender, Work and Organization*, 10 (1): 65–93.

Perrons, Diane (2004a) *Globalisation and Social Change. People and Places in a Divided World* (London: Routledge).

Perrons, Diane (2004b) 'Equity and representation in the new economy', in John Kelly and Paul Willman (eds), *Union Organization and Activity. Leverhulme*, Volume 2 (London: Routledge): 51–72.

Perrons, Diane (2005) 'Gender mainstreaming in European Union policy. Why now?', *Social Politics*, 12 (3): 389–411.

Perrons, Diane, Linda McDowell, Colette Fagan, Kath Ray and Kevin Ward (eds) (2006) *Gender Divisions and Working Time in the New Economy. Public Policy and Changing Patterns of Work in Europe and North America* (Cheltenham: Edward Elgar).

Peters, Julie and Andrea Wolper (eds) (1995) *Women's Rights, Human Rights. International Feminist Perspectives* (London: Routledge).

Pfarr, Heide (ed.) (2001) *Ein Gesetz zur Gleichstellung der Geschlechter in der Privatwirtschaft* (Düsseldorf: Hans-Böckler-Stiftung).

Pfarr, Heide and Klaus Bertelsmann (1989) *Diskriminierung im Erwerbsleben. Ungleichbehandlung von Frauen und Männern in der Bundesrepublik Deutschland* (Baden-Baden: Nomos).

Pfau-Effinger, Birgit (2000) *Kultur und Frauenerwerbstätigkeit in Europa. Theorie und Empirie des internationalen Vergleichs* (Opladen: Leske and Budrich).

Pierson, Paul (1994) *Dismantling Welfare States? Reagan, Thatcher and the Politics of Retrenchment* (Cambridge: Cambridge University Press).

Pierson, Paul (2000) 'Three worlds of welfare state research', *Comparative Political Studies*, 33 (6/7): 791–821.

Pierson, Paul (2001a) 'Introduction: investigating the welfare state at century's end', in Paul Pierson (ed.), *The New Politics of the Welfare State* (Oxford: Oxford University Press): 1–14.

Pierson, Paul (2001b) 'Post-industrial pressures on the mature welfare states', in Paul Pierson (ed.), *The New Politics of the Welfare State* (Oxford: Oxford University Press): 80–104.

Piketty, Thomas and Emmanuel Saez (2003) 'Income inequality in the United States', *Quarterly Journal of Economics*, 118 (1): 1–39.

Pillinger, Jane (1992) *Feminising the Market. Women's Pay and Employment in the European Community* (Basingstoke: Macmillan).

Piore Michael J. and Charles F. Sabel (1984) *The Second Industrial Divide. Possibilities for Prosperity* (New York: Basic Books).

Pitt-Catsouphes, Marcie and Leon Litchfield (2001) 'How are small businesses responding to work and family issues?', in Rosanna Hertz and Nancy L. Marshall (eds), *Working Families. The Transformation of the American Home* (Berkeley: University of California Press): 131–51.

Pollack, Mark A. and Hafner-Burton, Emilie (2000) 'Mainstreaming gender in the European Union', *Journal of European Public Policy*, 7 (3): 432–56.

Porat, Marc (1977) *The Information Economy* (Washington DC: US Government Printing Office).

Powell, Walter W. and Paul J. DiMaggio (eds) (1991) *The New Institutionalism in Organizational Analysis* (Chicago: Chicago University Press).

Pries, Ludger (2002) 'Transnationalisierung der sozialen Welt?' *Berliner Journal für Soziologie*, 12 (2): 263–72.

Pries, Ludger (2004) 'Change of employment interests regulation forms?', in *Limits of the Disintegration of Work Boundaries. The Necessity of a New Form of Labour*, Research Proposal for the Federal Ministry for Education and Research.

Prism Research (2000) *Homecare Workers Recruitment and Retention Study. Draft Final Report* (Brighton: Prism Research).

Quack, Sigrid (1997) *Karrieren im Glaspalast. Weibliche Führungskräfte in europäischen Banken*, FS I 97-104 (Berlin: WZB).

Quack, Sigrid (1999) 'Unternehmensreorganisation, Karrierewege und Geschlecht. Banken im internationalen Kontext', in Hildegard Maria Nickel, Susanne Völker and Hasko Hüning (eds), *Transformation – Unternehmensreorganisation – Geschlechterforschung* (Opladen: Leske): 109–30.

Quack, Sigrid and Glenn Morgan (2000a) 'Institutions, sector specialisation and economic performance outcomes', in Sigrid Quack, Glenn Morgan and Richard Whitley (eds), *National Capitalisms, Global Competition and Economic Performance* (Amsterdam, Philadelphia: John Benjamins): 27–52.

Quack, Sigrid and Glenn Morgan (2000b) 'National capitalisms, global competition and economic performance: an introduction', in Sigrid Quack, Glenn Morgan and Richard Whitley (eds), *National Capitalisms, Global Competition and Economic Performance* (Amsterdam, Philadelphia: John Benjamins): 3–24.

Quah, Danny (1996) *The Invisible Hand and the Weightless Economy*, Centre for Economic Performance, Occasional Paper No. 12, London School of Economics, http://cep.lse.ac.uk/pubs/download/occasional/OP012.pdf, accessed 14 October 2005.

Quah, Danny (2003) *Digital Goods and the New Economy*, London School of Economics, Economics Department, December 2002, http://econ.lse.ac.uk/staff/dquah/p/dp-0212hbne.pdf, accessed 14 October 2005.

Quinn, James Brian (1992) *Intelligent Enterprise. A Knowledge and Service-Based Paradigm for Industry* (New York: Free Press).

Rabe-Kleberg, Ursula (1993) 'Frauen auf dem Weg zur Bildungsbiographie?', *Frauenforschung*, 11 (4): 5–16.

Randall, Vicky (2000) 'Childcare policy in the European states: limits to convergence', *Journal of European Public Policy*, 7 (3): 346–68.

Rathmell, John M. (1966) 'What is meant by services?', *Journal of Marketing*, 30 (4) (October): 32–6.

Regini, Marino, Jim Kitay and Martin Baethge (eds) (1999) *From Tellers to Sellers. Changing Employment Relations in Banks* (Cambridge, Mass. and London: MIT Press).

Rehberg, Frank, Ursula Stöger and Detlef Sträter (2002) 'Frauen in der Medienwirtschaft: Chancen und Hemmnisse für Frauenerwerbstätigkeit in einer prosperierenden Zukunftsbranche', *Bayrische Landeszentrale für neue Medien Series*, 69 (München: BLM).

Reich, Robert B. (1991) *The Work of Nations. Preparing Ourselves for the 21st Century Capitalism* (London: Simon and Schuster).

Reich, Robert B. (2001) *The Future of Success Work and Life in the New Economy* (London: Heinemann).

RNGS (2005) *Research Network on Gender Politics and the State*, http://libarts.wsu.edu/polisci/rngs, accessed 12 February 2006.

Rieger, Elmar and Stephan Leibfried (2003) *Limits to Globalization* (Oxford: Polity Press in association with Blackwell Publishing Ltd).

Ritzer, George (2000) *The Macdonaldization of Society*, 3rd edition (Pine Forge Press).

Roberson, James and Nobue Suzuki (eds) (2002) *Men and Masculinities in Contemporary Japan. Beyond the Salaryman Model* (London and New York: Nissan Institute/Routledge).

Roberts, Glenda S. (1994) *Staying on the Line. Blue-Collar Women in Contemporary Japan* (Honolulu: University of Hawaii Press).

Roberts, Glenda S. (2002) 'Pinning hopes on angels: reflections from an aging Japan's urban landscape', in Roger Goodman (ed.), *Family and Social Policy in Japan* (Cambridge: Cambridge University Press): 54–91.

Roberts, Glenda S. (2003) 'Globalisation and work/life balance: gendered implications of new initiatives at a US multinational in Japan', in Heidi Gottfried and Laura Reese (eds), *Equity in the Workplace: Gendering Workplace Policy Analysis* (Lanham, Boulder, New York, Toronto and Oxford: Lexington Books): 294–314.

Robinson, Peter (1999) 'Explaining the relationship between flexible employment and labour market regulation', in Alan Felstead and Nick Jewson (eds), *Global Trends in Flexible Labour* (London: Macmillan): 84–99.

Rodosho Joseikyoku (Ministry of Labour, Women's Bureau) (ed.) (2000) *Fuamirii Furendorii' Kigyo o Mezashite: 'Fuamirii Furendorii' Kigyo Kenkyukai Hokokusho* (Aiming for 'Family Friendly' Firms: a Report from the Study Group on 'Family Friendly' Firms) (Tokyo: Okurasho Insatsukyoku).

Rodrigues, Maria João (2002) 'Introduction: for a European strategy at the turn of the century', in Maria João Rodrigues (ed.), *The New Knowledge Economy in Europe. A Strategy for International Competitiveness and Social Cohesion* (Cheltenham: Edward Elgar): 1–27.

Rodrigues, Maria João (2003) *European Policies for a Knowledge Economy* (Cheltenham: Edward Elgar).

Rose, Nikolas (1999) *Powers of Freedom. Reframing Political Thought* (Cambridge: Cambridge University Press).

Rubery, Jill and Colette Fagan (1994) 'Does feminisation mean a flexible labour force?', in Richard Hyman and Anthony Ferner (eds), *New Frontiers in European Industrial Relations* (Oxford: Blackwell): 140–66.

Rubery, Jill and Damian Grimshaw (2001) 'ICTs and employment: the problem of job quality', *International Labour Review*, 140 (2): 165–92.

Rubery, Jill, Mark Smith and Colette Fagan (1999) *Women's Employment in Europe* (London: Routledge).

Rupp, Leila (1997) *Worlds of Women. International Women's Organizations 1888–1945* (Princeton: Princeton University Press).

Ruppert, Uta (ed.) (1998) *Lokal bewegen, global verhandeln. Internationale Politik und Geschlecht* (Frankfurt and New York: Campus).

Sainsbury, Diane (ed.) (1994) *Gendering Welfare States* (London: Sage).

Sainsbury, Diane (1996) *Gender, Equality and Welfare States* (Cambridge: Cambridge University Press).

Sainsbury, Diane (ed.) (1999) *Gender and Welfare State Regimes* (Oxford: Oxford University Press).

Sassen, Saskia (1999) 'Embedding the global in the national: implications for the role of the state', in David A. Smith, Dorothy J. Solinger and Steven C. Topik (eds), *States and Sovereignty in the Global Economy* (London: Routledge): 158–71.

Sato, Hiroki (2001a) 'Nihon ni okeru "Fuamirii Furendorii" Seisaku no Genjo to Kadai' (Current Situation of 'Family Friendly' Policies in Japan), *Kikan Kakei Keizai Kenkyu* (Seasonal Journal of Household Economics): 11–17.

Sato, Hiroki (2001b) 'Is "atypical employment" a flexible form of working life?', *Japan Labour Bulletin*, 40 (4) (April 1): 6–10.

Sato, Hiroki and Emiko Takeishi (2004) *Dansei no Ikujikyuugyou. Shain no niizu, kaisha no meritto* (Men's Childcare Leave. Needs of the Employees and Merits to the Firms) (Tokyo: Chuukoushinsho).

Satzer, Ralf (2001) 'Nicht nur Traumjobs – vom Arbeiten und Verdienen in den Medien', *Research Project of connexx.av (ver.di)* (Frankfurt a. M.: connexx.av).

Schäfer, Reinhild (2001) *Demokratisierung der Geschlechterverhältnisse. Politische Strategien der Neuen Frauenbewegung gegen Gewalt* (Bielefeld: Kleine Verlag).

Schmidt, Verena (2000) 'Zum Wechselverhältnis zwischen europäischer Frauenpolitik und europäischen Frauenorganisationen', in Ilse Lenz, Michiko Mae and Karin Klose (eds), *Frauenbewegungen weltweit* (Opladen: Leske and Budrich): 199–232.

Schmidt, Verena (2005) *Gender Mainstreaming as an Innovation? The Institutionalisation of Gender Mainstreaming in the European Commission* (Leverkusen: Barbara Budrich Verlag).

Scholte, Jan Aart (2000) *Globalization. A Critical Introduction* (Basingstoke: Palgrave Macmillan).

Schon, Donald A. (1983) *The Reflective Practitioner. How Professionals Think in Action* (London: Ashgate).

Schon, Donald A. (1987) *Educating the Reflective Practitioner* (San Francisco: Jossey-Bass).

Schoppa, Leonard (2006) *Race for the Exits. Women, Firms, and the Future of Social Protection in Japan* (Ithaca: Cornell University Press).

Schulz, Kristina (2002) *Der lange Atem der Provokation. Die Frauenbewegung in der Bundesrepublik und in Frankreich 1968–1976* (Frankfurt: Campus Verlag).

Schulze Buschoff, Karin (2005) 'Von der Scheinselbstständigkeit zur Ich-AG – neue sozialpolitische Weichenstellungen?', *Zeitschrift für Sozialreform*, 51 (1): 64–93.

Scott, Joan W. (1988) 'Deconstructing equality-versus-difference: or, the uses of post-structuralist theory for feminism', *Feminist Studies*, 14 (1): 33–49.

Scott, W. Richard (1995) *Institutions and Organizations* (Thousand Oaks: Sage).

Scrinzi, Francesca (2003) 'The globalisation of domestic work: women migrants and neo-domesticity', in Jane Freedman (ed.), *Gender and Insecurity. Migrant Women in Europe* (Vermont: Ashgate): 77–90.

Segal, Lynne (1987) *Is the Future Female? Troubled Thoughts on Contemporary Feminism* (London: Virago).

Seifert, Wolfgang (1997) *Gewerkschaften in der japanischen Politik: der dritte Partner?* (Opladen: Westdeutscher Verlag).

Sen, Amartya (1984) *Resources, Values and Development* (Oxford: Blackwell).

Sen, Amartya (1999) *Development as Freedom* (Oxford: Oxford University Press).

Sennett, Richard (1998) *The Corrosion of Character* (London: W. W. Norton and Company).

Serrano-Pascual, Amparo and Lilja Mósesdóttir (2003) 'The implications of the KBS for employment and gender relations: towards a conceptual and analytical framework', *WELLKNOW-HPSE-CT-2002–00119, Project report No. 1* (Brussels: European Trade Union Institute).

SEU (2000) *Closing the Digital Divide: ICT in Deprived Areas* (London: Stationery Office).

Shakai Hoken Kenkyûjo (2002) *Josei to Nenkin: josei no raifu sutairu Lifestyle no henka nado ni taiôshita nenkin no arikata ni kansuru kentôkai hôkokusho* (Tokyo: Shakai Hoken Kenkyûjo).

Shardlow, Steven and Mark Doel (1996) *Practice Learning and Teaching* (BASW).

Shire, Karen (2000) 'Gender organization and workplace culture in Japanese customer services', *Social Science Japan Journal*, 3 (1): 37–58.

Shire, Karen (2005) 'Die Gestaltung der Kundeninteraktionen in wissensbasierter Dienstleistungsarbeit: eine empirische Studie', in Heike Jacobsen and Stephan Voswinkel (eds), *Der Kunde in der Dienstleistung*. Beiträge zur Soziologie der Dienstleistung (Wiesbaden: VS): 219–40.

Shire, Karen and Jun Imai (2000) 'Gender and the diversification of employment in Japan', in Hanns-Georg Brose (ed.), *Reorganisation der Arbeit* (Frankfurt: Campus Verlag): 117–36.

Shire, Karen, Cornelia Bialucha and Katrin Vitols (2002) 'Women and the new economy in Germany', presented at the GLOW Workshop at the University of Tokyo, September.

Shire, Karen A., Ursula Holtgrewe and Christian Kerst (2002) 'Re-organising customer service work: an introduction', in Ursula Holtgrewe, Christian Kerst and Karen A. Shire (eds), *Re-organizing Service Work. Call Centres in Germany and Britain* (Aldershot: Ashgate): 1–16.

Siaroff, Alan (1994) 'Work, welfare and gender equality', in Diane Sainsbury (ed.), *Gendering Welfare States* (London: Sage): 82–100.

Smeaton, Deborah (2003) 'Self-employed workers: calling the shots or hesitant independents? A consideration of the trends', *Work, Employment and Society*, 17 (2): 379–91.

Smith, Vicki (2001) *Crossing the Great Divide. Worker Risk and Opportunity in the New Economy* (Ithaca: Cornell University Press).

Smith, Vicki and Heidi Gottfried (1998) 'Flexibility in work and employment: the impact on women', in Birgit Geissler, Friederike Maier and Birgit Pfau-Effinger (eds), *FrauenArbeitsMarkt. Der Beitrag der Frauenforschung zur sozio-ökonomischen Theorieentwicklung* (Berlin: Sigma): 95–125.

Social Trends (2001) Table 4.12.

Social Trends (2002) Table 3.17.

Soete, Luc (2001) 'ICTs, knowledge work and employment: the challenges to Europe', *International Labour Review*, 140 (2): 143–63.

Sôrifu danjo kyôdô sankakushitsu (yearly) *Danjo kyôdô sankaku hakusho* (Tokyo).

Soskice, David (2005) 'Varieties of capitalism and cross-national gender differences', *Social Politics*, 12 (2): 170–79.

Special issue of *Social Politics* (2005) 'Gender, class, and capitalism', *Social Politics*, 12 (2) (Summer).

Spellman, Elizabeth (1988) *Inessential Woman. Problems of Exclusion in Feminist Thought* (Boston: Beacon Press).

Stäheli, Urs (1998) 'Zum Verhältnis von Sozialstruktur und Semantik', *Soziale Systeme*, 4 (2): 315–40.

Standing, Guy (1999) *Global Labour Flexibility* (New York: St. Martin's Press).

Statistisches Bundesamt (2005) *Leben und Arbeiten in Deutschland. Ergebnisse des Mikrozensus 2004* (Wiesbaden: Statistisches Bundesamt) http://www.destatis.de/presse/deutsch/pk/2005/MZ_Broschuere.pdf, accessed 19 October 2005.

Steinberg, Ronnie J. and Deborah M. Figart (eds) (1999) 'Emotional labour in the service economy', *Annals of the American Academy of Political and Social Science*, 561 (January) (Sage Publications).

Steinmueller, W. Edward (2002) 'Knowledge-based economies and information and communication technologies', *International Social Science Journal*, 54 (171): 141–53.

Stetson, Dorothy McBride (1995) 'The oldest women's policy agency: the women's bureau in the United States', in Dorothy Stetson and Amy Mazur (eds), *Comparative State Feminism* (Thousand Oaks: Sage): 254–72.

Stetson, Dorothy McBride and Amy Mazur (eds) (1995a) *Comparative State Feminism* (Thousand Oaks: Sage).

Stetson, Dorothy McBride and Amy Mazur (1995b) 'Introduction', in Dorothy McBride Stetson and Amy Mazur (eds), *Comparative State Feminism* (Thousand Oaks: Sage): 1–21.

Stewart, Kitty (2005) 'Changes in poverty and inequality in the UK in international context', in John Hills and Kitty Stewart (eds), *A More Equal Society* (Bristol: Policy Press).

Stichweh, Rudolf (2000) 'Semantik und Sozialstruktur. Zur Logik einer systemtheoretischen Unterscheidung', *Soziale Systeme*, 6 (2): 237–50.

Storey, John, Adrian Wilkinson, Peter Cressey and Timothy Morris (1999) 'Employment relations in UK banking', in Marino Regini, Jim Kitay and Martin Baethge (eds), *From Tellers to Sellers. Changing Employment Relations in Banks* (Cambridge, Mass.: MIT Press).

Strack, Guido (2003) 'High-tech and knowledge-intensive sectors creating employment in Europe', *Eurostat Statistics in Focus*, Theme 9-10.

Strack, Guido (2004) 'High-tech trade, employment and value added in high-tech industries and knowledge-intensive services', *Eurostat Statistics in Focus*, Theme 9-2.

Streeck, Wolfgang (1992) *Social Institutions and Economic Performance. Studies of Industrial Relations in Advanced Capitalist Economies* (London and Beverly Hills: Sage).

Streeck, Wolfgang (1999) *Korporatismus in Deutschland. Zwischen Nationalstaat und Europäischer Union* (Frankfurt/Main: Campus-Verlag).

Streeck, Wolfgang and Kozo Yamamura (eds) (2002) *The Origins of Non-Liberal Capitalism: Germany and Japan in Comparison* (Ithaca: Cornell University Press).

Sturdy, Andrew, Irena Grugulis and Hugh Willmott (eds) (2001) *Customer Service. Empowerment and Entrapment* (Basingstoke and New York: Palgrave Macmillan).

Styhre, Alexander (2004) 'Rethinking knowledge: a Bergsonian critique of the notion of tacit knowledge', *British Journal of Management*, 15 (2): 177–88.

Suzuki, Fujitaku (2005) 'Corporate governance reform and individual democracy in Japan', *Japan Labour Review*, 2 (1) (January): 81–104.

Swank, Duane (2002) *Global Capital, Political Institutions, and Policy Change in Developed Welfare States* (Cambridge: Cambridge University Press).

Swart, Juani and Nicholas Kinnie (2003) 'Sharing knowledge in knowledge-intensive firms', *Human Resource Management Journal*, 13 (2): 60–75.

Tabata, Hirokuni (1998) 'Community and efficiency in the Japanese firm', *Social Science Japan Journal*, 1 (2): 199–215.

Tachibanaki Toshiaki (1998) *Nihon no Keizai Kakusa* (Economic stratification in Japan) (Tokyo: Iwanami Shinsho).

Takanashi, Akira (ed.) (1994) *Kawaru nihon-gata koyo* (Changing Japanese-style employment) (Tokyo: Nihonkeizai shinbunsha).

Takahashi, Hiroyuki (1998) 'Working women in Japan: a look at historical trends and legal reform', *Japan Economic Institute Report*, 42.

Tamiya Yuko (2003) 'Kotekinenkinseido no Hensen, Jenda-shiten karano Saikou' (Transformation of the public pension system in Japan: rethinking from a gender perspective), *Journal of the National Women's Education Centre of Japan*, 7: 57–68.

Tanaka, Kazuko (1999) 'Kiki wo Kouki to Surutameni' (The employment of women at a critical juncture), *Women's Studies*, 7: 112–30.

Tanaka, Yukiko (1995) *Contemporary Portraits of Japanese Women* (Westport, Connecticut: Praeger).

Taylor, Mark C. (2004) 'What Derrida really meant', *The New York Times* (14 October): A29.

Taylor, Phil and Peter Bain (1998) 'An assembly line in the head: the call centre labour process', presented at the 16th Annual International Labour Process Conference, 7–9 April, Manchester, UK.

Theobald, Hildegard (2003) 'Care for the elderly: welfare system, professionalisation and the question of inequality', *International Journal of Sociology and Social Policy*, 23 (4/5): 159–85.

Thompson, Graham (2004) 'Getting to know the knowledge economy: ICTs, networks and governance', *Economy and Society*, 33 (4) (November): 562–81.

Thompson, Paul and George Callaghan (2002) 'Skill formation in call centres', in Ursula Holtgrewe, Christian Kerst and Karen A. Shire (eds), *Re-organizing Service Work. Call Centres in Germany and Britain* (Aldershot: Ashgate): 105–22.

Thompson, Paul, George Callaghan and Diane van den Broek (2004) 'Keeping up appearances: recruitment, skills and normative control in call centres', in Stephen Deery and Nicholas Kinnie (eds), *Call Centres and Human Resource Management. A Cross-national Perspective* (Basingstoke: Palgrave Macmillan).

Thompson, Paul, Chris Warhurst and George Callaghan (2000) 'Human capital or capitalising on humanity? Knowledge, skills and competencies in interactive service work', in Craig Prichard, Richard Hull, Mike Chumer and Hugh Willmott (eds),

Managing Knowledge. Critical Investigations of Work and Learning (Basingstoke: Palgrave Macmillan): 122–40.

Tienari, Janne, Sigrid Quack and Hildegard Theobald (1998) *Organizational Reforms and Gender. Feminisation of Middle Management in Finnish and German Banking*, FS I 98-105 (Wissenschaftszentrum Berlin für Sozialforschung), http://skylla.wz-berlin.de/pdf/1998/i98-104.pdf, accessed 20 October 2005.

Titmuss Richard (1974) *Social Policy. An Introduction*, ed. Brian Abel-Smith and Kay Titmuss (London: George Allen & Unwin).

Toffler, Alvin (1990) *Powershift. Knowledge, Wealth and Violence at the Edge of the 21st Century* (New York: Bantham Books).

Tomlinson, Jennifer (2004) 'Part-time workers and the EU Directive', unpublished PhD, University of Leeds, School of Sociology and Social Policy.

Toynbee, Polly (2005) 'Gender inequality: old patterns, new challenges', *Ralph Miliband Lectures on Inequalities: Dimensions and Challenges*, LSE, 3 February.

Tsuboi Hidetaka and Takagi Takeshi (2000) 'Gekiron Nihon Ishikai wa oboka', *Ronso* (May): 172–89.

Tsuchida, Tomoko (2004) *Nihon Jendâ byôdô seisaku to seisaku netowâku*, Institute of Social Studies, Tokyo University.

Tyler, Melissa and Steve Taylor (2001) 'Juggling justice and care: gendered customer service in the contemporary airline industry', in Andrew Sturdy, Irena Grugulis and Hugh Willmott (eds), *Customer Service. Empowerment and Entrapment* (Basingstoke: Palgrave Macmillan): 60–78.

UNDP (2004) *Human Development Report* (New York: Oxford University Press).

Unesco Institute for Statistics (2000) 'International flows of selected cultural goods 1980–89', *United Nations Report* (Paris: United Nations).

Ungerson, Clare (2003) 'Commodified care work in European labour markets', *European Societies*, 5 (4): 377–96.

Unifem (2000) 'Progress of the world's women', *Unifem Biennial Report*, UN, New York.

United Nations (1995) *Report on the Fourth World Conference on Women*, A/CONF.177/20 (Beijing, 4–15 September 1995).

United Nations (1999) '1999 world survey on the role of women in development – globalisation, gender and work', UN, New York.

United Nations (2000) 'The world's women 2000', *Trends and Statistics* (New York).

UN Statistics Division (2005a) *Information Sector*, http://unstats.un.org/unsd/cr/registry/docs/i31_information.pdf, accessed 13 December 2005.

UN Statistics Division (2005b) *Information and Communication Technology (ICT)*, http://unstats.un.org/unsd/cr/registry/docs/i31_ict.pdf, accessed 13 December 2005.

Upham, Frank K. (1987) *Law and Social Change in Post-war Japan* (Cambridge, Mass.: Harvard University Press).

Uzuhashi Takafumi (1997) *Gebdai Fukushikokka no Kokusaihikaku, Nihon Moderu no Ichiduke to Tenbou* (Tokyo: Nohonhyoronsha).

Vargas, Virginia and Saskia Wieringa (1998) 'The triangles of empowerment: processes and actors in the making of public policy', in Geertje Lycklama a Nijeholt, Virginia Vargas and Saskia Wieringa (eds), *Women's Movements and Public Policy in Europe, Latin America and the Caribbean* (New York: Garland): 3–23.

Verloo, Mieke (2005) 'Reflections on the Council of Europe approach to gender mainstreaming and gender equality', *Social Politics*, 12 (3): 344–65.

Vitols, Sigurt I. (2003) 'Changes in Germany's bank-based financial system: a varieties of capitalism perspective', *WZB Discussion Paper SP II 2004-03* (Berlin: WZB).

Voss-Dahm, Dorothea (2003) 'Zwischen Kunden und Kennziffern – Leistungspolitik in der Verkaufsarbeit des Einzelhandels', in Markus Pohlmann, Dieter Sauer, Gudrun Trautwein-Kalms and Alexandra Wagner (eds), *Dienstleistungsarbeit. Auf dem Boden der Tatsachen. Befunde aus Handel, Industrie, Medien und IT-Branche* (Berlin: Sigma): 67–111.

Wajcman, Judy (1998) *Managing Like a Man. Women and Men in Corporate Management* (Cambridge: Polity Press).

Walby, Sylvia (1986) *Patriarchy at Work* (Cambridge: Polity Press).

Walby, Sylvia (1990) *Theorizing Patriarchy* (London: Blackwell).

Walby, Sylvia (1997) *Gender Transformations* (London: Routledge).

Walby, Sylvia (1994) 'Methodological and theoretical issues in the comparative analysis of gender relations in Western Europe', *Environment and Planning A*, 26 (9): 1339–54.

Walby, Sylvia (1999a) 'The new regulatory state: the social powers of the European Union', *British Journal of Sociology*, 50 (1): 118–40.

Walby, Sylvia (1999b) 'The European Union and equal opportunities policies', *European Societies*, 1 (1): 59–80.

Walby, Sylvia (2001) *Globalization and Regulation. The New Economy and Gender in the UK* (Wayne State University, USA: Working Paper Series).

Walby, Sylvia (2002a) 'Gender and the new economy: regulation or deregulation?', presented at the ESRC seminar 'Work, Life, and Time in the New Economy' (London: LSE). (October), www.lse.ac.uk/collections/worklife/Walbypaper.pdf, accessed 20 October 2005.

Walby, Sylvia (2002b) 'Feminism in a global age', *Economy and Society*, 31 (4): 533–57.

Walby, Sylvia (2002c) 'Women and the new economy in the UK', presented at the GLOW workshop at the University of Tokyo (September 2002).

Walby, Sylvia (2005) 'Gender mainstreaming: productive tensions in theory and practice', *Social Politics*, 12 (3): 1–25.

Walby, Sylvia (2007 forthcoming) *Complex Social Systems in a Global Era* (London: Sage).

Weathers, Charles (2005) 'In search of strategic partners: Japan's campaign for equal opportunity', *Social Science Japan Journal*, 8 (1): 69–89.

Webster, Juliet (1996) *Shaping Women's Work. Gender, Employment and Information Technology* (London: Longman).

Weeks, Jeffrey (1989) *Sex, Politics & Society. The Regulation of Sexuality Since 1800*, second edition (London: Longman).

Weir, Guy (2003) 'Self-employment in the UK labour market', *Labour Market Trends* (September): 441–51.

Whittaker, D. Hugh (1994) 'SMEs, entry barriers, and strategic alliances', in Masahiko Aoki and Ronald Dore (eds), *The Japanese Firm. The Sources of Competitive Strength* (Oxford: Oxford University Press): 209–32.

Wichterich, Christa (1996) 'Wir sind das Wunder, durch das wir überleben', *Die 4. Weltfrauenkonferenz in Peking* (Köln).

Wichterich, Christa (2001) 'From passion to profession. Mehr Fragen als Antworten zu Akteurinnen, Interessen und Veränderungen politischer Handlungsbedingungen der neuen internationalen Frauenbewegung', *Zeitschrift für Frauenforschung und Geschlechterstudien*, 19 (1 and 2): 128–38.

Wilz, Sylvia M. (2002) *Organisation und Geschlecht. Strukturelle Bindungen und kontingente Kopplungen* (Opladen: Leske).

Witz, Anne, Chris Warhurst and Dennis Nickson (2003) 'The labour of aesthetics and the aesthetics of organization', *Organization*, 10 (1): 33–54.

Wiredsussex (2004) *Wired Women – Women in Media Breakfast*, http://www.wiredsussex.com/events/0407/womenbreakfast.asp, accessed August 2004.

Woodward, Alison (2001) 'Die McDonaldisierung der internationalen Frauenbewegung: Negative Aspekte guter Praktiken', *Zeitschrift für Frauenforschung und Geschlechterstudien*, 19 (1 and 2): 29–45.

Woodward, Alison (2004) 'Building velvet triangles: gender and informal governance', in Simona Piattoni and Thomas Christiansen (eds), *Informal Governance and the European Union* (London: Edward Elgar): 76–93.

Yamamura, Kozo and Wolfgang Streeck (eds) (2003) *The End of Diversity? Prospects for German and Japanese Capitalism* (Ithaca: Cornell University Press).

Yokohama fôramu (ed.) (1992) *Shinpan. Onna no netowâkingu. Onna no grupu zenkoku gaido* (Tokyo).

Yuval-Davis, Nira (1997) *Gender and Nation* (London: Sage).

Zippel, Kathrin (2004) 'Sexual harassment policy in the EU', *Social Politics*, 11 (1): 57–85.

Index